Middle East Today

Series Editors
Fawaz A. Gerges
Department of International Relations
London School of Economics
London, UK

Nader Hashemi
Center for Middle East Studies
Josef Korbel School of International Studies
University of Denver
Denver, CO, USA

The Iranian Revolution of 1979, the Iran-Iraq War, the Gulf War, and the US invasion and occupation of Iraq have dramatically altered the geopolitical landscape of the contemporary Middle East. The Arab Spring uprisings have complicated this picture. This series puts forward a critical body of first-rate scholarship that reflects the current political and social realities of the region, focusing on original research about contentious politics and social movements; political institutions; the role played by non-governmental organizations such as Hamas, Hezbollah, and the Muslim Brotherhood; and the Israeli-Palestine conflict. Other themes of interest include Iran and Turkey as emerging pre-eminent powers in the region, the former an 'Islamic Republic' and the latter an emerging democracy currently governed by a party with Islamic roots; the Gulf monarchies, their petrol economies and regional ambitions; potential problems of nuclear proliferation in the region; and the challenges confronting the United States, Europe, and the United Nations in the greater Middle East. The focus of the series is on general topics such as social turmoil, war and revolution, international relations, occupation, radicalism, democracy, human rights, and Islam as a political force in the context of the modern Middle East.

More information about this series at
http://www.palgrave.com/gp/series/14803

Victor Gervais · Saskia van Genugten
Editors

Stabilising the Contemporary Middle East and North Africa

Regional Actors and New Approaches

palgrave macmillan

Editors
Victor Gervais
Emirates Diplomatic Academy
Abu Dhabi, United Arab Emirates

Saskia van Genugten
Ministry of Defence
The Hague, The Netherlands

Middle East Today
ISBN 978-3-030-25228-1   ISBN 978-3-030-25229-8   (eBook)
https://doi.org/10.1007/978-3-030-25229-8

© The Editor(s) (if applicable) and The Author(s), under exclusive license to Springer Nature Switzerland AG, part of Springer Nature 2020
This work is subject to copyright. All rights are solely and exclusively licensed by the Publisher, whether the whole or part of the material is concerned, specifically the rights of translation, reprinting, reuse of illustrations, recitation, broadcasting, reproduction on microfilms or in any other physical way, and transmission or information storage and retrieval, electronic adaptation, computer software, or by similar or dissimilar methodology now known or hereafter developed.
The use of general descriptive names, registered names, trademarks, service marks, etc. in this publication does not imply, even in the absence of a specific statement, that such names are exempt from the relevant protective laws and regulations and therefore free for general use.
The publisher, the authors and the editors are safe to assume that the advice and information in this book are believed to be true and accurate at the date of publication. Neither the publisher nor the authors or the editors give a warranty, expressed or implied, with respect to the material contained herein or for any errors or omissions that may have been made. The publisher remains neutral with regard to jurisdictional claims in published maps and institutional affiliations.

Cover image: © Aanas Lahoui/shutterstock.com

This Palgrave Macmillan imprint is published by the registered company Springer Nature Switzerland AG
The registered company address is: Gewerbestrasse 11, 6330 Cham, Switzerland

CONTENTS

1 Introduction   1
Victor Gervais and Saskia van Genugten

Part I Changing Contexts

**2 The Evolution of the Regional Security Complex
in the MENA Region**   19
Christian Koch

**3 Global Tipping Point? Stabilisation in Afghanistan
Since 2001**   41
Mark Sedra

4 A Diplomatic Perspective on Stabilisation   67
Bernardino León Gross

**5 Non-state Armed Actors: Lessons from Peace
Processes and Implications for Stabilisation**   95
Ed Marques and Sylvia Rognvik

vi CONTENTS

Part II New Actors

6 GCC Approaches to Stabilisation:
   Compatible or Competing?   121
   Timo Behr

7 Saudi Arabia, the UAE and Turkey: The Political
   Drivers of 'Stabilisation'   139
   Neil Quilliam

8 Beyond Daesh: The UAE's Approach and Contribution
   to International Stabilisation and Reconstruction
   Efforts in Iraq   163
   Victor Gervais

9 Economic Stabilisation of the MENA Region:
   'Old' vs. 'New' Actors   185
   Saskia van Genugten, with Neil Quilliam

Part III Emerging Issues

10 Urban Warfare: Stabilisation of Cities   207
   Virginia Comolli

11 Redrawing the Lines in the Sand? Quests
   for Decentralisation, Regional Autonomy
   and Independence Among Syrian Kurds
   and South Yemeni Separatists   233
   Leo Kwarten

12 Egypt and Turkey: Identity as a Source of Instability   259
   Steven A. Cook

13 Distributing Justice: Transitional Justice
   and Stabilisation in North Africa   281
   Zinaida Miller

CONTENTS   vii

**14 The Soldier and the Curator: The Challenges
of Defending Cultural Property in Conflict Areas**   307
Jean-Gabriel Leturcq and Jean-Loup Samaan

Index   331

Notes on Contributors

Timo Behr is co-founder of Westphalia Global Advisory, a diplomatic services consultancy. He served as an advisor with the Policy Planning Department of the UAE Ministry of Foreign Affairs from 2013–2018. He previously held positions with the Finnish Institute of International Affairs, Jacques Delors Institute, Global Public Policy Institute and EU Institute for Security Studies. He holds a Ph.D. from the Johns Hopkins University (SAIS).

Virginia Comolli is a Senior Fellow at The International Institute for Strategic Studies. She heads the Conflict, Security and Development Programme which studies armed conflict in its multiple forms and its inter-relationship with socio-economic development. Prior experience includes a secondment to the UK Ministry of Justice and working for a private security firm and a strategic intelligence company.

Steven A. Cook is Eni Enrico Mattei senior fellow for Middle East and Africa studies at the Council on Foreign Relations (CFR). He is an expert on Arab and Turkish politics as well as US-Middle East policy. Cook is the author of *False Dawn: Protest, Democracy, and Violence in the New Middle East; The Struggle for Egypt: From Nasser to Tahrir Square*, which won the Washington Institute for Near East Policy's gold medal in 2012; and *Ruling But Not Governing: The Military and Political Development in Egypt, Algeria, and Turkey*.

Victor Gervais is a Senior Research Fellow at the Emirates Diplomatic Academy (EDA) in Abu Dhabi, where he leads the MENA Peace and Security programme. Victor specialises in Middle Eastern regional security affairs, with a particular focus on Iraq, Iran and the Arab Gulf States. He previously held positions with the Institute of International and Civil Security in Abu Dhabi and the Kuwait Program at Sciences Po Paris. He holds a Ph.D. in political science from Sciences Po Paris.

Christian Koch is a Senior Advisor at the Bussola Institute in Brussels. His work focuses on the various international and foreign relations issues of the GCC states with a particular interest in GCC-EU Relations. Prior to his current assignment, Dr. Koch served as Director of the Gulf Research Center (GRC) Foundation in Geneva, Switzerland.

Leo Kwarten is an Arabist and Anthropologist (Leiden University, The Netherlands). He is a lecturer with the Clingendael Institute in The Hague, which is a think tank and diplomatic academy acting for the benefit of the Dutch government, international working professionals and general public. Being an analyst of Middle Eastern politics, he is professionally consulted by both private and public organisations and spends long periods in the region for writing and research.

Bernardino León Gross is Director General of the Emirates Diplomatic Academy in Abu Dhabi and lectures in universities in Europe and the United States. He previously served as United Nations Special Representative-Head of the UN Mission in Libya. He was the European Union Special Representative for the Southern Mediterranean 2011–2014; Secretary-General at the Spanish Prime Minister Office 2008–2011; and Secretary of State for Foreign Affairs in the Spanish government 2004–2008. From 1998 to 2001, he was a senior member of EU Middle East Peace Process ad hoc team. He has participated in several civil society peace and human rights initiatives.

Jean-Gabriel Leturcq art historian, is advisor at Louvre Expertise, Musée du Louvre, where he works on international cooperation and projects related to endangered heritage. He coordinated cultural heritage preservation and museums projects in the Middle East and Africa (Egypt, Sudan, Libya, Ethiopia, Lebanon, and United Arab Emirates) over the last decade. Between 2014 and 2018, he worked at the Agence France-Muséums leading on opening operations of the Louvre Abu Dhabi.

Ed Marques is the Interim Head of the MENA Programme at Crisis Management Initiative (CMI). He has previously served in various capacities related to peacebuilding, diplomacy and development. He holds an M.A. from the Department of War Studies at KCL, as well as a Ph.D. in Politics and International Studies from SOAS, looking at the diplomatic strategies of rebel groups.

Zinaida Miller is Assistant Professor at the School of Diplomacy and International Relations at Seton Hall University and Senior Fellow at the Institute for Global Law and Policy at Harvard Law School. She is the co-editor of *Anti-Impunity and the Human Rights Agenda* (with Karen Engle and Dennis Davis, Cambridge University Press, 2016). She holds a J.D. from Harvard Law School and a Ph.D. in International Relations from The Fletcher School at Tufts University.

Neil Quilliam is a Senior Research Fellow with the Middle East and North Africa (MENA) Programme at Chatham House and Director of Chatham House's Future Dynamics in the Gulf project. Neil has lived in Saudi Arabia, Jordan and the UAE and travelled extensively around MENA, working on various development, education and research projects.

Sylvia Rognvik is the manager of a dialogue initiative in Yemen for CMI. Previously, she has served in various capacities related to peace-building, SSR and mediation with the UN in New York, Libya, Yemen, Iraq and Jordan. She has also monitored the ceasefire agreement, and facilitated dialogue, in Eastern Ukraine for the OSCE. She holds an M.Phil. in Peace and Conflict Studies from the University of Oslo.

Jean-Loup Samaan is an associate professor in strategic studies for the United Arab Emirates (UAE) National Defense College. His research focuses on Middle Eastern strategic affairs, in particular Israel-Hezbollah conflict, and the evolution of the Gulf security system. Prior to his position in the UAE, he held positions with the NATO Defense College in Rome, Italy between 2011 and 2016 and the French Ministry of Defence from 2008 to 2011. Dr. Samaan holds a Ph.D. in political science from the University of Paris, La Sorbonne.

Mark Sedra is the President and co-founder of the Security Governance Group (SGG), a private consulting firm specialising on international security issues. He is also a Fellow at the Balsillie School of International Affairs. Mark's research focuses predominantly on peacebuilding and state-building processes in fragile and conflict-affected states.

Saskia van Genugten is Strategy Advisor at the Dutch Ministry of Defence. Before this role, she was a Senior Research Fellow in the Middle East and North Africa Peace and Security Programme at EDA in Abu Dhabi. She holds a Ph.D. from Johns Hopkins University's School of Advanced International Studies (SAIS) and is the author of *Western Relations with Libya: 1911–2011* (Palgrave Macmillan, 2016).

CHAPTER 1

Introduction

Victor Gervais and Saskia van Genugten

The first decades of the twenty-first century have been characterised by great strife and conflict in the broader Middle East and North Africa (MENA) region, leaving many of the previously prevailing internal and external political balances uprooted. Protracted wars in Afghanistan, Iraq, Syria, Libya and Yemen have further complicated the already delicate political and social fabrics of this region. Fuelled from within as well as from the outside, the current instability in the region is likely to continue for decades to come as old rivalries have flared up and new ones have emerged, exacerbated by the shocks of the uprisings in the Arab world that started in 2011. Within this context, traditional Western 'security exporters' have reviewed their engagement in the region, while regional players have stepped up their involvement as they have increased ambitions to influence the course and outcome of ongoing conflicts in their neighbourhood. As a consequence, international interventions in the MENA region are increasingly carried out by coalitions that bring together the traditional Western players, most notably the United States (US), the United Kingdom (UK) and France,

---

V. Gervais (✉)
Emirates Diplomatic Academy, Abu Dhabi, United Arab Emirates

S. van Genugten
Ministry of Defence, The Hague, The Netherlands

© The Author(s) 2020
V. Gervais and S. van Genugten (eds.), *Stabilising the Contemporary Middle East and North Africa*, Middle East Today,
https://doi.org/10.1007/978-3-030-25229-8_1

and regional states such as the United Arab Emirates (UAE), Saudi Arabia, Qatar and Turkey. This was the case in the intervention in Libya and to a lesser extent in Yemen, as well as with the broader Global Coalition against Daesh, where all these state actors have been united in a common goal that entails stabilising the MENA region—even if they at times disagree on what that means.

Two decades into this century, policymakers from across the political spectrum and in many different countries are increasingly united in advocating 'stabilisation' as the way to contain the security risks stemming from the region, including radicalism and excessive and uncontrollable migration. Gradually, the concepts of democratisation and liberalisation that had dominated the agenda moved further to the background, and the idea that what the region really needed was security and stability gained in prominence. Indeed, a new concept of 'stabilisation' has emerged in recent years as the central guiding rationale behind international interventions and as a 'platform for rethinking engagement in fragile settings'.[1] This new emphasis is not unique to the MENA region, with stabilisation activities taking place in contexts as different as Mali, Haiti and Sri Lanka. The first appearance of this emerging paradigm arguably came with the international reaction to the Balkan Wars of the 1990s, when, after the collapse of the Soviet Union and the end of the Cold War, there was a reduced threat of large interstate wars.[2] Instead, powerful players started focusing on consolidating fragile and failed states, as the real threat was believed to derive from ungoverned spaces that turned into safe havens for terrorism and transnational crime. Under the umbrella term of stabilisation, experiments with blending military, political, economic, humanitarian and developmental tools, as well as elements of (transitional) justice and reconciliation, became the norm. Predicated on the idea that development and security are mutually reinforcing, stabilisation efforts have striven to promote legitimate political authority in conflict-affected countries by using a range of integrated civilian and military instruments with the aim to reduce violence, give people basic livelihoods and lay the groundwork for longer-term recovery. In some cases, interventions have been rooted in the belief that peace and stability can be best achieved by 'tackling structural sources of conflict through the promotion of responsive institutions, human rights, rule of law, accountable security services and broad-based social and economic development'.[3]

But unfortunately, for all the experiments in Kosovo, Afghanistan, Iraq, Libya and elsewhere, the stated ambitions of stabilisation operations and the realities on the ground have remained far apart. International stabilisation efforts in the region tend to be costly, risky and in many regards, thankless. Especially in the wider MENA region, success stories, such as in parts of Afghanistan and initially in Iraq's Anbar Province, have remained short-lived.[4] Partly, this is explained by the fact that many of the conflicts are fuelled by root causes that are difficult to tackle and include a mix of political, socio-economic, demographic and religious-cultural factors. The ongoing diversification in the region in terms of political constellations and preferred external allies also plays a role. At the same time, it also likely indicates a mismatch of instruments and intentions at the level of those external actors engaged with stabilisation efforts. The past decades have generated a large number of case studies, insights and lessons learned to draw from in this regard.[5] With this edited volume, we aim at documenting and analysing some of these recent efforts and lessons, both those efforts undertaken and lessons learnt by traditional Western actors, and also those undertaken and learnt by regional actors that have more recently started to raise their profile.

Distinguishing Stabilisation as a Concept: The Primacy of Politics

While the concept of stabilisation has become highly popular in policy, security and donor circles, it has also raised new issues, with regard to both its practice and its conceptualisation. Indeed, despite some broad agreement over its parameters and its frequent use in relation to current international efforts to increase security in the broader MENA region and elsewhere, there seems to be no actual consensus on what is meant by 'stabilisation'. In particular, ambiguity prevails with regard to what the end goal is (other than an undefined state of stability), what activities it includes and when it begins or ends. Similarly, disagreement persists over whether stabilisation is a set of activities, a strategic objective or a combination of the two, which tends to generate confusion and exacerbate the core challenges of coordinating development, defence and diplomacy.[6]

There is also a lingering question about how stabilisation efforts differ from or are linked to other approaches and concepts. Most notably, the ways in which military force and development assistance are expected to translate into local support bear a striking resemblance to counter-insurgency (COIN) practices carried out throughout the past century, as well as to aspects of the colonial and post-colonial nation-building enterprise.[7] In recent military operations in Afghanistan and Iraq as well, stabilisation has often been defined within COIN doctrine's sequential steps of 'clear, hold and build'. Specifically, in the Afghan case, after military forces 'cleared' an area of insurgents, the area was then stabilised—or 'held'—and 'built' with longer-term recovery and development programmes aimed at fostering local resilience and legitimacy.[8] Yet, in recent years, the scope of stabilisation activities has greatly expanded. Moving away from mid-conflict, military-centric responses akin to counter-insurgency, stabilisation operations of the past decade have come to encompass a wide range of policies and practices intended to 'fix' conflict-affected or fragile countries. They have also drawn on a wider variety of actors—from police personnel and specialists to urban planners, relief workers, developments experts, diplomats, (state-led) businesses and others—and have often entailed a wider transformation in local patterns of governance than the more traditional civilian-led activities that supported COIN.

Similarly, the concept of stabilisation is often conflated with 'reconstruction'. While the distinction between the two concepts is not always instructive,[9] key differences can be identified. Stabilisation activities are designed to address short-term priorities and focus on contested or recently secured areas, while development is regarded as a more long-term endeavour and focuses on already secured areas. Also, while reconstruction and stabilisation projects and programmes can be similar, they are usually undertaken for different reasons. As a recent report issued by the Special Inspector General for Afghanistan Reconstruction (SIGAR) clearly puts it: 'a development programme might build a school because education triggers a process that leads to greater long-term prosperity and development – educated children are more likely to grow up to be healthier and more qualified to administer government, succeed in business, and help grow the economy. In contrast, a stabilisation programme might build a school to trigger a process that leads to improved security: the school would demonstrate the government is working on behalf of the community, the local population would come to prefer government services over the return of insurgents, and insurgents would lose control over territory (they previously held)'.[10] As such, while development work usually requires a degree of insulation from political dynamics, combined with clear frameworks of operation to guarantee both effectiveness and accountability for longer-term objectives, stabilisation programmes, for their part, necessitate both direct political control and maximum flexibility.[11]

Part of the same overlapping continuum, the distinction between humanitarian response and stabilisation is also often blurred. According to the OECD, humanitarian assistance is 'short-term help that saves lives, alleviates suffering, and maintains human dignity through the provision of shelter, food and water, hygiene, and urgent health care'.[12] In this regard, the key distinction between humanitarian and stabilisation activities seems to be that the former is based strictly on need, while stabilisation tends to prioritise assistance primarily intended to bolster governing capacity (e.g. the ability of authorities to deliver services) and legitimacy.[13] Whereas humanitarian responses are universal and non-judgmental, stabilisation responses thus come with a political agenda. The stabilisation discourse is just as well linked to the literature around state resilience, which deals with the vulnerability of a country's key institutions to external and internal shocks.[14] In a 'resilient' democratic system, for example, general elections would not lead to the breakdown of state institutions, as happened in Libya after its June 2014 parliamentary elections. Bringing in 'resilience' adds a certain level of sustainability to the end goal of stability.

Taking the above comparisons into consideration, the primacy of politics could be seen as the starting point of any attempt to identify the foundational dimensions of stabilisation. As one author puts it, 'stabilisation is, in essence, about powerful states seeking to forge, secure or support a particular "stable" political order, in line with their particular strategic objectives'.[15] The UK's Stabilisation Unit, for instance, recognises that 'stabilisation is inherently a political intervention by a political actor within a political context'.[16] Any stabilisation action is thus to be 'planned and implemented with an overtly political objective in mind, ideally with a means of identifying success and a process of transition to longer-term recovery'.[17] Furthermore, as the objective is political, stabilisation remains flexible on design and implementation, and does not predetermine the sectors or means involved. Indeed, as Zyck and Muggah explain, stabilisation gives 'no a priori preference to security sector governance, justice reform and national as well as localised ceasefires and peace talks'.[18] Stabilisation can therefore be seen as a process, not an end in itself, with military, social and other efforts undertaken to promote stability being transitory and primarily aimed at increasing the political space for the negotiation and eventual establishment of a durable political settlement.[19]

The Challenge of (Institutionalising) Civilian and Military Coordination

Reflecting a growing preoccupation with state weaknesses and fragility, stabilisation efforts of the past two decades have typically involved integrating 'hard' and 'soft' forms of intervention, blending military means with non-military tools of statecraft and foreign policy. Having made the case that 'fragility' poses a security and development challenge, it is now widely accepted that integrated civil and military intervention policies, planning and operations are the key to the success of stabilisation operations. However, ideas differ regarding which non-military policy instruments should be part of the stabilisation toolbox, which instrument should be leading, what the priorities are and whether a specific sequencing is appropriate. In many cases, the assumption is that the military and security aspects are dominant and seen as a prerequisite, which often has led to complaints by the aid community about the securitisation of aid or the 'weaponisation' of foreign assistance.[20] At the same time, most military documents and doctrines on stabilisation operations recognise the primacy of politics and the need to engage alongside civilian experts in promoting stability. For instance, the US Joint Doctrine (JP 3-07) describes how political settlements that deliver lasting stability are ultimately accomplished 'through civil, military, and diplomatic activities that are carefully synchronized to reinforce each other and support a stabilization narrative'.[21] Within this volume, the focus is specifically on these non-military policy instruments that are considered part of the stabilisation toolbox, including political efforts, economic, humanitarian and developmental assistance, as well as on the interaction of these instruments and the engagement of non-military communities with the military side of stabilisation.

In fact, while modalities of stabilisation activities vary across countries, in most cases the primary challenge appears to be in promoting coherence and integration between a wide variety of actors with different, and sometimes contradictory, rationales for engaging in fragile settings. To make this possible, governments with experience leading stabilisation responses have often opted for 'integrated', 'comprehensive' or 'whole-of-government' approaches to plan and manage these activities. In particular, they have developed multi-agency bureaucratic units and funding mechanisms to lay out strategies, identify cross-sector priorities and integrate a range of policy communities and organisations with unique professional cultures, world views and overall objectives.[22] Looking across different governmental experiences, a variety of institutional models have emerged in recent years, ranging from the more integrated models adopted by the UK and the Netherlands to the more decentralised and broadly voluntary set-ups based on cross-departmental and inter-ministerial cooperation established by the French government, with both Canada and the United States standing mid-way between these models.[23] Once established, these structures have been tasked with producing concept papers and doctrines on stabilisation to guide policies and define what they are about.

Yet, while there is only limited empirical evidence of what works best with these approaches,[24] the challenges of bringing the military and non-military aspects of external policies together appear nonetheless to have been grossly underestimated. In particular, building coherence in support of joined-up stabilisation operations has faced three primary barriers: (1) a strategic gap affecting the integration of political, security and development strategies at the planning and prioritisation stage; (2) a civilian gap of inadequate capabilities and resources at the implementation stage; and (3) a cultural gap impending integration across government, with disagreement on principles, policies and practice.[25] For instance, the 2018 US Stabilisation Assistance Review (SAR), co-issued by the Department of State, USAID and the Department of Defense, concludes that 'performance of US stabilisation efforts has consistently been limited by the lack of strategic clarity, organisational discipline, and unity of effort' in how these missions were approached.[26]

Similarly, the possibility of balancing short-term imperatives with long-term needs remains widely misunderstood. While the modalities for overcoming the main challenges at each stage of the process are not in dispute, there is still a great deal of uncertainty about how 'quick impact' projects can be effectively linked with the broader tools of development cooperation. For instance, past stabilisation operations in countries such as Bosnia-Herzegovina, Haiti and Liberia have highlighted the tensions between short-term stabilisation imperatives and longer-term state-building objectives.[27] Indeed, in these cases, these two objectives were not always aligned and, in fact, sometimes contradictory, with the priority of ensuring immediate stability often undermining prospects for securing a sustainable, long-term peace. In this regard as well, the cultures and approach of different communities involved with stabilisation (humanitarian, developmental, military) seem to not always align.

Regionalisation of the Stabilisation Agenda

Thus, despite the widespread adoption and institutionalisation of the concept, stabilisation continues to be surprisingly elastic both in form and in content. The relative lack of clarity on the nature of the task and the goals to be achieved means that, in practice, the concept of stabilisation often implies different things in different contexts. In particular, disagreement persists over whether stabilisation efforts should be defined more narrowly—as the management of acute crises—or more broadly, portraying state fragility as the main challenge.[28] Yet, in recent years, there has been a distinct trend towards more realistic, less ambitious goals for stabilisation activities. Indeed, after years of limited success, experts and practitioners alike agree that, even under the best circumstances, the objectives set out by the broader approach to stabilisation appear hardly feasible. Nor do they seem necessary: in most cases, the normal instruments of bilateral and multilateral diplomacy, development and military cooperation have proved more successful in dealing with the multidimensional challenges of state fragility.[29] As such, while the stabilisation agenda of the post-Cold War era had ambitious goals, with envisioned end states of increased democracy and market liberalisation, it is increasingly conceived as short-term efforts to move on from situations of acute crises and large-scale violence in conflict-affected countries.[30] Following the Iraq and Afghanistan experience, Western capitals in particular have been promoting stabilisation as a form of intervention that offers a less costly and more responsible way to address the complex realities of state fragility. In the United Nations as well, the recent turn to stabilisation appears in practice to signal a departure from complex, multidimensional peace-keeping operations of the past decade to more modest security and development packages, conceived as part of a wider 'exit' or 'consolidation' strategy that might facilitate a way out of prolonged peace support operations.[31] As Lisa Grande, UN Humanitarian Coordinator in Yemen, describes it, referring to the emerging consensus in the UN around the operational parameters of stabilisation activities: 'to be successful, stabilisation efforts should not be about long-term development, but need to be fast, simple, well sequenced, and have immediate impact'.[32]

The increasing reticence of Western states and intergovernmental bodies to engage in complex military operations 'out-of-area' has several consequences. The most important one for the MENA region is arguably that it has contributed to the emergence of new regional actors to support state-building, peacebuilding and development activities in conflict-affected states. With important resources and an interest in advancing regional stability, the Arab Gulf States in particular have seized this opportunity to advance a new level of engagement in stabilisation operations, developing their own tailored policies and approaches. Stressing the political nature of stabilisation activities, these new interactions have been guided by the political and strategic interests of those involved. The heightened activity in this area by the Arab Gulf States, for example, cannot be detached from the way they experienced the 2011 Arab uprisings and their aftermath. At the same time, regional actors have learned to play into the lexicon used by powerful extra-regional security providers to recast their own policies and interventions as legitimate 'stabilisation' efforts or 'anti-terror' operations. As a result, various conceptions of stabilisation (as a process) and stability (as an objective of stabilisation efforts) have emerged, with regional actors frequently adapting both the nature and the objectives of their stabilisation efforts to contrasting, and sometimes rapidly changing, local and regional realities. Arguably, this pattern is also reinforced by the low level of institutionalisation and definition of stabilisation activities by these new regional actors. Indeed, in most cases, the assumptions and expectations associated with stabilisation have thus far remained largely implicit, although a number of countries in the region, such as the United Arab Emirates, have expressed a desire to build the conceptual and institutional toolkit they would need for stabilisation activities. While still loosely defined, a nascent 'stabilisation agenda' is thus being advanced by regional countries to tackle a range of immediate as well as structural sources of fragility in the MENA region. Within this edited volume, we try to clarify and explain the views, activities and growing footprint of new regional actors involved in efforts to build regional stability, as well as what the consequences are for the political objectives traditional Western security providers might have for the region.

Understanding Stabilisation Efforts in a Changing MENA Region

This edited book aims at providing a critical overview of the current thinking and practice related to stabilisation efforts in a changing MENA region. The book brings together recognised scholars and practitioners in the field and aims at clarifying the debate on stabilisation, focusing primarily on trends and developments that have been underexplored in the literature on contemporary stabilisation efforts in the MENA region. It does so by focusing on three broad aspects of these trends. In the first part of the book, the chapters deal with the changing contexts, with regard to both the regional dynamics and the evolution of the practice of stabilisation. In this part, Christian Koch provides an analysis of the geopolitical changes that have taken place in the MENA region over the past decade with an emphasis on the consequences for established actors and the new opportunities arising for new actors to establish themselves within the existing geopolitical spaces. In particular, Koch highlights three factors that can be identified as critical in terms of understanding the current transition. First is the fear of domestic uprisings or disturbances. Second is the growing concern among the Arab states of the MENA region of an expanding Iranian power especially through the use of non-state actors and proxy forces. Third is the fear of US abandonment or reorientation. He observes that, within these changing parameters, a number of regional countries, among them the GCC states, are placing increased emphasis on the terminology of stabilisation and looking at options for a regional framework wherein regional as well as international actors can come together to bring about a more stable environment.

Mark Sedra continues with setting out how the international intervention in Afghanistan represents a tipping point in global thinking on exogenous stabilisation processes in conflict-affected and fragile states. He notes how the Afghanistan stabilisation and state-building project has struggled to achieve sustainable change. This disappointing outcome has triggered a backlash in many Western states towards intensive, open-ended stabilisation missions in conflict-affected states. The setbacks experienced in Afghanistan, notes Sedra, can be attributed to both inherent flaws in the overarching stabilisation concept and poor implementation on the ground. Surveying stabilisation programming throughout the intervention, Sedra identifies in particular six primary lessons from the Afghan stabilisation experience with the potential to inform more effective programmes in comparable contexts.

In Chapter 4, Bernardino Leon makes the argument that the recent emergence of a stabilisation discourse has downgraded the role of international diplomacy, including in the MENA region. In this critical note, Leon questions the usefulness and the operational success of the concept of stabilisation, which he sees as directly linked to the unilateralism of the US that led to the wars in Iraq and Afghanistan. His plea is to regrant—slightly reformed—diplomacy centre stage as a natural and necessary coordinator between different policy communities, including the military and those practising international development, as well as between the different state actors involved in an area requiring stabilisation. The chapter also presents some positive examples of the UN-sponsored stabilisation approach to Libya as an essentially diplomatic process of stabilisation.

Concluding the first part, Ed Marques and Sylvia Rognvik provide us with an in-depth understanding of the (growing) role of non-state armed actors (NSAAs) in political transitions in the broader MENA region. Over the past decade, the MENA has indeed seen a proliferation of NSAAs—which has led to the emergence of alternative forms of governance and the realisation that NSAAs cannot be ignored. Indeed, the success or failure of peace processes increasingly depends on the effective engagement and inclusion of the different facets of society. In this context, Marques and Rognvik describe the different roles NSAAs can play in decentralised states and analyse the complicated relationships between NSAAs and peace processes, offering some lessons learned as to how they can be best engaged, while highlighting what the implications of such engagement are for stabilisation efforts in the MENA region.

The contributions in the second part of the book deal with the emergence of new regional actors alongside Western actors in their quest to stabilise the MENA region on their own terms, the Arab Gulf States in particular. Timo Behr provides an analysis of how the GCC countries, above all the UAE, Saudi Arabia, and Qatar, have filled in an increasingly important role in regional stabilisation efforts in the wider Middle East. While these actors often do so co-jointly with other international actors, their concept and practice of stabilisation do not always conform with that of their international partners. This chapter analyses the GCC countries' gradual emergence as stabilisation actors, the political objectives and theoretical frameworks that inform their actions and the impact their policies have had on a number of crisis countries. The chapter also compares GCC approaches to stabilisation with those of other major international actors in order to come to a better understanding of how far they are compatible or competing.

In the next chapter, Neil Quilliam provides an analysis of the engagement of several new actors of stabilisation (Saudi Arabia, the UAE and Turkey) in the Horn of Africa and Syria. Looking at the diplomatic, military and development assistance efforts, he concludes that as new actors, these states have yet to develop a coherent approach to stabilisation. At the same time, however, it seems unclear whether more seasoned stabilisation actors have really developed a coherent approach. He argues that, to a large extent, Saudi Arabia, the UAE and Turkey benefit significantly from operating in their own backyards as they are fully familiar with the environment, while a lack of familiarity with the local context is one of the major constraints that international actors such as the US and UK have faced in their deployments.

Victor Gervais reviews the support provided by the UAE to post-Daesh stabilisation and reconstruction efforts in Iraq from 2014 to 2018. As part of recent attempts by some Arab Gulf States to re-engage with Baghdad, Gervais finds that the UAE's commitment to post-Daesh efforts in Iraq has been intertwined with broader foreign policy initiatives aimed to build regional stability. Yet, whereas in most areas of regional unrest the UAE authorities have been inclined in recent years to adopt a narrower understanding of stability, framed as the absence of acute crises or large-scale violence, Gervais suggests that, in the case of Iraq, they have instead chosen to promote a transformative agenda predicated on the idea that building a more inclusive, viable and unified state represents the best way to regain a degree of influence in a complex and divided society that cannot simply or easily be controlled. In this context, what is meant with stabilisation remains unclear, with regional countries with an interest in advancing stability adapting both the nature of the task and the goals to be achieved to contrasting, and sometimes rapidly evolving, regional dynamics and realities.

In Chapter 9, Saskia van Genugten argues that the differentiation between 'traditional' and 'new' actors comes most to the fore in the economic dimension of stabilisation. Western actors tend to focus on creating the right political and governance conditions for a private sector to flourish and economic growth to happen—in line with their own liberal market views. New actors, in particular China and several Gulf actors, challenge that static approach and are instead promoting a different model, thereby putting more emphasis on economic instruments of stabilisation, including bilateral loans, investments by state-led companies and large construction projects—reflecting their own views on economic development. Given the fact that many of the underlying problems of the MENA region are economic in nature, the impact of stabilisation in this area should not be underestimated and in fact deserves more attention among Western actors as well.

The third and last part includes contributions that deal with emerging and/or underexplored issues and themes within the stabilisation discourse/toolbox. Virginia Comolli assesses the specificities and challenges of stabilisation efforts in cities. Building on an overview of demographic and urbanisation trends and on a discussion of urban warfare, the author highlights the growing need for developing effective stabilisation operations that take into account specific pressures felt by cities such as rising populations, migration patterns, ethnic tensions, weakening of urban services and infrastructure, institutional deterioration, and the presence and role of non-state (armed) groups, among other factors. Given the multifaceted challenges presented by urban conflict and post-conflict scenarios, Comolli contends that military or security interventions on their own are insufficient. Instead, she finds that conflict cities would benefit from 'area-based' approaches, involving targeting aid and other interventions to promote the recovery of specific areas such as building public services in a given neighbourhood.

In Chapter 11, Leo Kwarten focuses on the quests for decentralisation, regional autonomy and independence among Syrian Kurds and South Yemenis. Noting that the Arab uprisings in 2011 gave impetus to certain regions and political groups in the Middle East to accelerate their strife for regional autonomy or independence, Kwarten argues that these breakaway groups stand little chance of success of militarily attaining their political goals. To their foreign backers, they are allies of convenience, not conviction. He illustrates this argument with two case studies: the Syrian Kurds and the separatists in South Yemen. Taken into consideration local factors, regional involvement and international reactions, the author concludes that the reluctance of the international community to involve these breakaway groups in stabilisation efforts may well create a league of party spoilers to any future peace deal.

Steven Cook then offers a critical reading of the recent political developments in Egypt and Turkey and indicates that they manifest a complex set of problems that have undermined social cohesion. After examining the common and divergent social, economic and political dynamics in these countries that are driving instability and the export of this problem to the region, Cook explores the issue of identity as a critical factor in Egyptian and Turkish instability. This is an issue that is understudied in previous analyses of stabilisation and suggests that the problem of instability in both countries will be enduring.

Zinaida Miller, in Chapter 13, turns to yet another under-researched instrument of the stabilisation toolbox: transitional justice mechanisms. She identifies ways in which transitional justice in the post-2011 MENA region has affected stability, shaped change and allocated power. Using examples drawn from Libya, Tunisia and Egypt, Miller identifies the factors that shape the stabilising or spoiling potential for transitional justice in the MENA region. She focuses on the conditions of transition, the choice of justice practices, the treatment of economic harms and the relationship between time and justice. In doing so, she argues for a view of justice projects as distributional and political—and thus as critical sites of social contestation—rather than inherently stabilising or destabilising. As the chapter demonstrates, in certain circumstances, transitional justice can generate a persistent confrontation with a violent past as well as a space to challenge an unequal present. It can also, however, be instrumentalised on behalf of the powerful, deployed against the weak, or defanged and delegitimised.

In the last chapter, Jean-Gabriel Leturcq and Jean-Loup Samaan look at the link between stabilisation and the protection of cultural heritage in conflict areas. Over the last years, the wave of terrorist attacks against cultural artefacts in Mali, Iraq or Syria has put the defence of cultural heritage on the diplomatic agenda. In the eyes of decision-makers, these destructions demonstrated that heritage was not a collateral damage of war but one of its ostentatious targets. While these developments have triggered a momentum on the international stage to launch new policy initiatives, the creation in 2017 of an International Alliance for the Protection of Heritage in Conflict Areas, Leturcq and Samaan note that major challenges remain, including the issue of governance among all the stakeholders, the cultural clash between curatorial and military communities, the applicability of the legal framework in the current security environment and finally the operational complexity of defending artefacts in conflict zones.

NOTES

1. Robert Muggah, ed., *Stabilization Operations, Security and Development: States of Fragility* (Routledge, 2014), 3.
2. Roger Mac Ginty, "Against Stabilization," *Stability: International Journal of Security and Development*, no. 1 (2012): 20–30.
3. Steven A. Zyck, Sultan Barakat, and Sean Deely, "The Evolution of Stabilisation Concepts and Praxis," in Muggah (ed.), op. cit., 15.
4. Ben Barry, *Harsh Lessons: Iraq, Afghanistan and the Changing Character of War*, The International Institute for Strategic Studies (Routledge, 2017).
5. For instance, Greg Shapland, "Elite Bargains and Political Deals Project: Iraq's Sunni Insurgency (2003–2013) Case Study," *Stabilisation Unit*, UK Government, February 2018; "Stabilization: Lessons from the U.S. Experience in Afghanistan," *Special Inspector General for Afghanistan Reconstruction*, May 2018, 6; and "Stabilization Assistance Review: A Framework for Maximizing the Effectiveness of U.S. Government Efforts to Stabilize Conflict-Affected Areas," State Department, DOD, USAID, 2018.
6. Zyck, Barakat, and Deely, op. cit., 17.
7. Sultan Barakat, "Stabilisation," *GSDRC*, no. 47, University of Birmingham, July 2016, 1.
8. "Stabilization: Lessons from the U.S. Experience in Afghanistan," op. cit., 6.

9. Gilles Carbonnier, "Humanitarian and Development Aid in the Context of Stabilization: Blurring the Lines and Broadening the Gap," in Muggah (ed.), op. cit., 35–55.
10. "Stabilization: Lessons from the U.S. Experience in Afghanistan," op. cit., 5.
11. Philipp Rotmann, "Towards a Realistic and Responsible Idea of Stabilisation," *Stability: International Journal of Security and Development*, vol. 5, no. 1 (2016): 9.
12. "Humanitarian Assistance," *OECD*, 2016, quoted by Shelly Culbertson and Linda Robinson, "Making Victory Count After Defeating ISIS. Stabilization Challenges in Mosul and Beyond," *Rand*, 2017, 8.
13. Ibid.
14. Volker Boege, M. Anne Brown, and Kevin P. Clements, "Hybrid Political Orders, Not Fragile States," *Peace Review*, vol. 21, no. 1 (2009): 13–21.
15. Susanne Collinson, et al., "States of Fragility: Stabilization and Its Implications for Humanitarian Action," Overseas Development Institute, 2010, 7. https://www.odi.org/sites/odi.org.uk/files/odi-assets/publications-opinion-files/5978.pdf.
16. "UK Principles for Stabilisation Organisations and Programmes," *Stabilisation Unit*, UK Government, 2014, 6.
17. "The UK Government's Approach to Stabilisation," *Stabilisation Unit*, UK Government, 2014, 5.
18. Robert A. Muggah and Steven Zyck, op. cit., 3.
19. "UK Principles for Stabilisation Organisations and Programmes," op. cit.
20. Sarah Collinson, Samir Elhawary, and Robert Muggah, "States of Fragility: Stabilisation and Its Implications for Humanitarian Action," HPG Working Paper, ODI, May 2010.
21. Along these lines, stabilisation is defined as "the process by which military and non-military actors collectively apply various instruments of national power to address drivers of conflict, foster host-nations resiliencies, and create conditions that enable sustainable peace and security". "Stability", Joint Chiefs of Staff, JP 3-07, August 2016, I-5. Stressing the primacy of politics as 'guiding lights' of stabilisation operations, it also concludes that "instability is the symptom of a political crisis rooted in how political power is distributed and wielded, and by whom". Ibid., X.
22. For governments involved in stabilisation efforts, this has highlighted the challenge of establishing clear processes to identify and manage possible tensions and trade-offs between different, sometimes contradictory, rationales for engaging in fragile settings, in particular between the conservative objectives of stabilisation and the transformative objectives of early recovery and development. Barakat, op. cit.; Becky Carter, "Multi-Agency Stabilisation Operations," GSDRC, February 2015, 3.

23. Philipp Rotmann, and Lea Steinacker, "Stabilization: Doctrine, Organization and Practice," Global Public Policy Institute, 2013; also, Gervais (2018).
24. Robert Muggah, "Introduction," in Muggah (ed.), op. cit., 4–5.
25. Serefino et al., 2012, cited by Carter, op. cit., 3.
26. "Stabilization Assistance Review: A Framework for Maximizing the Effectiveness of U.S. Government Efforts to Stabilize Conflict-Affected Areas," op. cit., 1.
27. Blair, Stephanie, Fitz-Gerald, Ann, op. cit., 13.
28. Philipp Rotmann, 2016, op. cit., 6.
29. Philipp Rotmann, 2016, op. cit., 6.
30. Ibid.
31. Ibid.
32. Lisa Grande, "Session II: Regional Approaches to Postconflict Stability and Reconstruction," UAESF 2018, Abu Dhabi, 9 December 2018.

PART I

Changing Contexts

CHAPTER 2

The Evolution of the Regional Security Complex in the MENA Region

Christian Koch

INTRODUCTION

This chapter will look at the geopolitical changes that have taken place in the MENA region in the period since 2010 with a focus on the consequences for established actors and the opportunities for new actors to establish themselves within the existing, yet evolving, geopolitical space. The Middle Eastern strategic regional environment is undergoing a widespread transition with the ultimate outcome still unknown. Traditional external powers such as the United States or regional powers such as Egypt are adjusting their roles and changing their focus. Non-state actors have proliferated forcing established states into forging new policy responses. Moreover, new issues have emerged or taken on renewed urgency, such as the need for economic diversification and the rising concern over cybersecurity threats to name just a few, that are broadening the overall security agenda of the states in the region.

C. Koch (✉)
Bussola Institute, Brussels, Belgium

© The Author(s) 2020
V. Gervais and S. van Genugten (eds.), *Stabilising the Contemporary Middle East and North Africa*, Middle East Today,
https://doi.org/10.1007/978-3-030-25229-8_2

19

While this transition opens the space for regional actors to play a different and, one could argue, a more central role in determining their own affairs than has been the case in the past, the new emerging environment also requires greater adjustment and flexibility than was probably initially thought of. It certainly suggests a different, fluid and potentially more volatile environment that carries with it both opportunities and greater risks especially given the fact that any vacuums will be quickly filled by actors willing to take those risks. The evolving regional security complex is further accompanied by a breakdown in the general consensus of what the order should look like as well as competing and different conceptions of existing and emerging threats.[1] For some of those threats, no ready policy responses exist.

To make better sense of the implications of the evolution of the regional complex in the Middle East, this chapter will focus on three factors that can be identified as being particularly critical in terms of understanding the transition underpinning the current regional security environment. The first is the overall domestic volatility that has resulted in a combination of uprisings, revolutions and even civil wars impacting in one way or another virtually all states in the Middle East. The series of upheavals that erupted in late 2010 starting in Tunisia have swept through the entire region and have led regional actors to respond in a variety of ways. While some states took immediate action to prevent domestic uprisings or disturbances, others found themselves quickly at the mercy of an increasingly uncontrollable situation with state power being virtually eradicated and non-state actors rapidly filling corresponding vacuums. The starting point of any analysis on the changing regional security complex in the Middle East thus has to be the domestic level.

The second factor is more of a regional nature and involves the role of non-Arab states, especially Iran and Turkey. A primary concern for the Arab states of the MENA region in the past decade has been the issue of expanding Iranian power throughout the region at their expense, especially through the use of non-state actors and proxy forces. The greater influence that Iran is able to exert is the direct result of the fact that traditional power states such as Egypt, Syria and Iraq are for the moment no longer geostrategic players in the region. To some degree, the Arab Gulf states—primarily Saudi Arabia and the UAE—have moved into the prevailing space, but their own domestic issues as well as overall state capacity has meant that gaps remain. In addition to Iran, Turkey under the leadership of Recep Tayyip Erdogan has equally indicated a willingness and readiness to spread its influence into the Middle Eastern region from both an ideological and nationalist neo-Ottoman perspective. Yet Iranian and Turkish incursions have not produced any stability in the Middle Eastern region. In fact, it can be argued that their policy prerogatives have been to prevent the region from returning to stability as Ankara and Tehran benefit from a certain degree of volatility in the Arab state system. In addition to Arab vs. Persian and Arab vs. Turkish ethnic rivalries, the regional dimension is also marked by increased sectarianism at the Sunni vs. Shia level which tends to frame regional competition in a 'with-us-or-against-us' framework. At the onset of 2019, there is little to suggest that such competition will soon dissipate. The role of Israel must also be considered in this context as due to rising concerns about Turkish and Iranian ambitions, there has been a convergence among Arab states with Israel on common objectives. While the continued intransigence of the Israeli government over a resolution to the Palestinian issue prevents such convergence from transitioning into a new alliance mechanism, the outlook and direction of Israeli policy are naturally tied to considerations related to the broader regional and international dimension.

The third factor lies at the international level and involves the changing role of the United States in the region and the return of great power competition with Russia's re-emergence through its intervention in Syria. For US allies in the Middle East, there is a concrete fear that the US is not only recalibrating its policies towards the region but that, in fact, Washington has begun a more widespread withdrawal given the growing war fatigue back home and a shift of priorities to Asia where, as some have argued, the core strategic interests for the US are greater.[2] A direct result of this shift is that Middle Eastern geopolitics has placed greater emphasis on the role of regional forces whose foreign and security policy now stands more in the forefront than at any other time in recent decades. The more immediate impact has been an increase in regional tensions with the further possibility that those tensions could escalate into confrontations whether in direct form or through proxy forces as the previous determination of the US to prevent such escalations withers away. Combined with the domestic and regional factors mentioned earlier, a strong argument can be made for the fact that the power constellations in the Middle East region are indeed witnessing a dramatic shift. Equally relevant is the growing role of Russia as a factor with Moscow making a determined push not to be sidelined when it comes to the overall power game of international relations in the Middle East. The resulting shift to greater multipolarity has created additional opportunities as well as challenges for regional states who find themselves engaged in balance-of-power efforts in one effort to enlarge their own strategic autonomy. A key question mark when it comes to external involvement in the Middle East hangs over the future role of China given its high economic and strategic dependency on Gulf oil resources and China's own determination to see its increasingly global interests being protected and advanced through a more proactive security policy. To be sure, China is poised to be more influential in the near future given the high stakes involved.

All three factors outlined above—on the domestic, regional and international levels—come together to present a different picture of the MENA region than existed during the Cold War or in years prior. The overarching transformation taking place has, in turn, a direct impact in terms of how stabilisation strategies for both short-term security and medium- to long-term development are conceived of and implemented by actors within the same domestic, regional and international context. The uncertainty about the role of traditional external actors such as the United States or individual European countries when it comes to outlining the contours of an emerging regional order, for example, forces regional states to step up to the plate and fill the vacuum with their own responses given both their own national interests and the fear that inaction will result in competing agendas dominating the future discourse. As such, the political context plays an even greater role especially given the stakes involved, i.e. the future regional order. The emphasis in stabilisation approaches tends to also shift to the more immediate impact of one's policies on the ground and away from the long-term focus on sustainability given the rapidly shifting local and regional realities.

Overall, it can be stated that the Middle East region is experiencing a multiple set of transitions (James Dorsey has referred to it being 'enmeshed in a lengthy period of transition'[3]) that, for the moment, have not resolved themselves. As Vali Nasr has stated: '… today, the foundations of the region's political structure are in flux … this is a fundamental reorganization of power in the region in a manner that we actually don't know where the dust will settle'.[4] As a result, there is an urgent need to find new mechanisms for order that would at least prevent further upheavals and widespread violence and allow for political space in which a new organising principle can be developed and ultimately agreed upon. Looking at the shifting regional security order, one aspect that is evident is that a few regional actors, led by some of the GCC states, are trying to re-establish a degree of stability in those areas defined by lawlessness, chaos and state decay in recent years. Those approaches are outlined in more detail towards the end of this chapter after a closer look at the three factors that has gotten the region to the point where it finds itself at present.

ALL POLITICS IS LOCAL

The speed with which the revolts of the Arab uprisings spread throughout the region underlined the vulnerability and fragility of most of the existing ruling systems in the Middle East. To be sure, no state in the Middle East has been left untouched by the rising domestic volatility of the past decade. While protests and revolts in some countries resulted in actual changes in government (Tunisia, Egypt, Libya, Yemen), in others the governments were forced to respond to mounting issues of contestation (Bahrain, Oman, Jordan, Iran and Morocco, for example). Even in countries that did not experience any clear outbreak of unrest (primarily Kuwait, Qatar, Saudi Arabia and the United Arab Emirates), there was an immediate recognition that reform efforts, in particular at the economic level, needed to be undertaken with greater urgency.[5] In the immediate aftermath of the Arab uprisings, there was a shift in the local discourse away from the threat of the external environment for domestic security and towards a greater emphasis on local and regional issues within which the security paradigm would be framed. On the one hand, the predominant concerns of the states in the region were to preserve the existing social and political structures as well as protect the existing compact between the ruling elite and the population at large. On the other, there was also a growing recognition that reform would have to be an essential part of the process of maintaining the status quo. This was due to the ongoing transition occurring at the broader social level where a younger generation, supported by better education opportunities and, even more important, greater connectivity, no longer felt bound to previous unspoken agreements and traditions that had existed in governing arrangements with the result that this generation began pushing for the rewriting of the existing social contract. With a determined push emerging from below, it became clear to many ruling authorities that in order to preserve some level of communal consent and legitimation of existing authority, domestic issues would have to be tackled head-on.[6]

Within the context of increased domestic political contestation, some of the states in the Middle East were able to respond better than others. Outside of Bahrain, the GCC states largely withstood the Arab uprising's wave because of the ruling regimes' high degree of legitimacy and their ability to quickly respond to rising discontent levels and because they used the large financial resources at their disposal for the very visible transformation of their countries thereby further underscoring their legitimacy. Yet, even being in a comfortable economic situation has not prevented domestic issues from emerging, causing these countries to respond with a variety of reform efforts that are mostly encapsulated in so-called vision programmes such as Saudi Vision 2030 or the UAE Vision 2021.[7] Combined with the fact that much of the impetus for change and reform is because the GCC states have witnessed the emergence of a new generation of rulers, the outlook tends to be forward-looking and pre-emptive. The question that remains for the GCC states in the current environment is how much change their societies can absorb in a short period of time before the change itself becomes a destabilising factor.

In contrast to the GCC states, the wider Middle East has also seen the emergence of the so-called 'chaos states' marked by a complete breakdown of internal order and increased domestic fragmentation.[8] Egypt, Syria, Libya and Yemen are barely functioning with, in particular, the latter three countries experiencing power vacuums that have been filled by various non-state actors often with the support of other regional or external states. In turn, throughout much of the region political turmoil remains persistent as the initial transition that emerged out of the Arab uprisings have failed to proceed in a linear, stable and expected fashion. As a result, the countries mentioned above will continue to be consumed by domestic conflict for many years to come, meaning that they will also be unable to project sufficient power outside of their territories. The proliferation of weak and shattered states has therefore changed the structural dynamics of the region's politics or as Marc Lynch has framed it: 'The new order is fundamentally one of disorder'. As regional states and external powers grapple with this new environment, the need for new policies and multipronged approaches has grown, underpinned by the realisation that preventing further domestic chaos is closely linked to better stabilisation policies within the greater region. It is this line of thinking that underpins what has been termed the activism of the GCC states' foreign policy, i.e. the determination to actively engage in regional affairs in order to be able to shape certain outcomes.[9]

The concern over domestic instability has, for example, directly led to the deep split among regional Middle Eastern actors about the rise of so-called political Islam as the organising principle for the future politics of the region. For the UAE and Saudi Arabia, for instance, any form of militant Islamism is seen as an existential threat whose imposition will result in permanent insecurity in the volatile region as a whole.[10] The role played by radical extremism has become a key driver of policies within states in the Middle East as well as the key regional foreign policy driver with new constellations of states forming around this growing divide not unlike the 'Arab Cold War' that followed the rise of Nasserism but with a different alignment of players. Notwithstanding the normal caveats surrounding unique national situations, this issue has certainly exposed fissures that will need to be resolved if a stable regional order is to re-emerge.

The bottom line is that the new volatility exemplified by the outbreak of the Arab uprisings brought the danger closer to home in the form of diverse threats no longer limited to state-to-state interactions. For most of the region, the volatility continues to persist as governments struggle to re-establish themselves and their legitimacy. As such, the potential for new revolts remains an ever-present reality. This is due to the fact that many of the issues that were seen as causes for the Arab uprisings—ranging from prevailing socio-economic disparities and the inability to promote sustainable development plans to questions over citizen dignity as well as the failure to construct coherent national identities—remain unresolved with few of the underlying causes having been addressed.[11] As Marc Lynch has aptly described it: 'In almost every [Middle Eastern] country, the economic and political problems that drove the region towards popular uprising in 2011 are more intense today than they were seven years ago'. As a result, he concludes that Arab regimes continue to be confronted with the 'condition of profound perceived insecurity'.[12] The Arab uprisings were thus not so much about the birth of freedom but about the collapse of central authority with little to replace it.

Yet the developments in the GCC states have underlined the fact that the current debate is also about active citizenship in which people contribute to the development of their society in the full sense. This does not mean that citizens are necessarily ready to challenge and overturn the system as it currently exists. As Sultan al-Qassimi stated: 'Taxation in exchange for ensuring the security of citizens in an increasingly dangerous neighborhood might be the new accepted social contract'.[13] On the other hand, the short-term path of stability chosen over accommodating social change underscores the current constant pressure on ruling legitimacy. With the youth becoming increasingly economically and socially empowered, governments are compelled to gradually open the spaces in which the new generation that is emerging can put the tools that they have been given through better access to education and closer links established through globalisation to optimal use. To their credit, the GCC governments see the emerging youth as a huge resource that must be fully integrated in the overall effort to secure continued stability and viability.

IRAN, TURKEY AND THE MENA REGION

The second factor that must be examined in the context of regional security is the role being played by non-Arab regional states in the developments of the past decade. As already mentioned, the civil wars that have devastated the Middle East have created vacuums that have been filled by both regional and external actors. On the regional level, what the Middle East region has experienced as a result is a new tripartite competition between the Arab states, Turkey and Iran for power and influence. To some degree, this can also be classified as a competition between revisionist and status quo powers to determine the type of regional order that should emerge. The US-led invasions of Afghanistan in 2001 and Iraq in 2003 opened the door for Iran to break out of its isolation and once again propose itself as an alternative model for the rest of the region. Almost overnight, two key enemies of the Islamic Republic, the Taliban in Afghanistan and the Saddam Hussein regime in Iraq, were removed from power. While Iran took advantage and solidified its influence in the western parts of Afghanistan, its reach into Iraq was much more extensive, and Iranian-sponsored and supported groups soon began to dominate the domestic political scene in Iraq while American troops got increasingly dragged into a war of attrition that ultimately cost the US more than 4000 lives and over a trillion dollars in economic losses.[14] It was in this context that former Saudi Foreign Minister Saud Al-Faisal said, 'We fought a war together to keep Iran out of Iraq after Iraq was driven out of Kuwait ... Now we are handing the whole country over to Iran without reason'.[15]

In 2011, the protests that erupted in Syria gave Iran an additional opportunity to come to the aid of its ally Bashar Al-Assad and through political and military support aid the Syrian regime. Ultimately, the Assad regime was able to prevail (also due to the Russian intervention discussed later), and Iran saw its position further strengthened inside Syria and in the region. The spread of Iranian influence in Arab affairs was, at the same time, seen as being detrimental to overall Middle Eastern stability as outside the Syrian case, Iran tended to support non-state actors like Hizbollah in Lebanon, militias like the Hashd al-Shaabi in Iraq and the Houthi in

Yemen, actively undermining the stability of the given state in an effort to strengthen Tehran's own influence. In Lebanon, Hizbollah has taken the Lebanese state hostage and prevented the election of a president for more than 2 years from May 2014 until October 2016. Such examples, together with statements that reiterated Iran's intention to continue with the export of the Iranian revolution to the neighbourhood and other statements by Iranian officials that more Arab states would soon fall under Iranian control, caused deep concern in much of the Arab world. Soon a determination was made by some Arab states, led by Saudi Arabia and the UAE, that a more substantive shift in policy was needed to curtail and push back on Iranian intentions. The overall assessment was that a continued wait-and-see approach would be too dangerous and that in addition to one's own domestic security, regional security would be endangered as well.

From Iran's perspective, Saudi Arabia and the UAE are seen as primarily leading the creation of an anti-Iran coalition with the support of the Trump administration and Israel that exaggerates the threat emanating from Tehran in terms of stability in the Middle East.[16] It is therefore its response to carefully cultivate a network of state and non-state regional allies that Teheran can deploy in the defence of its interests. Some have described this as a forward defence strategy.[17] In order to counter a perceived encirclement, Iran's emphasis is on asymmetric military capabilities and increasing the so-called strategic depth of the Islamic Republic. At the same time, with the consolidation of power by Recep Tayyip Erdogan in Turkey over the past decade, Turkey is aspiring to be 'the only logical leader' of global Muslims and the dominant power in the Middle East.[18] In the light of the announcement of the Trump administration in early January 2019 that the US would be withdrawing its troops from Syria, President Erdogan is said to have told President Trump that 'It's our neighborhood' and as such there is no reason for the US to be there.[19] While Iran is often seen as overextended and struggling under the new sanctions, Turkey as a member of NATO sees itself as playing a more direct role in some Arab affairs especially as far as Syria and Iraq are concerned. A driving factor here is the Kurdish question with Turkey determined to quell any form of rising Kurdish nationalism and prevent the formation of a united front among Kurdish groups that would strengthen their case for independence and separate nationhood. Here, Turkey has similar interests to those of Iran and the majority of the Arab states. However, in terms of regional security, Turkey is not necessarily seen as a stabilising force by much of the Arab world. Its promotion of political Islam as an organising force as well as its transition from a parliamentary to a strong presidential system under President Erdogan tends to suggest that Ankara is more interested in seeing its own influence extended rather than promoting regional security. In that context, Turkey has emerged more as a competitor bidding for regional hegemony rather than a potential partner with whom Arab countries could work to re-establish security in the Middle East and contain Iranian ambitions. The lack of a regional order mechanism has, therefore, tended to push Turkey forward to try and achieve its own strategic ambitions at the expense of others in the broader Middle East.

What has occurred at the regional level in the past decade is an increased discrepancy between the simultaneous fragmentation and interconnectedness of the regional order. While territorial borders remain largely intact, national sovereignty as a concept has seen its manoeuvring room curtailed.[20] Yet what happens on the ground in one part of the Middle East is seen as having an impact on the security perceptions of all regional actors, and as such, the forces of disorder and interdependence must also be seen as going hand-in-hand. Furthermore, the created strategic spaces that have resulted from the increased turmoil have become the areas where increased competition between various regional forces is being played out. In that context, the regional security picture has become more complex than ever before.

THE CHANGING ROLE OF THE UNITED STATES

The third factor into the equation comes at the international level. For the past four decades, and some would argue even longer than that, the United States has played the pivotal role as an external actor in the Middle East. In particular, following the end of the Cold War and the US-led operation Desert Storm that evicted Iraq from Kuwait in 1990, the US held the position of the hegemon of the region. While regional power dynamics remained stable in the two decades after the end of the Cold War, recent developments have transformed those dynamics. Here, in addition to the regional upheavals and revolutions discussed previously, the changing role of the US as the core security guarantor for Middle East allies is a key factor.

Three main issues can be identified as influencing the reorientation that the US has initiated following the developments of the past decade. First, there is widespread war fatigue following the long-drawn-out and not very successful campaigns in Afghanistan and Iraq following September 11, 2001. As it stands, the US public is simply not willing to commit large amounts of resources for foreign campaigns in which the American public sees little substantive progress or results being made.

Second, a reorientation is taking place towards other areas of engagement which indicates that the Middle East is slowly losing the vital national security classification that it once held within US strategic thinking. Coupled with the development of shale oil and the increased energy independence of the US, the emphasis on protecting the free flow of energy from the Gulf region is no longer considered a vital strategic interest by planners in Washington. Instead, the increased power competition with Russia and China in the Asian theatre is being given higher degrees of attention. As Martin Indyk argues, the perceptions of a US withdrawal and retrenchment from the Middle East can as a result be deemed as accurate.[21] Or, as the former US ambassador in the region, Jeffrey Feltman has stated: 'The region is still important, but not as critically important to us as it was ten or fifteen or twenty years ago'.[22] Kuwaiti commentator Abdullah Al-Shayeji has referred to 'a non-committed, wavering, fatigued US' when it comes to its regional Middle East policy.[23] There seems to be a growing US hesitation on further engagement in a region that has not led to expected returns and an increased preference to stay in the background when it comes to the daily developments on the ground. As an alternative, political scientists John Mearsheimer and Stephen Walt have pleaded for a policy of 'off-shore balancing' as a way to keep US interests protected.[24]

Third, it is felt that a shift in capabilities is needed that caters for the move away from specifically large-scale military engagement to a more diverse and technologically driven hybrid form of warfare. Part of this is related to the war weariness mentioned previously as rising death tolls have an immediate impact on domestic political sentiment. Modern forms of warfare now allow for greater distance to the actual battlefield as well as place the emphasis on battlefield containment rather than having actual boots on the ground. Thus, while a vital national security interest of the US is the elimination of terrorism and the prevention of another attack on the US homeland, military planners see such an objective being largely accomplished through drone attacks on militant groups abroad coupled with surveillance technology and immigration procedures that protect US borders and prevent infiltration. However, in terms of developments in the Middle East, those capabilities are not suitable to determine the outcome in places such as Syria, Libya or Yemen. Instead, what has become clear during both the Obama administration and the Trump administration is the increased emphasis from the US side that in such cases, regional allies should have their forces on the ground with the US playing merely a supporting role. It is in line with this view that President Trump has favoured the establishment of the Middle East Strategic Alliance or asked Saudi Arabia for a \$4 billion contribution to the stabilisation of Syria.[25] The overall consensus in Washington is that America's allies have relied too much on the US to solve regional problems and have too little contribution to the problems at hand.

With domestic issues being in the forefront and foreign policy decisions being made on the basis of domestic priorities, there is an increasingly restricted room to manoeuvre as far as US administration is concerned. The Arab uprisings forced the Obama administration to confront a familiar US policy dilemma but one of unprecedented magnitude, scope and complexity: determining whether and how, in each case, to support Arab popular aspirations while at the same time protecting America's strategic interests. Overall, President Obama embraced a gradualist approach to democratic change, marked by an emphasis on universal rights, rule of law, institutional reform, economic development and poverty alleviation. This was due to Obama's views about the US role in world affairs and his thinking about the limits of American power and influence. Obama's policies subsequently manifested themselves in a decided preference for region-based solutions, multilateral action, 'low visibility' American leadership and cautious incrementalism. Strategic considerations remained, including cooperation on counterterrorism, reliable access to oil, countering Iran and ensuring Israel's national security. But these were radically tempered by an approach that sought to get away from the neo-conservative push for interventionism under Obama's predecessor. In Libya, for example, one witnessed a clear determination within the US policy community to let others take the lead. All of this has a direct consequence, as Robert Malley, the President of the International Crisis Group, outlined at the start of 2019. He stated:

> As the era of largely uncontested US primacy fades, the international order has been thrown into turmoil. More leaders are tempted more often to test limits, jostle for power, and seek to bolster their influence – or diminish that of their rivals – by meddling in foreign conflicts. Multilateralism and its constraints are under siege, challenged by more transactional, zero-sum politics ... The danger of today's free-for-all goes beyond the violence already generated. The larger risk is of miscalculation. Overreach by one leader convinced of his immunity may prompt an unexpected reaction by another; the ensuing tit

for tat easily could escalate without the presence of a credible, willing outside power able to play the role of arbiter.[26]

For US allies in the region, especially the GCC states, the changing US role in the Middle East brings them face-to-face with certain dilemmas. Most importantly, in terms of their own security, they continue to see the US as the only power militarily capable of protecting their territorial sovereignty and reversing situations like the invasion by Saddam Hussein of Kuwait in 1990. Up until recently, the common view held has been that when Arab states needed outside support, the US stood ready to provide such support.[27] With recent action and policy statements, such support can no longer be seen as a given. A key question being asked in the region is whether the US is still both willing and able to provide in particular its regional Gulf allies those capacities which they themselves lack but which are essential for their own survival and security. Marc Lynch has argued that 'the Arab regimes no longer see the United States as a reliable guarantor of regime survival or their foreign policy interests'. He concludes that the US simply 'no longer has the power or the standing to impose a regional order on its own terms'.[28] The UAE Minister of State for Foreign Affairs Anwar Gargash also stressed his belief that the UAE can no longer completely rely on its Western allies but he has tied this assessment to the case that the Arab states themselves need to invest in their capabilities as a result. He stated in July 2018: 'In this current international system, it is no longer "write a cheque and someone is going to come and secure the stability in the region." You have to do some of the burden-sharing'.[29] One direct consequence therefore is that US allies in the Middle East have either built up or are putting together a level of capabilities that allows them to act in a more independent fashion and not rely as much on the US as has been the case in the past.

Another aspect is that the previous era of US unipolarity failed to offer any alternative to the existing regional order. Regional US allies have also been forced to re-examine their overall regional and international positions as a reaction to the changed circumstances. As Cafiero and Shakespeare have argued: 'In light of the financial crisis of 2008 and the uncertainty of US foreign policy during Donald Trump's presidency, Gulf Arab States are increasingly determined to counter-balance their dependence on Washington as a security guarantor by broadening their diplomatic relationships'.[30] Issues such as the debate on the so-called pivot to Asia have been highly disconcerting for the Gulf region even though such a debate should also be seen in the context of a move away from the interventionist policies of the previous decade. For the GCC states, however, recent developments have underlined the critical need for building different partnerships for the maintenance of regional security. While in regional terms this means establishing a new balance in relations with powers such as Iran, Turkey and Israel, on the international level, countries such as Russia, China and India are beginning to play a more central role in overall policy deliberations. Given the fact that regional actors are beginning to have to confront theatres such as Syria without necessarily having the right tools to determine developments on the ground, the need to show that one can talk to others and that there is no longer an exclusive dependence on the US when it comes to their own security is an important element in the new strategic thinking being found among US Arab allies. In that context, it must be asked if indeed the first two years of the Trump administration represent a high point in relations between the Arab Gulf states and Washington. One commentator recently referred to the current situation as that of a 'mutual sobering' where both sides do not see the other as investing enough resources and the Arab Gulf states, in particular, increasingly hedging against an unpredictable United States.[31] And while the main line of argument has been that the reorientation away from the Middle East occurred under the Obama administration, there is enough evidence to suggest that the shift is even clearer under the Trump administration.[32]

Another direct consequence of the American policy reorientation has been the re-emergence of Russia as a power player on the Middle East chessboard, first in Syria but later also across other theatres. With the US unwilling to enforce stated red lines as a great ambivalence began to gather that questioned overall US interventionist policy, a strategic opening was presented to Moscow that it quickly capitalised on. In Syria, Russia was able to reassert itself in the Middle East without much US objection. While the US did continue to assert itself as a player on the ground, it did so almost exclusively under the premise of fighting the Islamic State (Daesh) and not in terms of guiding regional developments towards the emergence of a new regional security mechanism. In this context, the decision by the US in early January 2019 to withdraw its forces from Syria has further benefited Moscow. The decision has forced Syrian Kurds from once again seeking an alliance with the Assad regime due to fears about a potential Turkish invasion against them, an alliance that Moscow favours, and it has left Moscow as the only force in Syria that could potentially restrain Syria as well as serve as a bulwark against Ankara. Russia's policies have been noticed by US Arab allies. King Salman's landmark visit to Russia in October 2017 as well as the signing of a declaration of strategic partnership between the UAE and Russia in June 2018 underscores the readiness to engage with Russia as a strategic factor in regional affairs.[33] As such, it has been argued that 'Russian-Gulf Arab relations may be better than at any time in the past'.[34] In similar vein, an approach has also been made towards China. While China is currently not a strategic actor as far as the Middle East is concerned, there is a growing consensus in the region that Beijing is poised to become a more influential actor especially if the US umbrella for ensuring the free flow of energy from the Gulf region begins to be drawn in. Here again, the UAE and China have agreed to establish a comprehensive strategic partnership,[35] while Jordan, Saudi Arabia and Oman have all strengthened their bilateral ties with Beijing. Through its Belt and Road Initiative, China seeks to establish a firm foothold covering the regions of the Gulf, the Arabian Sea, the Horn of Africa and the Sea.

The changing external involvement in Middle East strategic affairs is the third pillar impacting the regional security complex. The age of US unipolarity is coming to an end and being replaced by a return to great power politics and greater multipolarity. America's Middle East allies are adjusting to the new realities by diversifying their own foreign relationships and positioning themselves within the emerging framework. While the new environment makes the search for new regional order mechanisms more complex, it also opens a space for regional actors to see their own policy prerogatives being included in the overall debate. As such, the impetus for further regional activism when it comes to Middle East developments will remain a key element in future alignments.

Conclusion

The regional security environment in the Middle East is in transition—to some degree, it is in fact up for grabs. Some of the vacuum created by the decline of state control and a less unilateral international order has been filled by violent non-state actors that operate in a different space. Yet the shift also opens the space for regional actors who with determined leadership as well as institutional capabilities can have an impact on the direction of the transition that is taking place. No doubt, the changing regional scene carries with it both opportunities and risks. The combination of the breakdown of regional consensus and US reorientation can be classified as a sea change. On the one hand, it takes away the obstacles to regional integration (i.e. the US umbrella) while, on the other, it prevents integration due to the rising lack of prevailing consensus over the future direction of the Middle East as a whole. While the era of US dominance was one of greater simplicity, the involvement of a number of traditional as well as newly emerging factors introduces new complexities to an already difficult search for order. The GCC states may be in the unique position to stamp their own impression on the direction of future shifts and outcomes. While the event around the Arab uprisings has had a profound impact on their domestic developments, the GCC states have emerged as functioning and stable states that can respond to the challenges with which they are presented. On a regional level, the GCC states are starting to take initiatives on many fronts within the context of promoting a new security paradigm, taking the Arabian Peninsula as a whole as their point of departure when referring to regional security.[36] And internationally, the GCC states are forging new partnerships that broaden their strategic choices while still emphasising the relevance of the United States and key European states to achieving stability within the Middle East region.

Within the changing parameters, some of the GCC states are placing increased emphasis on the terminology of stabilisation in a regional context and looking at options for a regional framework wherein regional as well as international actors can come together to bring about a more stable environment. Key components to be pursued in areas where instability and volatility remain high include ensuring the delivery of public services so as to maintain overall public support; stabilising the economy both as a means to deliver on the service front but also to provide a basis for medium- to long-term stability; and finally, establishing security on the ground so that the implementation of public service delivery and economic stability can be followed up on. There is an awareness that stabilisation measures must achieve progress in all three areas simultaneously and that all of them are interconnected. As the state is essential for the provision of security, a high degree of trust by the population in the state is a needed element for relevant security measures to be effectively implemented. That trust is grounded in the provision of public services which in turn operate efficiently in a well-structured and functioning economy. One key aspect of the approach on the regional level is centred on the provision of humanitarian assistance and development aid.[37] Such approach, however, again has stability as a prerequisite for a successful implementation process.

In the future, efforts to set a new agenda for regional cooperation could see a move towards an Arab-led security architecture for the Middle East that is largely free from interference by outside actors. A key battleground in this context lies in the Levant region especially in Iraq given that Syria is likely to need decades in order for the semblance of a state to re-emerge that could reassert its role at a regional level. An emphasis on Iraqi national interests, Arab character and its ties to the Arab world is increasingly seen as critical when it comes to the overall security of the Middle East. Yet Syria will also remain critical. The re-engagement of the GCC states with Syria, including the re-opening of embassies by the UAE and Kuwait as well as the re-admission of Syria into the Arab League as of early 2019, is a clear recognition that isolating the Assad regime and keeping one's distance from Damascus is not conducive to moving the region to greater stability. The ultimate goal, however, has to be an arrangement that also includes the non-Arab states of Turkey, Iran and Israel as well as the key international actors such as the United States, Russia, China and Europe. A good starting point could be going back to the speech that former Saudi Foreign Minister Saud Al-Faisal delivered at the inaugural Manama Dialogue in 2004. Arguing for a framework structured around sub-national, regional and international inter-dependent components, the foreign minister called for 'meaningful political, economic, social and educational reforms and not merely cosmetic changes', 'a regional security framework that includes all the countries of the region' and 'international guarantees ... provided by the collective will of the international community through a unanimous declaration by the Security Council ...'.[38] Given the interlocking transitions occurring at the domestic, regional and international levels in the Middle East security environment at the moment, these views put forward by Saud Al-Faisal would be worthwhile re-visiting once again.

NOTES

1. On the regional security complex and its theoretical underpinnings, see Buzan and Waever (2003).
2. Martin Indyk has made this point along with the suggestion that one of the most important interests the United States had in the Middle East, ensuring the free flow of oil from the Gulf at reasonable prices, is no longer a vital strategic one. See Feltman et al. (2019).
3. See Dorsey (2018).
4. See "The Frontline Interview: Vali Nasr," 20 February 2018.
5. In these countries, the governments responded with immediate economic packages that addressed issues of unemployment, housing and the rising cost of living. Public sector salaries for nationals, for example, were

increased, and additional public sector jobs were created for the region's large youth population. See Colombo (2012) as well as Ulrichsen (2018).

6. This was highlighted Mohammed Bin Rashid Al-Maktoum, the Prime Minister in the UAE who stated: "change or you will be changed eventually." See "The Region Is Not on My Agenda: It Is My Agenda," *Newsweek*, 27 October 2015.

7. The Saudi Vision 2030 can be found at https://vision2030.gov.sa/en while the UAE's Vision 2021 is available at https://www.vision2021.ae/en. In fact, all the GCC states have issued their reform programmes under the headings of so-called vision programme including Oman 2040 Vision (https://www.2040.om/en/national-priorities/), Kuwait Vision 2035, Bahrain Economic Vision 2030 (https://www.bahrain.bh/wps/wcm/connect/38f53f2f-9ad6-423d-9c96-2dbf17810c94/Vision%2B2030%2BEnglish%2B%28low%2Bresolution%29.pdf?MOD=AJPERES) and Qatar National Vision 2030 (https://www.mdps.gov.qa/en/qnv1/pages/default.aspx). All websites were accessed 2 February 2019.

8. Peter Salisbury defines the chaos state as "Fragmented internally to the point they no longer exist as unified entities in reality and require highly sophisticated, multipronged policy responses." See Salisbury (2018).

9. There is much literature on this subject. See, for example, Young (2013) or Ragab and Colombo (2017).

10. Nael Sharma, "Commentary: Ambitious UAE Flexes Military Muscle," *Reuters*, 27 August 2018.

11. See Khoury (2018). Or as Florence Gaub has stated: "All the principal factors which sparked the Arab Spring in 2011 [have] grown progressively worse." See Gaub (2019, 37).

12. See Lynch (2018).

13. See Al-Qassemi (2016).

14. The military conflict from 2003 until 2011 is said to have cost $1.06 trillion and resulted in 4423 casualties for the US military. See https://www.thebalance.com/cost-of-iraq-war-timeline-economic-impact-3306301 and https://dod.defense.gov/News/Casualty-Status/. Accessed 2 February 2019.

15. Saud Al-Faisal, "The Fight against Extremism and the Search for Peace," Remarks at the Council on Foreign Relations, 20 September 2005.

16. See Barzegar (2018).

17. Adnan Tabatabai, "Why Iran Is Not a Mideast Hegemon," Lobelog.com, 6 February 2018.

18. See Ibish (2019).

19. See Wright (2018).

20. Galap Dalay, 17 August 2017.

21. See Feltman et al. (2019, 5).

22. Quoted in Wright, "The Shrinking US Footprint in the Middle East."

23. Quoted in Victor Gervais, "The Changing Security Dynamic in the Middle East and Its Impact on Smaller Gulf Cooperation Council States' Alliance Choices and Policies," in Almezaini and Rickly (2017, 39).
24. See Mearsheimer and Walt (2016, 70–83).
25. "Trump Asked for $4 Billion from Saudis for Syria," *Stars & Stripes*, 16 March 2018. See also, "Trump Seeks to Revive 'Arab NATO' to Confront Iran," *Reuters*, 27 July 2018. Ray Takeyh of the Council of Foreign Relations characterised the speech by US Secretary of State Mike Pompeo delivered in Cairo on 10 January 2019 as being largely about burden-sharing. See https://www.cfr.org/article/middle-east-burden-sharing. Accessed 3 February 2019.
26. See Malley (2019).
27. See Ross Harrison, "Shifts in the Middle East Balance of Power: A Historical Perspective," Al-Jazeera Center for Studies, 2 September 2018, 4, available under http://studies.aljazeera.net/en/reports/2018/09/shifts-middle-east-balance-power-historical-perspective-180902084750811. html. Accessed 19 January 2019.
28. Lynch, "The New Arab Order."
29. "UAE Ready to Take on Greater Security Burden in Middle East: Minister," Reuters, 26 July 2018.
30. Giorgio Cafiero and Victoria Shakespeare, "Oman's Port Strategy," Lobelog.com, 31 August 2018.
31. See Guzansky (2018).
32. The withdrawal of the US from the Joint Comprehensive Plan of Action (JCPOA) represents another dilemma for the GCC states. President Obama did not see the Iran-Saudi rivalry as being necessarily a zero-sum game. Moreover, as has been pointed out, "the willingness of the United States to play a leading role could have made a difference in terms of countering Iran in the region." Yet the withdrawal from the Iranian nuclear agreement also has put the reliability of the US as a party to international agreements into question. See Feltman et al. (2019, 16–17).
33. "UAE, Russia Forge Strategic Partnership," *Gulf News*, 1 June 2018.
34. See Katz (2019).
35. "UAE and China Declare Deep Strategic Partnership as State Visit Ends," *The National*, 21 July 2018. For a more in-depth analysis, see Janardhan (2018).
36. The concept of a new regional security paradigm was the subject of a seminar held at the Bussola Institute in Brussels on 24 October 2018. For more information, see https://www.bussolainstitute.org/news/1007/. Accessed 3 February 2019.
37. See Salisbury (2018).
38. "Towards a New Framework for Regional Security," Statement by HRH Prince Saud Al-Faisal, Minister of Foreign Affairs, Saudi Arabia, The Gulf Dialogue, Manama, 5 December 2004.

BIBLIOGRAPHY

Almezaini, Khalid S., and Jean-Marc, Rickli (eds.). *The Small Gulf States: Foreign and Security Policy Before and After the Arab Spring*. London: Routledge, 2017.

Al-Qassemi, Sultan. "The Gulf's New Social Contract." *Middle East Institute*, 8 February 2016.

Barzegar, Keyhan. "Regional Viewpoints: Iran." *European Council on Foreign Relations*, May 2018.

Buzan, Barry, and Ole, Waever. *Regions and Powers: The Structure of International Security*. Cambridge: Cambridge University Press, 2003.

Colombo, Silvia. "Unpacking the GCC's response to the Arab Spring." Sharaka Commentaries No. 1, 2012.

Dorsey, James M. "Transition in the Middle East: Transition to What?" *National Security* (Online), vol. 1, no. 1 (2018): 84.

Feltman, Jeffrey, et al. "The New Geopolitics of the Middle East: America's Role in a Changing Region." *The Brookings Institution*, January 2019.

Gaub, Florence. "What If … "There Is Another Arab Spring." In Florence Gaub (ed.), *What If …? Scanning the Horizon: 12 Scenarios for 2021*. Challiot Paper no. 150, *European Union Institute for Security Studies*, January 2019.

Guzansky, Yoel. "US-Gulf States Relations: Mutual Sobering?" *INSS*, 27 August 2018.

Ibish, Hussein. "Gulf Re-Engagement with Assad Regime Signals New Phase in the Struggle for Syria." *Arab Gulf States Institute* in Washington, 15 January 2019.

Janardhan, N. "Gulf's Pivot to Asia: Contextualizing 'Look East' Policy." Eda Working Paper, February 2018.

Katz, Mark. "Is US Withdrawal from Syria Pushing Gulf Arabs Closer to Moscow?" Lobelog.com (Online), 17 January 2019.

Khoury, Rami G. "The Implications of the Syrian War for New Regional Orders in the Middle East." Menara Working Papers no. 12, September 2018.

Lynch, Marc. "The New Arab Order." *Foreign Affairs*, 97, no. 5 (September/October 2018).

Malley, Robert. "10 Conflicts to Watch in 2019." *Foreign Policy*, 28 December 2018.

Mearsheimer, J.J., and Walt, S.M. "A Case for Offshore Balancing." *Foreign Affairs*, vol. 95, no. 4 (July–August 2016): 70–83.

Ragab, Eman, and Colombo, Sylvia (eds.). *Foreign Relations of the GCC Countries: Shifting Global and Regional Dynamics*. London: Routledge, 2017.

Salisbury, Peter. "Aiding and Abetting? The GCC States, Foreign Assistance, and Shifting Approaches to Stability." *James A. Baker Institute for Public Policy*, 28 August 2018.

Ulrichsen, Kristian Coates. "Economic Inclusion in Gulf Cooperation Council (GCC) States." Rice University, Baker Institute for Public Policy, 2018.

Wright, Robin. "The Shrinking US Footprint in the Middle East." *The New Yorker*, 21 December 2018.

Young, Karen. "The Emerging Interventionists of the GCC." LSE Middle East Centre Paper Series No. 2, December 2013.

CHAPTER 3

Global Tipping Point? Stabilisation in Afghanistan Since 2001

Mark Sedra

INTRODUCTION

In 2019, it is hard not to be pessimistic about the situation in Afghanistan. Eighteen years of international engagement has seen the investment of tens of billions of dollars of reconstruction assistance and the deployment of hundreds of thousands of foreign soldiers, yet conditions on the ground worsen with each passing year. Despite some progress in peace negotiations between the Taliban and the United States, the facts on the ground are grim: the Taliban control more territory today than at any time since their ouster in 2001 and the Islamic State now has a foothold in the country; the economy is slowing considerably from the heady days of double-digit economic growth in the early 2000s, with the international drawdown causing parts of the aid economy to burst, and the political situation remains precarious with the national unity government deeply divided and public attitudes towards the state plummeting due to endemic corruption and dysfunctional governance.[1] The international intervention in Afghanistan

---

M. Sedra (✉)
Security Governance Group, Kitchener, Canada

© The Author(s) 2020
V. Gervais and S. van Genugten (eds.), *Stabilising the Contemporary Middle East and North Africa*, Middle East Today,
https://doi.org/10.1007/978-3-030-25229-8_3

41

has not just failed to achieve its goals; in some areas, it has seemed to have done harm.[2]

In many ways, Afghanistan's war-to-peace transition represents a tipping point in global thinking on exogenous stabilisation and state-building processes in conflict-affected and fragile states. For the United States, the leader of the external intervention in Afghanistan, the doctrine of stabilisation has over the past decade defined not only their engagement in Afghanistan, but their approach to fragile and conflict-affected states writ large. The Afghan case demonstrated, however, that this approach may be faulty. The failings of stabilisation programming can be attributed to both inherent flaws in the overarching stabilisation concept and poor implementation on the ground. Compounding these problems was the immensely challenging nature of the context in Afghanistan. While many global actors including the United States have turned away from stabilisation in the wake of the Afghanistan experience, the concept still has some merit. By highlighting lessons from the Afghan process, this paper hopes to contribute to dialogue that will coalesce around a new set of best practices for stabilisation missions.

The very meaning of the stabilisation concept is not always clear, even among governments and agencies that have endorsed the concept. The first section of the paper will briefly explore some of the conceptual and definitional challenges that have marred implementation. However, even when a coherent vision of stabilisation is seized upon, donors face the challenge of appropriately calibrating the scale and scope of the intervention in line with conditions and needs on the ground. If the footprint of the stabilisation mission, in terms of both aid and military deployments, is too large, it can inhibit local initiative and capacity building and arouse public resentment; if the footprint is too light, it may not be sufficient to facilitate meaningful change. Although the Afghanistan stabilisation and state-building processes may have begun with a 'light footprint' approach, dictated primarily by America's shifting attention to Iraq, it would evolve into a 'heavy footprint' mission, involving massive resource flows and troop commitments. What seems clear is that neither approach struck the right balance to address the challenges that existed in Afghanistan. The second section of the paper will survey stabilisation programming throughout the intervention, identifying six lessons that can elucidate its meagre impact. The paper will conclude with some brief reflections on how those lessons can be employed to inform new stabilisation strategies by both traditional stabilisation donors and emerging interveners. The increasing reticence of Western states to engage in complex stabilisation operations opens the door for other, non-traditional donors to support state-building, peacebuilding and development activities in conflict-affected states. For instance, the Gulf States and other regional organisations and blocs of countries have an opportunity to advance a new level of engagement in stabilisation operations in their spheres of influence. They could fill the growing void being left by Western donors by developing and implementing their own tailored civil-military and development frameworks that move beyond the mere deployment of military assets.

CONFLICTING CONCEPTS OF STABILISATION

The stabilisation concept has gradually grown in stature in the international peace and security field since the mid-1990s. Its first breakthrough came with the formation of the Stabilisation Force (SFOR) for Bosnia and Herzegovina in 1996.[3] Within a decade, the concept would be mainstreamed in international policy and embraced with particular zeal by Western donor states, with the majority of UN, EU and NATO interventions explicitly referencing stabilisation in their mandates and resolutions.[4] Donor infrastructure to facilitate stabilisation operations gradually emerged in the early 2000s, including the Office of the Coordinator for Reconstruction and Stabilisation (S/CRS) in the US State Department—a body that later evolved into a larger Bureau for Conflict and Stabilisation Operations—and a cross-departmental Stabilisation Unit in the UK. Despite the wide endorsement of the concept in Western donor circles, there was not always a clear consensus on its definition. As Roger Mac Ginty explains, 'many of the definitions lack precision and resemble a hodge-podge of words around the general areas of peacebuilding, security and development' (Mac Ginty 2012, 24).

In 2018, the US government defined stabilisation as: 'A political endeavour involving an integrated civilian-military process to create conditions where locally legitimate authorities and systems can peaceably manage conflict and prevent a resurgence of violence'. They saw it as a transitional project that could 'include efforts to establish civil security, provide access to dispute resolution, and deliver targeted basic services, and establish a foundation for the return of displaced people and longer-term development'.[5] With a civil-military partnership at the core of the concept, stabilisation donors have often differed on the level of attention or onus placed on military versus civilian tools to achieve its fundamental goals. While the US definition has the flavour of a civilian-centric concept, in practice it is the military that has been the decisive actor in driving programming, as the Afghan case will demonstrate.

The UK Stabilisation Unit identifies three core tasks for stabilisation operations: to 'protect political actors, the political system and the population; promote, consolidate and strengthen political processes; [and] prepare for longer-term recovery'.[6] By emphasising efforts to enable local political processes, the UK approach seeks to situate ownership and agency for the process with local stakeholders. However, in practice, stabilisation processes have often been driven by external security priorities, undercutting local agency. Mac Ginty decries 'the nannyish instincts of stabilization', which he sees as undervaluing 'the agency that national elites and local communities have in interpreting, delaying, modifying and mimicking inputs from international peace-support and state-building actors'.[7]

The problem, as Christian Dennys sees it, is that stabilisation programmes have been too closely linked to counter-insurgency (COIN) activities.[8] Indeed, as the US Special Investigator General for Afghanistan Reconstruction (SIGAR) recognises in a landmark 2018 report evaluating the US stabilisation experience in Afghanistan: 'stabilization was often framed as the civilian component of COIN' and 'conceptually nested within COIN doctrine's sequential steps of 'clear, hold, build''.[9] Dennys is adamant that political engagement be accorded a position of primacy in stabilisation missions, because 'local stability stems from the way in which local political elites are structured, the manner in which they co-opt or control the state (and vice versa) and the way in which the population is treated over the medium term'.[10]

Addressing the apolitical approach of stabilisation operations in many contexts, David Keen and Larry Attree show how 'the focus on weakening or eliminating' perceived spoilers through predominantly military means often 'take[s] attention away from the wider project of pushing for political changes (within the relevant state or neighbouring states) that might help to undermine the 'spoiler''.[11] This effort to employ security instruments to achieve political ends, points to one of the main criticisms of the ostensibly civilian-led concept: its securitisation. Many critics of the stabilisation project see it as a thinly veiled effort to securitise development and reconstruction assistance.[12] Rather than being a people-focused and politically sensitive process that collaborates with military actors on a limited level to achieve desired change, the process has often become a means to advance kinetic military objectives.

It is important to remember that stabilisation is distinct from traditional security operations and development activity in terms of intent. While the intent of a military operation is to employ force to pacify an area, eliminate threats and win the hearts and minds of local populations, stabilisation operations employ a wide range of civilian and military tools to establish security and political order and lay the groundwork for sustainable economic development. By contrast, traditional development activities implement programmes to advance long-term economic and social well-being irrespective of the local political and security environment. These distinctions are important in evaluating the impact of stabilisation activities on the ground.

USAID, which oversees civilian stabilisation efforts for the United States, defined stabilisation in the Afghan context as: 'Strengthening the reach and legitimacy of the central government in outlying regions ... to improve security, extend the reach of the Afghan government, and facilitate reconstruction in priority provinces'.[13] This definition provides a clear framework for stabilisation operations in Afghanistan; however, as the following analysis will show, the difficult conditions on the ground coupled with confusion over stakeholder roles often marred its application.

Brief Overview of the Afghanistan Intervention

Before outlining the principal lessons that can be drawn from stabilisation programming in Afghanistan, it is worthwhile to briefly look at the origins of the international intervention. In October 2001, a US-led coalition intervened in Afghanistan to overthrow the Taliban regime. Triggered by the 9/11 terrorist attacks in the US, the stated goal of the intervention was to remove the Taliban from power and prevent the country from being utilised as a sanctuary for terrorist groups like al-Qaeda. However, as Barnett Rubin states, 'the main goal of US policy in Afghanistan was not to set up a better regime for the Afghan people. If the United States had wanted to do that, it could have done it much more easily and more cheaply earlier'.[14] In fact, the US was so eager to avoid entangling itself in a grand reconstruction project that it barred its first military and civilian personnel deployed to the country from using the term 'nation building'.[15] The so-called light footprint strategy for Afghanistan's transition that would be adopted by Western donors in 2001, predicated on the notion that the international community should be relegated to a supporting rather than a trusteeship role in the reconstruction process, was a natural evolution of this outlook.[16]

Over time the international intervention would undergo a transformation from a light to a heavy footprint. The slow pace of change and the rising tide of insecurity began to convince Western donors that a more conventional, externally led reconstruction project was indeed a necessity to stabilise Afghanistan.[17] It was from that point forward that Western support for state-building and stabilisation activities increased massively in scale and scope.

Despite escalating levels of violence in Afghanistan in the wake of the Taliban's ouster in 2001, the external troop presence in Afghanistan, in the form of the UN-mandated International Security Assistance Force (ISAF) and a separate US contingent under the auspices of Operation Enduring Freedom (OEF), was modest in numbers, mandate, and geographic scope. This was particularly so in the first eight years of the process, during which its force numbers typically ranged from 30,000 to 65,000 troops. The ISAF mission, established by UN Security Council Resolution 1386 in December 2001, was initially confined to Kabul and its immediate environs. NATO assumed control of the force in August 2003 and began a phased expansion across the country, achieving nationwide coverage in October 2006. Even after ISAF's expansion, its troop levels, which reached a high-water mark of 128,000 in 2012, were never sufficient to project influence across the entire national territory and arrest insecurity. For its part, the mandate of US forces under OEF was limited to hunting and disrupting al-Qaeda and the Taliban; they were not concerned with expanding the sovereignty of the national government, advancing stabilisation or facilitating development and reconstruction.

The international troop presence, particularly in the critical early stages of the intervention, was insufficient to provide stabilisation programming with the security buffer it needed. Insecurity grew steadily with each passing year, defying the post-conflict label. Demonstrating the tenuous nature of the security situation, over 550 civilians were killed in violent incidents across the country between October 2003 and April 2004.[18] That number would increase to 929 in 2007, 3133 in 2011, and 3438 in 2017.[19]

Complicating the adverse security environment, the broader political settlement in Afghanistan was always contested. The Taliban were not consulted at Bonn and have resisted the political transition ever since. Beyond the Taliban, several other spoiler groups have expressed opposition to the new political dispensation.[20] This has hampered efforts to foster meaningful political consensus on the reform agenda and give it vital public legitimacy, with regime opponents framing reforms as foreign impositions.

Frantic efforts by the international donor community to make up for early underinvestment and stem the rising tide of the Taliban-led insurgency, resulted in too much aid being dispatched to the country. Between 2009 and 2012 alone, the US spent roughly US\$37.5 billion on the Afghan National Security Forces (ANSF), an amount both the Afghan state and donor missions on the ground lacked the capability to absorb and disburse effectively.[21]

The massive increase in aid in a very short period of time had the perverse effect of encouraging grand corruption within the Afghan state— crowding-out reformist elements—and fostering aid mismanagement and leakage among donor agencies. For instance, it is believed that up to US\$200 million from the UNDP-managed Law and Order Trust Fund for Afghanistan (LOTFA) meant to underwrite crucial reforms in the Afghan police sector was lost to fraud, corruption and mismanagement.[22] The accelerated infusion of donor money may have fostered the perception in Western capitals that the deficiencies of the Afghan stabilisation mission were being addressed, but in reality, it compounded them. It became clear that too much money, delivered amidst the wrong political and security conditions, can be as damaging as too little.

The significant drawdown of international military forces by 2014 facilitated a significant increase in insecurity across Afghanistan. More than 100 Afghan soldiers and police died on a weekly basis in the summer of 2014 alone, prompting the Afghan defence and interior ministries to cease releasing casualty data.[23] Major setbacks for the ANSF in 2015—including the temporary fall of Kunduz city to the Taliban, the near collapse of the ANSF in Helmand province, and the growing presence of the Islamic State—prompted the US to beef up its military presence, deploying limited air power and special operations troops to support the floundering ANSF. In another sign of the worsening security environment, the conflict in 2015 triggered the internal displacement of 335,000 Afghans, a 78% increase from the previous year, as well as the exodus of more than 213,000 refugees to Europe.[24] Security and political conditions continued to deteriorate in 2018, marked by a major insider attack in Kandahar in October, which saw the entire leadership of Kandahar province, the Governor, Police Chief and intelligence head, killed in a single Taliban attack, with the Commander of US and NATO forces narrowly escaping without injury.[25] The incident, which sparked new levels of political uncertainty nationally, highlighted the perilous security situation on the ground.

As this overview demonstrates, the conditions in Afghanistan posed a major challenge for the internationally supported stabilisation process. SIGAR holds that those challenges 'make it difficult to discern whether and how the problems seen in Afghanistan were specific to the environment or systemic to stabilization'.[26] Nonetheless the next section identifies six lessons from the Afghan case that can help not only to understand the trajectory of the Afghan transition over the past decade but also inform future stabilisation programming.

Lessons from Afghanistan

Understand the Context

Donors in Afghanistan never fully understood the country's complex political and power dynamics, particularly the patronage and clientelistic networks that run through Afghan society. They failed to grasp that violence in many parts of the country had nothing to do with the Taliban but was rather an outgrowth of local disputes and grievances that were often inflamed by poorly constructed and ill-advised donor programming. Donors also failed to comprehend the scope and character of factionalism within the state, causing some key donor stakeholders to inadvertently signal support for some factions over others. This had the effect of disrupting power balances and creating new fault lines of conflict. This lack of knowledge meant donors were often 'flying blind' when designing and implementing stabilisation operations. The experience shows that stabilisation donors must invest greater resources to understand the contexts in which they are working and tailor their strategies accordingly. Stabilisation operations do not take place in a vacuum; they must reflect the socio-political milieu in which they are being implemented. In other words, it is better to delay programme design to nurture this understanding, than rush programming and get it wrong.

In Afghanistan, the pressure to achieve rapid change after the fall of the Taliban regime seemingly overshadowed the need for knowledge accumulation, rigorous data collection and careful analysis. As one donor official remarked about efforts to reform the Afghan security sector: 'Often in Afghanistan you are creating policy without the necessary data. The donor community has made pledges and contributions of funds without knowing what the needs are'.[27] This reality on the ground in Afghanistan prompted SIGAR to recommend 'taking the time to understand the complex political terrain' even if it means implementing fewer and more modest stabilisation initiatives in the short- to medium-term.[28]

A senior US military official, speaking about the necessity of good data underpinning stabilisation processes, told SIGAR that they required 'a level of local knowledge that I don't have about my hometown'.[29] The complexity of contexts such as Afghanistan can create a high bar for donors to comprehend local conditions, but they have been guilty of failing to conduct even rudimentary baseline data collection and political analysis. This has made interveners prone to manipulation by local actors eager to instrumentalise stabilisation programmes to strengthen their own political and economic positions at the expense of their rivals. As one US civil-military planner noted, 'we were played all the time by the Afghans. If you didn't understand what had come before, rolling in with some help wasn't going to do very much. Clear, hold, and build doesn't work if you don't have an underlying political understanding and a grasp of the human terrain'.[30]

The US military sought to address this knowledge shortfall by deploying Human Terrain Teams (HTT), comprising social scientists from different disciplines with knowledge of local political, cultural and historical dynamics. They were intended to help US forces, mostly at the brigade and regiment level, to better understand and disentangle complex local political dynamics and assist the military to form more fruitful local relationships. However, the HTTs had mixed effectiveness. While valued by US military commanders, 'the program was controversial, poorly managed, and faced many of the personnel issues that troubled the civilian agencies'.[31]

A broad example of the lack of sophistication with which the stabilisation mission engaged the local context can be found in its treatment of civil society, particularly Islamic actors. In Afghanistan, a devout Muslim country, the religious establishment is an important component of civil society. Thomas Barfield notes how Islam 'permeates all aspects of everyday social relations, and nothing is separate from it...Afghanistan is a place where the concept of Islamic politics is little debated, but only because its people assume there can be no other type'.[32] William Maley argues that a 'lack of sensitivity to the centrality of Islam in Afghan politics and society among Western interveners' has consistently antagonised and even alienated Afghans, setting back the state-building and stabilisation processes.[33] 'The behaviour of Westerners in Afghanistan has shown a lack of sensitivity towards local customs', Vice-president Khalili claimed in a 2006 interview, speaking both about religious and traditional customs.[34] There are many examples of how the international interveners have been insensitive to local religious and cultural norms, from the failure to construct adequate mosque facilities on the new bases of the Afghan national security forces to unnecessary 'intrusions of homes and mosques' in counter-insurgency operations.[35] Moreover, the international community missed an opportunity to legitimatise their mission by reaching out to religious authorities. The Afghan constitution (Ch. 1, Art. 3) enshrines Islam as the state religion and affirms that 'no law shall contravene the tenets and provisions' of Islam. In spite of this, religious actors are rarely consulted on stabilisation activities by the donor community at the national, regional or local level.

Accentuating the problem of inadequate understanding of the local environment was the failure of donors to erect comprehensive monitoring and evaluation (M&E) systems to track the progress of stabilisation initiatives. M&E gives donors the evidence and insights needed to flexibly adapt programmes to changing conditions on the ground and correct inefficiencies in real time to minimise resource waste and maximise impact. SIGAR reveals that 'efforts by U.S. agencies to monitor and evaluate stabilization programs were generally poor'.[36] The challenges of monitoring programmes in adverse security environments meant that donors tended to assess their performance on the basis of inputs, such as money spent, infrastructure built and civilians employed, rather than impacts on local security, political and economic conditions. This undercut programme flexibility in a highly fluid environment. The bottom line is, as SIGAR notes, 'while the high number of variables in stabilization environments makes it difficult to discern cause and effect, programming should not take place in areas where it is impossible to monitor and evaluate it'.[37]

To fully grasp the level to which the Afghan stabilisation mission has been decontextualised and out of touch with local circumstances, it is instructive to look at donor-supported initiatives to build and empower non-state, informal security structures. Instead of working with different forms of locally legitimate informal security and justice structures, they manufactured new non-state entities, or gravitated to existing predatory non-state actors on an ad hoc opportunistic basis to serve short-term specific security goals.

The practice of mobilising and manufacturing militia structures to supplement and reinforce formal security bodies has been commonplace since 2002.[38] For instance, the UN hired militias to assist in the provision of security for polling stations for the 2004 presidential elections and the UN Protection Unit that secured UN facilities across the country largely comprised former militiamen.[39] This practice, however, hit centre stage with the formation of the Afghan National Auxiliary Police (ANAP). In late May 2006, the Afghan government announced that the president had approved a plan to mobilise militia forces to address the growing security crisis caused by the upsurge of insurgent activity. The plan called for 11,271 auxiliary police to be mobilised and deployed in 124 insecure districts of 21 provinces, mainly in the south and east (ICG 2007, 13). The purpose of the force was to secure static checkpoints and provide community policing, freeing up the regular police to support counterterrorism and COIN operations.[40] US officials continually referred to the programme as a 'temporary' or 'stop-gap' measure, revealing their lack of faith in its sustainability.[41] Although all recruits were vetted using the same system employed by both the army and police, US trainers still suspected that as many as one in ten of the recruits were Taliban agents.[42] They performed poorly, had a minimal positive impact on the security terrain and were widely distrusted by the population.

In contrast to previous historical periods in Afghanistan where the state made mini-compacts with traditional authority in the periphery to provide security and order, the US in the post-2001 period has sought to construct new informal militias that are intricately intertwined with warlord shadow networks. Despite the failures of past experiments (that bear a striking resemblance to current initiatives), and the reticence of Afghans to support them, such structures have been seen by donors as a panacea. By contrast, many Afghans see the strategy of employing militia groups 'as a distressing step backward' to 'the anarchic '90s, when warlords and militias terrorized the country'.[43]

Engage the Political Sphere

Ethan B. Kapstein, in a wide-ranging review of US stabilisation programming in Afghanistan for the United States Institute for Peace (USIP) explains that the 'fundamental conflict drivers in Afghanistan are inherently political: ethnic grievances, inter- and intra-tribal disputes, fights over shares of resources, and the like'.[44] Just as the roots of conflict in Afghanistan are fundamentally political in nature, stabilisation operations must be endowed with the political focus and tools to succeed. A publication of the US Joint Chiefs of Staff on stabilisation operations released in August 2016 astutely recognised that 'instability is a symptom of a political crisis rooted in how political power is distributed and wielded, and by whom'. Addressing this situation demands that stabilisation programmes endeavour 'to reshape the relationships with the indigenous populations and institutions, the different communities that make up the [host-nation] populace, and elites competing for power'.[45]

One prominent example of how donors have tended to get the politics of stabilisation wrong is how they approached the indispensable goal of encouraging local ownership of the process. After the collapse of the Taliban regime, the international community clearly selected local owners on the basis of both expediency and shared interests and values. There were two sets of favoured local owners: the Tajik-led Northern Alliance that represented the main anti-Taliban grouping at the time of the US decision to invade Afghanistan, and the Afghan expatriate technocrats living in the West who returned to the country after the Taliban ouster. These two groups of elites occupied places on opposite ends of the political spectrum. Each faced significant legitimacy problems within Afghanistan, the Northern Alliance *jihadi* groups, because of their human rights records and role in wartime atrocities, and the Western technocrats because of the public perception that they had abandoned the country during the civil war for greener pastures abroad. Relying so heavily on these particular local partners may have complicated efforts to advance a stabilisation project with broad-based legitimacy and ownership.

The partnership between former Northern Alliance commanders and the US-led coalition moved beyond the overthrow of the Taliban and the establishment of the Afghan government; the US routinely supported local commanders in areas with a Taliban presence to act as counter-insurgent proxies. According to one civil society representative speaking in 2005, the US was supporting certain warlords in the south with financial stipends of up to US$1600 per day for the use of their militias.[46] A prominent human rights activist, Ahmad Nader Nadery, detailed in 2012 that 'the United States embraced nearly any party that would oppose the Taliban, regardless of their human rights records' and political orientation.[47] SIGAR shows how 'power brokers and predatory government officials with access to coalition projects became kings with patronage to sell, and stabilization projects sometimes created or reinvigorated conflicts between and among communities'.[48] The result was that 'Afghans who were marginalized in this competition for access and resources found natural allies in the Taliban, who used that support to divide and conquer communities the coalition was keen to win over'.[49]

The reality is, as SIGAR resolutely states, 'stabilisation is an inherently political undertaking'. Yet the US and its key international and domestic partners failed to adopt a sophisticated and nuanced strategy that could cultivate and galvanise local political will for change. In fact, their adoption of short-term expedient strategies did more to alienate parts of the Afghan political establishment and population than to build the legitimacy of the new political dispensation.

Prioritise Governance

Governance has received inadequate attention in stabilisation programming in Afghanistan. In many areas of the country, Afghans view dysfunctional and predatory state institutions as a greater threat than the Taliban and other anti-government armed groups. A common sentiment in Afghanistan is that the majority of the population have not seen a peace dividend in terms of more effective, accessible, transparent and accountable government services. Even the Taliban, have sought to fill the governance void by providing public goods, primarily their harsh brand of security and justice, in the growing number of districts where they have been able to maintain a presence. The inability of the government to expand and improve service delivery since 2001 has alienated large segments of the Afghan population and driven some, principally out of desperation and fatigue, to support the Taliban.

Donors came to Afghanistan with a 'turn-key approach to governance', something that was later referred to in the field as 'governance in a box'.[50] The idea was that you could rapidly implant sound governance structures then hand them over to local administrators. It assumed that the presence of competent local bureaucracies would be sufficient and largely ignored the normative and political dimensions of governance, seeing it as a purely technical exercise. SIGAR has concluded that 'successful stabilization depends on the existence of some local governance already in place' that is competent, legitimate and committed to reform, something that was often lacking.[51]

As one Western police adviser put it, governance reforms have 'been structurally oriented, more about hardware than software'.[52] The focus was on building infrastructure and transplanting foreign bureaucratic models rather than developing human capacity and political will for change. The strategy ignored local political dynamics and underappreciated the challenges of quickly erecting governance structures that lacked local roots or traditions. One of the obstacles to improving governance under the auspices of stabilisation, as one senior UNAMA official plainly stated in 2005, is that 'the main motivation for international support has been counter-terrorism', a situation that was unchanged more than a decade later.[53] This drew vital resources and attention away from efforts to improve local governance and service delivery, and often worked at cross-purposes. As one 2010 report aptly argued, the long-term goals of rule of law reform efforts in Afghanistan were characteristically 'co-opted by counterinsurgency strategies that require immediate results'.[54] This short-termist agenda, driven by external strategic interests rather than local imperatives, undercut the ability of interveners to deliver on the people-centred stabilisation vision. SIGAR recognises that in Afghanistan 'disillusionment with formal governance was often based not on the government's absence, but rather on its behaviour when present, and stabilisation tended to exacerbate this dynamic'.[55] Even when coalition forces could clear a target area of insurgents, the government lacked qualified and capable administrators to fill the void. Accordingly, 'when the promise of improved services raised expectations and failed to materialize, Afghans who saw more of their government through stabilisation projects actually developed less favourable impressions of it'.[56] These dashed expectations opened the door for the Taliban and other anti-government armed groups to return, a vicious cycle that has churned for years, stalling momentum for countrywide stabilisation.

Demonstrating the crucial significance of good governance promotion to the consolidation of the post-Taliban regime, the Taliban have adapted their own governance strategy. Over the past two years, they have increasingly sought to frame themselves as a 'government in waiting'. As Ashley Jackson states, 'what began with a gradual recognition that unbridled violence would hurt the Taliban's battle for popular support grew into a sophisticated governance structure, including the management of schools, clinics, courts, tax collection, and more'.[57] In many areas of the country, one of the principal goals of the Taliban seems to be to 'out-govern' the Kabul administration. As the US and Afghan forces pull back into major urban centres, the Taliban have filled the void and sought to present themselves as a capable administrator of services.[58] Predictably, they have placed specific attention on justice and security, seen by Afghans as harsh but largely incorrupt and better than no justice at all.

Even in urban centres like Kunduz, the Taliban exact taxes and adjudicate disputes. High levels of corruption have created a fertile ground or at least receptivity to Taliban governance. According to one estimate, '80 percent of state teachers must pay bribes to get their positions'.[59] The Taliban have quashed such corrupt practices in areas under their control. While estimates of Taliban territorial control vary widely, in January 2018 a BBC study speculated that it was 'openly active' in up to 70% of the country.[60] With civilian casualties from Coalition airstrikes hitting an all-time high in 2017, more Afghans are turning away from the embattled international intervention.[61] The Taliban have even collaborated with government actors in some areas and softened their most hardened positions, such as their prohibitions on girl's primary education and women occupying particular professions, to curry favour with the Afghan public.[62] In effect, the Taliban have adopted their own brand of stabilisation rooted in their own brand of justice, security and good governance, in many ways a curative or reaction to the failures of the internationally supported mission.

When It Comes to Aid, Less Can Be More

The international community has funnelled vast amounts of aid into Afghanistan, far more than the Afghan state ever had the ability to absorb and disburse. This massive outlay has inadvertently driven corruption and clientelism and even fuelled the insurgency, as leaked aid and security equipment have frequently found their way into the hands of the Taliban and other anti-government armed groups.[63] Combatting corruption is a daunting task for donors in fragile and conflict-affected states, with some level of aid malfeasance rightly viewed as a cost of doing business on the ground. However, donors can minimise entry points for corruption by following development best practices, including limiting money flows when aid management and monitoring capacity is weak and underdeveloped. With the immense pressure on donors, particularly the United States, to spend money in Afghanistan, this basic tenet of development has often been ignored. Accordingly, a US Joint Center for Operational Analysis (JCOA) report concluded that 'the deluge of military and development spending which overwhelmed the absorptive capacity of the Government of Afghanistan created an environment that fostered corruption'.[64]

One of the principal objectives of stabilisation and state-building processes is ensuring that their impacts are sustainable over the medium- to long-term, creating fertile ground for development, public order and political normalisation. A look at the donor intervention in the Afghan security sector shows that this sustainability imperative has often been an afterthought. The donor community has fostered the creation of security institutions that the Afghan government will not be able to independently afford for the foreseeable future. Without long-term external subsidies, the security sector will likely break down, with disastrous consequences for the state and public security. Short-term thinking coupled with the flawed idea that massive amounts of aid can paper over programmatic deficiencies and weak political will has created a sustainability time bomb.

With the Afghan government lacking stable sources of revenue following the fall of the Taliban regime due to weak systems for tax collection, massive corruption and endemic poverty, the stabilisation and state-building processes were inevitably going to be reliant on external resources. The problem was that external aid was slow to materialise at the beginning of these processes. Illustrating the early paucity of resources, the initial lead donor for police reform, Germany, dedicated only a single adviser to support reforms in the entire Ministry of Interior in 2003, one of the largest and most complicated ministries in the government, employing tens of thousands of civilian staff and police personnel.[65]

Efforts by the international donor community to make up for the early under resourcing of Afghanistan's transition and to stem the rising tide of the Taliban-led insurgency, paradoxically resulted in too much aid being dispatched to Afghanistan. Instead of giving a much-needed boost to the flagging stabilisation process, massive increases in donor aid had the perverse effect of driving corruption, clientelism and state disfunction. The Afghan case provides yet more proof that in the absence of appropriate enabling conditions, most notably stable institutions with a base level of absorptive capacity, more aid will at best have no impact and at worst do harm. One of the lessons that the dramatic rise of corruption in Afghanistan taught stabilisation practitioners is that under difficult conditions it may be advisable to keep programmes small in scope and modest in scale. As Kapstein explains, 'large programs appeared to be much more susceptible than their smaller counterparts to negative forces such as corruption and violence'.[66] Smaller projects keep civilian expectations in check, are easier to monitor, and carry less risk in terms of vulnerability to corruption. In other words, less aid used for more modest purposes can be more impactful than major initiatives and infusions of assistance. While donors will never be able to eliminate corruption in complex stabilisation processes like Afghanistan, reducing it by all means necessary has to be a bigger priority as it has a cascading effect on all other aspects of the process. As Kapstein concludes, corruption is 'a key issue, if not the single most important one, affecting support for the Afghan government, support for insurgents, and attitudes toward foreign forces'.[67]

Avoid the Temptation for Quick Fixes

If you look at the lack of coherence and consistency in the way the Afghan stabilisation and state-building processes were planned and implemented, they appear more like several one to three-year engagements than a single seventeen-year mission. The constant focus on quick wins coupled with short-term deployments of personnel had counterproductive effects on stabilisation mission planning. In Afghanistan, planning cycles tended not to exceed two or three years, and donor staff tended only to stay 'in-country' for six months to one year before being rotated out, far too short to establish institutional memory, programme consistency and durable relationships with local stakeholders. These programme limitations bred short-termism in the stabilisation and state-building initiatives, which came to be more preoccupied with shaping the immediate conditions for a NATO exit than constructing a stable foundation for a long-term peace.

This exit strategy mentality was reflected in a myriad of ways from the creation of fiscally unsustainable institutions to the employment of hastily assembled militias to backstop NATO military operations.[68] It is accurate, as Kapstein explains stabilisation activities are principally 'designed to achieve short-term stability rather than long-term' change.[69] However, if that stability is to be sustained, it is essential that stabilisation programmes are grounded or rooted to longer-term processes of change. Otherwise, any positive effects these programmes produce will be fleeting at best.

The manner in which aid donors supported the Afghan security sector further demonstrated its damaging short-termist outlook. According to every fiscal projection, the Afghan state will not be able to afford the security apparatus being constructed for it for at least a generation. The most enduring legacy of the SSR programme may be to cement Afghanistan's place as a semi-permanent rentier state. As Ghani, Lockhart and Carnahan explain: 'No state can be sovereign while it relies on an external source to fund its on-going operations'.[70] The post-2001 dependency relationship forged between Afghanistan and the West is all the more problematic because the Western commitment to Afghanistan's future looks distinctly cloudy in 2018. The US$4 billion per annum subsidy that Afghanistan will require merely to keep its security sector afloat for the foreseeable future is far from assured given shifting geopolitical priorities.

The sustainability issue provides clear evidence how the security sector reform programme has not only failed to deliver on its aims, but may in fact be doing harm. There are several precedents since the beginning of the modern Afghan state in the nineteenth century of political order crumbling when vital external rents, whether British or Soviet, dried up.[71] A RAND Corporation report drawing lessons from US security assistance programmes in Afghanistan since 2002, concluded 'that central among the lessons of security sector reform is the requirement to establish systems and approaches that fit with the needs and capabilities of the country in question...and are based on realistic understandings of what is sustainable 'financially, operationally, and logistically".[72]

Focus on Low Hanging Fruit First

One of the overarching strategic mistakes made by the US stabilisation mission relates to its sequencing of programming. It targeted the most insecure and unstable districts of the country first in the hope that it would deal a severe blow to the Taliban-led insurgency. However, as SIGAR notes, the adoption of this strategy meant that the mission 'struggled to clear priority districts of insurgents', creating a situation where 'Afghans in those or other districts' lost confidence 'that the government could protect them if they openly turned against the insurgents'.[73] Accordingly, one of the overarching goals of stabilisation operations, to extend the writ of the state and bolster its legitimacy, could not be achieved. Kapstein's analysis shows that 'stabilization aid reduces violence only when administered in districts controlled by pro-government forces'.[74] Given that the stabilisation activities were never able to secure unambiguous control of many key districts, the overall impact of the programme was limited. Stabilisation programming still had 'a small but positive, short-term impact'[75] in these areas, but its full potential was never realised. Any impacts it had were limited and transitory rather than deep and enduring.

Instead of focusing attention on stable districts featuring permissive security climates in order to build countrywide momentum for programming, the opposite approach was adopted from its outset. SIGAR describes the typical outcomes of this sequencing decision: 'Afghans were often too afraid to serve in local government, Afghan civilians had little faith their districts would remain in government hands when the coalition eventually withdrew, implementing partners struggled to implement projects amid the violence, and U.S. government agencies were unable to adequately monitor and evaluate the projects that were implemented'.[76] It didn't have to be this way. Security conditions have varied widely across Afghanistan; there were many more secure districts that could have been targeted first to test the programme and established its legitimacy. A window of opportunity early in the transition process to stabilise better performing districts closed gradually over time in line with deteriorating countrywide security conditions. Had the stabilisation process taken advantage of more secure and well-performing districts at an early stage of its roll-out, achieving demonstrable successes that could be sold to more precarious regions of the country, it may have had a more profound impact. Future stabilisation missions should be cognisant of the need to be opportunistic and exploit any openings to demonstrate programme efficacy and legitimacy.

Conclusion

The former Special Representative of the UN Secretary General in Afghanistan, Nicholas Haysom, admitted in a March 2016 briefing to the UN Security Council, that with Afghanistan facing 'a contracting economy characterised by low growth and high unemployment; an intensifying insurgency regarded by some as an eroding stalemate; and an increasingly fractious and divided political environment' the mere act of 'survival will be an achievement' for the Afghan government.[77] If anything, conditions in the country have deteriorated in the two years since Haysom made those remarks. An October 2018 New York Times article captured very well the sense of 'peril and hopelessness' that engulfs Afghanistan: 'If there is a common theme in this upswell of alarm and worry that seems so widespread, it is a sense that no one sees any clear path through a minefield of crises'.[78] The 18-year state-building and stabilisation project appears to be in serious trouble.

What becomes clear in the analysis of the lessons from the Afghan experience is that critical preconditions for effective stabilisation were absent in large parts of the country from the outset of the transition. These include a permissive security environment; a base level of local governance capacity; robust political will to drive change among key local and external stakeholders; and a durable commitment of resources from external actors. However, the lack of fertile conditions for the stabilisation project did not guarantee its failure. In fact, some minimal progress has been achieved, with important advancements in private sector development, primary education and health. The stabilisation mission was also undermined by poor strategic and tactical decisions by donors, notably their move to concentrate resources on stabilising the most challenging and insecure districts of the country first rather than building momentum in better performing areas, and the failure to inform programming with a comprehensive evidence base and track it with appropriate M&E instruments.

Traditional stabilisation and state-building activities will bear little fruit in Afghanistan until there is a shift in the overarching political and security environment. In fact, there are three shifts that need to materialise to create more conducive conditions for change. First, a peace agreement has to be reached with the Taliban that will end the insurgency and permit their re-entry into the political process. This will give Afghanistan the indispensable political settlement that was always lacking. Second, key regional actors, notably Pakistan, Iran, the Central Asian States, the Arab Gulf States, Russia and China, along with the UN, NATO and the United States need to come together to develop a regional framework to ensure non-interference in Afghanistan's affairs and support its long-term reconstruction. Third, key international donors must commit to subsidising the Afghan security sector for the foreseeable future. Without guaranteed subsidies, the Afghan state, particularly the security forces as they are currently constructed, will be prone to collapse with devastating consequences for the country's security. Geopolitical currents and domestic political conditions in Afghanistan seem to indicate that these shifts will be a tall order, but they are critical for the future stability of the country. Many donors have interpreted the Afghan experience as an indictment of the overarching and overlapping concepts of stabilisation and state-building, indicating their bankruptcy as instruments of change. Contrary to this view the Afghan case demonstrates that a reconfigured strategy could achieve better success under the right conditions. Donors have to accept that stabilisation operations may not be appropriate in every circumstance, particularly in areas where a political settlement is lacking, and high levels of insecurity persist. Where there are enabling conditions, a strategy carefully calibrated to the local environment that is flexible, politically attuned, and properly sequenced, meaningful results could be achieved.

With traditional stabilisation stakeholders retreating from the concept, opportunities exist for new actors to reinvigorate it and put their stamp on it. One type of stakeholder that will likely assume an even greater role in the stabilisation field in the future are regional organisations and blocs of states, such as the African Union, the Organisation of American States and Arab Gulf States. We have already seen the African Union assume a major role in peace and security issues on the African continent, with significant Western donor assistance, developing its own norms and infrastructure to support peacebuilding and stabilisation processes. Regional bodies have the advantage of local knowledge and existing political capital in the target countries that international actors often lack. Of course, regional states could be an existing party to those conflicts as well, complicating their involvement in reconstruction. The Arab Gulf States could leverage their considerable financial and political assets to develop tailored strategies and infrastructure to advance stabilisation operations in various Middle East hotspots, beyond narrow military engagements which we have seen recently in Libya, Iraq and Yemen. This is a crucial period of transition and change for the stabilisation concept and the broader peace and security field; there are distinct entry points for new stakeholders and a need for new ideas. Those new stakeholders must learn the lessons of cases like Afghanistan if they are to succeed in improving the fortunes of the stabilisation model.

NOTES

1. See UNSG (2018).
2. See Kolenda et al. (2016).
3. See Mac Ginty (2012, p. 23).
4. See Herbert (2013, p. 2).
5. Quoted in SIGAR (2018, p. vi).
6. See Keen with Attree (2015, pp. 1–2).
7. See Mac Ginty (2012, p. 28).
8. See Dennys (2013, p. 2).
9. See SIGAR (2018, pp. 6, 8).
10. See Dennys (2013, p. 5).
11. See Keen with Attree (2015, pp. 1–2).
12. See Mac Ginty (2012).
13. See SIGAR (2018, p. 5).
14. See Rubin (2004, p. 167).
15. See Sedra (2017, p. 164).
16. Ibid.
17. Ibid., p. 165.
18. See Sedra (2004, p. 1).
19. See Sedra (2017, p. 168) and Janjua (2017).
20. See Sedra (2017, p. 170).
21. See SIGAR (2012, p. 175).
22. See Lynch (2014).
23. See UNAMA (2015).

24. Ibid.
25. See Shah and Mashal (2018).
26. See SIGAR (2018, p. xi).
27. See Sedra (2017, p. 249).
28. See SIGAR (2018, p. 141).
29. Ibid., p. 169.
30. Ibid., p. 170.
31. Ibid., p. 171.
32. Quoted in Long and Radin (2012, p. 120)
33. See Maley (2009).
34. See Sedra (2017, p. 248).
35. See Ahmad (2012).
36. See SIGAR (2018, p. 181).
37. Ibid., p. 188.
38. See Sedra (2017).
39. Ibid., p. 250.
40. See Hignite (2007).
41. See US DoD (2007).
42. See Sand (2007).
43. See Mogelson (2011).
44. See Kapstein (2017, p. 4).
45. See US Joint Chiefs of Staff (2016).
46. See Sedra (2017, p. 237).
47. See Nadery (2012).
48. See SIGAR (2018, p. 192).
49. Ibid.
50. See Sedra (2017, p. 68).
51. See SIGAR (2018, p. 171).
52. See Sedra (2017, p. 68).
53. Ibid., p. 236.
54. See CIGI (2010, p. 15).
55. See SIGAR (2018, p. 149).
56. Ibid., p. 152.
57. See Jackson (2018).
58. Ibid.
59. Ibid.
60. See Sharifi and Adamou (2018).
61. See UNAMA (2018).
62. See Jackson (2018).
63. See Bhatia and Sedra (2008).
64. See JCOA (2014, p. 1).
65. See SIGAR (2012, p. 57).
66. See Kapstein (2017, p. 8).

67. Ibid., p. 9.
68. See Katzman (2012, p. 15).
69. See Kapstein (2017, p. 6).
70. See Ghani et al. (2006, p. 112).
71. See Hanifi (2008) and Oliker (2011).
72. See Kelly et al. (2011, p. 9).
73. See SIGAR (2018, p. 181).
74. See Kapstein (2017, p. 4).
75. Ibid.
76. See SIGAR (2018, p. 181).
77. See UNAMA (2016).
78. See Mashal (2018).

BIBLIOGRAPHY

Ahmed, Javid. "Cultural Sensitivity Key to U.S. Role in Afghanistan." *CNN*, 31 August 2012.

Bhatia, Michael Vinay, and Sedra, Mark . *Afghanistan, Arms and Conflict: Armed Groups, Disarmament and Security in a Post-war Society*. London: Routledge, 2008.

Centre for International Governance Innovation (CIGI). *Security Sector Reform Monitor: Afghanistan*, No. 4. Waterloo, ON, Canada: CIGI, 2010.

Dennys, Christian. "For Stabilization." *Stability: International Journal of Security and Development*, vol. 2, no. 1 (2013): 1–14.

Ghani, Ashraf, Clare Lockhart, and Michael Carnahan. "An Agenda for State-Building in the Twenty-First Century." *The Fletcher Forum of World Affairs*, vol. 30, no. 1 (Winter 2006): 101–123.

Goode, Steven M. "A Historical Basis for Force Requirements in Counterinsurgency." *Parameters*, vol. 39 (Winter 2009–2010): 45–47.

Hanifi, Shah Mahmoud. *Connecting Shared Histories in Afghanistan: Market Relations and State Formation on a Colonial Frontier*. Stanford: Stanford University Press, 2008.

Herbert, Siân. "Stability and Stabilisation Approaches in Multinational Interventions." GSDRC Helpdesk Research Report. Cranfield, UK: GSDRC, 2013.

Hignite, Greg. "On Patrol: Newest ANAP Graduates Provide Security in Kandahar." In *CSTC-A, Defence and Security Highlights Afghanistan*. Kabul: CSTC-A, 2007.

International Crisis Group (ICG). *Reforming Afghanistan's Police*. Asia Report No. 138. Brussels: ICG, 2007.

Iyengar, Radha, Shapiro, Jacob N., Crisman, Benjamin, Singh, Manu, and Mao, James. *Stabilization in Afghanistan: Trends in Violence, Attitudes, Well-Being and Program Activity*. Rand Working Paper. Santa Monica: Rand Corporation, 2017.

Jackson, Ashley. "The Taliban's Fight for Hearts and Minds." *Foreign Policy Magazine*, 12 September 2018.

Janjua, Haroon. "'Unspeakable Numbers': 10,000 Civilians Killed or Injured in Afghanistan in 2017." *The Guardian*, 16 February 2018.

Joint and Coalition Operational Analysis (JCOA). *Operationalizing Counter/Anti-Corruption Study*. Suffolk, VA: JCOA, 2014.

Kapstein, Ethan B. *Aid and Stabilization in Afghanistan: What Do the Data Say?* USIP Special Report No. 405. Washington, DC: USIP, 2017.

Katzman, Kenneth. *Afghanistan: Post-Taliban Governance, Security and U.S. Policy*. CRS Report for Congress 7-5700. Washington, DC: Congressional Research Service, 2012.

Keen, David with Larry Attree. *Dilemmas of Counter-Terror, Stabilisation and State-building*. London: Saferworld, 2015.

Kelly, Terrence K., Bensahel, Nora , and Oliker, Olga. *Security Force Assistance in Afghanistan: Identifying Lessons for Future Efforts*. Santa Monica, CA: RAND, 2011.

Kolenda, Christopher D., Reid, Rachel, Rogers, Chris, and Retzius, Marte. *The Strategic Costs of Civilian Harm: Applying Lessons from Afghanistan to Current and Future Conflicts*. New York: Open Society Foundations, 2016.

Long, Austin, and Radin, Andrew . "Enlisting Islam for an Effective Afghan Police." *Survival*, vol. 54, no. 2 (2012): 112–128.

Lynch, Colum. "U.S. Watchdog: U.N. Misspent Hundreds of Millions of Dollars in Afghanistan." *Foreign Policy Magazine*, 6 October 2014.

Mac Ginty, Roger. "Against Stabilization." *Stability: International Journal of Security and Development*, vol. 1, no. 1 (2012): 20–30.

Maley, William. *The Afghanistan Wars*. 2nd ed. London: Palgrave Macmillan, 2009.

Mashal, Mujib. "In Afghanistan's Season of Crisis, 'Words Do Not Have the Strength.'" *The New York Times*, 17 October 2018.

Mogelson, Luke. "Bad Guys vs. Worse Guys in Afghanistan." *The New York Times*, 19 October 2011.

Nadery, Ahmad Nader. "Getting Human Rights Wrong is not an Option." *Foreign Policy Magazine*, 17 May 2012.

Oliker, Olga. *Building Afghanistan's Security Forces in Wartime: The Soviet Experience*. Santa Monica, CA: RAND, 2011.

Rubin, Barnett R. "(Re)Building Afghanistan: The Folly of Stateless Democracy." *Current History*, vol. 103, no. 672 (April 2004): 165–170.

Sand, Benjamin. 'Afghan Government Recruiting Thousands of Auxiliary Police to Battle Insurgents', *Voice of America*, 10 January 2007.

Sedra, Mark. *Are the Taliban Really 'Gone'?* Silver City, NM and Washington, DC: Foreign Policy In Focus, 2004.

———. *Security Sector Reform in Conflict-Affected Countries: The Evolution of a Model*. London: Routledge, 2017.

Shah, Taimoor, and Mashal, Mujib. "An Afghan Police Chief Took on the Taliban and Won. Then His Luck Ran Out." *The New York Times*, 18 October 2018.

Sharifi, Shoaib, and Adamou, Louise. "Taliban Threaten 70% of Afghanistan, BBC Finds." *BBC*, 31 January 2018.

Special Inspector General for Afghanistan Reconstruction (SIGAR). *Stabilization: Lessons from the U.S. Experience in Afghanistan.* Arlington, VA: SIGAR, 2018.

Special Investigator General for Afghanistan Reconstruction (SIGAR). *Quarterly Report to the United States Congress* (April 2012). Arlington, VA: SIGAR, 2012.

United Nations Assistance Mission in Afghanistan (UNAMA). *Afghanistan: Protection of Civilians in Armed Conflict Report 2014.* Kabul: UNAMA, 2015.

———. *Afghanistan: Protection of Civilians in Armed Conflict Report 2017.* Kabul: UNAMA, 2018.

United Nations Assistance Mission in Afghanistan (UNAMA). *Briefing to the United Nations Security Council by the Secretary-General's Special Representative for Afghanistan, Mr. Nicholas Haysom.* New York, 15 March 2016.

United Nations Secretary General (UNSG). *The Situation in Afghanistan and Its Implications for International Peace and Security.* A/73/374-S/2018/824. New York: United Nations, 2018.

US Army. *Field Manual 3-24, Counterinsurgency.* Washington, DC: Headquarters Department of the Army, 2006.

US Department of Defense (US DoD). *News Briefing with Maj. Gen. Robert Durbin and Deputy Minister Abdul Hadir Khalid from the Pentagon.* Transcript, 9 January 2007.

US Joint Chiefs of Staff. Joint Publication (JP) 3-07, Stability. Washington, DC: US Joint Chiefs of Staff, 2016.

CHAPTER 4

A Diplomatic Perspective on Stabilisation

Bernardino León Gross

INTRODUCTION

Stabilisation represents, in a way, an alternative to diplomacy. In the past, states operated along a binary set of international affairs: either it was peacetime, or it was a time of war. Reflecting this organisational principle, states tended to focus on two key approaches in their external engagements: they projected power abroad through their armed forces in times of war, or through their diplomatic and commercial networks in peacetime. This toolkit was adequate for such a binary, clearly demarcated set of situations. However, in the last three decades, various strategists and academics have introduced a new kind of external projection: a hybrid approach that reflects the way in which post-Cold War conflicts are usually described. A grey zone is conceived between war and peace and new modes of external engagements have emerged, with fading diplomacy and a new emphasis on the concept of stabilisation. We have seen the growth of the use of concepts such as 'whole-of-government' and 'civil-military action', generally driven by administrative coordination units, or by the military. In the US, for instance, it has been called kinetic diplomacy, which has often translated in

B. León Gross (✉)
Emirates Diplomatic Academy, Abu Dhabi, United Arab Emirates

© The Author(s) 2020
V. Gervais and S. van Genugten (eds.), *Stabilising the Contemporary Middle East and North Africa*, Middle East Today,
https://doi.org/10.1007/978-3-030-25229-8_4

67

more deployments of special forces and less presence of diplomats abroad.[1] This new approach does not necessarily deny classic diplomacy a role, but places it within a toolkit of other necessary instruments of external policy actions, including security and development aspects of conflict resolution, and weakens its pre-eminence and coordinating role between communities and policies. Different from classic diplomacy, this new mode of intervention is predominantly unilateral in nature, at least as a strategic concept. To a large extent, this is the case because of a belief that once deployed on the ground, civilian or military units of allied states operate with similar objectives, thereby minimising the need for diplomatic coordination. In sum, the focus on stabilisation relegates diplomacy to a less prominent level.

This trend from a narrower emphasis on multilateral diplomacy to a broader emphasis on more unilaterally implemented stabilisation packages should come as no surprise. Although the history of contemporary stabilisation operations can be traced back to colonial conflicts, such as the counter-insurgency operations of the US in the Philippines after the war against Spain in 1898, or that of France in the War of Independence in Algeria,[2] its most recent version has been shaped in Afghanistan and Iraq, reflecting operations initiated by the US. These military interventions signalled a new approach—maybe a paradigm shift towards unilateralism, as the US and its allies started to question prevailing multilateral institutions and the international law underpinning them. These institutions, outcomes of decades-long diplomatic efforts, are being considered, in a certain way, increasingly outdated.

Diplomacy is a *continuum* that tries to understand with a long-term vision the causes and consequences of problems and considers the divergence of interests as normal, but the conflict as abnormal. This chapter argues that we should bring diplomacy back to the central stage. Undoubtedly, the practice of diplomacy needs to be reformed, but it remains useful and potentially indispensable. Its natural capacity to operate during a conflict and represent all sectors of administration and society is an asset. Effective diplomacy is inherently more multilateral than stabilisation approaches are. It proposes policies and plans in situations of misgovernment and disorder that are sustained over time and supported by a broad set of countries and organisations. Diplomacy tends to understand the difference between reality 'on paper' and 'on the ground'.[3] Institutions and international development agencies will often be travelling companions and, in times of acute crisis, it might be necessary to incorporate military elements.[4]

Ultimately, it is a matter of dosage of each element,[5] which remains one of the great challenges of stabilisation.

Stabilisation operations tend to be focused on the short term. They do not seem to pursue, as for example in the case of normalisation,[6] a return to a situation of generalised order, but rather aim at the recovery of some vital survival constants for a state. It is a kind of declaration of a state of emergency that might allow an interruption of the application of international and national legislation, somehow dictated from abroad, which creates a situation of absolute exceptionality, whose governance is uncertain.[7]

In the classical binary system of war and peace, international diplomatic law applies in peacetime, while during a conflict, combatants apply international humanitarian law. Some of nowadays stabilisation operations have instead worked in a *limbo* of ambiguous legal foundations. Allegations of violations of international law and human rights by those who were called to restore them in Iraq are a testimony in this regard. This challenge was compounded by the fact that the historically difficult relations between the promoters of major stabilisation operations of the early 2000s and the UN, a classical diplomatic institution, has led to the paradoxical situation that stabilisation often denies the involvement of the UN, while the UN often denies stabilisation as a valid conflict resolution approach. In this context, if the debate does not leave the political-bureaucratic and academic environments in which it is currently confined and is fully integrated into global and regional international organisations, it is difficult to imagine the viability of the concept in the medium and long term. This will involve a thorough and painful debate that will bring important modifications with respect to the concept we have known up to the present, which is desirable if it provides greater precision and global acceptability, so that stabilisation will not remain an 'elusive concept'.[8] There seem to be compelling reasons for diplomacy to occupy a central place in the debate on the future of the concept of stabilisation. Diplomatic actors are permanently on the ground and develop a long-term relationship with all sectors of a state and society. Therefore, it is not entirely a *foreign body* and is by nature multilateral and open to work with development organisations. But when we say more diplomacy, we do not mean only on the ground. We mean that diplomacy is a complex organic system in which all parts are interconnected. It works locally and globally.

Effective diplomacy does not only work with global actors (it is essentially transactional, synallagmatic), but also tries to incorporate regional actors. Neighbouring countries of that area or country facing serious challenges to its political, economic or security governance tend to share these challenges to a greater or lesser extent. Chapter VIII of the UN Charter has codified the prominence of regional involvement. If Afghanistan, for example, is unstable, so will be Pakistan, and its other neighbours, China, and even India, will be affected. If Iraq, Syria, Yemen, Libya or Mali are unstable, so will their neighbours, and they must be the first ones concerned with trying to find an end to a crisis. This principle of classical diplomacy is still pertinent and regional organisations must claim and be granted a greater role in the debate.[9] This holds in particular true in the Middle East and North Africa (MENA) region, where efforts to stem that instability should include a return to classical diplomacy, as a way to facilitate the application of remedies that are agreed collectively, in accordance with ethical codes and a multilateral approach.

When we speak of diplomacy, we mean renewed diplomacy, with a new toolkit that enhances negotiation and consensus, preferably through multilateral institutions, though also bilateral diplomacy enhances the role of local actors.

This chapter has three parts. First, it will describe the need for diplomacy at a *macro*-level to reach viable parameters for stabilisation. This means working on general principles and international law and considering the role of United Nations. Secondly, it will posit the reflection from the MENA region perspective, in which the diplomatic conversation must incorporate its own characteristics and toolkit in order to be considered as an option in one of the most challenging backgrounds one can imagine for stability. Finally, the chapter will present some thoughts on the experience of Libya as an essentially diplomatic and political process of stabilisation, which was strongly indigenous in nature.

The Uncomfortable Diplomatic Agenda: Between 'Stabilisation' and Multilateral Diplomacy

A point has arrived at which intense diplomatic work is needed to build consensus *for* stabilisation and *within* stabilisation. In recent decades, there have been disagreements among policy communities and organisations involved in stabilisation efforts that help explain the problematic situation in which we find ourselves today. Stabilisation is an unstable concept designed to help countries emerge from situations of acute crises and large-scale violence, which has created its own legal and political disorder. Different initiatives and processes converge in the diffuse practice of stabilisation, and all of them have been the object of struggles between different policy objectives that have deepened in a specific area without extending to the rest, although all of them overlap. Therefore, given the confluence of political, legal, military and communication aspects of different actors and levels, there is a need for a diplomatic process based on international law principles and legitimacy. Indeed, only dialogue and agreement can allow a solution, not so much to the problem of the definition of stabilisation, but to the dysfunctions that the lack of common understanding might represent for human security. In the following pages, the way this process could be articulated is being outlined.

The Debate on the Foundations: International Law

When assessing the possibility of articulating a coherent diplomatic perspective on stabilisation, the key question remains whether it is possible to address new challenges, in particular those associated with the issue of interventions in 'fragile' settings, while reinforcing multilateral organisations and the UN Charter. The process will involve reflecting on the constitutional foundations of the global order, sovereignty, international humanitarian law, human rights and the Responsibility to Protect. Very profound changes have happened since the end of the Second World War and this means we are facing a great effort of adaptation. The nature of the prevailing conflicts in recent decades requires a new type of peace operation, so closely connected, after all, to stabilisation. Only a diplomatic effort similar to that made at the 2005 UN World Summit[10] would allow us to re-establish such an important issue on sound foundations, and today it can be assumed that it will be a more complex task given the global changes and subsequent breaches of confidence.[11] The debate should include, *inter alia*, concepts such as sovereignty, fragility and the use of force and should involve the insights of civil society and NGOs, as their support is crucial. The coordination of the debate should be in the hands of diplomats, as diplomacy is better suited to be the pivot of a dialogue in which all parties are involved. Diplomats' relationship with development institutions and NGOs is more 'natural' than that of the military, since they are usually integrated into the same ministries and are accustomed to working in close coordination. Arbitrating a fluid relationship between the 'three D's' (diplomacy, defence, development), but with respect to the nature and function of each one,[12] may seem less tempting than strong action to 'win hearts and minds', but it will probably be to a wider benefit of all involved.

With regard to the concept of sovereignty, the focus should be on finding a new consensus that the entire international community can agree with. Sovereignty is the principle that has dominated international law in its evolution since the times of the founding fathers, elevated to 'doctrine' when Brierly explained Bodin and Hobbes.[13] It also attracts great interest given its recent evolution. Beyond its recognition as a principle on which the UN is 'based', and the frequent assertion that authoritarian regimes hide behind it to commit all kinds of abuses and produce instability, in the last decades limitations have been added that portray sovereignty as a non-absolute principle, for example, through the creation of law by international organisations, the development of institutions such as the European Union, the actions of the International Courts and the development of Human Rights regimes (including emerging and promising proposals on non-state actors responsibilities). But it must be remembered that Article 2.1 of the UN Charter speaks of the 'Principle of sovereign equality', which should apply *equally* to all subjects of international law, since both principles must be considered together, as Kelsen famously put it.[14] No *laudatio* to the outdated principle is needed, but it can be celebrated that in recent years progress has been made towards ideas of cooperative sovereignty such as those advocated by Chayes and Chayes.[15] Conversely to frequent criticism from the North, G77 countries have accepted this evolution, for example, in the case of the principle of the Responsibility to Protect as an expression of twenty-first-century sovereignty.[16]

It is of vital importance today to recover that consensus, to build a concept of sovereignty that, based on equality, does not divide the international community between states that can afford to decide unilaterally when other states are dysfunctional and project their power, and those who cannot. The Security Council and regional international organisations, in accordance with Chapters VII and VIII of the UN Charter, are the ones who must determine when collective action must be taken in the face of threats to international peace and security. Also, when talking about the toolkit of stabilisation operations, it is important to include *legitimacy*, which must accompany legality. Sometimes, a simple agreement between two states may allow for the second, but it is the intervention of the relevant international organisations that bolster the first. Thus, while the question of sovereignty may seem too broad in the face of stabilisation debates, both appear to be closely interrelated.

When it comes to the concept of fragility, the debate should focus on agreeing on concrete criteria about the nature of fragility and when these would become candidates for stabilisation measures. Fragility is a popular term, but is very controversial and has no legal translation, despite its success in different circles. However, *fragility* does have a place in multilateral organisations such as the World Bank or the OECD, which has published an index since 2005 and for which these states are characterised by risk and lack of capacity.[17] Although the OECD has made recent North-South transversal efforts, and the final end is to prevent vulnerability to a range of shocks, it continues to be looked upon with suspicion. Fragility is a policy-oriented label, value-burdened, confusing and superficial. The international community needs to operate on clear concepts, and not uncertain labels. Edward Said explained in *Orientalism* the risks of building such discourses[18] and then apply them as a filter to look at the world. Concepts evolve and new elements continue to feed stereotypes, think of Paul Collier's 'greed', or Kaplan's 'scarcity, crime, overpopulation, tribalism and disease'. Allegedly, the new concept of fragility has its roots in the idea of the 1990s of the *failed* state and Liberal Peace.[19] Also the *War on Terror* has had an inevitable overlap in the debate on stereotypes, since it changed *all*, the whole perception of security, overlapping with conflicts of all kinds, ethnic, generated by failed states, genocides, ecological wars, natural resources, etc.[20] All this should be considered when stating that insecurity or terrorism stems from poverty or fragility.

The interest for international law is not a philosophical debate but is based on the tendency to consider *fragility* as the assumption that justifies stabilisation operations.[21] Numerous voices have shown their concern about this issue, *who* and based on *which criteria* decides what is fragility, given the important consequences of the debate. The Group of 77 (G77) accepted, in a certain way, a concept of a *failed* state: those who commit 'genocide, war crimes, ethnic cleansing and crimes against humanity', as the international community unanimously accepted at the 2005 Summit.[22] Those states that have signed or ratified the Rome Statute, including many members of the G77, have also accepted limitations for their leaders and officials. The same holds true for the states party to the American Convention and the African Charter on Human Rights. Therefore, there is enough basis to think that it would be possible through wide diplomatic consultations to pave the way for the establishment of an objective and consensual understanding of the concept of fragility that could inform stabilisation practices.

The debate should also consider finding consensus on the prerequisites for the use of force. If sovereignty is the *basis* of the UN, the Charter affirms in its first article that its *raison d'être* is the maintenance of international peace and security through 'effective collective measures'. This refers not only to acts of aggression, but also to 'other breaches of the peace', which should make it possible to consider other assumptions, such as severe instability, or the presence of terrorist or criminal groups that threaten collective security. When the Charter prohibits in its Article 2.4 the use of force, it specifies that such use may affect the territorial integrity, but also the 'political independence' of a state, or any other aspect that is incompatible with 'the purposes of the United Nations'. The last twenty years have shown very interesting advances in which the Security Council has adapted to new situations, understanding that phenomena such as humanitarian crises or *coups d'état* can also constitute threats to international peace and security, and it has included novel mechanisms, such as humanitarian corridors, no-fly zones or safe havens, and individualised smart sanctions.[23]

Yet, much remains to be done: Chinkin and Kaldor have highlighted the criticism for the possible loss of legitimacy, or the insufficient incorporation of civil society,[24] especially since the proposals to reform the use of the veto by permanent members of the UN Security Council have not gone very far. However, the work done up to the present has been of value, and the Security Council began a reflection on the eve of 9/11 proposing modifications to international law. These advances demonstrate that the objectification of criteria is possible, but it requires, again, a diplomatic process without which it would be impossible to modify one of the fundamental constitutional concepts of the international community.

Overall, the debate should also address the fundamental question of the relationship between security and development (and its *political* meaning).[25] This is a quasi-constitutional debate that has been ongoing for decades and has been a source of many controversies and misunderstandings.[26] From the 1991 Boutros Ghali document,[27] much has been written about the need (almost 'orthodoxy'[28]) of every society to advance in both vectors. This does not mean, however, that the actions of the international community in countries considered *fragile* can automatically assume the objectives and initiatives of military forces and development institutions and organisations, public and private, to be aligned with one another. It has occurred in exceptional cases in the past and, in addition to generating strong criticism in the international cooperation community, it has largely failed to produce the expected results, either in terms of security or development, as detailed case studies have shown.[29] There are guiding principles that must be taken into consideration, like the Red Cross Code of Conduct, Sphere Humanitarian Charter or MSF Chantilly Principles and La Mancha Agreement.

Within the debate, a key question is to what extent development and security can be linked. The SDGs have allowed a sophisticated metric that shows, through multiple indicators, that all countries suffer some fragility, both in the North and in the South, and therefore we must avoid any confusion between vulnerabilities in the field of development and in that of security. The SDGs also offer a toolkit, with guidelines and *Soft Law* tools to work on them, and an elaborate vision of what *resilience* means,[30] a success of international diplomacy and the UN, which also should remain the forum for this debate. SDG16 proposes a way to rethink the divide between development and security. Coordination approaches of state apparatuses are welcome, but proposals such as the whole of government and civil-military cooperation make more sense as organisational principles for more effective bureaucracies,[31] than as models of action in the field. It is therefore of the utmost importance to maintain security and development as interconnected principles whose instruments on the ground are distinct and can work independently (although coordinated).

The Debate on Implementation: United Nations Security Council

Since Dag Hammarskjold proposed the three criteria for peacekeeping missions—consent, impartiality and non-use of force except in self-defence—the international community has known moments of consensus and dissent about UN peace missions and has learned that the latter is frustrating and sterile, and that the periods of disagreement require a return, sooner or later, to the agreement. All stakeholders have to be involved in defining—or perhaps redefining—the limits, actors and assumptions for peacemaking, peacebuilding, peacekeeping and, where and if appropriate, peace-enforcing, a large-scale diplomatic project, as Carl Bildt explained.[32] It can be understood that it is a debate that would directly affect stabilisation missions, and it is critical to understand that this is a normative and an operational issue, and not only the latter.[33]

The world and its conflicts have changed, and, after tragic failures in some of these *new wars*,[34] many requested more effective UN missions in a debate with blurred lines between peacebuilding and peacekeeping on the one hand, and peace enforcement. This is why Secretaries General Kofi

Annan and Ban Ki-moon have commissioned reports on this type of missions. The 2000 *Brahimi Report* addressed many of the challenges related to stabilisation operations, and, if it had been fully implemented, perhaps it might have shaped more successful operations. But the post-9/11 scenario was more conducive to stabilisation missions. The Brahimi report emphasises diplomacy, since its philosophy is that more robust use of force must be accompanied by more robust diplomacy for peacebuilding, through the development of the Department of Political Affairs and instruments such as enhanced fact-finding missions. The report also insisted on a more political role of the Secretariat in cases similar to Kosovo. Mandates should be carefully addressed, in a credible and achievable way, for the maintenance of a peace agreement. The use of force would be required in more complex scenarios to protect civilians, peacebuilders and UN staff, missions should be impartial and have the consent of the parties and receive better training and support (including information gathering) tools. Civilian, police and rule of law components were heightened. All this should require more coordination through Integrated Mission Task Forces and a Peacebuilding Unit.

Although many aspects that justify stabilisation missions were there, there was no proper follow up for most of these recommendations. After the previously described *confrontational* years, in 2015, the 'Review of the Question of Peacekeeping Operations in all its aspects, the Special Political Missions and the Reinforcement of the UN System' was published by a UN panel chaired by Jose Ramos Horta. It reiterated that the orientation must be essentially political in the design and development of peace operations, although flexible to adapt to the needs on the ground, and always seeking an association for global and regional peace and security, vindicating equally more diplomacy. It also insisted that mediation should be the priority element, along with a central obligation to protect civilians in a realistic convergence of expectations and capabilities.

The UN needs clarity regarding the possibilities of using force and the relationship with other forces present in conflicts, recalling that what maintains peace agreements and reinforces them is, above all, political action. The report does not ignore the ecosystems in which *stabilisation* is predicated, and in its points 11–14 describe the situation of states with little resilience or in a post-conflict situation, where terrorist and other violent groups are present, and cases in which poor governance produces devastating effects, but in point 14 it points out that the strategies focused on these environments have not had the expected success and the approaches must change. UN peacekeepers cannot respond to 'all threats' (point 17).

The 2015 Report of the High-Level Independent Panel on Peace Operations (HIPPO) launched a challenge to international diplomacy and the academic and legal world in its paragraph 111: 'The Panel also notes that in the last decade, the Security Council and the Secretariat have used the term "stabilisation" for a number of missions that support the extension or restoration of state authority and, in at least one case, during ongoing armed conflict. The term stabilisation has a wide range of interpretations, and the Panel believes the use of this term by the UN requires clarification'. This is not a concept of minor importance in the UN system, since it has served to define some important and delicate missions between 2004 and 2014, such as MONUSCO, MINUSTAH, MINUSCA and MINUSMA. Although it is hard to imagine how it was possible to agree on the fundamental meaning of these missions without a consensus on their denomination, it is even more difficult to imagine that this practice can be maintained in the future, especially after the 2015 report. The—probably intended—constructive ambiguity that has allowed to reach this point does not hide, however, a 'doctrinal change' that could have 'unforeseen consequences'.[35] It may be useful to inquire into the nature of these missions to begin this orientation exercise. MONUSCO's mandate allows for a robust peacekeeping and proactive defence of civilians, in addition to the creation of a Brigade of Intervention Force, conceived especially to confront the M23 guerrilla. MINUSCA and MINUSMA present similar characters, and MINUSTAH has a robust mandate to confront organised crime in Haiti. This has led some observers to point out that the HIPPO might have assumed that the prevailing interpretation in these missions has been the 'Western' one.[36]

The positions of the main country groups involved seem quite different. We can essentially divide them into three major camps: the main Western countries that have individually developed their own doctrines of stabilisation (and the organisations in which these countries are integrated), the candidate countries to receive at some point such missions and their allies, and other states. Western countries have accumulated some experience in this type of missions, showing clear support, which is even more marked in the case of Eastern European countries.[37] Authors such as Curran and Holtom, or De Coning, have attributed an outstanding persuasion work to the three Western permanent members, frequent *penholders* in many of these resolutions.[38] The term is applied with nuances to NATO and the EU (who have their own experience in the region[39]), but with a more restricted sense. Among the Latin American countries, more doubts are recorded (lower in the case of MINUSTAH) and likewise the Africans, who do not include stabilisation operations in the equivalents of the AU African Standby Force.[40] In 2010, Morocco stated on behalf of the Non-Aligned Movement that peacekeeping was sufficiently robust, and South Africa underlined that they should not be used for peace enforcement.[41] The Arab countries showed little enthusiasm in 2004 through the SG of the LA, as we will see later. On the other hand, the states that most contribute to the PKOs have also shown their concern[42] (importantly, parallel to a certain Western intervention fatigue). Russia, India and other Asian countries have expressed similar doubts in recent years.[43]

The problem is of enormous importance, because the Security Council is the *legitimate authority* to authorise the use of force and must have precise criteria to do so. After the rejection of the Bush administration's proposal for Iraq and subsequent events, there was a rupture that could have been overcome at the 2005 Summit. But, as has been indicated, another rupture would arise in 2011 after events in Libya. The model used in the past is exhausted. All countries have understood the lesson: no state, nor the most powerful, can sustain this type of operations in the long run (and here there is no short term). However, if we accept that these ecosystems tend to spread, in the medium-term new such situations will emerge, and the tendency should be the multilateralisation of *fully legitimate* operations. Some of the national stabilisation doctrines are gradually converging towards that vision, but they need to affirm it more soundly, and the distance with the G77 and UN reports is still perceptible. Others are evolving in a more counterproductive direction.[44] Diplomatic agreements will be required in the Security Council for the construction of a large consensus that avoids ambiguities, contradictions or absences in similar cases, the use of a concept that has a value implication, and strategic and legal consequences of relevance. We must avoid placing ourselves in a 'no man's land' where there is no 'operational concept-guide'.[45]

Diplomacy for a Consensual Concept of Stabilisation

Discussions on both the normative and operational aspects of peace and stabilisation missions will continue in the Security Council, for a broader concept or for ad hoc decisions.[46] Yet, the Council is not the right place for academic debates, since it operates with a hectic agenda and must deal with all kinds of global crises. Such debates should therefore take place in a diplomatic and academic dialogue on concepts. It is here that the contributions of academics and think tanks can be highly valuable and support the dialogue in the Security Council and other organisations and states which should try to converge towards a broadly acceptable definition and guidelines, following the excellent example of international humanitarian law for the past 150 years.

For this to happen, it might be necessary that academics also progress in their own 'diplomatic' dialogue, since it is not possible to speak of a widely accepted definition of stabilisation in the literature either, as can be concluded from the introductory chapter of this book. For some, it is simple counter-insurgency or counterterrorism; for others, it is the state-building aspect that prevails. Some highlight the 'three Ds' (diplomacy, defence, development), for others the concept must be more restricted. As such, Robert Muggah's work, or the concept proposed by Zyck, Barakat and Deely can be good starting points: 'a process involving coercive force in concert with reconstruction and development assistance during the immediate aftermath of a violent conflict in order to prevent the continuation or recurrence of conflict and destabilising levels of non-conflict violence'.[47] There is also a school of thought which is highly critical of the idea, including authors such as Duffield, who frames it in neo-colonial and neoliberal mindsets that delegitimise these operations, or Mac Ginty, who criticises the insistence on control and securitisation—instead of peace—and the prevailing 'good enoughery' in state-building, after setbacks in the last twenty years, instead of more local involvement.[48] Also Paris and Sisk have analysed the contradictions of stability and state-building and suggested they have to be rethought.[49]

Developing a concept with wide acceptance and overcoming the *misunderstandings* and *misinterpretations*[50] is so complex that it is worth considering Rotmann's approach, which identifies two thresholds, a more limited concept and a broader one, that gravitate precisely around this complex conjunction of the military and development. The 'broad' vision focuses on the challenge represented by fragility, lack of goods and services, political instability and unspecified violence of high or low intensity: in this case, stability must produce a lasting ('sustainable') peace, stability, security and prosperity. Faced with this concept 'without limits', a more realistic version appears that contemplates stabilisation as 'appeasement of crisis': it would try to avoid that crises reach a very acute character and contribute to generate resilience. If the state in question has the capacity to avoid extreme situations of violence, it is understood that problems may persist within its political system and its capacity to offer services to citizens, but these must be addressed in the long term and using other instruments. Most of the states that have been involved in the debates on 'stabilisation' seem to move in this direction.[51] Another approach is that of Barakat, who suggests the presence of criteria such as a clear mandate, early intervention, specificity of context and a clear transition strategy.[52] Dennys has proposed focusing on sub-national levels of stability.[53] Whichever approach is chosen, a potential academic convergence will have a high value in the current international context. It may serve as inspiration to crystalise current approaches or perhaps see how the stabilisation concept is blurred in the negotiations in the UN Security Council before new crises arise, and a new consensual vision of stabilisation takes over.

DIPLOMACY VS. STABILISATION IN THE MENA REGION

Putting diplomacy centre stage in the MENA region is as necessary as it is urgent and undoubtedly more pressing than in other areas of the globe. The region has witnessed three stabilisation operations that have generated the most controversy in recent decades, those of Iraq, Afghanistan, and Libya in 2011 and in addition to paying for actions generated in its midst, MENA countries pay a high price for the mistakes that others make on their soil. Currently, parties involved do not all opt for diplomacy. So far, at this historical moment characterised by a more prominent role for regional actors, a double focus has prevailed: firstly, international actors consider the region as a chessboard, where the progress of some is done to the detriment of the resources or the tactical position of others. Second, when it is inevitable, conflicts are started, mainly by involving proxies. Regional powers are not only competing among themselves, there is also a continuing interest of global powers in the MENA region, with sometimes opposing interests, as developments in Syria have shown.

However, the greater international assertiveness of regional actors is accompanied by interesting diplomatic initiatives that show new capabilities. From the diplomatic intervention of the UAE in Ethiopia-Eritrea to the Saudi plan for the Middle East, from the initiatives of Oman and Kuwait to those of Qatar, it is no longer the traditional Egyptian or Algerian diplomats that are the only players active in this field. Diplomacy has, in this sense, unprecedented opportunities in the region. But this would require a level of mutual confidence that does not exist today. Suffice it to recall the rejection of Iran to involve other regional actors in the Joint Comprehensive Plan of Action (JCPOA), something that had been accepted by the other negotiators and which perhaps today would have given the agreement greater strength. This is not only a quantitative issue—more local diplomacy—it is also a qualitative one, since regional diplomacy will require a specific toolkit. Working with local diplomats and tools increases the likelihood of success. The advantages of more local approaches and the understanding of specificities are necessary for a viable implementation of stabilisation.[54]

The problem of current day instability is not limited to specific territories or countries in the MENA region, it is a regional issue. Cold War formulas and stabilising policies have been left behind, and more recent ones have proven ineffective and controversial. Today local stabilisation is hardly conceivable without addressing the stabilisation of the region as a whole. Also for this objective, more homegrown diplomacy is needed. This raises the big questions about the appropriate forum, the extension and whether to include only Arab countries or adopt a broader scope. Equally important is the question about the notion of regional stabilisation and whether this should be a Westphalian concept based on hard sovereignty, which simply stops conflicts with limited intra-stabilisation efforts. Or a more structured and interventionist concept like that of the Congress of Vienna? Or perhaps a more cooperative vision with formulas such as the Helsinki Act or the first agreements of the European Community? Obviously, whatever the choice is, it should not be an *imported* one, but a localised one. Without answering these major questions, it is difficult to conceive stabilisation operations with a deployment of military, humanitarian and diplomatic forces. As has happened in the Security Council with other operations, it is not excluded to continue operating with ad hoc formulas, but it will be increasingly difficult. The states of the region should not only build a position *ad intra*, it would also be desirable to build it *ad extra*, as a regional consensus would result in greater possibilities for a consensus in the Security Council, whose decisions will undoubtedly continue to affect the region, a region that vitally needs the mistakes of the past not to be repeated.

Among the pending tasks of global diplomacy, is the implementation of a more effective division of labour with regional organisations, in accordance with Chapter VIII of the Charter. In the MENA region, this would have important implications for the Arab League. In 2004, the Secretary General of the Arab League, Amre Moussa, clearly showed the dissatisfaction of the regional organisation with the predominant stabilisation concept:

Is stabilisation an objective in itself? Is the purpose to cool down conflicts that are growing? Sometimes we find that, even when a situation is calm and when concerns are allayed, danger will remain if the status quo continues. The notion that stability will lead to peace and reconstruction has yet to be confirmed. It is in fact possible to take the opposite course: first to establish peace in order to ensure the success of peacekeeping operations, and then to pursue security, reconstruction, reconciliation and stability.

The next paradigm shift necessary is moving towards a positive concept of stabilisation. This means not only observing international developments, but also developing political and academic concepts from the region, to which this book aims to contribute. A regional vision of stabilisation would not be very different, but undoubtedly it would pay more attention to certain aspects. One of them would be sectarianism. The region has rejected *orientalising* tendencies, but such tendencies have multiplied since 9/11 and the beginning of the so-called War on Terror. For many in the US and other countries, the idea of terror is totalising.[55] In the region, there is a similar risk today due to the spread of sectarian violence. Often the same terrorist groups that seek with their attacks to consolidate a confrontation between the Judeo-Christian West and Islam, also seek to consolidate a sectarian confrontation in the MENA region between Sunnis and Shiites, which would amount to orientalising the East. Related to this aspect, stabilisation in the region will require a more effective fight against extremism, for which diplomacy can and should have sophisticated instruments and institutions (an organisation such as Hedayah is a good example[56]). To the extent that we have understood that there is no possible stabilisation in the short term, we must be aware that there is no stabilisation without tolerance and reconciliation.

Putting diplomacy centre stage in the MENA region must also involve the evolution of diplomacy towards twenty-first-century forms, in which *inclusion* can become one of its most valuable assets. History teaches us that inclusive diplomacy is more effective.[57] All the states of the region have a role to play in the process, although concentric circles may be established because some will have more impact than others. But inclusion today also implies working with civil society, at all levels, with different settings, from individuals to NGOs (including those of development, an area that has seen an impressive increase with some countries in the region in positions of global leadership). Since 2011, a vibrant civil society has been seen in the region asking to be heard, and this may be the best time to do so.

And, in a wider sense, cultural diplomacy is another interesting tool. In the Middle East, Western commentators often understate the importance of long-standing Arab cultural stabilising factors—the *majlis*, community and tribal links, etc. They often wrongly characterise Arab societies as being too hierarchical. In reality, there are checks and balances (in most) but they operate in less visible ways to our own. A twenty-first-century stabilisation approach might draw from these models as much as global ones, but the main goal should be to find the region's homegrown 'natural equilibrium',[58] in an inclusive way, without external interference.

Another issue of enormous importance in the region is human rights. Frequently, stabilisation operations originate in an environment characterised by serious violations of human rights. In turn, subsequent interventions have often produced new cases that further complicate the solutions, of which Iraq is a good example. Regional human rights institutions have developed impressively, for example, in Latin America or Africa. In the MENA region, it is still a pending issue. From a disappointing text agreed in 1990,[59] the region moved to the 2004 Arab Charter on Human Rights, which has also received justified criticism. The Arab Court of Human Rights is another step, but still insufficient and will take time to consolidate. There will not be any stability if it is not in a climate of strict respect for human rights. This should be a precious element in the regional diplomatic toolkit. Democratic societies with freedom of expression and free press will not only be more stable, they will prevail. Only by assuming certain great principles will it be possible to move to a second stage, where more delicate and complex issues that have already been evoked can be addressed, such as the development of an Arab League Standby Force, and the design and implementation of regional stabilisation missions.

A CASE STUDY OF POLITICAL-DIPLOMATIC STABILISATION IN THE MENA REGION: LIBYA

It is not the subject of this chapter to provide an in-depth analysis of the case of Libya. This book contains excellent case studies on the region and this chapter's goal is only to address the value of diplomacy as a central element in the construction and implementation of stabilisation formulas that work in the long term. For this, diplomacy and development must be maximised, promoting internal security and minimising external interventions, together with 'strategic patience', and allowing regional diplomacy to take the lead. These elements were present in the UN-sponsored stabilisation approach to Libya and offered a clear opportunity for stabilisation that today, after Khalifa Hafter operation in Tripoli, is likely to turn into instability and chaos.

In Libya, it is easy to see the glass half empty. The situation is far from stable, given the difficulties for political understanding, the threats that still remain in different areas, the profound differences of vision between different international actors and the existence of problems, such as the drama of smuggling and human trafficking, that produces a large number of deaths at sea every day, very serious abuses of human rights on land, and difficulties for European countries to pursue a unified vision within a rightly questioned externalisation. Unfortunately, there is no immediate short-term solution to these problems, but the principle that Libyans solve Libya's problems remained a priority in the Skhirat agreement (conceived as a first step towards stabilisation) and, it should remain a priority in the future. UNSMIL had an excellent team of diplomats, mainly from the region.

In 2014, Libya presented a very sombre situation of instability, with great fragmentation and a risk that the confrontations in Benghazi and Tripoli would end up becoming an all-out civil war in the country. In that reign of chaos, Daesh found the best breeding ground to build a large base of operations in the centre of the Mediterranean and close to Tunisia (whose democratic experience it wanted to destroy) and Europe, a priority target for their terrorist attacks. Different countries were considering political actions and studying possible military contingency plans. But Libya is an immense country, which poses logistical difficulties equally immense. After the summer confrontations, the options for the Libyans and the international community were *victor* or *virtue*, an elitist peace dictated by the *victors* (*Fajr Libya* in the West and Karama-LNA in the East) or a broad national agreement in which all Libyans could recognise themselves and subscribe to. The first option did not seem the most promising and would have represented offering military winners the possibility of dictating an agreement without having won the battle throughout the country. It would not have been a very stable and sustainable formula. An agreement drawn up with criteria of indigenous deliberative democracy might seem unorthodox, but it offered a perspective of stability built from bottom-up and top-down perspectives, that could work for society and for the elites.

The presence of Daesh and al-Qaeda, and their attacks against Egypt and Tunisia, the use by AQIM[60] of Libyan territory as an entry point to Algeria and the attacks against Western tourists, all augured some kind of more robust intervention in line with the last two decades practices (there were several aerial actions against specific objectives) and exhausted the patience of many, but finally diplomacy prevailed, perhaps making virtue of necessity. Diplomacy offered the Libyans a platform for a first stage of stabilisation, from which to begin to operate and act against other instability factors such as Daesh. Despite many shortcomings in the process and the current situation, it is worth remembering some of the fundamental principles of this inclusive political dialogue that could be part of a diplomatic stabilisation strategy.

First of all, given the controversial precedents in the Security Council in 2011, the country's projection of instability towards the African continent, the Middle East and Europe, the strategic interest of the great international powers and the weight of Libyan oil in the international markets, it came as no surprise that the Council considered the situation of the country as a threat to international peace and security. The UN-led process progressed in close coordination with regional organisations, in particular the AU, the Arab League and the EU. But the international aspects were balanced with strong local components. The talks included five groups, with different political, institutional and social actors, women groups, municipalities, militias and tribes. It was, following Mac Ginty's distinction, indigenous (but not strongly traditional,[61] since the deliberate annihilation of the local political culture by the Qaddafi regime and the difficulties in identifying tribal representatives prevented more tribal involvement). But to a large extent this role was played by municipalities and local communities, so active that, at difficult moments, they saved the talks. It was a highly customised process, in which this local approach was prioritised by the UN, making it compatible with some elements of sustainable peace. The country could not build stability out of the neo-Darwinian, exclusively internal, factors without external support.[62]

Secondly, the international consultation was structured in concentric circles, in which work from within the country was accompanied by the initiative of neighbouring countries—directly and deeply affected by the instability—a second circle of other regional actors, and international powers and organisations, especially interested in the process. The former were asked to freeze their peace and stabilisation efforts (such as the initiative of the Six Neighbours, driven mainly by Algeria and Egypt, or the dialogue initiatives in Algiers and Khartoum), but allowing their active involvement in the process (Morocco, Algeria and Tunisia were hosts of important negotiating groups in the UN process, and Egypt should have hosted a forum of Libyan tribes). The ambassadors of the so-called five-plus-one group (EU,

US, UK, France, Italy and Spain, later also Portugal and some Scandinavian countries), as well as the ambassadors of other interested countries (most regularly those of Russia, Egypt, Saudi Arabia, Turkey, United Arab Emirates, Qatar) accompanied informally the process, providing advice and support. All of them coordinated a stabilisation strategy that should start with an interim political agreement that would allow for two years consensual governance acceptable to the main actors with a single and inclusive government, a formula for institutional cooperation, and the participation of the main cities, political parties, members of civil society, women and youth, tribes, among other groups, which would decrease (as it was) the confrontations between militias, whose demobilisation could allow to start later a process of disarmament and reintegration (still one of the great challenges for deeper stabilisation).

Thirdly, the *political* nature of the mission was fundamental. The international community was never seen as a threatening actor that could propose an intervention with military elements (something to which the Libyans were very suspicious and that could generate more security problems than it solved). The Security Council and all regional actors involved unanimously supported the agreement, which indicates that regional consensus is possible through intense diplomatic efforts. This all allowed for a more effective action by maintaining a single multilateral process, not without challenging phases, essentially diplomatic, led by the UN, in which many of the recommendations and the spirit of legitimacy, credibility and local ownership of the Brahimi and Ramos Horta reports were present.

Providing security was the aspect of instability that concerned most actors inside and outside Libya. The problem of building state institutions was serious, but in a continent-country, cities were used to functioning as true city-states and many governance problems get solved locally. On the other hand, the three major national institutions, the Central Bank, the National Oil Company and the Libyan Investment Authority, continued to operate trying to maintain the balance between the different contenders. For that reason, the most formidable challenge was the existence of thousands of militias (some of only a few members, and, others, true armies with thousands of fighters). Added to those was the increasing presence of Daesh (which ended up having more than 6000 members in the Sirte area), training bases of al-Qaeda, and also the gradual presence of organised crime gangs from different origins. Within this context, the first step after the ceasefire was to address the political problem to reduce the risks of direct confrontation between the larger groups of militias, something that the political agreement achieved. There was still insecurity and a need for policing,[63] but it was a first step that created the conditions for the Libyans themselves to defuse the threat of terrorist groups in the centre and east of the country (what the militias of Misrata did against Daesh and the forces of Khalifa Hafter in other areas). Work is still pending on organised crime groups, on which much less progress has been made.[64] The great local actors have also acted on those smaller groups that interfered in the national management of oil. The militias played an important role in the first stage of stabilisation, although they should have been a key component of the following stages through DDR and SSR processes, which were not possible in the first stage. What Coletta calls 'Interim Stabilisation Measures' should wait in this case, since militias, once returned home, still had to play a defensive-police role in many areas, given the total collapse of the former state security apparatus.[65] The inability of the Libyan government, militia leaders and international community to agree on a way forward has contributed to create conditions for Khalifa Hafter to launch an operation which might reinforce militias instead of weakening them. Arguably, one of the downsides of political missions without a strong military component is the limited clout on such groups. But at the same time, the UN has conducted hundreds of meetings with different militia leaders, explaining the political process and gaining support.[66]

Finally, the Libyan Political Agreement maintains its validity and fragile stabilising role until this day, almost four years later, as a roadmap to solve difficult issues through dialogue and consensus. And this will be the case after current military operations by Hafter reach deadlock. Paradoxically, a non-elected PM leading a highly inclusive and plural council, agreed through the Skhirat agreement, has been more stable than the previous ones, elected by democratic, albeit highly polarised, parliaments. Even some of the hardliners who rejected the text accepted it later, totally or partially. Amendments are debated, while the Constitution is still pending, and possible elections are discussed, which is a good sign, although any step has to be weighed very carefully because in such situations it is easy to lose momentum. The country remains vulnerable to the threat of terrorism and organised crime and has other outstanding pending tasks. Probably a greater involvement of a more united international community—specially in state-building—and a regional consensus would have made it possible to move forward with greater strength, but, with all its shortcomings, the Libyan experience is better than that of other crises in the region and offers valuable lessons in the prioritisation of political dialogue and local and regional diplomacy in unstable contexts.

CONCLUSION

The international community needs a consensual concept of stability that, in no case, can be a euphemism for intervention that simply tries to avoid the negative burden of this concept. If stabilisation can be a viable formula for dealing with new conflicts, it will require clearer parameters and rationales. The delimitation of the concept requires work at the level of international law and institutions, and also on the ground, which only diplomacy can provide with its wide presence in both spaces, and permanence. But also for its openness to the local and the global-multilateral, and its teamwork with development and state-building organisations. This has to be a rule- and legitimacy-based dynamic, where principles like sovereign equality, inclusion and the priority of politics and dialogue are crucial.

The consensus should also address new wars and effective international institutions and rules to deal with it, and what has been called *fragility*. This can only be done through a contemporary reading of constitutional principles, which need to be adapted, but also respected, and a discussion about the role of the UN and the meaning of stability in UN Peace missions. Meanwhile, situations on the ground will continue to request urgent answers, and academia can shed light in a conversation with practitioners. Reports elaborated by Brahimi or Ramos Horta committees can be interesting references. UN needs to find ways to implement more effectively lessons learned.

Threats on civilians and international staff can be a pressing security concern where international support—including military—might be needed urgently. This is also true for cases of massive human rights violations. However, state-building and development is a long-term challenge, and tools to deal with both should be coherent, but keeping their distinct structures and rules. It is a fundamental debate at the level of principles and on the ground. Coordination of different actors will continue to be the main challenge.[67] While diplomacy will make stabilisation more viable, it will need the support of the critical areas of government—meaning head of government offices—to allow the right decision-making.

Instability is present all over the world, but it is especially serious in the MENA region. It is an endemic instability, with distinctive local characteristics. After the failures of international formulas, it is time for the region to apply its own, for which it has an increasingly active and capable diplomacy. It will not be easy to address many key questions like the forum, the actors and the principles, a MENA stabilisation concept, the role of regional organisations, the tools to deal with sectarianism, extremism, terrorism, and reach stability, inclusion and reconciliation, the relevant role of human rights. Importantly, CSO have to be relevant actors in the process. Libya not only offers a good example on how to maximise local political dynamics, while keeping international support, but also about working in concentric circles (local, neighbouring, regional and global). Using a UN political mission facilitated this approach. As it happens in all stabilisation operations, experience—both successes and failures—offers valuable lessons. Challenges through the use of force will produce more instability, only political and diplomatic formulas can work in the medium and long term.

Notes

1. See Monica Duffy Toft, "Fewer Diplomats, More Armed Force Defines US Leadership Today," The Conversation, Tufts University, 26 March 2018. https://theconversation.com/fewer-diplomats-more-armed-force-defines us-leadership-today-92890.
2. See Barakat et al. (2010).
3. See Carter (2013).
4. In particular, if there are massive attacks against civilians or serious human rights violations, which in recent years have come to be considered by the Security Council as threats to international peace and security.
5. See Muggah and Zyck (2015).
6. See Lemay-Hébert and Visoka (2017).
7. Arguably there could be a connection with Foucault or Agamben. See for example Tom Frost (2010).
8. See Van Genugten (2018).
9. Groups of developing states, such as the G77, must also have a greater role in the stabilisation debate, as it should not be a polarising question between the North and the South.
10. 2005 World Summit, which agreed the *Millennium Declaration*. A very encouraging example of good diplomacy is the diplomatic process that former Foreign Ministers of Canada, Gareth Evans, and Algeria, Mohamed Sahnoun carried out to build a global consensus on one of the relevant principles in this debate: the Responsibility to Protect. That debate allowed, after four years, to move from a Global South frontal rejection (to a concept considered synonymous with the 'right of humanitarian intervention'

imposed by the West) to a very promising consensual principle in international law in 2005, although this consensus was broken following the intervention in Libya in 2011.

11. As highlighted by Gareth Evans. See Evans (2012).
12. See Collinson et al. (2010, p. 14).
13. See Clapham (2012). Brierly understood well the need to adapt sovereignty to modern times. See Brierly (2012, p. 7)
14. See Kelsen (1944, p. 207).
15. See Slaughter (2004, p. 288).
16. To the frustration of those who wanted to go further, it had the virtue of convoking a great international consensus. This valuable consensus was lost after the intervention in Libya, which provoked a bitter rift between some Western countries and the BRICS/G77 (supported by with the support of other Western countries).
17. Fragility is defined as "the combination of exposure to risk and insufficient coping capacity of the state, system and/or communities to manage, absorb or mitigate those risks. Fragility can lead to negative outcomes including violence, the breakdown of institutions, displacement, humanitarian crises or other emergencies". See, OECD "States of Fragility" report (2016, p. 22).
18. See Said (1979).
19. See Duffield and Hewitt (2009).
20. See Butler (2009, p. 40).
21. See Collinson et al. (2010, p. 3).
22. See, Resolución sobre la Cumbre Mundial de 2005 (A/60/L.1), p. 30.
23. See Chinkin and Kaldor (2017, p. 72).
24. Ibid., pp. 74–76.
25. See Collinson et al. (2010, p. 3).
26. See Duffield and Hewitt (2009).
27. See Ghali (1992).
28. See Carter (2013).
29. See Iyengar et al. (2017).
30. See Sachs (2015, p. 355).
31. See Miles (2014).
32. See Bildt (2011, p. 5).
33. See S. Von Billerbeck, "All Talk and No Action or No Action Without Talk? UN Peacekeeping and Internal Legitimacy," *Dag Hammarskjöld Foundation blog.* https://www.daghammarskjold.se/peacekeeping-legitimacy/.
34. See Kaldor (2013).
35. See Karlsrud (2015, p. 41).
36. See Curran and Holtom (2015, p. 5).
37. Ibid., p. 9.
38. Ibid.

39. See Lucarelli et al. (2017).
40. See Curran and Holtom (2015, pp. 5, 9).
41. See Karlsrud (2015, p. 43).
42. Ibid., p. 49.
43. Ibid., p. 10.
44. See Karlsrud (2019, p. 15).
45. See Ruggie (1993, p. 26), quoted by Karlsrud (2015, p. 48).
46. In 2013, France indicated that it acted in Mali "pour empêcher les groupes terroristes lies à Al Qaida de prendre le contrôle du pays," and three days later got the unanimous endorsement of the Security Council. Experience shows that, in a temporary and brief manner, exceptional situations requiring very urgent action (with very serious human rights violations, attacks against civilians or terrorism) can occur.
47. See Zyck et al. (2014, p. 19).
48. See Mac Ginty (2012).
49. See Paris and Sisk (2009).
50. See Dennys (2013).
51. See Rotmann (2016, p. 4).
52. See Barakat (2016, p. 3).
53. Ibid.
54. See Dennys (2013, p. 3).
55. See Butler (2009, p. 40).
56. http://www.hedayah.ae/.
57. Some historians have observed that the success of the Congress of Vienna was largely to the inclusion of all European actors following precisely the formula of concentric circles, for example, Paul Meerts, "Persuasion Through Negotiation at the Congress of Vienna" 1814–1815, *DiPLO*. https://www.diplomacy.edu/resources/general/persuasion-through-negotiation-congress-vienna-1814-1815.
58. See Mac Ginty (2012, p. 28).
59. Cairo Declaration of Human Rights in Islam.
60. Al-Qaeda in the Islamic Maghreb.
61. See Mac Ginty (2008).
62. See Weinstein (2005, p. 29).
63. See Caan (2005, p. 2).
64. It has evolved into a systemic issue in Libya's transition but that has its roots outside of the Skhirat process.
65. See Colletta (2014).
66. UN Facilitated and supported numerous ceasefires and dialogue with armed actors. More recently this was done by Ghassan Salame in the summer of 2018.
67. See Paris (2009).

BIBLIOGRAPHY

Barakat, Sultan. *Stabilisation*. GSDRC Professional Development Reading Pack no. 47. Birmingham, UK: University of Birmingham, 2016.

Barakat, Sultan, Deely, Sean, and Zyck, Steven A. "'Tradition of Forgetting': Stabilization and Humanitarian Action in Historical Perspective." *Disasters*, vol. 34, no. 3 (2010): S297–S319.

Bildt, Carl. "Dag Hammarskjöld and UN Peacekeeping." *UN Chronicle*, United Nations, vol. XLVIII, no. 2 (2011).

Boutrous-Ghali, Boutrous. *An Agenda for Peace: Preventive Diplomacy, Peacemaking and Peace-Keeping*, UN, A/47/277, 1992.

Bull, Hedley. *The Anarchical Society: A Study of Order in World Politics*. London: Macmillan, 1977.

Butler, Michael J. *International Conflict Management*. London: Routledge, 2009.

Caan, Christina. "Post-conflict Stabilization and Reconstruction: What Have We Learned from Iraq and Afghanistan." USIPeace Briefing, *USIP*, 22 April 2005.

Carter, William Robert. "War, Peace and Stabilisation: Critically Reconceptualising Stability in Southern Afghanistan." *Stability: International Journal of Security and Development*, vol. 2, no. 1 (2013).

Chinkin, Christine, and Kaldor, Mary. *International Law and New Wars*. Cambridge: Cambridge University Press, 2017.

Clapham, Andrew. *Brierly's Law of Nations: An Introduction to the Role of International Law in International Relations*, 7th edition. Oxford: Oxford University Press, 2012.

Colletta, Nat. "Promoting Interim Stabilization in Fragile Settings: From Theory to Practice." In Muggah (ed.), *Stabilization Operations, Security and Development: States of Fragility*. London: Routledge, 2014.

Collinson, Sarah, Elhawany, Samir, and Muggah, Robert. "States of Fragility: Stabilisation and Its Implications for Humanitarian Action." HPG WP, May 2010.

Curran, David, and Holtom, Paul. "Resonating, Rejecting, Reinterpreting: Mapping the Stabilization Discourse in the United Nations Security Council, 2000–14." *Stability: International Journal of Security and Development*, vol. 4, no. 1 (2015).

Dennys, Christian. "For Stabilization." *Stability: International Journal of Security and Development*, vol. 2, no. 1 (2013).

Duffield, Mark, and Hewitt, Vernon (eds.). *Empire, Development and Colonialism: The Past in the Present*. Woodbridge and Rochester, NY: James Currey, 2009.

Evans, Gareth. "The Responsibility to Protect after Libya and Syria." Annual Castan Centre for Human Rights Law Conference, Melbourne, 20 July 2012.

Frost, Tom. "Agamben's Sovereign Legalization of Foucault." *Oxford Journal of Legal Studies*, vol. 30, no. 3 (2010): 545–577.

Iyengar, Radha, Shapiro, Jacob N., and Hegarty, Stephen. "Lessons Learned from Stabilization Initiatives in Afghanistan: A Systematic Review of Existing Research." RAND Working Paper, *WR-1191*, June 2017.

Kaldor, Mary. *New and Old Wars: Organised Violence in a Global Era*, 3rd edition. Cambridge: Polity, 2013.

Karlsrud, John. "The UN at War: Examining the Consequences of Peace Enforcement Mandates for the UN Peacekeeping Operations in the CAR, the DRC and Mali." *Third World Quarterly*, vol. 36, no. 1 (2015): 40–54.

———. "From Liberal Peacebuilding to Stabilization and Counterterrorism." *International Peacekeeping*, vol. 26, no. 1 (2019): 1–21.

Kelsen, Hans. "The Principle of Sovereign Equality of States as a Basis for International Organization." *The Yale Law Journal*, vol. 53, no. 2 (March 1944): 207–220.

Lemay-Hébert, Nicolas, and Visoka, Gëzim. "Normal Peace: A New Strategic Narrative of Intervention." *Politics and Governance*, vol. 5, no. 3 (2017): 146–156.

Lucarelli, Sonia, Marrone, Alessandro, and Moro, Francesco N. "Projecting Stability in an Unstable World." *Istituto Affari Internazionali*, University of Bologna, 2017.

Mac Ginty, Roger. "Indigenous Peace-Making Versus the Liberal Peace." *Cooperation and Conflict*, vol. 43, no. 2 (2008): 139–163.

———. "Against Stabilization." *Stability: International Journal of Security and Development*, vol. 1, no. 1 (2012): 20–30.

Miles, Renanah. "The Foreign Policy Essay: The (Many) Hurdles to US Stabilization Operations." *Lawfare*, 2 February 2014.

Muggah, Robert. "Reflections on United Nations-Led Stabilization. Late Peacekeeping, Early Peacebuilding or Something Else?" In R. Muggah (ed.), *Stabilization Operations, Security and Development: States of Fragility*. New York: Routledge, 2014a.

——— (ed.). *Stabilization Operations, Security and Development: States of Fragility*. New York: Routledge, 2014b.

Muggah, Robert, and Zyck, Steven A. "Preparing Stabilization for 21st Century Security Challenges." *Stability: International Journal of Security and Development*, vol. 4, no. 1 (2015).

OECD. *States of Fragility: Understanding Violence*, 2016.

Paris, Rolland. "Understanding the 'Coordination Problem' in Postwar Statebuilding." In R. Paris and T. D. Sisk (eds.), *The Dilemmas of Statebuilding: Confronting the Contradictions of Postwar Peace Operations*. London: Routledge, 2009.

Paris, Roland, and Sisk, Timothy D. *The Dilemmas of Statebuilding: Confronting the Contradictions of Postwar Peace Operations*. London: Routledge, 2009.

Rotmann, Philipp. "Toward a Realistic and Responsible Idea of Stabilisation." *Stability: International Journal of Security and Development*, vol. 5, no. 1 (2016).

Ruggie, John Gerard. "Wandering in the Void: Charting the UN's New Strategic Role." *Foreign Affairs*, vol. 72, no. 5 (1993): 26–31.

Sachs, Jeffrey. *The Age of Sustainable Development*. New York: Columbia University Press, 2015.

Said, Edward. *Orientalism*. Vintage Books, 1979.

Slaughter, Anne-Marie. "Sovereignty and Power in a Networked World Order." *Stanford Journal of International Law*, vol. 40, no. 2 (2004): 283.

Tobias, Pietz. "Flexibility and 'Stabilization Actions': EU Crisis Management One Year After the Global Strategy." Policy Briefing, *Center for International Peace Operations (ZIF)*, September 2017.

Van Genugten, Saskia. "Stabilization in the Contemporary Middle East and North Africa: Different Dimensions of an Elusive Concept." Working Paper, *Emirates Diplomatic Academy*, March 2018.

Weinstein, Jeremy. "Autonomous Recovery and International Intervention in Comparative Perspective." Working Paper no. 57, *Center for Global Development*, April 2005.

Zyck, Steven A., Sultan Barakat, and Seán Deely. "The Evolution of Stabilisation Concepts and Praxis." In Robert Muggah (ed.), *Stabilization Operations, Security and Developments*. London: Routledge, 2014.

CHAPTER 5

Non-state Armed Actors: Lessons from Peace Processes and Implications for Stabilisation

Ed Marques and Sylvia Rognvik

INTRODUCTION

Most conflicts today take place within the borders of a state, and they often involve at least one non-state armed actor (NSAA) fighting another armed group or state security forces.[1] NSAAs, of which the Middle East and North Africa (MENA) region saw a proliferation in the wake of the 'Arab Spring' in 2011, are defined as organised armed groups operating outside of state control that use force to achieve their ostensibly political objectives.[2] This development further weakened the central state, and consequently, a plethora of alternative forms of governance emerged. In parallel, regional actors have taken a more proactive role in the conflicts in the Middle East by supporting NSAAs and establishing proxy forces, often divided along Sunni and Shia lines.

Engaging with armed groups is rarely straightforward and often risky and highly political, and the international community is therefore understandably reluctant to engage with non-state armed groups. But when managed

---

E. Marques (✉) · S. Rognvik
Crisis Management Initiative (CMI), Helsinki, Finland

© The Author(s) 2020
V. Gervais and S. van Genugten (eds.), *Stabilising the Contemporary Middle East and North Africa*, Middle East Today,
https://doi.org/10.1007/978-3-030-25229-8_5

properly, the potential benefits outweigh the costs of not engaging—you cannot make peace without talking to the groups that are fighting. It is increasingly acknowledged that since armed groups are a part of the problem, they also need to be a part of the solution. Armed groups left out of the ecosystem of a peace process can easily become spoilers of that process and jeopardise the chances of attaining a sustainable peace. It is also recognised that when military options for stabilisation are applied on their own, they rarely create the requisite foundations for lasting peace. This view has increasingly been accepted, as conflicts over the past decades have become more complex and actors and sources of grievance have proliferated. However, governments and official political actors remain reluctant to engage with armed actors, as they fear the political risks of doing so, and the legitimacy that such engagement could potentially bestow on groups that utilise violence to advance their goals.

When the initiative is first taken towards stabilisation, international actors must initially make a strategic decision of engagement or non-engagement. Arriving at this decision also entails finding ways of dealing with the risks and challenges related to the chosen strategy. The operative question addressed in this chapter is how can we constructively engage with NSAAs in peace processes, and what are the implications of such engagement for international stabilisation efforts? We seek to address this by providing some insight into the way that NSAAs reshape realities on the ground during conflicts, assessing the role they play in peace processes and offering some lessons learned from international experiences of engaging with them.

In the first section we describe the characteristics of NSAAs in the MENA and the positive and negative aspects of international community engagement with them. In the second section, we discuss the various roles NSAAs can play in decentralised states and the implications of this for international stabilisation efforts. In the third section, we analyse the complicated relationship between NSAAs and peace processes, drawing some lessons learned from various experiences of engaging with NSAAs during the different stages of peace processes—highlighting the need for either deliberate and active engagement at an appropriate level or a conscious and strategic decision of non-engagement.

Engaging with NSAAs

One of the many repercussions of the 'war on terrorism' was the criminalisation of engagement with many NSAAs. This has had the detrimental knock-on effect of limiting the ability of international actors to understand how they can effectively engage with NSAAs.[3] Most commonly, NSAAs are conceptualised within the framework of 'fragile states'—where they are perceived as scavengers of the state, perpetuating its fragility and serving as spoilers of any peace and stability efforts. At the same time, linkages between the role of NSAAs in governing the spaces they occupy during a conflict and how this shapes the post-conflict order are increasingly being recognised both in academia and among practitioners.[4] This is not an either-or argument, as NSAAs are often both spoilers and governance actors—very often at the same time.[5] A recent study by the UK government's Stabilisation Unit argues for the need to engage effectively with both local elites and armed actors to achieve sustainable peace and stability.[6] The challenge remains how to put this recommendation into practice, particularly in a policy context where political, security and developmental challenges are intertwined.

Peacebuilding and mediation professionals, alongside the broader set of international actors working in conflict and post-conflict environments, need to better understand NSAAs and their potential role in achieving or undermining sustainable peace.[7] Steps have been taken to this end by various UN agencies, for instance by compiling guidelines on how to interact with NSAA's in various domains, or through initiatives like UNESCO's Culture of Peace and Non-Violence programme which promoted dialogue among social, political and armed groups.[8] Furthermore, non-governmental organisations, such as Conciliation Resources, have extensively researched ways to better understand and engage with NSAAs in peace processes.[9]

In their review of options and strategies for engaging NSAAs in state-building and peacebuilding efforts, Claudia Hofmann and Ulrich Schneckener highlight that distinct types of organisations unwittingly use different strategies to influence NSAAs.[10] The rule of thumb is that officially mandated and supported stabilisation missions tend to be more coercive, whereas non-official missions are able to engage with greater agility and focus. These different approaches emanate from the fact that non-official, private diplomacy actors do not have access to the leverage that state- or UN-sponsored stabilisation missions do. Recent reviews of large-scale multinational stabilisation missions have highlighted how more coercive official approaches have had mixed results at best. According to one such report by the Government of Norway, reviewing their support to stabilisation efforts in Afghanistan, state-building efforts were not successful at all vis-à-vis NSAAs:

> Despite more than fifteen years of international effort, the situation in Afghanistan remains discouraging. Militant Islamist groups still have a foothold in parts of the country and the Taliban are stronger now than at any time since 2001.[11]

The political leverage that comes with the 'whole-of-government' approach and the need to balance political, military, development strategies with other states can hinder the capabilities of willing official actors to engage with the changing political landscape. Norway's own efforts to engage with NSAAs in Afghanistan, and foster a negotiated solution, were undercut by the political realities of a large multinational and integrated stabilisation mission:

> There was little interest among coalition partners in negotiation in the early years when the Taliban were relatively weak. In later years, however, the desire for negotiation gained momentum as Taliban military capability and power increased.[12]

There are different degrees of engagement with NSAAs, ranging from informal conversations at the one end to having them represented as a party at the negotiation table, and even building their capacity to take part in negotiations at the other. In fact, 'capacity building' of NSAAs can be crucial to the sustainability of a peace process, and their political maturity/immaturity is a considerable factor in whether NSAAs can be constructive parts of political systems. A channel of communication should be a minimum requirement, as it is essential to understanding their dynamics, motivation and appetite for dialogue. These channels can also facilitate humanitarian access to areas under their control. An established but latent channel can be activated or broadened during official negotiations. Alongside these benefits, engagement with NSAAs poses a whole range of challenges and raises questions that need to be taken into consideration. It is imperative to assess who would be the key interlocutors to engage with, and whether they possess the necessary authority or represent the interests of the members, given the internal coherence and structure of the group. For instance, following the chaos after the Libyan uprising of 2011, a major challenge for the UN-led efforts on initiating dialogue with armed groups was to identify the right groups and people to bring around the table, as there was a plethora of militias, all of which were fragmented to varying degrees.

Sometimes incumbent governments are perceived as having insufficient territorial control, and NSAAs will seek talks with regional or international actors instead. For instance, in Afghanistan the Taliban has insisted on talking to the US, mainly due to their demands of the withdrawal of foreign troops and the delisting of Taliban members. In Yemen, Ansar Allah said they engaged in indirect talks with Saudi Arabia leading up to the official Kuwait talks in 2016.[13] The challenge that comes with such dialogue is that while it may offer the benefit to international actors of direct engagement, it can inadvertently legitimise the armed group in question. In an arena where a multiplicity of actors is competing for influence as legitimate national actors, international acknowledgement of local actors can carry significant weight. In reality, the actors most impacted by such dynamics are non-state *unarmed* actors, who fear that such interaction will weaken their influence. This is often one of the reasons why NSAAs would often be most willing to start talks with powerful regional or international entities.

The Role of NSAAs in Areas of Limited Statehood[14]

The shifts in the political landscape during periods of conflict can precipitate a change in the panoply of actors, empowering new entities while disempowering old ones. For instance, the reach of the government may shrink, which can draw in non-state actors to fill the gap and can transform the landscape of social and political relations in those areas. Sociologist Timothy Wickham-Crowley identifies an 'implicit social contract' emerging between NSAAs and civilians in the territories under their control.[15] In general, the governance efforts of NSAAs are increasingly recognised in literature on civil wars. Zachariah Mampilly highlights that much of the reluctance to observe the broader capacities of NSAAs is related to a state-centric conception of governance that is pervasive across political analysis in general, not just among researchers of civil war. He notes that in studies of government 'scholars thus far have not adequately accounted for the performance of governmental functions by non-state actors'.[16] For Mampilly, the existence of NSAA governance is a form of 'counter-state sovereignty' which exists in competition with the state, seeking to mimic the state and adopt functions of a state, and they can even attempt to claim recognition within the international community.

In asserting control over territory, NSAAs often take it upon themselves to administer these areas. Most commonly, NSAAs serve as important providers of basic services, like Hamas in Gaza, or may take it upon themselves to defend against foreign enemies, maintain internal order and contribute to the 'material security of the populace'—all of which are responsibilities that are commonly attributed to the state.[17] NSAAs do not necessarily usurp or displace government services. In areas where basic services do not exist or suffer from explicit neglect, it is not just shrinking state control, but also areas of dubious control to begin with. Attempts by NSAAs to administer areas will not necessarily be welcomed by the populace at large, as they may be coercive or discriminatory. Daesh, which at one point controlled an area the size of the UK stretching over large parts of Iraq and Syria, serves as an interesting case. Daesh's goal was to establish a caliphate with strict sharia law, and their tactics included brutal methods such as beheadings, taking of slaves and expelling of other religious groups such as the Yazidis.[18] At the same time, they acted much in the same way as other NSAAs and created an administrative system of taxation, garbage collection and issuance of birth and marriage certificates under the caliphate.[19] At times they offered better services than the Iraqi government, they had replaced.[20]

Research on NSAA governance highlights that NSAAs adopt governance responsibilities in a broader context of interactions with the political landscape around them. This is dependent on both their relationship with the incumbent state and how they organise and sustain themselves. One factor that cuts across the analysis of several analysts is that the reach of the state, where one exists, and the presence of other non-state actors both locally and abroad can vastly alter the need for NSAAs to administer the areas they control.[21] Moreover, NSAAs governance and military functions are interconnected, and NSAAs commitment to governance is often pragmatic rather than altruistic. An NSAAs ability to govern the areas it controls can change based on a number of factors, including 'ideological conviction, relative military strength, dependence on civilian material assistance, and need for accommodation with civilian preferences in its operational area'.[22] The divergences and unpredictability in how NSAAs govern, and how they balance governance with their political agenda, means that they are intrinsically complicated actors to engage with.

NSAAs can also take on a role as security providers in areas outside the reach of any centralised security structures. In Afghanistan, for instance, local structures like the *Arbakai*—community militias controlled by the elders (*Jirga*)—have a long history in the Pashtun areas. During the stabilisation mission in Afghanistan, these structures were supported by the international mission. This collaboration was initially considered successful but faced several challenges when the model was replicated in non-Pashtun areas, when the president decided that the commanders should be appointed by the Ministry of Defence, instead of the tribal leaders, and when the *Arbakai* was supported in Pashtun areas while other tribal groups and areas were subject to disarmament processes.

NSAAs ensure financial sustainability through various means. They rely on generating resources to continue to operate and support their actions, to pay their soldiers, to ensure means of transport and communication, as well as to acquire weapons and other equipment. Funds can be generated through taxation of the population, through the illicit economy or via foreign support. In Yemen, Ansar Allah has taken control over most of the national economy in the areas they control by working with those ministers and managers that have pledged their allegiance to the group since then it took control of the capital Sana'a. The UN Panel of Experts for Yemen has estimated that a minimum of 14% of the state budget might be under the control of Ansar Allah. Telecommunications companies constitute a major source of revenue, alongside tax and customs on tobacco sales and black-market fuel and oil products.[23] In Libya, from 2012 to early 2014, the primary source of income for NSAAs was direct payments from the Ministry of Defence and Interior. These payments were initially targeted at those who participated in the 2011 uprising. These 'revolutionary' brigades were paid two to three times the salary of regular military personnel, which not only removed all incentives to reintegrate into official state structures but also led to a massive increase in the number of people claiming to be 'revolutionaries'. These numbers rose from, at the start, a figure of around 20,000 to somewhere between 250,000 and 400,000 at its peak. As this funding source decreased, militias have adopted increasingly criminal methods to generate revenue, such as operating protection rackets, and financially motivated kidnappings. In 2018, the control of the Libyan capital, Tripoli, was divided between four militias—the Special Deterrence Force (SDF), the Tripoli Revolutionary Battalion (TRB), the Nawasi Battalion and the Abu Slim Unit of the Central Security Apparatus—all of which are nominally loyal to the government but in reality undermine it.

Despite this misalignment, they have occupied official administrative positions and continue to control large parts of the banking sector and the black market.[24]

NSAAs in many cases also rely on the mobilisation of resources from abroad, in the way that, for example, Hezbollah receives financial and political assistance from Iran. Resources can come from states, but they can also come from transnational political groups or diaspora groups.[25] The effective mobilisation of resources from abroad can also be politically and economically expedient, for instance because it can play a central part in NSAAs' attempts to supplant an incumbent state's relations with external states.[26] International support can also have the effect of reshaping the domestic political landscape. Where NSAAs play a strong governance role, the provision of foreign resources to NSAAs can create dependencies that detach NSAAs from local political realities and prevent them from establishing effective relations with the communities around them. Such a dynamic can diminish their need to cater to local political demands and subsequently undermine whatever local control of these entities might exist. NSAAs' increased access to resources and their ability to control official sources of revenue, like in Yemen and Libya, gives them a position of significant power and economic leverage. When they benefit from the status quo both financially and politically, there are few incentives for NSAAs to engage in peace talks or to be brought under democratic control, a situation which has major implications for international stabilisation efforts. Identifying and creating the incentives that can ensure that NSAAs engage constructively, in both peace processes and broader stabilisation, is a great challenge, but nonetheless paramount to any stabilisation efforts.

NSAAs and Peace Processes

The term 'peace process' refers to varied mechanisms that are used to move communities from violent or frozen conflict towards greater consensus and peace. This usually will include dialogue at various social and political levels, which may include mediation by a third party. What is essential for reaching sustainable peace is that all relevant parties are involved in developing solutions to issues affecting their society. These parties and stakeholders may be armed or unarmed.[27] NSAAs may be one of the major parties to a peace process, or they may be facets within a broader landscape of political actors. The relationship between the unarmed and armed actors is often, however, unclear. Not only is the line between NSAAs and unarmed actors often blurred, but unarmed actors may find themselves unable to exert control over armed actors during the talks or to ensure compliance after an agreement is reached. This means that it is difficult to validate their inclusion or exclusion 'around the table' on such considerations alone. It also means that even if NSAAs are excluded, they may still play a role in the broader political landscape in which the peace process operates.

Given this background, we would like to suggest that there are three factors that should be taken into account when seeking to engage with NSAAs: (1) their political agenda; (2) their direct relevance to the process; and (3) their indirect relevance to the process. Despite legitimate concerns about the inclusion of NSAAs, if they are politically relevant, they *will* need to be dealt with somehow. Not including them in the process risks inviting them and the different actors associated with them to undermine the process. Exclusion of NSAAs (albeit on good grounds) can perpetuate insecurity, as they tend to demonstrate their clout by ramping up their military action when they are ignored. NSAAs are often perpetrators of violence in civil wars and therefore play a critical role in efforts to end it. Although the distinction is not seamless, what marks them out from organised criminal actors are their political aspirations and the way they organise and engage with the communities around them to achieve these. NSAAs may have deeply ingrained political aspirations, or these may develop over time, influenced by the context in which they operate. NSAAs' political aspirations are not only a motivating factor behind their actions, but they may directly challenge the authority and legitimacy of the incumbent government or other political actors. NSAAs aspirations therefore often form a central element of the dynamics of the conflict in which they are present.

In designing and coordinating a peace process, a mediator will have to ascertain how to deal with political aspirations of NSAAs. There are situations when strategies for the consideration of NSAAs' political aspirations will have to be devised, and also situations when they should probably be disregarded—for example when there is a political organisation that seeks to advance the same goal and is considered equally or more legitimate by the broader population. Offering NSAAs some sort of influence in the process, either through a place at the table or other ways, is often argued to be the only way to prevent them from undermining it. For instance, during the Burundi Arusha Peace Talks between 1998 and 2000, where the main NSAAs were reluctant to attend, the talks went on, and a Comprehensive Peace Agreement was signed without them under the behest of Nelson Mandela, former president of South Africa, and the former president of Tanzania, Julius Nyerere. It was only after continued instability that Thabo Mbeki and his successor Jacob Zuma, with support from the region, the UN and the AU, engaged the two main armed groups, CNDD-FDD (*Conseil National Pour la Défense de la Démocratie–Forces pour la Défense de la Démocratie*) and FNL (*Forces nationales de liberation*), and succeeded in bringing them into the fold, thus completing the Burundi Peace Process in 2006.

NSAAs are often highly controversial actors. Mediators may be reluctant to engage with them, not least due to concerns over illegal acts that they may have carried out, which may pose legal implications for those that engage with them. However, the preference to avoid contact may come most strongly from local actors, who risk being marginalised by the inclusion of the armed groups in the peace process. For instance, the Libyan Political Dialogue was vehemently criticised by local groups as pandering to an armed coalition who had asserted control over the capital city.[28] Furthermore, it is often the case that NSAAs refuse to sit around the same table with other NSAAs, claiming they are the 'exclusive' owners of a cause. This can fragment the peace process, complicating and delaying the settlement and increasing the human and material cost of the conflict.

There are different ways to judge the relevance of engagement with NSAAs. Some approaches suggest that groups should commit to certain principles, such as the resolution of conflict through dialogue, or to human rights. More commonly the focus is on more pragmatic considerations, such as the NSAA's size or centrality within the conflict dynamics. One consideration that needs to be made clear is that many armed groups, although locally rooted, may not be widely representative, or essential parties to include in a political settlement. NSAAs are not static actors, and there are likely to be different narratives operating within the organisation, each advocating for different approaches to realise their political aspirations. The cost–benefit calculation of fighting or negotiating is a constant for NSAAs throughout a conflict, which may sometimes lead to internal divisions between 'moderates' and 'hardliners', or between the political leadership and the military leaders on the ground. The decision between fighting and negotiating becomes explicitly tangible during an active peace process. Hardliners are generally identified as those who would seek to fight rather than negotiating. Initial divisions may cement into clear fault lines within the movement, with armed factions continuing to operate separately from the factions deciding to engage in negotiations. For instance, in Afghanistan, in 2018, parts of the Taliban were seeking to engage in dialogue and negotiations with the US, while other factions continued fighting.

The exclusion of particular NSAAs, or factions of NSAAs, from peace processes will not make them disappear from the political landscape. Isolation can embolden hardliners and increase their influence within NSAAs, having the knock-on effect of increasing violence. By the same token, isolation can, in the long term, also prevent NSAAs from accruing political skills and knowledge. Delayed engagement with both the Irish Republican Army (IRA) and ETA (*Euskadi Ta Askatasuna*), in Ireland and Spain, respectively, contributed to the prolongation of the conflicts, and it was only once these groups were engaged with that progress towards peace was possible. The buy-in of an established and credible government was essential in both the case of ETA and the IRA and was arguably a crucial to the success of the respective peace processes. Both cases have been lauded as highlighting the benefits of engaging with armed groups; however, both cases involved conflicts between territorially defined movements and established and strong states. The same approach needs to be different where the state is very weak.

In contexts where stabilisation missions are established, the state and the government are weak—a characteristic reflected in the need to establish a mission in the first place. Stabilisation missions are often invited by the government and mandated with supporting state functions such as strengthening the security sector and supporting political processes. Arthur Boutellis, however, argues that stabilisation is often confused with the restoration of state authority, and that such a conflation may undermine the mission's strategy if the weak and contested state authority is a major part of the problem.[29] Often, weak governments do not provide effective counterparts to NSAAs in negotiations and may lend NSAAs credence where they otherwise would not have received it. For instance, in Afghanistan President Karzai was throughout his time in power described by the Taliban as a puppet of the West, which meant that from the Taliban's point of view any talks with the government would suggest an admission that the Afghan government was legitimate.

Direct Relevance to the Peace Process

NSAAs are the most likely parties needed to reach and implement a cessation of hostilities or a ceasefire agreement. Such agreements are, however, only the precursors to the much longer sets of negotiations required to carry out a peace process. In the longer term, as belligerents, NSAAs will be required to address and take part in these longer discussions, at least regarding security sector reform, and the demobilisation or reintegration of their ranks within formal structures in the national security sector. NSAAs' buy-in, participation and cooperation in discussions and negotiations are critical to the implementation of any agreements. NSAAs consent may be crucial to establish a secure environment for government to operate. For instance, in Libya, an extensive (and ongoing) dialogue with the militias in control of the capital Tripoli, carried out by third-party mediators, was required to ensure that the Government of National Accord (GNA) was capable of slowly moving there.

But NSAAs are not necessarily just belligerents. The way they organise, the way they administer the areas in which they are present or which they control, as well as the way that they alter the social contract that exists between the governors and the governed during periods of conflict, all engender changes in the political landscape which need to be taken into account in peace processes. NSAAs may provide services themselves or may provide consent for others to provide services in the areas they control. There may also be *ad hoc* systems of governance or security provision. Some NSAAs may also transition into political parties and/or lay down their arms if given the opportunity to advocate for their cause through political channels. The reality is that the transition to becoming political parties is not automatic; many will transform into a political party, but will also keep an armed contingent as continued leverage in a predatory political system. NSAAs may have effective control over vast swaths of a country, they may *de facto* govern these areas, and they may even do so effectively, but by the same token their perceived options and their capacities to convey their positions in a peace process may be extremely limited. This may be due to their lack of exposure to political processes, or lack of interest in dialogue, or the lack of the willingness of international actors to engage with a specific group. For instance, in Yemen prior to and during the National Dialogue Conference (NDC) both local and international actors had very limited contact with Ansar Allah. This is one of the reasons why the nuances to their perspectives, positions and goals were not well known or understood despite the inclusion of the group being paramount to a sustainable peace process. In general, the lack of awareness may be directly related to the fact that they are listed entities, where direct engagement with them can have legal and security ramifications. Yet such a lack of appreciation may have a direct impact on the sustainability of a peace process. The means through which NSAAs convey their opinions may also be very limited even in the case of other domestic political actors, and because of their partisan nature. Awareness of their precise positions is likely to be highly uneven, causing NSAAs to face challenges in communicating with a variety of actors in peace processes.

INDIRECT RELEVANCE TO THE PEACE PROCESS

NSAAs can be of crucial relevance for peace and stability efforts although they are not directly involved in the national cessation of hostilities. They may become spoilers to the process, if they have no incentives to participate or they believe that they are representing an important constituency in the conflict. As previously highlighted, NSAAs may have a pervasive, if less direct, role in the illicit trade that tends to form a staple part of the conflict economy. Vested interests that emerge during conflict can quickly become ingrained, and NSAAs—or their leaders or individual members— may themselves enjoy a substantial profit. Peace processes may in these cases not serve the NSAAs interests, as they are benefiting financially from the *status quo*. This may lead to them becoming spoilers of the process. NSAAs may even be major recipients of social benefits, especially through veterans' organisations and other local and foreign sources. These privileges may be a major point of contention for the population at large, as financial empowerment of the armed groups may lead to further insecurity in the local communities. NSAAs, understandably, will quickly become dependent and will be reluctant to give these up.

NSAAs can emerge because of social grievances, but can also appropriate such grievances strategically as a way to build their support base. In either case, NSAAs are not self-sufficient and will always rely on the communities around them for economic and political nourishment. In Palestine, for instance, Hamas enjoy a wide level of support across the nation, as they have come to represent resistance to occupation. If an NSAA has a strong support base as well as a cohesive structure, this can mean that it may be able to effectively act as a proxy and convey the views of key constituencies to a peace process, or conversely, it may otherwise have the capacity to act as the spoiler of a peace process. Ansar Allah in Yemen took advantage of widespread discontent generated by the long-standing political deadlock, limited statehood and post-2011 chaos, to expand their support base and gain further territory. The support of Ansar Allah was broadened as a part of these dynamics when significant segments of the society, including tribal leaders, and former President Ali Abdallah Saleh allied with them. Furthermore, an NSAA's support base can extend beyond national borders. Where an NSAA relies heavily on transnational, foreign government, or private support to mobilise resources, or is linked to a community transcending national borders, it may be able to convey the views of these constituencies which through the conflict have become part of the political landscape within a certain country. Support can come from proxy actors such as diaspora communities, or from external nation states and lobby groups with a strategic interest in the conflict.

NSAAs are central to both the conduct and sustainability of peace processes of all kinds. We should understand their capacities and their potential contribution to ending violence and supporting other political and security processes in the post-conflict environment. As a part of the altered political landscape, the changed governance structures, as well as the war economy, they are likely to influence peace processes and their implementation in a variety of ways. The consideration is not simply whether they should be at the table or not, but what sort of ways that they can be creatively engaged with within a peace process to constructive ends. As belligerents in a conflict NSAAs may be unable to effectively convey their positions, especially to those beyond their immediate constituencies. This means that engagement with them needs to be targeted and deliberate. Moreover, in some cases, for instance with extremist groups, their values and views are irreconcilable with the incumbent government and the majority of the local population. Stabilisation missions may still engage in dialogue with the groups to facilitate humanitarian access, while any further engagement or inclusion is in these cases unreasonable.

Principles for Engagement with NSAAs

Based on previous engagements with NSAAs, there are some lessons learned that can be identified that offer practical guidance. As peace processes can take many forms, we would like to offer some broad principles that we believe are relevant in a variety of contexts. We have clustered these around three phases: (1) the pre-negotiation period, being the period of research and outreach leading to the preparation of the process; (2) the negotiation period, where the process is undertaken; and finally, (3) the implementation period, where we have drawn attention to the ways that NSAAs will likely have to play a part. In reality, these periods are overlapping and do not always follow one another in a linear order, and other periods can be added to this, but for the sake of simplicity, we will offer a succinct 'before, during and after' perspective. It is also worth noting that strategies presented under a certain phase may be applicable also during other phases. Furthermore, the type of support that is most conducive to NSAAs' inclusion in a peace process in any phase is heavily dependent on the context.

Lessons Learned: Pre-negotiation

NSAAs should be mapped, and interaction has to take place through carefully determined entry points. It is important to understand the NSAA itself, how it operates, and if and how it can be engaged with. It is essential to understand the actors involved and how they can contribute to a peace process. In Eastern Ukraine in 2015, a local ceasefire agreement in an area with frequent shelling came into place between the Luhansk Peoples Republic (LPR) and the governmental forces without the knowledge of the higher-ranking commanders. Understanding the chain of command, and the degree of autonomy they operate within, is particularly important because different strategies are necessary depending on the NSAAs' organisation. At times, lower-ranking commanders will be reluctant to cooperate or to talk, and in such cases, it will be useful to move up the ranks. At other times, lower-ranking commanders will be willing to speak and even to initiate dialogue with counterparts and may have the autonomy to make those decisions without the prior approval of higher-ranking officials. However, all levels would eventually need to be engaged for a more sustainable agreement, and therefore, a mediator needs to identify the right entry point and look for creative ways to engage the various levels. Such considerations should be a starting point but can be overtaken by circumstances. In Lebanon in 1990, for instance, a ceasefire agreement had to be renegotiated when lower-ranking soldiers felt they were outside of the agreement, although their commanders had initially been part of the negotiations.

Trust and confidence-building are paramount after deciding to include NSAAs in peace processes. The decision to include NSAAs implies that they are perceived as a key actor in the process, and without trust between an NSAA and the supporting organisation or between the negotiating parties, an essential precondition for provision of any type of support is lacking. A common feature of armed groups is the high level of mistrust towards external actors. Trust between NSAAs and other parties can be built through increasing the flow of information at an early stage or conducting confidence-building measures such as transfer of detainees, prisoner exchanges or the implementation of a ceasefire agreement or the cessation of hostilities.

The effective flow of information is particularly important in the pre-negotiation period. It allows for NSAAs to have a better idea of what is actually going on in the political sphere, and to start creating space for improved understanding between the conflicting parties. One way to do this is through the inclusion of NSAA representatives in informal dialogue platforms with other political and civil society groups. NSAAs, as with the other parties around the table may mistrust other groups, doubt their sincerity and their willingness to deliver on commitments, and such dialogues provide an opportunity for all parties to understand each other's perceptions and objectives. Informal, multi-party and bilateral dialogues between the Ansar Allah and other domestic political groups were helpful in building a degree of trust, paving the way for the NSAA's engagement in Yemen's 2013–2014 NDC. Such engagement provides an opportunity for other domestic groups as well as those working on the process to learn more about the NSAA's perceptions, positions and interests. Equally important is the flow of information between those working on the peace process itself and those working directly with the NSAAs, as actors involved in different aspects of a peace process may have very limited contact with the group, and there may be considerable differences in understanding. The exchange of analysis between international actors on NSAAs and their positions can increase the awareness and understanding they have of NSAAs, as well as ensure that any misunderstandings are worked through early on.

A strategy of engagement or disengagement should be deliberately determined. The increased flow of information early on provides opportunities to those working on a peace process to understand NSAAs' interests and will help those designing the process itself to determine the appropriate engagement strategy. NSAAs should not be excluded from nor included in a peace process on principle. The decision whether to engage with NSAAs should be made pragmatically and deliberately from the standpoint of strengthening sustainable peace. Pragmatic reasons for NSAA's inclusion can be based on different motivations. The choice may be simple where the group is large and cohesive, and provides a coherent bloc to negotiate with, and clearly represents a significant segment of the society. However, more often the reality is much more complex. Identifying the right actors to bring to the table is key. In the case of Libya, there were a plethora of militias operating after the 2011 uprising, many of them with loose or shifting alliances, and many of the groups overlapping. In all cases, but specifically in contexts where there are numerous NSAAs, effective mapping of their size, reputation and even electoral success is valuable to help determine an appropriate strategy.

The selection of groups that accept certain principles may also be important. For instance, some private diplomacy actors working on the Israeli-Palestinian conflict have determined engagement with NSAAs based on their commitment to certain principles or norms—political partnership, dialogue rather than violence as a basic principle for conflict resolution, and relevant international norms such as the resolutions of the UN Security Council. Such criteria are often used to ensure that informal dialogues have real prospects to make progress and produce outcomes acceptable to all sides. Early engagement may also provide an opportunity to convey these norms and their relevance to NSAAs. Mediators will need to be creative and shrewd when the up-front inclusion of these principles may limit engagement with recalcitrant NSAAs. A further consideration, which is extremely difficult to measure, is an assessment of the *sincerity* of the NSAA. In some cases, NSAAs express willingness to pursue political engagement and seem in principle open to political dialogue, but international actors need to judge that they are not using the opportunity of participation to gain legitimacy and recognition in the eyes of other international actors without making necessary concessions. Even where they are acting 'insincerely' it will be up to the mediator to judge if this is palatable, and where it is simply to extract gains that would enable them to continue the conflict. This is a dynamic consideration, and sincerity may accrue over time through participation, as the process moves forward and their trust in the supporting organisation and other parties become stronger.

Lessons Learned: Negotiation

One should engage pragmatically and contextually with NSAAs. NSAAs that are not part of negotiations do not necessarily need to be completely excluded from them, as there are many ways for NSAAs to be involved in peace processes, without necessarily 'sitting at the table'. There may be other representatives involved that can function as a channel of communication between the NSAA and the official peace process, and that represent their interests. Likewise, NSAAs that are part of negotiations may require support to engage effectively.

NSAAs should also be assisted in engaging effectively through capacity building and advice on constructive engagement. In Palestine, private diplomacy actors have worked with NSAAs to support them in defining political goals, as well as to support inclusion in informal dialogue platforms. In one instance, this was done by creating a dedicated security sector dialogue group with a number of representatives of the main Palestinian factions. This enabled initial confidence-building to be carried out among the factions through this process, and more importantly to formulate and suggest initiatives and proposals that would contribute to the removal of security sector-related challenges that stood in the way of a comprehensive national reconciliation agreement. The work of the group was supported through a team of experts in the security sector who offered perspectives to the group during the sessions. In the same instance, this was combined with a workshop aimed at conveying the experiences that NSAAs had both during and after the peace process in Ireland and during the democratic transformation in South Africa.

Informal dialogue should be facilitated throughout. Alternative avenues for dialogue will often be required to ensure that issues and tensions that arise during political negotiations can be addressed. Given NSAAs' often limited experience in participating in political processes, their commitment to resolve disputes through negotiations may waiver as the political process moves forward and difficulties arise. Several times during the NDC in Yemen, tensions flared up between various factions. These tensions were for the most part mitigated through the facilitation of targeted bilateral dialogues conducted by international actors preventing their further escalation and potential negative impact on the discussions within the simultaneous NDC. Likewise, in periods when Ansar Allah boycotted the NDC sessions, international actors played a crucial role in ensuring that channels of communication both to other parties and to the NDC representatives themselves were maintained.

The full range of issues that relate to NSAAs should be engaged. To pre-empt the role that NSAAs will be required to play during the implementation, it is paramount to deal comprehensively with the full range of issues that relate to NSAAs. This will be different in each instance, depending on shifts in the political landscape that have taken place during the conflict, but should typically include items outside the sphere of security arrangements alone, as NSAAs are rarely if ever just military actors alone.

LESSONS LEARNED: IMPLEMENTATION

NSAAs can play important roles in the implementation phase of a peace agreement. The successful implementation of a peace agreement should not automatically mean the disappearance of NSAAs. Paradoxically, in many cases, stability may require their continued presence albeit in a different relationship with the state and the people. It is important to think beyond the perceived conventional roles of armed groups, to fully understand the various social contracts that NSAAs operate under, and the potential role they can play in the implementation phase of a peace agreement. These roles include integration into the central army, disarmament and reintegration into civil society, or transformation into a political party, or continuation as a non-armed social movement.

NSAAs can provide administrative or governance services. For instance, in some contexts NSAAs will continue to need to fill the void in areas of limited statehood by providing administrative services, such as running schools and collecting garbage. NSAAs will very likely have to play a role in the security sector. Some armed groups have the potential of serving as constructive contributors in the provision of security—again in a context where states are weak and do not hold a monopoly of violence. This is particularly relevant in decentralised and tribal societies such as Yemen and Libya but may also be a factor in more centralised societies. In Palestine, any sustainable agreement is likely to involve NSAAs or their factions playing a central role in the provision of security, simply due to the fact that Hamas is currently in charge of security in key areas. To this end, security dialogues have been convened in Palestine by private diplomacy actors, involving relevant NSAAs to develop security-related policies and draft laws for the security sector, which have been approved by members of the Hamas Legislative Council.

NSAAs relationship with the communities around them is dynamic. The implementation of a peace process will inevitably not mean a return to a pre-war order; neither will it mean the erasure of all the changes in the political landscape that the conflict generated. Such changes may be profound and difficult to undo, especially as regards the war economy. For the state to slowly re-establish control over NSAAs, stop-gap measures may be required. In the security sector, local control mechanisms are one way that can serve, in the transitional period, until local institutions are strengthened to ensure accountability. In Afghanistan, local governance structures were invoked to oversee the activities of local community militias.

There are clear lessons learned which favour pragmatic engagement with NSAAs in the design and conduct of peace processes, aware that they are able to add value to the process as a whole, and aware that stability generally requires their participation in some way in the implementation of peace agreements. Such lessons are broad and general and do not fully account for the range of strategies available in peace processes, nor the great many risks that are inherent in engaging with NSAAs. These risks are not only related to practical challenges, but also the political and normative trade-offs related to engaging with NSAAs and the wider implications for society. By including NSAAs in peace processes, and in inclusive or multi-layered governance structures, there is a risk related to the values they may represent. For instance, empowering a group like the Taliban could lead to repression of women and the undermining of basic human rights. Whether NSAAs disappear or not is conditioned by their own resilience and ability to survive and sustain themselves in adverse conditions. They can continue to exist in name, even after having played their part in a peace process, but this does not necessarily guarantee their integrity and cohesion.

Conclusion

It is true that the capacities, resources, and ambitions of large-scale stabilisation efforts undertaken by official actors, such as UN organisations, and the targeted interventions of private diplomacy actors may differ considerably. The varying strength is also why they complement each other in important ways. The red thread that runs through both is the assumption that external involvement can in some way help to achieve sustainable peace. Independent organisations, because of their smaller size, and the fact that they do not represent official state actors, have much greater flexibility in dealing with NSAAs. Informal actors may have leverage through relationships and access built over time with the conflicting parties, or through highly respected personalities representing the organisation. Informal actors may also include insider mediators, such as individuals from the country or region in conflict. There may be cases where stabilisation missions are not mandated to engage with the NSAAs, and there is no political will for taking on the risks involved in such a course, although the necessity and benefits may be acknowledged. In such cases, engagement with the NSAAs may be outsourced to other actors to ensure an informal channel.

NSAAs are part of the political landscape and can play a positive role, or become spoilers, in peace processes. However, because of their official nature, stabilisation missions face an even greater risk of legitimising NSAAs by simply engaging with them, than private diplomacy actors do. This can be dealt with creatively through careful, deliberate and pragmatic engagement with NSAAs in relation to the role they play in society, and careful coordination and smart cooperation between official and unofficial support actors. Engagement on issues central to the peace process through an informal track may be appropriate where NSAAs are large and cohesive. Engaging on thematic issues with defined objectives may be appropriate where NSAAs play a strong governance role. In certain contexts, where central state structures are nominal, NSAAs may serve the purpose of providing administrative and security services in transitional periods. The challenge in stabilisation interventions remains to ensure mechanisms of accountability to assert a certain degree of control over the NSAAs and identifying incentives for the NSAAs to yield parts of their authority to a centralised system. Finding ways of disentangling the NSAAs from the war economy, so they are incentivised to become constructive contributors in the post-war agenda and bringing parallel government and security structures under democratic control, is essential in ensuring stability.

The post-conflict order usually has its origins in the political landscape as it has been altered through conflict, and creative engagement with this context rather than attempting to ride roughshod over it provides the best chances for sustainable peace. There is, in other words, a need to think more creatively about models of statehood and challenge traditional notions of a centralised state. With NSAAs, it is typically assumed that over time they would be either absorbed into shared state frameworks by agreement or faded into irrelevance by circumstance or defeat—their continued existence alongside state structures is typically not considered. In some cases where state structures are controlled by single political actors, or where state structures are extremely weak and contested, it may not be realistic to assume that NSAAs could be either absorbed in state structures or be necessary for resolving violent conflict. This has ramifications for stabilisation engagement as well.

NOTES

1. See DCAF (2011).
2. Ibid.
3. See McQuinn and Oliva (2014).
4. See Huang (2012).

5. See Schneckener (2009).
6. See http://www.sclr.stabilisationunit.gov.uk/publications/elite-bargains-and-political-deals.
7. Ibid. The research project from the UK Government's Stabilisation Unit points to the balance that needs to be struck: 'Moving too quickly to promote inclusive development and alleviate poverty can destabilise elite bargains, which are founded on providing elites with more stable and predictable power, political clout and access to economic resources'.
8. See OCHA (2006), UNICEF (2011), DPKO (2014), UNHCR (2006, 2012), UNSG (2009), and UNESCO (2013).
9. See http://www.c-r.org/accord/engaging-armed-groups/case-engagement-interview-president-carter/understanding-armed-groups.
10. See Hofmann and Schneckener (2011).
11. See https://www.regjeringen.no/en/dokumenter/nou-2016-8/id2503028/sec5.
12. Ibid.
13. "Yemen Militia Leaders Says Holding Indirect Talks with Saudi Arabis," *The Jordan Times*. http://www.jordantimes.com/news/region/yemen-militia-leader-says-holding-indirect-talks-saudi-arabia.
14. See Risse (2013). The idea of modern statehood has been challenged by the pervasiveness of instances of 'limited statehood'. Risse and the contributors to the volume highlight that governance models in areas of limited statehood are the predominant and fundamental reality of politics, and one that has largely been immune to modernisation.
15. See Wickham-Crowley (1987).
16. See Mampilly (2015).
17. See Wickham-Crowley (1987).
18. A Kurdish religious minority that believe in a peacock angel, and are, by Daesh considered devil worshippers.
19. See Huang (2012); also, "The Islamic State as an Ordinary Insurgency," *The Washington Post*, 14 May 2015. https://www.washingtonpost.com/news/monkey-cage/wp/2015/05/14/the-islamic-state-as-an-ordinary-insurgency/.
20. Rukmini Callimachi, "The ISIS Files," *New York Times*, 4 April 2018. https://www.nytimes.com/interactive/2018/04/04/world/middleeast/isis-documents-mosul-iraq.html.
21. See Mampilly (2015).
22. See Kasfir (2005).
23. Report of the UN Panel of Experts on Yemen (2018). http://www.un.org/en/ga/search/view_doc.asp?symbol=S/2018/594.
24. See Al-Idrissi and Lacher (2018).
25. See Adamson (2005).
26. See Connelly (2003).

27. Unarmed actors may include, government representatives, political parties, unions, dissidents, and other organisations or individuals perceived to represent a constituency crucial to resolving the conflict.
28. The Libyan Political Dialogue had the dual problem of dealing with the overwhelming prevalence of NSAAs in all aspects of the political landscape, combined with the challenge of including them in what was initially an intra-legislative process.
29. See Boutellis (2015).

Bibliography

Adamson, Fiona B. "Globalisation, Transnational Political Mobilisation, and Networks of Violence." *Cambridge Review of International Affairs*, vol. 18, no. 1 (2005): 31–49.

Al-Idrissi, Alaa, and Lacher, Wolfram. "Capital of Militias, Tripoli's Armed Groups Capture the Libyan State." Briefing Paper, *Small Arms Survey*, June 2018.

Boutellis, Arthur. "Can the UN Stabilize Mali? Towards a UN Stabilization Doctrine?" *Stability: International Journal of Security and Development*, vol. 4, no. 1 (2015): p.Art.33. http://doi.org/10.5334/sta.fz.

Connelly, Matthew. *A Diplomatic Revolution: Algeria's Fight for Independence and the Origins of the Post-Cold War Era*. Oxford: Oxford University Press, 2003.

DCAF. "Armed Non-state Actors: Current Trends & Future Challenges." Horizon Working Paper Series no. 5. Geneva: Geneva Center for the Democratic Control of Armed Forces, 2011. http://www.dcaf.ch/content/download/53925/812465/le/ANSA_Final.pdf.

DPKO. *Understanding and Integrating Local Perceptions in Multi-Dimensional UN Peacekeeping*. United Nations, 2014.

Hofmann, Claudia, and Schneckener, Ulrich. "Engaging Non-state Armed Actors in State- and Peace-Building: Options and Strategies." *International Review of the Red Cross*, vol. 93, no. 883 (September 2011): 603–621.

Huang, Reyko. *The Wartime Origins of Postwar Democratization: Civil War, Rebel Governance, and Political Regimes*. PhD thesis. Columbia University, 2012. file:///C:/Users/eda013/Downloads/Huang_columbia_0054D_10688.pdf.

Kasfir, Nelson. "Guerrillas and Civilian Participation: The National Resistance Army in Uganda, 1981–86." *Journal of Modern African Studies*, vol. 43, no. 2 (2005): 271–296.

Mampilly, Zachariah Cherian. *Rebel Rulers: Insurgent Governance and Civilian Life During War*. Ithaca: Cornell University Press, 2015.

McQuinn, Brian, and Oliva, Fabio. *Preliminary Scoping Report: Analyzing and Engaging Non-state Armed Groups in the Field*. Turin: United Nations System Staff College, 2014.

OCHA. *Humanitarian Negotiations with Armed Groups: A Manuel for Practitioners*. United Nations, January 2006.

Risse, Thomas (ed.). *Governance Without a State? Policies and Politics in Areas of Limited Statehood*. New York: Columbia University Press, 2013.

Schneckener, Ulrich. "Spoilers or Governance Actors? Engaging Armed Non-state Groups in Areas of Limited Statehood." SFB-Governance Working Paper Series no. 21, October 2009.

UNESCO. *Culture of Peace and Non-violence: A Vision in Action*. United Nations, 2013.

UNHCR. *Operational Guidelines on Maintaining the Civilian and Humanitarian Character of Asylum*. United Nations, 2006.

UNHCR. *Dangerous Liaisons? A Historical Review of UNHCR's Engagement with Non-state Armed Actors*. United Nations, 2012.

UNICEF. *Programme Guidance Note on Engaging with Non-state Entities in Humanitarian Action*. United Nations, November 2011.

UNSG. *Enhancing Mediation and Its Support Activities*. United Nations, 2009.

Wickham-Crowley, Timothy. "The Rise (and Sometimes Fall) of Guerrilla Governments in Latin America." *Sociological Forum*, vol. 2, no. 3 (1987): 473–499.

PART II

New Actors

CHAPTER 6

GCC Approaches to Stabilisation: Compatible or Competing?

Timo Behr

INTRODUCTION

Over the past decade, Arab Gulf countries have emerged as increasingly proactive and influential foreign policy actors in the Middle East and North Africa. No longer content to be mere 'payers' that are subject to the regional ambitions of others, they have increasingly turned into active 'players' on the regional chessboard, willing to shoulder greater regional responsibilities and confidently shaping regional outcomes. There are many different reasons for this development, including the increasing sophistication of their governance systems and state institutions, the evolving structures of global politics, the diminishing role of traditional regional powers, and the evolution of the regional threat environment, resulting from the atrophy and collapse of state structures, the rise of extremist actors, and growing regional competition.

As Gulf Cooperation Council (GCC) States have sought to navigate the new regional landscape and redefine their wider role, one issue in particular

---

T. Behr (✉)
Westphalia Global Advisory, The Hague, The Netherlands

© The Author(s) 2020   121
V. Gervais and S. van Genugten (eds.), *Stabilising the Contemporary Middle East and North Africa*, Middle East Today,
https://doi.org/10.1007/978-3-030-25229-8_6

captured their imagination and became a core foreign policy objective—the restoration or promotion of 'regional stability'. This reorientation coincided on the one hand with the collapse of a number of Arab regimes and the general climate of insecurity and instability following the so-called Arab Spring. On the other hand, it benefitted from a growing scepticism of grand state-building exercises in the West in general and the US' abnegation of its traditional Middle Eastern role in particular. Both of these trends naturally meshed with the traditional inclinations of the Gulf monarchies and the new and emerging concept of stabilisation. Stabilisation, as a concept, therefore provided a natural tool for Arab Gulf States to connect with and align their own regional agendas with those of their traditional international partners, while pursuing their emerging foreign policy interests.

However, their willing embrace of 'stability' as an end state, and 'stabilisation', as a process, has not been based on an easily identifiable and carefully defined stabilisation doctrine. Even more than in the case of Western countries, GCC States have remained vague about the way they conceptualise and operationalise 'stabilisation' processes. Thus, unlike some of their western counterparts, GCC States have not issued stabilisation strategies to underpin their actions at a strategic or operational level. While this may have allowed them greater flexibility in their actions, it also means that they ceded the theoretical ground to others. At the same time, there are noticeable differences both among GCC States, as well as between GCC States and their Western partners, concerning the content and definition of domestic and regional stability.

This chapter seeks to address this gap in the academic literature by tracing the evolution of GCC approaches towards regional stability. It starts by analysing the gradual evolution of foreign aid, the traditional soft power tool of GCC States for promoting political stability. It then provides an overview of the wider contributions that GCC States are making to regional stabilisation efforts, which include an increasingly broad set of soft and hard power tools. The chapter then looks at the case of Libya, which marks the emergence of Arab Gulf States as independent actors on the stabilisation scene, before it tries to derive some general principles that characterise the way that GCC States have approached stabilisation as a process. The last part of the chapter looks at some of the differences between GCC States and their international partners when it comes to the concept of state stability, as the end goal of any stabilisation efforts, before drawing some general conclusion about the compatibility of their approaches.

Gulf Assistance: Traditional Focus and Characteristics

While the concept of 'stabilisation' is a recent addition to the academic and policy literature and Arab Gulf actors are relatively new to international peacekeeping and stabilisation operations, GCC States have a long tradition of promoting political stability in the Arab world through the use of generous overseas development assistance funds.[1] GCC States' use of foreign assistance is partly rooted in Islamic traditions, as well as based on the general sense of insecurity felt by GCC States after their emergence as fully independent countries in a hostile regional environment. Although GCC aid has fluctuated significantly over time and data limitations complicate a systematic analysis and comparison of assistance flows and trends, it is clear that already between 1974 and 1994, Saudi Arabia, Kuwait and the UAE, ranked among some of the world's most generous providers of overseas development assistance, as measured by gross national income (GNI), when compared with their Western counterparts.

Gulf State assistance has traditionally been defined by a number of characteristics that have been noted throughout the academic literature and remain of relevance today.[2] First, Gulf assistance has fluctuated strongly in line with the oil price. As a percentage of GNI, Gulf assistance started from a very high level in the 1970s, decelerated sharply in the 1980s and 1990s and has risen again in the 2000s, but remains below the level of the 1970s. Second, a majority of Gulf assistance (50–60% by some accounts) has traditionally been directed to Arab countries. In particular, a majority of Gulf aid has traditionally been disbursed to what has been largely the same group of countries since the 1970s, which includes Algeria, Egypt, Jordan, Morocco, Sudan, Syria, Tunisia and Yemen. Third, Gulf aid has traditionally been bilateral in nature and has shunned multilateral channels and processes. Thus between 1995 and 2004, some 85% of aid was disbursed through bilateral channels, while Gulf donors largely stayed clear of UN Funds. Fourth, much of Gulf assistance has been provided in the form of concessionary loans and direct budgetary support, with some also being channelled towards large-scale infrastructure projects. This contrast with a focus on service provision amongst OECD DAC countries in areas such as education and health care, as well as their provision of debt-relief. Fifth, while the traditional motives for providing assistance have included support for commercial penetration and the spread of Islam, the promotion of regional, and especially political, stability has been a long-standing preoccupation of GCC States. Finally, unlike many western assistance programmes, Gulf aid has been 'unconditional', at least when it comes to promoting concepts of liberalism and democratisation or enforcing specific good governance criteria. Instead, its overarching goal was to support regional political stability, by strengthening the legitimacy of a specific government or regime.[3]

Recent empirical research suggests that Gulf assistance has had a very real impact on the level of political stability in the region, with there being a direct causal link between the decline in Gulf assistance to Arab countries in the 1980s and the increase of political violence in the Arab world during the same period.[4] However, this analysis also cautions that while Gulf aid may have contributed to political stability by strengthening government capacity in the short run, it may have laid the seeds for future conflict and eventual state failure, by sustaining a pseudo-stability that quickly collapsed, once the transfer funds were no longer sustained.[5]

THE TRANSFORMATION OF GULF ASSISTANCE

Since the late 2000s, there has again been a growing focus on the role and changing character of Gulf development assistance, with some researchers identifying a specific '*khaleeji* mode' of development aid that sets itself apart from established Western and even Chinese approaches to development.[6] Academic attention to the role and impact of Gulf assistance has spiked since 2011, with a particular focus being devoted to the impact that Gulf assistance and investments are having on Arab countries in transition.[7]

While at some level, there has been a remarkable continuity in the trajectory and focus of Gulf development assistance after 2011, there have also been some notable changes, not all of which can be directly related to the challenges posed by the 2011 protests. First, there has been a clear decoupling of the scale of Gulf assistance from oil prices. Despite the oil price decline in the 2010s and its continued stagnation, Gulf development and stabilisation spending have remained steady or increased.[8] This suggests not only a growing concern about the impact that regional instability is having on GCC States, but could also reflect the growing diversification of GCC economies, where public funding is not solely driven by oil prices and can draw on large buffers of available funding. Second, even though the Arab world remains the predominant focus of Gulf assistance, there is a rising interest and attention on countries in sub-Saharan Africa, which seems to be clearly led by the changing commercial and geopolitical interests of GCC States. Third, while there continues to be a clear preference for bilateral forms of funding, there is an increasing willingness to contribute to multilateral funding tools, particularly in areas where GCC States seek greater international donor engagement, such as Yemen. Fourth, GCC States are increasingly aware and confident about their new role in international development assistance and are no longer shy to flex their 'aid muscle'. This has led to some accusations that Arab Gulf donors, in particularly Saudi Arabia, are using crowding-out tactics to influence and attach their own conditions to UN programmes, including the obligation to work with vetted implementing agencies (from the GCC) on the ground. This greater awareness of their overall weight contrasts with another trend in Gulf funding, namely that some Arab Gulf actors are becoming more transparent about their funding by releasing more detailed statistics and data, as well as the fact that there is some re-balancing in the focus of their programmes, with education and health also an increasingly important focus, apart from direct support and large-scale projects. Finally, since the late 1990s, GCC States have started to mix their traditional focus on foreign assistance with other soft power and increasingly more hard powers tools, in particular by making limited contributions to some international peacekeeping missions and by offering themselves as 'neutral' mediators in regional conflicts, with the ability to facilitate negotiations through side payments and consolidate agreements by making large-scale investments.

This shift is clearly discernible in the case of the UAE and Qatar. The UAE, as the only Arab country, dispatched peacekeepers to Kosovo in 1999 and later followed suit by sending forces to Afghanistan in the early 2000s, where they served alongside US and other international forces.[9] Qatar, on the other hand, has invested heavily into establishing itself as a 'non-stop' mediator, facilitating talks between Hamas and Fatah, trying to bring the US and the Taliban together at various stages, resolving tensions in Lebanon and mediating in Yemen and Darfur, among others.[10] This approach benefitted from Doha's close relations with a wide spectrum of regional actors and its willingness to maintain an open channel with some extremist parties across the region. Overall, Gulf assistance clearly became more targeted and strategic throughout the 2000s, while GCC States have started to experiment and develop other soft power tools. Moreover, these soft power tools have increasingly been placed in the service of a well-defined and comprehensive foreign policy strategy that serves their respective regional interests and go beyond some nominal support for the regional status quo.

Gulf Contributions to Stabilisation: Multifaceted and Growing

From 2011, starting with the crisis in Libya, it is possible to observe a clear shift in the way GCC States approach issues of regional stability. In particular, it is possible to see their departure from a singular reliance on 'soft' power tools such as generous development assistance and conflict mediation to address regional crises. Instead, starting with the Libyan conflict, GCC States have increasingly drawn on a comprehensive toolbox of 'soft' and 'hard' power tools to pursue their respective visions of regional stability and have taken an increasingly proactive and confident approach in pursuing their interests. As a result of this shift, GCC States are now central contributors to various aspect of regional stability.

To realise their regional relevance, it is worth considering how comprehensive their efforts have become. Humanitarian funding has been one of the areas where Arab Gulf countries are playing a particularly disproportionate role. On their own account, members of the Coalition for Legitimacy in Yemen have contributed some US$18 billion in funding to the conflict since its start in 2015.[11] Saudi Arabia and the UAE alone were the second and third largest contributors to the UN Humanitarian Relief Fund for Yemen in 2018 and have further increased their pledges in 2019. Similarly, Saudi Arabia reports that is has provided US$2.35 billion to Syria between 2007 and 2017, the UAE contributed US$976 million between 2012 and 2019, and Qatar claims to have given US$1.6 billion between 2012 and 2015. These large sums of humanitarian assistance have been overshadowed by the significant structural funding that Arab Gulf countries have provided at various stages across the region, in particular to countries like Egypt, Jordan, Bahrain, Morocco and Oman. Between July 2013 and February 2015, Egyptian officials declared they had received over US$23 billion in assistance from friendly Arab Gulf countries, followed by another aid package of US$12.5 billion, as well as several other contributions. In June 2018, Saudi Arabia, Kuwait and the UAE pledged US$2.5 billion in aid to Jordan, following other previous pledges.[12] In October 2018, the UAE, Kuwait and Saudi also pledged some US$10 billion to Bahrain.[13] What makes these contributions somewhat different than more traditional GCC foreign assistance is their scale and timing. In all cases, the funding was meant as a direct stopgap to an urgent economic and political crisis. Moreover, much of the funding came with a new level of oversight, to ensure that money was being well spent and was having a tangible impact on the affected parties on the ground.

While GCC States have been resistant to granting refugee status to many of the individuals fleeing conflict in the region, they have provided temporary shelter to growing numbers and have supported refugee issues across the region. Estimates of Syrian refugee entries to Saudi Arabia since 2011 range from just over 400,000 to 2.5 million (Government figures), while the UAE has provided over 100,000 residence visas to Syrians and promised to take on a further 15,000 from refugee camps. GCC States are also providing funding for a number of refugee camps in Jordan, Lebanon, Turkey and even Greece. Although the verifiable refugee numbers remain modest compared with the burden carried by some other countries in the region, they nevertheless indicate a growing Gulf contribution.

In addition to some of their financial contributions, GCC States are also making a growing military contribution to various crises in the region. During the Libyan conflict, both the UAE and Qatar made substantial contribution to the NATO no-fly zone.[14] In 2011, the UAE and Saudi Arabia deployed Peninsula Shield forces to Bahrain, in response to a request of the Bahraini Government. Saudi Arabia and the UAE are leading a Coalition of Arab countries in Yemen, which includes contributions from Bahrain and Kuwait, as well as Qatar, until 2017. Several GCC States have also contributed forces to the military efforts of the Global Coalition against Daesh in the early phases of the operation. Arab Gulf countries are also increasingly deploying their forces out of territory, with the UAE and Qatar having pledged smaller contingents to NATO's Operation Resolute Support in Afghanistan and Qatar previously deploying peacekeepers in Eritrea. Saudi Arabia and the UAE also maintain military bases across the Red Sea, providing them with strategic depth.[15]

In parallel to their military deployments abroad, Arab Gulf countries have provided training and support to foreign military forces from crises countries. Qatar and the UAE have provided trainers to the Somali National Forces, with the UAE mission ending in 2018. Qatar has also trained Libyan opposition fighters during the 2011 uprising, while Saudi Arabia has reportedly provided training to Syrian opposition fighters.[16] Both Saudi Arabia and the UAE have also provided structured training programmes for Yemeni troops in Yemen and abroad.

On the political level, Arab Gulf countries have made various efforts to mediate regional conflicts. In Libya, the UAE has played an active role hosting meetings between key Libyan players to support the UN process and remains an active participant in various multilateral efforts to address the crisis. Oman has used its neutral status to host negotiations on Yemen, Iran and Libya. Kuwait played host to the first UN dialogue between the Houthis and the Yemeni Government and has played the role of the mediator in the Gulf crisis. Saudi Arabia has organised the Syria I and II Conferences of the Syrian opposition. Qatar has facilitated the Arab Peace Plan for Syria and hosts negotiations with the Taliban. While many of these efforts have ultimately been unsuccessful, they demonstrate the growing role that GCC States seek when it comes to shaping political outcomes.

Arab Gulf countries have also taken a leading role as part of multilateral stabilisation efforts. For instance, the UAE has been the Co-Chair of the Working Group on Stabilisation and the Working Group on Strategic Communications of the Global Coalition against Daesh, where Saudi Arabia is the Co-Chair of the Working Group on Terrorism Financing.[17] The UAE has also been a co-founder of the Syria Recovery Trust Fund (SRTF), to which it contributed US$18.7 million, while various GCC States have made smaller contributions to the UN's Funding Facility for Stabilisation in Iraq, a key stabilisation tool.

While this brief overview touches only on some of the more critical aspects of the GCC States growing engagement to promote regional stability, it is clear that their contribution has become increasingly substantial, both in terms of soft and hard power. This is not to deny the critical role played by external, in particular Western actors, who have mobilised a lion's share of the military, diplomatic and financial muscles that is being used to address the crises in Syria and Iraq, and who remain important players in both Yemen and Libya. However, the growing size and multifaceted nature of their engagement means that GCC States have an increasingly important voice on how these crises develop—and eventually conclude.

Embracing Regional Stabilisation: The Case of Libya

As GCC States opted for an increasingly proactive and forward-leaning foreign policy approach in the region, they were forced to give greater definition to their views on regional stability and stabilisation.[18] In the process, some clear differences emerged with the views of their Western and international partners, as well as among each other. The fulcrum of the new Arab Gulf States activism on regional issues was the crisis in Libya, which revealed deep divisions among Arab Gulf actors when it comes to the means and the ends of stabilisation efforts. To gain a better understanding of the gradual emergence of Arab Gulf countries as stabilisation actors and to analyse their divergent approaches, it is therefore helpful to start with their engagement in the Libyan conflict.

As already noted, the Libyan crisis was one of the first times that Arab Gulf countries shifted from a largely passive foreign policy approach that was focused on the use of soft power and financial means, towards a more proactive and increasingly aggressive engagement. This was helped by the lack of strong international leadership when it comes to the Libyan conflict, in the light of the US reluctance to engage and deep European division over the file, thus opening spaces for GCC States to adopt a more entrepreneurial approach. In Libya, Qatar was initially the most proactive in defining a new role and direction for its foreign policy. Qatar was the first Arab state to abandon the Qaddafi regime and to recognise the Libyan National Transitional Council (NTC) and played an important role in pushing other Arab League countries to follow suit.[19] Qatar was also among the first to provide large-scale assistance to the plethora of fighting groups and revolutionary forces battling the Qaddafi regime, providing them with significant military and economic support.[20] For the first time, Qatar also directly engaged in the operational aspects of a 'stabilisation operation', by providing air support for the NATO no-fly zone. In addition, it has been widely acknowledged that Qatari Special Forces have given military training and logistics support to rebel forces and were directly engaged in some of the confrontations at the tail end of the conflict. Former Qatari chief of staff, Major-General Hamad bin Ali Al Atiya, acknowledged as much, stating that 'hundreds' of Qatari forces had been deployed.[21] Throughout the conflict, as well as in its aftermath, Qatari support was channelled through Libyan exiles who had developed close links to Qatar. Many of these were directly connected to 'Islamist' political groups, including some with an extremist background, such as members of the former Libyan Islamic Fighting Group (LIFG).[22] In the aftermath of the conflict, Qatar is thought to have maintained close contacts with revolutionary and Islamist actors in particular in Benghazi, Derna and Misrata and has used its influence with these groups in order to try and shape post-conflict political developments.

The UAE, similarly, shifted towards a more proactive and multifaceted stabilisation engagement in the course of the Libyan crisis.[23] Like Qatar, the UAE supported political change in Libya and made a significant contribution to the NATO no-fly zone. While there is less direct evidence of UAE military engagement on the ground early on in the crisis, media reports have suggested that the UAE provided substantial assistance, training and logistical support to a variety of, mainly, tribal actors, as well as some elements of the former Libyan military that had abandoned the Qaddafi regime.[24] After the overthrow of Qaddafi, the UAE continued to engage with tribal and nationalist elements to promote a 'Libyan-led' solution, while simultaneously seeking a political consensus that sidelines Islamist actors that the UAE considers as incompatible with, and opposed to, efforts to build a modern nation state. As Libya's conflict endured and the country began to fragment, the UAE established itself as a key interlocutor, taking a leading role in multilateral efforts, such as the P3+3 (US, UK, France, Egypt, Italy, UAE), and co-hosting a number of meetings of the main protagonists in Abu Dhabi.[25]

While both Qatar and the UAE have recognised, publicly acknowledged, and in some ways contributed, to successive UN frameworks for resolving the Libyan conflict, both have simultaneously sought to promote outcomes that serve their wider political goals and strategic visions. To this end Qatar, in coordination with Turkey, has continued to assist certain groups on the ground, while the UAE, in coordination with Egypt, has worked with others. In the process, they have reinterpreted the conflict to fit their respective regional visions, as defined by competing Islamist and anti-Islamist forces.

Saudi Arabia, while remaining largely in the background, has intermittently engaged in the crises on the side of the UAE and maintains some links with another important conflict party, in form of the Madkhali Salafists. However, Saudi Arabia's engagement has recently grown, as it sought to contribute in a more structured way to some of the multilateral processes surrounding the crisis by engaging a leading Libyan protagonist.[26] Other Arab Gulf actors, including Oman, Kuwait and Bahrain, have tended to take a more hands-off approach, lacking the resources, structures and strategic ambitions of their neighbours. The role that these other GCC countries adopted in Libya has largely defined their foreign policy posture going forward. Thus, Oman, in line with its traditional role as a neutral mediator, has briefly sought to facilitate a dialogue on the Libyan Constitution, but has otherwise abstained from the conflict, while neither Kuwait or Bahrain claimed a role.

GCC States as Stabilisation Actors

When considering the engagement of GCC States in the Libyan crises, it is possible to identify a number of key characteristics that have been largely confirmed in some of their other stabilisation efforts, directed at the various other regional conflicts that followed. First, GCC States consider stabilisation as quintessentially political in nature. For both Qatar and the UAE, the focus has not solely been on addressing immediate gaps in local security and governance, but on shaping a long-term political settlement that reflects their political preferences and visions. This is in line with the aforementioned approach of the UK Government that any stabilisation action is to be 'planned and implemented with an overtly political objective in mind'.[27] As such, it is clear that neither of them considers stabilisation as an a-political activity that is limited to restoring local security and basic services in a post-conflict setting, but rather as the first step of a long-term, state-building exercise that requires building local influence and a support base on the ground with the aim of directly shaping national bargaining processes to ensure preferred outcomes.

Second, GCC States stabilisation engagement in Libya has been comprehensive, combining both hard and soft power tools, in terms of military support and humanitarian and development financing. However, in the case of Libya, these actions were rarely integrated, in the sense of civil and military efforts reinforcing each other. In fact, GCC States contributions to civilian aspects of crisis management in Libya have been very limited. None of the GCC States participated in efforts to manage migration and trafficking challenges, including through the EU's Operation Sophia; there has been limited real cooperation on issues such as border management, coastguard training and police training, and demobilisation efforts have been subject to ideological differences.

Third, while GCC States have started to make large contribution to some multilateral UN instruments (as is the case in Yemen), they continue to prefer bilateral means of engagement in some other cases, which provide them with greater leverage and serve their view of stabilisation as a largely political tool. This is confirmed by the fact that in Libya, GCC States have made no contribution to the UN's Stabilisation Facility for Libya, rather preferring to provide assistance directly and to selected groups.[28] Similarly, despite a plethora of multilateral initiatives on Libya, GCC States have displayed a preference for taking actions bilaterally, instead of aiming for broader multilateral compromises. The UAE's efforts to bridge differences among some of the Libyan protagonists—including LNA Commander General Khalifa Haftar, Presidency Council Head Faiez Serraj and House of Representatives President Ageelah Saleh—while aimed at supporting the UN process, have taken place in a bilateral setting in Abu Dhabi.[29]

Fourth, GCC States have focused on engaging and co-opting selected local partners, when it comes to distributing assistance and support and to build their influence and leverage, consisting of like-minded tribes, religious groups, ethnic groups and political parties. This approach has made Arab Gulf States important interlocutors in any conflict resolution effort, as some of these groups command significant spoiler potential. This has been the case in Libya, where the UAE, Saudi Arabia and Qatar have worked with different tribes and political groups, as well as in Yemen, where tribal fighters represent the core of the Coalition's fighting power. Similarly, in Syria, Saudi Arabia, Qatar and others have consistently provided support to different sides of the opposition, at times complicating opposition efforts to form a united front against the Assad regime. While this approach has wielded political influence on the ground, it can encourage political fragmentation.

Fifth, GCC States have placed a premium on legitimacy and the preservation of core state institutions, when seeking to determine winners and losers; even if the basis of legitimacy in some cases is not clear-cut and its contestation is a key driver of some of the crises. In Yemen and Bahrain, GCC States support has been for the internationally recognised legitimate authorities; in the case of Libya, there has been an emphasis on the domestic legitimacy of the Libyan National Army and the House of Representatives, over that of the Presidency Council, which derives its legitimacy from a UN process. In Syria, GCC States contested the legitimacy of the regime, a decision that some have reversed, but were less outspoken over the legitimacy of state institutions, in particular the armed forces. In many cases, including in Bahrain and Egypt, the emphasis has been on preserving state institutions against internal enemies. Even though there is a willingness to foster some forms of internal compromise, as evidenced for example by the UAE's bridge-building efforts in Libya, in general Arab Gulf States have tended to adopt a rigid definition of legitimacy, which favours zero-sum outcomes that tend to produce clear winners and losers. While this approach has the potential to lead to strong and centralised governance structures and favours insiders and established institutions, it risks entrenching the opposition of those that are being excluded; whether former Qaddafi-supporters, Islamists or civil society activists, who have no direct claim to legitimacy or authority.

Finally, even though it is possible to discern some commonalities in the approach of GCC States towards stabilisation issues, there are clear differences in the way in which different Arab Gulf countries approach this subject. While Saudi Arabia, Qatar and the UAE, each have taken a strongly proactive approach, their neighbours have remained a lot more passive. Oman has largely abstained from directly engaging in regional crises in order to preserve its traditional neutrality and to serve as a mediator, as it has done on occasions in the case of Yemen, Libya and Iran. Kuwait has pursued a somewhat similar approach, but has combined its mediation efforts with generous aid contributions, including through more multilateral channels. Thus, while there are some broad principles on which GCC States have based their stabilisation approaches, there are also significant differences. Moreover, just as GCC States have not always been aligned on the processes of stabilisation, they have also differed with regard to their views on stability—both among each other and with their partners.

Conclusions: Divergent Visions of Stability and the State

The preservation and promotion of stability have been a long-standing priority for Arab Gulf States. This focus on regional stability, while long established, has received a new dynamism and greater definition, following the 'Arab Spring' in 2011. However, despite their almost continuous focus on the promotion of regional stability as a core aim of foreign policy, both the concept of 'stability' and the action of 'stabilisation' remain surprisingly elusive and ill-defined. While the concept of 'stabilisation' has in general been enthusiastically embraced by Arab Gulf countries, there are no publicly available strategies or doctrines on stabilisation that have been issued by any of their governments, even though there are ongoing efforts in the UAE to develop a more strategic approach to stabilisation issues. This lack of a well-defined doctrine makes it difficult to fully analyse their views on 'stabilisation' issues. Still, based on their record of engagement, it is possible to derive some general principles that have characterised their stabilisation approaches. While these principles, summarised in the above, do not make for a clear and coherent doctrine, they do largely fit within one of the prevailing strategies of stabilisation identified in the literature.

According to Philipp Rotmann, it is possible to distinguish between two separate approaches Western governments have taken towards stabilisation—'stabilisation as peace-making' and 'stabilisation as crisis management'.[30] While the former seeks to fix failing states by permanently tackling the sources of fragility, the latter is limited to managing fragility within the specific institutional and political context of the state. After the failure of previous state-building exercises, Western countries have gradually adjusted their doctrines to reflect the more realistic goal of managing fragility, by defusing crisis.[31] The weakness of this approach is that it hinges on cooperation with local elites—sometimes the very purveyors of instability—over which outsiders often lack sufficient influence.

Despite a lack of public doctrines, strategies or positions, based on an analysis of their recent engagement, it seems clear that GCC States likewise have embraced a narrow concept of 'stabilisation', with a focus on managing 'fragility' and building the resilience of states to crises. This has been the gist of the approaches adopted by the UAE and Saudi Arabia in places like Libya, Yemen and Bahrain. Rather than a fundamental overhaul of state structures or an uprooting of the system of governance, their efforts are usually aimed at rescuing state institutions and creating a local balance of power that is able to guarantee a base stability—which falls in line with their own regional and international interests.

Where GCC States perhaps differ from some prevailing Western approaches is in the scale and scope of their engagement and ambitions. While their efforts are not aimed at changing the formal system of governance or state institutions of fragile states, their engagement, intentionally or not, contributes to a reshuffling of the local power coalitions that underpin these structures. Whether in Yemen, Libya or Syria, their approach has been focused on building a local balance of power that favours those groups that share their own political views and regional outlook. Western countries, in contrast, have focused on mediating, but largely abstained (not always successfully) from interfering, in local power dynamics. While these different approaches can perhaps be explained by a lack of local knowledge or a limitation of resources on part of Western countries, just as important, it suggests different visions and concepts of the state.

On the one hand, there is the view of the state as consisting of various distinct groups, tribes and ethnicities that continuously compete for resources. According to a large body of academic literature on the Middle East, this is the basis of the tribal state and society, where politics is often considered as a zero-sum game, which delivers clear winners and losers.[32] Stability is guaranteed by the victory and supremacy of one coalition of groups over the other. This view of the 'tribal state' is generally juxtaposed with that of a modern, Weberian state, which is bound by institutions and values and where conflict is resolved through compromise. Differences over whether the concept of the tribal or the concept of the modern state represent a more fitting model and reality for the Middle East run deep and have a long tradition. For some, the Arab Spring has been about the continuing effort to replace one model of governance with the other. For others, the Arab Spring demonstrated the failure of trying to enforce a western model of modernity and governance on the Middle East.

The emergence of stable and cohesive states in the Arabian Gulf raises questions over this bifurcated model of statehood. While Arab Gulf leaders have acknowledged and embraced the underlying tribalism of their societies and Middle Eastern society at large, they have simultaneously demonstrated that well-managed tribalism, by competent authorities, can be a source of stability. In contrast, countries like the UAE and Saudi Arabia have viewed all efforts to change traditional institutions and state structures through revolutionary rather than evolutionary means to lead to chaos and sedition. In a wide-ranging interview with the Council of Foreign Relations in 2017, the UAE's Minister of State for Foreign Affairs, Dr Anwar Gargash, reiterated this point of view. In his view, the Middle East resembles a vulnerable 'mosaic of ethnicities and sects and cultures'.[33] Once this mosaic is shattered by revolutionary forces, widespread violence and chaos is bound to follow. This surge of violence is likely to target the region's minorities in particular, creating a space for extremists to exploit. According to Gargash, democratic experiments in the region have largely disappointed. Instead, young Arabs consider the Gulf, with its combination of good governance, state effectiveness, legal security and traditional forms of legitimacy, as the most attractive models of governance to embrace, as successive youth surveys confirm.[34]

This fusion of elements of the modern Weberian state and the parochial tribal state appear to be at the basis of the stabilisation efforts of some of the GCC States. It suggests that tribalism and social segmentation do not have to be a source of social tension and violence, as long as they are well managed and pluralism and diversity are protected by effective state institutions. This vision is deeply rooted in the national development of the GCC States. However, whether it can be easily transferred and is able to provide a basis for sustainable stability in other Middle Eastern countries remains yet to be seen.

NOTES

1. See World Bank (2010) and Villanger (2007).
2. See Isaac (2014, 2015) and World Bank (2010).
3. See Isaac (2015, p. 263).

4. See Ahmed and Werker (2015).
5. Ibid., p. 181.
6. See Tok and D'Alessandro (2017).
7. See Sons and Wiese (2015).
8. UAE foreign aid, for example, has fluctuated somewhat but has remained consistently over 1% of GNI since 2011, reaching 1.31% of GNI in 2017. From 2015 to 2018, the UAE has been the world's largest donor of development assistance in proportion to GNI, according to OECD DAC, despite a trough in oil prices. See: *WAM*, "UAE Named World's Largest Humanitarian Donor for Fifth Straight Year," 9 April 2018. http://wam.ae/en/details/1395302680710.
9. See Ibish (2017) and Ulrichsen (2016).
10. See Barakat (2012, 2014).
11. Announcement by the Embassy of Saudi Arabia in Washington, DC, "Saudi Arabia Donates an Additional USD $500 Million to Yemen Humanitarian Response Plan," 26 February 2019. https://www.saudiembassy.net/news/saudi-arabia-donates-additional-usd-500-million-yemen-humanitarian-response-plan.
12. See *Reuters*, "Gulf States Pledge $2.5 Billion Aid Package to Jordan," 11 June 2018. https://www.reuters.com/article/us-jordan-protests-gulf/gulf-states-pledge-2-5-billion-aid-package-to-jordan-idUSKBN1J7026.
13. See *Reuters*, "Saudi, Kuwait, UAE to Sign $10 Billion Bahrain Aid Deal: Kuwait Newspaper," 4 October 2018. https://www.reuters.com/article/us-bahrain-economy/saudi-kuwait-uae-to-sign-10-billion-bahrain-aid-deal-kuwait-newspaper-idUSKCN1ME0GC.
14. See Chivvis (2013).
15. See Ibish (2017).
16. See Barakat (2012) and Schanzer (2012).
17. See Chapter 8 of this volume—Victor Gervais, "Beyond Daesh. The UAE's Approach and Contribution to International Stabilisation and Reconstruction Efforts in Iraq."
18. See Pinto (2014).
19. See Barakat (2012, p. 12). For a general overview of Qatari policies during the Arab Spring, see Ulrichsen (2012).
20. See Barakat (2012).
21. See, Ian Black, "Qatar Admits Sending Hundreds of Troops to Support Libya Rebels," *The Guardian*, 26 October 2011. https://www.theguardian.com/world/2011/oct/26/qatar-troops-libya-rebels-support.
22. See Fishman (2017).
23. See Pinto (2014).
24. See Fishman (2017).

25. See, for example, *The National*, "Libyan PM and Commander Khalifa Haftar Agree to National Election at Abu Dhabi Meeting," 28 February 2019. https://www.thenational.ae/world/mena/libyan-pm-and-commander-khalifa-haftar-agree-to-national-election-at-abu-dhabi-meeting-1.831556.
26. See Karasik and Cafiero (2019).
27. See, "UK Principles for Stabilisation Organisations and Programmes," Stabilisation Unit, UK Government, 2014, p. 6.
28. See, UNDP, "Germany Contributes €15 Million More to the Stabilization Facility for Libya," 26 February 2019. http://www.ly.undp.org/content/libya/en/home/presscenter/pressreleases/2018/Germany-contributes-15-million-more-to-the-Stabilization-Facility-for-Libya.html. While Qatar earlier announced that it would contribute €2 million to the initiative, it is no longer listed as a funder for the Stabilisation Facility for Libya.
29. *The National*, "Libyan PM and Commander Khalifa Haftar Agree to National Election at Abu Dhabi Meeting," 28 February 2019. https://www.thenational.ae/world/mena/libyan-pm-and-commander-khalifa-haftar-agree-to-national-election-at-abu-dhabi-meeting-1.831556.
30. See Rotmann (2016, p. 11).
31. Ibid., p. 5.
32. See Khoury and Kostiner (1990) and Salzman (2008).
33. See Council on Foreign Relations (2018).
34. Ibid.

BIBLIOGRAPHY

Ahmed, Faisal Z., and Werker, Eric D. "Aid and the Rise and Fall of Conflict in the Muslim World." *Quarterly Journal of Political Science*, vol. 10, no. 2 (2015): 155–186.

Barakat, Sultan. "The Qatari Spring: Qatar's Emerging Role in Peace-Making." LSE Research Paper, No. 24, Kuwait Programme on Development, Governance and Globalisation in the Gulf States, July 2012.

———. "Qatari Mediation: Between Ambition and Achievement." Brookings Doha Center Analysis Paper 12. Washington, DC: Brookings Institute, November 2014.

Chivvis, Christopher S. *Toppling Qaddafi: Libya and the Limits of Liberal Intervention*. Cambridge: Cambridge University Press, 2013.

Council on Foreign Relations. "A Conversation with Anwar Mohamed Gargash." 27 September 2018. https://www.cfr.org/event/conversation-anwar-mohammed-gargash.

Fishman, Ben. "The Qatar Crisis on Mediterranean's Shores." *Washington Institute for Near East Policy*, Policy Watch 2830, 12 July 2017.

Ibish, Hussein. "The UAE's Evolving National Security Strategy." Issue Paper No. 4, *Arab Gulf States Institute*, April 2017.

Isaac, Sally Khalifa. "Explaining the Patterns of the Gulf Monarchies' Assistance After the Arab Uprisings." *Mediterranean Politics*, vol. 19, no. 3 (2014).

———. "Gulf Assistance Funds Post 2011: Allocation, Motivation and Influence." IEMed Mediterranean Yearbook 2015, *European Institute of the Mediterranean*, 2015, pp. 262–265.

Karasik, Theodore, and Cafiero, Giorgo. "Libya General Haftar's Visit to Saudi Arabia." *Gulf State Analytics*, 2019.

Khoury, Philip S., and Kostiner, Joseph. *Tribes and State Formation in the Middle East*. Cambridge, MA: MIT and Harvard University Press, 1990.

Pinto, Vania Carvalho. "From 'Follower' to 'Role Model': The Transformation to the UAE's International Self-Image." *Journal of Arabian Studies*, vol. 4, no. 2 (2014).

Rotmann, Philipp. "Toward a Realistic and Responsible Idea of Stabilisation." *Stability: International Journal of Security & Development*, vol. 5, no. 1 (2016): 1–14.

Salisbury, Peter. "Aiding and Abetting: The GCC as Quiet Giants and Emerging Players in Aid and Overseas Developments Assistance." Issue Brief, *Baker Institute*, 28 August 2018.

Salzman, Philip Carl. *Culture and Conflict in the Middle East*. Amherst, NY: Humanity Books, 2008.

Schanzer, Jonathan. "Saudi Arabia Is Arming the Opposition; What Could Possible Go Wrong?" *Foreign Policy Magazine*, 27 February 2012.

Sons, Sebastian, and Wiese, Inken. "The Engagement of Arab Gulf States in Egypt and Tunisia Since 2011—Rationale and Impact." DGAP Analyse, no. 9, October 2015.

Tok, M. Evren, and D'Alessandro, Cristina. "The Khaleeji Mode of Development Cooperation." *Gulf Affairs*, Autumn, 2017.

Ulrichsen, Kristian Coates. *Qatar and the Arab Spring*. Oxford: Oxford University Press, 2012.

———. *The United Arab Emirates: Power, Politics and Policy-Making*. London: Routledge, 2016.

Villanger, Espen. *Arab Foreign Aid: Disbursement Patterns, Aid Policies and Motives*. Bergen: Chr. Michelsen Institute (CMI Report), 2007.

World Bank. *Arab Development Assistance: Four Decades of Cooperation*. Washington, DC: World Bank, 2010.

Young, Karen E. "The Interventionist Turn in Gulf States' Foreign Policies." Issue Paper No. 4, *Arab Gulf States Institute*, June 2016.

CHAPTER 7

Saudi Arabia, the UAE and Turkey: The Political Drivers of 'Stabilisation'

Neil Quilliam

INTRODUCTION

Saudi Arabia, the UAE and Turkey are not new actors when it comes to intervening (directly and indirectly) in other countries. Although Turkey has a longer track record of direct military intervention than Saudi Arabia and the UAE, both of which have tended to be 'status quo' powers in the past, all three have made significant interventions since the advent of the Arab uprising in late 2010.[1] However, it is important to draw a clear distinction between an intervention and stabilisation efforts. The former ordinarily refers to a short and targeted effort at achieving a specific goal and often, but not always, comes in the form of a military intervention. The latter, as described below, refers to an approach that draws on different government agencies, often civilian-led, and coordinates a response aimed at supporting stabilisation through a series of measures, including diplomatic, military, humanitarian and economic support. As such, stabilisation serves

---

N. Quilliam (✉)
Chatham House, London, UK

© The Author(s) 2020   139
V. Gervais and S. van Genugten (eds.), *Stabilising the Contemporary Middle East and North Africa*, Middle East Today,
https://doi.org/10.1007/978-3-030-25229-8_7

as a short-term measure on the road to stability. Arguably, these countries are 'new actors' with regard to stabilisation.

Former US President Barack Obama's 'pivot to Asia' challenged the states of the region, especially the Arab Gulf States, to take on the burden of responsibility for stability and security in the Middle East.[2] His successor, President Donald Trump, has made the call for more 'solutions in the region' even louder. To that end, both Saudi Arabia and the UAE have stepped up the nature of their intervention in the region and beyond (Afghanistan, Sudan and the Horn of Africa) and put into practice the semblance of stabilisation.[3] As such, they have deployed more of a 'whole-of-government approach' to their interventions and pursued methods akin to the stabilisation approaches of the UK, German and US governments, through with varying degrees of coherence and success.

The author has chosen to analyse three case studies: Saudi Arabia's stabilisation efforts in the Horn of Africa; the UAE's stabilisation efforts in the Horn of Africa; and Turkey's stabilisation efforts in Syria. The purpose of the chapter is to compare each state's approach to stabilisation, notably, within its own immediate region and better understand how leadership in Riyadh, Abu Dhabi and Ankara conceive of stabilisation and implement it. While it would have been tempting to analyse their approaches to stabilisation in one sub-region, for example, in the Horn of Africa, where Saudi Arabia and the UAE compete with Turkey for influence, the author believes the analytical value of the chapter is best served by examining cases where each state's approach to stabilisation is both more advanced and of immediate interest to its leaders. Saudi Arabia and the UAE's competition for influence in the Horn of Africa has been examined by detail by academics and think tank analysts elsewhere.[4] The case study of Turkey's stabilisation efforts in Syria provides for a rich comparison. At the same time, the different approaches adopted by Saudi Arabia and the UAE are highlighted through their separate case studies in the Horn of Africa. As this chapter shows, the degree to which policies support stabilisation are carefully calibrated and coordinated remains uncertain. The context that has shaped Saudi Arabia, the UAE and Turkey's efforts to stabilise countries in the Middle East and North Africa (MENA) and, more importantly for this chapter, states that encompass the Red Sea pertains both to their domestic agendas and changes to the regional and international order.

Saudi Arabia: Motivations and Priorities

Riyadh's motivation and priorities for supporting stabilisation in the Horn of Africa should be understood against the backdrop of its intervention in Yemen. There is a strong linkage between Saudi Arabia's interests in Yemen and the Horn of Africa, given their proximity and the strategic value of that sub-region. Therefore, it is useful to consider in brief, Riyadh's objective in intervening in the Yemen conflict. There is neither scope nor space to address it in any depth, other than to provide context to the subject matter. The stated goal of the Saudi government is to restore the legitimate government and help it stabilise the country, while severely curtailing the Houthis ability to exercise further political, military and economic power.[5] The primary objectives include dislodging the Houthi-led alliance from Sanaa, through military means, stabilising the country and restoring the Hadi-led government. Its other objective is to end Iranian influence in the country. Although Saudi Arabia and Iran have been locked into a struggle for influence for decades, the competition has intensified since the Arab uprisings in 2011. Since then, Iran has extended both direct and indirect influence in the region and in 2015 signed the Joint Comprehensive Plan of Action (JCPOA), which was reached between the Islamic Republic and the states of the P3 (US, Russia and China) and the E3 (UK, France and Germany).[6] Iran's apparent success has proven particularly irksome to Saudi Arabia and has resulted in its new leadership seeking to reverse Tehran's gains.

Saudi Arabia's extensive military campaign in Yemen has been studied in considerable detail elsewhere. Its air campaign has been criticised heavily, not only by human rights and humanitarian organisations, but also by leading members of the international community—deservedly so. In addition to the direct Saudi military intervention in Yemen, Saudi Arabia has engaged in supporting stabilisation efforts in Yemen. Although dwarfed by the scale of its military intervention and the humanitarian disaster left in its wake, the Saudi authorities committed, along with the UAE, to donate US$930 million to United Nations Office for the Coordination of Humanitarian Affairs (OCHA) for humanitarian aid[7] to support the United Nations Yemen Humanitarian Response Plan.[8] It deposited US$2 billion in Yemen's central bank to stabilise the Yemeni riyal[9] and donated US$35 million to a UNICEF-supported programme that pays salaries of Yemeni teachers.[10] These efforts appear to be overtly political in nature and more aimed at shoring up support for the Hadi government and demonstrating to both the international community and Yemeni public, Riyadh's commitment to alleviating humanitarian suffering, rather than supporting stabilisation in the country.

Riyadh's engagement in the Horn of Africa has followed a different pattern, which draws together political, diplomatic and economic Saudi agencies in supporting stabilisation. The conflicts in the Horn of Africa—that followed the end of the Cold War and included civil wars in Ethiopia (leading to the separation of Eritrea), Somalia and Sudan[11] and allowed for the emergence of Al Qaeda in Sudan, Somalia and Yemen—posed a peripheral threat to Saudi Arabia. However, the attacks carried out in the kingdom by Al Qaeda in the Arabian Peninsula (AQAP) between 2003 and 2007 precipitated a fundamental change in Riyadh's approach to counterterrorism and a review of policy towards the Red Sea states.[12] This has led to Saudi Arabia deepening its engagement with some fragile states in the Horn of Africa with the view to stabilising their political, social and economic environments in order to strengthen cooperation on counterterrorism, create investment opportunities, tighten economic links and draw them into its sphere of influence.

Saudi Arabia's particular motivation for supporting stabilisation in the Horn of Africa in various stages since the end of the Cold War can be best characterised as serving its strategic interests by ensuring Red Sea security; long-term food and water security; stemming migration; denying Iran strategic partnerships; and limiting Qatari influence. However, upon close examination (see below), it seems that Riyadh's approach to stabilisation was more ad hoc than coordinated among government agencies. The earlier efforts were driven more by individual ministries and agencies, whom were intent on serving their specific stakeholder interests. More recently, stabilisation has served Saudi, and Emirati, interests in providing bases from which they can prosecute the war in Yemen. Since 2015, the Saudi-led military coalition in Yemen has been overtly supported by the coastal governments of the region, namely Djibouti, Eritrea, Somalia, Somaliland and Sudan. Since 2011, Saudi Arabia has signalled strongly its desire to play a role in stabilising the Horn of Africa and becoming an indispensable peace-broker to the Red Sea region.[13] Previously, Qatar had positioned itself as the mediator to conflicts in the Middle East, Africa and even further afield, so it should be no surprise that both Saudi Arabia and the UAE now wish to play this role in place of Doha.[14] However, the move into mediation is not simply driven by a wish to eclipse Qatar, but more by a strategic ambition to tie the fortunes of the Horn of Africa states to Riyadh and Abu

Dhabi. This serves the purpose of securing Saudi Arabia's backyard not only from contemporary rivals, but also possible long-term rivals in the shape of China and India—both of whom are developing blue-water navies. As such, there is a long-term strategic dimension tied to the short-term goals of stabilisation.

The region provides Saudi Arabia points of access into East Africa and beyond, which it views as destinations for capital and also lucrative consumer markets. Hence, Saudi Arabia has pursued economic aims in the Horn, such as food production, regional trade and economic diversification, but perhaps more importantly political aims such as denying Iran a strong presence in the ports along one of the Gulf's main supply lines. Thus, Saudi Arabia has committed considerable resources to help stabilise states in the Red Sea basin, including Sudan, Ethiopia, Djibouti and Somalia. It has used a variety of instruments from its stabilisation toolbox to do so, including diplomatic efforts, military assistance and humanitarian and development aid.[15]

Diplomatic Efforts

Saudi Arabia has sought to advance peace agreements among the Horn of Africa states.[16] For example, alongside the UAE and the US, Riyadh supported the peace agreement reached between Ethiopia and Eritrea in September 2018 ending over 18 years of conflict.[17] Saudi Arabia also hosted direct talks between Eritrea and Djibouti in Jeddah following the signing of the peace agreement; Djiboutian President Ismail Omar Guelleh made clear that Saudi Arabia's role was key to normalising Djibouti's relations with Eritrea.[18] In the past, Horn of Africa states have proven adept at playing off the Gulf Arab states against Turkey and Iran and extracting maximum concessions from all parties. However, since the spat between Riyadh and Doha broke out in 2014 and the imposition of a Saudi-led blockade against Qatar in June 2017, the balance of power has shifted firmly into the hands of the Saudis vis-à-vis their partners in the Horn of Africa. It is symptomatic of the rising tensions between the two blocs in the Middle East region: the Saudi-Emirati-Egypt and Qatar-Iran-Turkey axes. It has led to a zero-sum approach to diplomacy; Saudi Arabia and the UAE have made it clear to their allies and partners that they must choose sides. This has become evident in Saudi Arabia's relationships with Sudan, Djibouti, Somalia and Eritrea; Riyadh has become a more demanding patron than in the past. For example, the Sudanese government broke off relations with

Iran in 2014 in order to improve relations with Saudi Arabia and receive economic assistance. Subsequently, Sudan has provided hundreds of troops to join the Saudi-led military alliance in Yemen. Djibouti and Somalia followed suit and cut ties with Iran in 2016.[19] Saudi Arabia has deployed financial support to shore up its political capital in the Horn of Africa. To that end, it has supported stabilisation through civilian-led channels, but they have been backed by military support.

Military Assistance

Saudi Arabia has invested in developing the security and military capabilities of some states in the Horn of Africa. Arguably, this has contributed towards stabilising those countries emerging from civil war or interstate conflict. For example, it has strengthened the security and military institutions of states where it has intervened and by doing so helped lower the prospect for domestic instability or conflict with neighbours. However, Saudi support has not followed the traditional pattern of supporting stabilisation, whereby donor countries encourage recipient countries to undergo the transformational processes of disarmament, demobilisation and reintegration (DDR). In the Saudi case, its investment in the militaries of some Horn of Africa states—be that investment in infrastructure, purchase of military hardware and materiel or training—has been to serve its own specific goals, rather than serving stabilisation in the recipient country. These include securing support for prosecuting the war in Yemen, developing bases and ports to serve its own long-term military purposes and strengthening the authority of central governments which will be more inclined to award contracts to Saudi own state-owned enterprises and investment vehicles.

The Saudi military presence along the Red Sea coast has grown considerably since its military intervention in Yemen in 2015. Saudi Arabia (like the UAE) has signed military cooperation agreements that have significantly increased military presence in Eritrea, Djibouti, Somaliland and Somalia.[20] It appears that their primary motive in doing so is to increase capacity to take control of the Yemeni coastline, cut off rebel supply routes and increase naval and aerial attacks against the Houthi-led forces along the southern flank.[21] In other words, the political motivation of stabilising these states has been less about stabilisation per se and more about securing bases and ports from which it can prosecute the war in Yemen. As such, there is a short-term stabilisation goal, but it does not purport to support long-term stability. Saudi Arabia and the UAE's accord with Eritrea in 2015 granted both countries a three-decade lease to use the port of Assab, a military airfield close to the port and other facilities on Eritrean-owned Hanish islands in the Red Sea. Eritrea has well-developed military facilities, experienced armed forces and is close to Yemen's important southern flank. Hundreds of Eritrean troops and special forces back the Saudi-led coalition in Yemen, in addition to other troops from Sudan and Somalia.[22]

Development and Humanitarian Assistance

Saudi Arabia has for a long time deployed financial support—in varying forms—to supports its own goals. It has used chequebook diplomacy to pursue its objectives, though the results have been typically mixed. For example, where Saudi Arabia does not possess the capacity (institutional or otherwise) to support its financial—charitable and humanitarian—objectives, it has often failed to translate its financial support into support for stabilisation. Overseas Development Assistance (ODA) by the Saudi Fund for Development to Horn of Africa states 2000–2017 was only US$36 million.[23] Saudi Arabia is the largest donor of the Islamic Development Bank (IDB),[24] which donated US$2061 million mostly for education, finance and health; it is an important donor to the other multilateral development funds.[25] The Jeddah-based Organisation of the Islamic Conference (OIC) provides Saudi Arabia with significant diplomatic leverage; moreover, its financial arm, the IDB with its capital base of more than US$150 billion allows for more developmental initiatives, driving development for recipient governments and supporting the wider geopolitical aims of its major donors, notably Riyadh. Saudi Arabia's charitable organisations are also an instrument of soft power. Unlike the investments deployed by Saudi Arabia's private sector actors, sovereign wealth funds or its central bank (Saudi Arabia Monetary Agency SAMA) Saudi charities for the most part target the wider population in most African states.[26] They typically focus upon on housing, schools and mosques.[27] Organisations such as Sultan bin Abdulaziz Al Saud Foundation and the Mecca-based Muslim World League and the Jeddah-based International Islamic Relief Organization are other instruments available to the Saudi state in supporting stabilisation. They seem to possess a capacity that is unique to oil-rich Arab Gulf States and deploy substantial financial support to recipient countries through multiple channels. Although they are not state entities, as such, and do not serve as development agencies either, as they serve broader state interests and even more so, following 9/11 and the universal clampdown on terrorist financing.

In sum, Saudi Arabia has used a number of instruments to support its stabilisation efforts in the Horn of Africa. These instruments have included diplomatic, military, financial and humanitarian support lent to select states in the region. The kingdom's deepening engagement in the Horn of Africa and Red Sea region forms part of its competition with Turkey and Iran, which has intensified with the emergence of Mohammed bin Salman as a transformational leader. It appears to have eclipsed Qatar as deal maker in the region having brought about a reconciliation between Ethiopia and Eritrea and investing in conflict-torn Somalia.

The UAE: Motivations and Priorities

Among the Arab Gulf States, the UAE has arguably been the most strategic in how it approaches stabilisation. Whereas Qatar has placed most of its efforts in mediation drawing upon its senior leadership to broker talks bankrolled by its LNG dollars and Saudi Arabia continues to muddle through, the Emirati leadership has made sure that it has not only acquired capacity to support stabilisation but has also gained first-hand experience in the field. Nonetheless, as shown below, the UAE's approach to supporting stabilisation in the Horn of Africa carries with it a significant risk, as its foreign aid policy is often driven by a transactional logic that seeks rapid returns on investment in spite of the country's longer-term strategic vision. One could argue that Abu Dhabi has long recognised the strategic significance of the Horn of Africa and has put in place a strategic plan to not only stabilise the sub-region, but also create a dependency or interdependency between the Emirates and the states of the Horn. In a bid to diversify international partners and in anticipation of a reduced US presence in the Gulf region and the entry of China in its wake, Abu Dhabi's Crown Prince Muhammed bin Zayed has undertaken to acquire his own string of pearls connecting the Indian Ocean and the Red Sea. With a long-term strategic vision, Abu Dhabi has invested heavily in Yemen and the Horn of Africa to secure access to ports and licence to build naval bases, which not only lend the UAE strategic depth, but also a means to make the country indispensable to developing China's Belt and Road Initiative (BRI). Therefore, while Abu Dhabi shares the same set of interests with Saudi Arabia (food security, migration, access to new markets, and offsetting Iranian and Turkish influence), it appears to have prioritised stabilising the sub-region in a bid to prepare for and profit from a new China-led international order. The following sub-sections outline the UAE's stabilisation efforts in the Horn of Africa. The UAE's stabilisation efforts, similarly to Saudi Arabia, materialise through diplomatic efforts, military assistance, economic support and humanitarian means.

Diplomatic Efforts

Abu Dhabi's exercise in diplomacy in the Horn of Africa has in some cases supported stability, notably in encouraging Ethiopia and Eritrea in beginning to reconcile their long-held differences. It has also contributed to lowering tensions between Ethiopia and Egypt over the Grand Ethiopian Renaissance Dam (GERD) project.[28] Nevertheless, the UAE's adventurous diplomatic moves towards the federal states of Somalia has increased tensions between Mogadishu and Somaliland and Puntland, which has encouraged the federal states to push more for independence. As such, the UAE's diplomatic manoeuvres could be considered as de-stabilising for both Somalia and the sub-region by pushing Mogadishu and the federal states towards serious conflict. Following the UAE's spat with Djibouti, Abu Dhabi prioritised its relationship with Ethiopia; and the emergence of reform-minded Prime Minister Abiy Ahmed meant that the two countries could more readily advance their partnership. The UAE has also sought to instrumentalise its relations with Egypt and new improved partnership with Eritrea to increase the prospect for cooperation between the two countries. Along with Saudi Arabia, the UAE's diplomatic intervention facilitated a series of meetings between Egyptian President Abdel Fattah el-Sisi and Abiy Ahmed, starting in Cairo in June 2018, aimed at assuaging Egyptian fears that the GERD will have a material impact upon its supply of water from the Nile. Consequently, Sisi has agreed to remove the military option from the table in working towards resolving the issue.[29]

Military Assistance

The UAE appears to be growing its military presence in the Horn of Africa to help protect trade flows through the Bab el-Mandeb strait, which is a key-shipping lane used by oil tankers and other cargo vessels en route to the Suez Canal; and to establish strategic footholds to support the Saudi Arabia-led war against Houthi forces in Yemen.[30] Abu Dhabi's short-term motivation for deepening military ties can be attributed to the war in Yemen and its goal of taking control of Yemen's coastline, cutting supply routes to the Houthi alliance and increasing capacity to carry out naval and aerial attacks against forces along the southern flank. Similarly, its objectives in training Somali armed forces and developing a naval base in Berbera suggest that Abu Dhabi intends to enhance counterterrorism competency in Somalia, checking the military influence of Turkey, which maintains a base in Mogadishu, and shoring up support from regional allies for its campaign in Yemen.

The UAE has been using its financial and military assets to support operations in Yemen, as well as to counter Iranian influence more broadly.[31] The cornerstone of that effort has been the forging of military basing agreements with friendly leaders and factions in several Horn of Africa states. For example, UAE forces deployed to Djibouti to support the Saudi-led intervention in Yemen in 2015, Abu Dhabi and Riyadh also established a logistics centre in Djibouti's Haramous facility near Camp Lemonier and stationed special forces there to help prosecute the war in Yemen. However, in mid-2015 a UAE-Djibouti dispute over funding arrangements was one of a number of factors that caused UAE (and Saudi) forces to begin using facilities in Eritrea instead.[32] This provides an early example of the UAE either (a) changing tactic in order to support a broader strategic goal (arguably, effective stabilisation); or (b) exhibiting impatience or naivety when working with local partners in the Horn of Africa, which carries risks to all parties (arguably, ineffective stabilisation). It is not clear, however, whether it was a change in tactic or an act of impatience, as information pertaining to Abu Dhabi's decision remains publicly unavailable.

Nonetheless, Djibouti and the self-declared Republic of Somaliland have openly declared support for Saudi and the UAE in their more recent dispute with Qatar. The former has since downgraded ties with Doha based on strategic and economic calculations around UAE and Saudi investments in ports and military bases.[33] As noted above, the 'Qatar crisis' has not contributed towards stabilisation in the Horn of Africa—it has, in many ways, forced states to choose between the two groupings (Saudi Arabia, UAE, Egypt and Bahrain) and Qatar, Turkey and Iran.

This division has manifested itself in particular in Somalia. Although difficult to orchestrate, the UAE has used a combination of diplomatic, political, military and financial capital to work with both the Federal Government of Somalia (FGS) and the authorities in the autonomous regions of Somaliland and Puntland.[34] For example, the UAE established a training facility for the Somali armed forces and, at the same time, it agreed to train the Puntland Maritime Police Force (PMPF). The UAE's state enterprise DP World further negotiated with the authorities in Somaliland to gain access to and upgrade Berbera port for US$442 million.[35] The UAE also established a base at the port of Berbera. The 30-year basing agreement reportedly includes UAE training for Somaliland military and police forces.[36] Under a separate agreement, Somaliland granted the UAE a 25-year lease to build a military base and use the Berbera airport. This is expected to give rise to at least US$1 billion in investments to develop and modernise infrastructure.[37] Expectedly, the agreement with Somaliland triggered a legal complaint from the government of Somalia in March 2018.[38] In mid-2015, the UAE had expanded its partnership with the fragile government in Somalia to open a new centre at which a few hundred UAE special forces trained Somali commandos to counter terrorist groups, particularly Al Shabab.[39] It bore the hallmarks of a stabilisation programme and demonstrated the UAE's growing stature amongst the international community. However, its rift with the government in Mogadishu, over UAE's agreement with Somaliland, led to a termination of the UAE training mission in Somalia in early 2018 and ultimately compromised the project.[40] This provides another example where the UAE's approach to stabilisation in the near-term appears somewhat short-sighted, despite it having a clear vision where its strategic interests lay.

Humanitarian and Development Aid

The UAE extends humanitarian aid primarily through key philanthropic organisations, such as the Zayed Charitable and Humanitarian Foundation, Abu Dhabi Fund for Development, Emirates Red Crescent, Dubai Cares, and Mohammed Bin Rashid Al Maktoum Humanitarian and Charity Establishment. According to UAE Foreign Aid 2015 Report, most of UAE aid (92%) was directed towards development, while only 6.7% went to humanitarian causes. This pattern was reflected in the UAE's provision of aid to the Horn of Africa states. According to the report, the UAE contributed the following: Sudan (US$108 million), Eritrea (US$36 million), Somalia (US$31 million) and Djibouti (US$14 million). While Africa was the main recipient of UAE aid in 2015, receiving almost 78% of total aid, nearly 97% of that aid went to North Africa, reflecting its massive financial support to Egypt and aid to allies in eastern Libya. East Africa received only 1.7%.[41]

The UAE provided substantial aid to Yemen, where it contributed US$908 million in 2015 to help with reconstruction, while also supporting sectors such as education, health, food aid, water and sanitation and economic recovery. In 2017, a report by the Emirate state news agency noted that incomplete figures indicated that expenditure on humanitarian and charitable activities by the UAE had exceeded US$536 million. This included the supply of 172,000 tonnes of food and over 100 tonnes of medicines and other medical supplies, and ambulances, with ERC medical teams also treating hundreds of thousands of patients.[42] While it is not surprising that the UAE would prioritise aid to Yemen, it is instructive that it places such a low priority on providing humanitarian support to the Horn of Africa. The UAE views the Horn as a strategic priority, but at present, views its partnerships through a transactional lens.

Thus, the UAE's motivation for wanting to support stabilisation in the Horn of Africa fits with its strategic goal of securing access to the sub-region and creating its own string of pearls ahead of China's BRI. To that end, it has pursued a policy likely to bear fruit. However, the UAE's transactional approach to foreign policy may well compromise its overall goal and undermine its effort to establish sustainable relationships with key partners in the region. As such, the UAE's stabilisation efforts, though more advanced than Saudi Arabia appear immature and possibly at risk, given they are tied to quick returns and early gratification.

TURKEY: MOTIVATIONS AND PRIORITIES

Although Turkey has deployed a number of policy instruments in the Horn of Africa, which mirror those of the Saudi Arabia and the UAE, this section will focus on Ankara's stabilisation efforts in Syria. The choice of Syria allows to draw upon different facets of Turkey's stabilisation efforts, which are not otherwise present in the Horn of Africa. Turkey's motivation and priorities for stabilisation, on the one hand, resemble those of Saudi Arabia and the UAE and, on the other, differ in design and implementation. Turkey's efforts at stabilisation in Syria are driven by two overriding factors: first, a desire to secure its borders and influence events in neighbouring territory; second, and linked to that, a goal to thwart Syrian Kurds ambitions to establish an autonomous region within adjacent Syria, with its own restive Kurdish population in eastern Turkey. The Turkish authorities consider the Syrian Kurdish population to pose a direct threat to Turkey's domestic security. Meanwhile, Turkey's NATO ally, the US, supported Syrian Kurds, in the form of the Syrian Democratic Forces, in fighting Daesh[43] until US

President Donald Trump announced that US forces would withdraw from Syria in early 2019.

There is pressing need upon Ankara to stabilise northern Syria, according to the explanation provided above, vis-à-vis the Kurdish community stretching across the Syrian and Turkish border areas. This has, therefore, led the Turkish authorities to develop a raft of stabilisation efforts that ultimately service Turkey's security interests. This sub-section considers a number of those stabilisation efforts in light of the discussion above on Saudi Arabia and the UAE's own stabilisation efforts in the Horn of Africa. The following sub-section, therefore, analyses the same set of instruments, diplomatic, military and humanitarian employed by Turkey in Syria. The following analysis offers a snapshot of Turkey's stabilisation efforts for comparative purposes for this chapter. The subject matter itself requires and deserves much closer scrutiny than this chapter can offer, but the comparative analysis with Saudi Arabia and Turkey, as new actors, offers valuable insights to our endeavour.

Diplomatic Efforts

Turkey's interests in Syria have remained the same (to maintain stability on its borders and fight Kurdish aspirations for independence), since the uprising in 2011, but it has changed its approach and tactics in reaction to events as they unfolded, including Assad's resistance to implement reforms, Russia's support to the Syrian government, pressure from the US to fight Daesh, and the attempted coup in Turkey. In the process, it arguably failed to grasp the regional demographic, religious and political interrelations, with deep sectarian fault lines, while overestimating its capacity to influence unfolding developments. Turkey's policy towards the Syrian conflict has been predicated on six main factors. First, it is committed to Syria remaining a unitary state with a strong central government based in Damascus—it actively opposes decentralisation within Syria. Second, Ankara has worked against the Assad regime by supporting the Free Syrian Army (FSA) and other opposition groups with the goal of instituting regime change. Third, since the Turkish Air Force struck down a Russian fighter plan in 2015, it has aligned itself closely with Moscow, especially following the latter's decisive military deployment in September 2015; as a result, Ankara has given full support to the Russian-led Astana process. Fourth, it has actively opposed US policy in arming and partnering with the People's Protection Units (YPG) in the fight against Daesh. Fifth, it has accommodated a significant number of Syrian refugees (over 3.6 million)[44] and provided humanitarian support both inside Syrian territory and in Turkey itself. Finally, it has sought, wherever possible, to undermine Kurdish autonomy in northern Syria, though has been forced to balance its desire to do so against Russia's own political agenda.[45]

Russia's decision to give Erdogan a green light on moving forces into Afrin probably had more to do with gaining concessions on the Astana process—such as Ankara's acquiescence on the Syrian regime's advances on Idlib—than any real sense of a Kurdish threat.[46] In the following subsection, the chapter analyses Turkey's military intervention in Afrin and evaluates its efforts at stabilising the parts of Syria under its control.

Military Assistance

The Turkish Armed Forces carried out Operation Euphrates Shield from August 2016 to March 2017 in the triangle between Azaz, Jarablus and al-Bab in northern Syria. While the stated goal of the operation was to stabilise the region, fight Daesh and Syrian Kurdish 'terror groups that threaten [the] country in northern Syria',[47] the operation eventually led to the Turkish occupation of northern Syria. In January 2018, Turkey then launched Operation Olive Branch in Afrin, which had until that point been controlled by the YPG. Afrin lies in the most western part of the Kurdish region in Syria but is isolated from the rest of the Kurdish-controlled zone liberated from Daesh since 2014. The Turkish government claimed that Operation Olive Branch specifically targeted the YPG, which it considers to be part of the United Nations proscribed-Kurdistan Workers Party (PKK). It was Ankara's second major incursion into Syria, but the Turkish army's first major confrontation with Syria's Kurdish forces. Ankara's goal was to begin stabilising the area with the creation of a 30 km-deep safe zone and eventually connect it to the Jarablus-Azez pocket, which had been controlled by the Turkish military since Operation Euphrates Shield. Consequently, Turkey began to stabilise Afrin and transform it into an enclave that would attract Syrian refugees to resettle while giving it leverage over the future of Syria. Over 140,000 Syrians arrived in the Afrin region during the early phases of the Turkish takeover. The Turkish authorities used two measures to draw in Syrian refugees: they empowered their local Syrian allies to take over the administration of the region and employed a relatively successful system of distributing humanitarian aid.[48] Turkey's military engagement and occupation of Syrian territory have compelled it to not only administer, directly and indirectly, the areas under its control, but also help local Syrian allies develop capacity to govern. In other words, Turkey has been actively involved in helping stabilise regions of northern Syria ahead of a resolution to the overall conflict. Its objective in doing so serves its strategic goal of eliminating the threat posed by Syrian Kurds to its own national security and shoring up its allies ahead of a resolution of the conflict to secure its influence in the post-conflict phase.[49]

As part of its stabilisation efforts, Turkey has tended to demilitarise the towns and villages it has occupied (or liberated) by removing military check-points and pushing local militias to camps outside population centres.[50] As noted below, Ankara provides financial support to help local councils provide education and health services, supports the local economy and trains new police forces.[51] The effort to stabilise in this environment clearly serves the interests of Turkey as an occupying force and resembles efforts made by the US and UK in Iraq following the 2003 war. In other words, Turkey is putting in place a political, security and economic system that will serve its own interests over the longer term, should it be sustained, rather than the broader interests of the different Syrian communities living in the locale. The case of Jarablus highlights the tensions between an occupying force attempting to impose a local solution upon populations, and, in doing so, bakes in the prospect for future destabilisation, as it expels and excludes target communities—in the case of northern Syria, Ankara's *bête noire*, Syrian Kurds belonging to the YPG.

Turkey's earlier intervention in Jarablus has been portrayed by Ankara as a success story in stabilising the area. It is now administered by a local council, which comprises professionals (teachers and engineers) many of whom joined the uprising against Assad in 2011. The local council faces a series of major challenges, including providing basic government services, such as healthcare, water and electricity, but receives support from Turkey in doing so. Turkish officials play an important role in local governance—most notably, the current deputy governor who remains responsible for coordinating reconstruction and managing the distribution of humanitarian aid. Subsequently, the administration has opened a hospital and over 100 schools. The Turkish military continues to provide security, but has trained the FSA to assume some of the responsibility.[52]

Following Operation Olive Branch, an interim local council was established in Afrin and included eleven Kurds, eight Arabs and one Turkmen.[53] Democratic Union Party (PYD) officials criticised the council and accused it of working with an occupying force. At the same time, Turkish forces began to implement a resettlement policy by moving fighters and refugees from southern Syria into the empty homes that belonged to displaced locals. The previous owners, many of them Kurds or Yazidis, were often prevented from returning to Afrin. Though some Kurdish militias of the Turkish-backed FSA (TFSA) and the Turkish-backed civilian councils opposed resettlement policies, some TFSA units supported the move. The Syrian Observatory for Human Rights reported that refugees from Eastern Ghouta had claimed that they were part of an organised demographic change intended to replace the Kurdish population of Afrin with an Arab majority.[54] Turkey's policy of stabilising those parts of Syria under its influence—direct or indirect—appear vulnerable to a project which while it brings together the facets of a whole-of-government approach to stabilisation, serves the narrow security interests of Ankara. By pursuing a partisan approach, it risks the very stabilisation it is seeking to achieve and appears to be sowing the seeds for further conflict and destabilisation.

Humanitarian and Development Assistance

State-run Turkish Cooperation and Coordination Agency (TİKA) leads Turkey's global outreach in humanitarian aid. It implements its humanitarian aid through its line ministries, for example, agriculture or health, and also through the Turkish Red Crescent. The conservative business community finances like-minded humanitarian NGOs, such as the Humanitarian Relief Foundation (IHH). Whether funded by and aligned with the conservative business community, the majority of Turkish humanitarian NGOs are faith-based. The Development and Justice (AK) party and the conservative business community with their respective operational partners finance and implement Turkish humanitarian assistance. To this end, Turkish humanitarian aid is nearly always politically oriented and intended to serve a clear political and/or faith-based objective.[55] According to figures in the 2013 Global Humanitarian Assistance Report, Turkey donated US$1 billion in emergency humanitarian aid in 2012, elevating Turkey to the highest league of donors and ranking it behind the US, the EU and the UK. And in 2017 Turkey was ranked the most charitable nation as it contributed nearly US$8.1 billion in humanitarian aid, which amounted to almost 30% of all international humanitarian aid according to the Development Initiative's (DI) Global Humanitarian Assistance Report. The country's humanitarian aid expenditures were nearly 1% of its gross domestic product (GDP) in 2017.[56]

Evidently, Turkey is a substantial humanitarian actor. It has demonstrated considerable capacity to not only distribute funds, but also find unique mechanisms to deliver aid. Its contribution towards Syria, of course, has been extraordinary in terms of accommodating so many Syria refugees, in spite of the complexities of distinguishing between refugees and guests and the country serving as an important bulwark for Europe. The close ties between Turkey's humanitarian sector and its business community has meant that the state and private sector have cooperated closely in consolidating advances inside Syria. As a result, there is close alignment amongst Turkey's political, security, humanitarian and business sectors in stabilising Syria and building influence through each channel to serve its long-term goals of remaining influential in post-conflict Syria.

Conclusion

Saudi Arabia, the UAE and Turkey are new actors in stabilisation and given their propensity to be active foreign policy players, they are likely to continue on their path and will become more mature actors over time. That said, the practice of contemporary stabilisation in its current form is also new and continuously draws upon the experiences gained in the field—and in most cases, those (Western) experiences did not lead to the expected outcomes.

Saudi Arabia has begun to develop a more integrated approach to stabilisation than in the past. It is not clear to what extent the approach is consciously integrated and represents a whole-of-government approach, but at the surface level, there appears to be a degree of coordination between government departments, private sector and civil society. Nonetheless, Saudi Arabia has long followed the practice of spending petrodollars to influence events on the ground; and this will likely remain the predominant mode of operation until it has acquired more experience and deepened capability. The shortcoming of chequebook diplomacy, however, is that influence dries up as funds run short; and competitors can make larger bids. In other words, it does not offer a sustainable means of engagement or support to stabilisation efforts, as it can be easily compromised by regional competitors. Clearly, Saudi Arabia is now an active foreign policy player and its new Crown Prince has transformed it from a status quo to an adventurous actor. This is manifest in various theatres, including Yemen, the Gulf, North Africa and the Horn of Africa. The Kingdom's deepening engagement in the Horn of Africa and Red Sea region forms part of its competition with

Turkey and Iran, which has intensified with the emergence of Mohammed bin Salman as a transformational leader. It appears to have eclipsed Qatar as deal maker in the region having brought about a reconciliation between Ethiopia and Eritrea and investing in conflict-torn Somalia. At present, Saudi Arabia is developing the tools of stabilisation but is still quite far from using them in a coherent manner and being in a position to deploy its own personnel to support stabilisation in conflict and post-conflict zones.

Whereas Saudi Arabia could be classified as a student of stabilisation, Abu Dhabi is best characterised as a recent graduate of stabilisation and is in the process of acquiring much needed experience. This means that for some time, it will struggle to apply theory to practice. The UAE has learned these lessons from its own major partners, the US and European states, so it is applying lessons learned in the neighbourhood. Nevertheless, the UAE has the instruments to help it become an effective stabilisation actor; and its natural resources, including a massive natural resource endowment, demography, geography and political system, can support that process. It is evident that the UAE is more advanced than Saudi Arabia in managing a close degree of coordination among state agencies and its active state-owned enterprises. It has also developed its own capability in some areas, so that it can deploy Emirati practitioners to support its stabilisation efforts. Nonetheless, there is a heavy emphasis on the role of the military in providing training, rather than focusing on SDR and DDR. The UAE's motivation for wanting to support stabilisation in the Horn of Africa fits with its strategic goal of securing access to the sub-region and creating its own string of pearls ahead of China's BRI. To that end, it has pursued a policy likely to bear fruit. However, the UAE's transactional approach to foreign policy and its desire to achieve quick wins may well compromise its overall goal and undermine its effort to establish sustainable relationships with key partners in the region, as policies tend to be quixotic or prone to sudden change.

Turkey at its turn has acquired stabilisation experience in a number of theatres, including northern Iraq, Libya, Syria and the Horn of Africa and has developed close coordination between its military, civilian administration and business sectors in supporting stabilisation efforts. However, Turkey's motivation and priorities in wanting to help bring about stabilisation in northern Syria will likely compromise not only its ability to support such stabilisation, but also sow the seeds for future conflict. Ankara's difficult relationship with its own Kurdish community and Syria's Kurds—at least those belonging to the PYD and YPG—could undermine a future resolution of the Syrian conflict, especially as and when Syria's Kurdish community reaches a Russian-brokered deal with Damascus. In other words, Turkey's motivation in northern Syria has made its objective of supporting stabilisation too narrow and focused upon its own direct security interests. While this is unsurprising given the proximity of the conflict, it does mean that Turkey remains a new actor in stabilisation, but one with many harsh lessons to learn.

In conclusion, Saudi Arabia, the UAE and Turkey are all new to stabilisation. As new actors, they have yet to develop a coherent approach to stabilisation. Having said that, it remains unclear whether more seasoned stabilisation actors have really developed a coherent approach, though they are at least fifteen years ahead from a conceptual and experiential perspective. One major constraint that international actors, such as the US and UK, have faced in their deployments in the past has been lack of familiarity with local context. To a large extent, Saudi Arabia, the UAE and Turkey benefit significantly from operating in their own backyards; they are fully familiar with the environment. However, that could also be their biggest challenge and ultimately undermine their success at supporting stabilisation. Being situated so close to the target country could compromise not only the motivations of the new actors, but also their short and long-term objectives. Consequently, the wider goals of stabilisation may well fall victim to the partisan objectives of Riyadh, Abu Dhabi and Ankara.

NOTES

1. See Miller (2016) and Ragab (2017).
2. See Goldberg (2016).
3. See Huliaras and Kalantzakos (2017) and Brewster (2018).
4. Rossiter and Cannon (2019), Lons (2018), Khan (2018a), and Soliman (2017).
5. CBN News, "How Yemen's Chaos Threatens US Security," 26 March 2015.
6. See Vakil (2018).
7. See Wintour (2018).
8. See "Yemen Comprehensive Humanitarian Operations (YCHO): Unprecedented Relief to the People of Yemen," *ReliefWeb*, 2018.
9. Ibid.
10. See "Saudi Arabia and UAE to Donate US$70 Million to Support Yemeni Teachers," *Arab News*, 23 October 2018.
11. See Mengistu (2015).

12. See Byman (2016).
13. See Manek (2018a).
14. See Soliman (2017).
15. See Meester et al. (2018).
16. See Lons (2018).
17. "Ethiopia, Eritrea Sign Peace Deal at Saudi Arabia Summit," *Al Jazeera*, 17 September 2018.
18. See Youssef (2018).
19. See Winsor (2016).
20. See Stevis-Gridneff (2018).
21. See Taylor (2016).
22. See Dudley (2018).
23. See Meester et al. (2018).
24. Saudi contribution to IDB capital amounts to 23.5%, see Islamic Development Bank, https://www.isdb.org/isdb-member-countries.
25. Meester et al. (2018).
26. Ibid.
27. See Williams (2018).
28. See Maasho (2018).
29. See International Crisis Group (2018b).
30. See Manek (2018a).
31. See Brennan (2018).
32. See Khan (2018a).
33. See Maru (2018).
34. See Khan (2018a).
35. See Khan (2018b).
36. See Cornwell (2018).
37. "Somaliland, UAE Sign Historic Economic and Military Pact," *The National*, 21 March 2018.
38. "Ethiopia, Eritrea Sign Peace Deal at Saudi Arabia Summit," *Al Jazeera*, 17 September 2018.
39. See Khan (2018a).
40. See Cornwell (2018).
41. See Ministry of Foreign Affairs and International Cooperation (2016).
42. See Mohamed and Ismail (2017).
43. See Lund (2018).
44. See UNHCR (2018).
45. See Ifantis and Galariotis (2017, pp. 27–35).
46. See Lund (2018).
47. See "Erdogan Says Syria Operation Aimed at IS Jihadists, Kurdish PYD," AFP, 24 August 2016.
48. See Çetinkaya (2018).
49. See Lund (2018).

50. See Al-Khateb (2017).
51. See Ashawi (2018).
52. See Gall (2018).
53. "Interim Local Council Established in Syria's Afrin," *Hurriyet Daily News*, 12 April 2018.
54. See Iddon (2018).
55. See Binder (2014).
56. "Humanitarian Aid Spending Makes Turkey Most Charitable Country," *Daily Sabah with AA*, 20 June 2018.

Bibliography

Al-Khateb, Khaled. "FSA Relocating to Outside Syria's Liberated Areas." *Al Monitor*, 12 September 2017.

Ashawi, Khalil. "Falling Lira Hits Syrian Enclave Backed by Turkey." *Reuters*, 28 August 2018.

Binder, Andrea. "The Shape and Sustainability of Turkey's Booming Humanitarian Assistance." *International Development Policy*, 2014.

Brennan, Andrew. "The UAE Weaves a Regional 'String of Pearls'." *Asia Times*, 26 May 2018.

Brewster, David. "Base Race in the Horn of Africa." *The Interpreter*, 7 February 2018.

Byman, Daniel. "The U.S.-Saudi Arabia Counterterrorism Relationship." *The Brookings Institution*, 24 May 2016.

Çetinkaya, Lokman B. "Turkey's Military Operations in Syria." *Ejil: Talk*, 20 February 2018.

Cornwell, Alexander. "UAE to Train Somaliland Forces Under Military Base Deal: Somaliland President." *Reuters*, 15 March 2018.

Dudley, Dominic. "East Africa Becomes a Testing Ground for UAE and Qatar as They Battle for Influence and Opportunity." *Forbes*, 4 April 2018.

Gall, Carlotta. "Emboldened Turkey Pushes Deeper into Syria, but Risks Abound." *The New York Times*, 22 March 2018.

Goldberg, Jeffrey. "The Obama Doctrine." *The Atlantic*, April 2016.

Huliaras, Asteris, and Kalantzakos, Sophia. "Gulf States and the Horn of Africa: New Hinterland?" *Middle East Policy Council*, vol. xxiv, no. 4 (Winter 2017).

Iddon, Paul. "Turkey Slowly Implementing Demographic Change in Afrin." *RUDAW*, 3 May 2018.

Ifantis, Kostas, and Galariotis, Ioannis (eds.). "Turkey's Foreign Policy Towards Syria, 2011–2017." *The Syrian Imbroglio: International and Regional Strategies*. Florence: European University Institute, 2017.

International Crisis Group. "Iran's Priorities in a Turbulent Middle East." Middle East Report No. 184, 13 April 2018a.

_____. "The United Arab Emirates in the Horn of Africa." Crisis Group Middle East Briefing No. 65, November 2018b.

Khan, Taimur. "Shifting Regional Dynamics Challenge UAE's Balancing Act in Somalia." *The Arab Gulf States Institute in Washington*, 26 April 2018a.

_____. "UAE and the Horn of Africa: A Tale of Two Ports." *The Arab Gulf States Institute in Washington*, 8 March 2018b.

Lons, Camille. "Saudi Arabia and the UAE Look to Africa." *Carnegie Endowment for International Peace*, 23 October 2018.

Lund, Aron. *Syria's Civil War: Government Victory or Frozen Conflict?* Swedish Defence Research Agency (FOI), 2018.

Maasho, Aaron. "UAE to Give Ethiopia $3 Billion in Aid and Investments." *Reuters*, 16 June 2018.

Manek, Nizar. "Saudi Arabia Brokers a New Ethiopia-Eritrea Peace Deal." *Bloomberg*, 17 September 2018a.

_____. "U.A.E. Military Base in Breakaway Somaliland Seen Open by June." *Bloomberg*, 6 November 2018b.

Maru, Mehari Taddele. "UAE and Its Relations with the Horn of Africa." *The Journal Discourse Affairs*, November 2018.

Meester, Jos, van den Berg, Willem, and Verhoeven, Harry. *Riyal Politik: The Political Economy of Gulf Investments in the Horn of Africa*, The Netherlands Institute of International Relations (Clingendael), April 2018.

Mengistu, Muhabie Mekonnen. "The Root Causes of Conflicts in the Horn of Africa." *American Journal of Applied Psychology*, vol. 4, no. 2 (2015): 28–34.

Miller, Rory. *Desert Kingdoms to Global Powers: The Rise of the Arab Gulf.* New Haven: Yale University Press, 2016.

Mohamed, Hatem, and Ismail, Esraa. "UAE National Day 46: WAM Report 6— UAE Aid to Yemen." 28 November 2017.

Ragab, Eman. "Beyond Money and Diplomacy: Regional Policies of Saudi Arabia and UAE After the Arab Spring." *The International Spectator*, vol. 52, no. 2 (2017): 37–53.

Rossiter, Ash, and Cannon, Brendon. "Re-examining the 'Base': The Political and Security Dimensions of Turkey's Military Presence in Somalia." *Insight Turkey*, vol. 21, no. 1 (2019): 167–188.

Soliman, Ahmed. "Gulf Crisis Is Leading to Difficult Choices in the Horn of Africa." *Middle East Eye*, 29 June 2017.

United Arab Emirates Foreign Aid 2015. Abu Dhabi: Ministry of Foreign Affairs and International Cooperation, 2016.

Stevis-Gridneff, Martna. "Middle East Power Struggle Plays Out on New Stage." *Wall Street Journal*, 1 June 2018.

Taylor, Magnus. "Horn of Africa States Follow Gulf into the Yemen War." *The Africa Report*, 22 January 2016.

UNHCR. "Syria Regional Refugee Response: Turkey." 2018.

Vakil, Sanam. *Iran and the GCC Hedging, Pragmatism and Opportunism.* London: Chatham House, September 2018.

Williams, Timothy. "The Middle East's Scramble for Africa: Building Bases and Instability." *Royal United Services Institute (RUSI)*, 26 February 2018.

Winsor, Morgan. "Saudi Arabia-Iran Rivalry in Africa: Sudan, Djibouti, Somalia Part Ways with Tehran as Riyadh Influence Grows." *International Business Times*, 7 January 2016.

Wintour, Patrick. "Saudis Demanded Good Publicity over Yemen Aid, Leaked UN Document Shows." *The Guardian*, 30 October 2018.

Youssef, Fatah Arahman. "President of Djibouti: Saudi Arabia Helped Us Open a New Page with Eritrea." *Asharq Al Awsat*, 25 September 2018.

CHAPTER 8

Beyond Daesh: The UAE's Approach and Contribution to International Stabilisation and Reconstruction Efforts in Iraq

Victor Gervais

INTRODUCTION

In Iraq, the military campaign to defeat Daesh, as well as the immediate post-conflict stabilisation efforts, have achieved notable successes.[1] Yet, as the post-2003 period has clearly shown, any meaningful victory over Daesh is likely to require far more than simply attempting to recover to pre-conflict levels. Stressing its commitment to avoid yet another resurgence of extremism, the Iraqi government unveiled in June 2017 a 10-year reconstruction plan for the country, aimed at achieving human, social and economic development, as well as the rehabilitation of infrastructure. The Iraqi authorities have also striven to muster the domestic and international support they need to ensure that short-term stabilisation programmes will be coupled with longer-term solutions that focus on the broader structural

---

V. Gervais (✉)
Emirates Diplomatic Academy (EDA), Abu Dhabi, United Arab Emirates

© The Author(s) 2020
V. Gervais and S. van Genugten (eds.), *Stabilising the Contemporary Middle East and North Africa*, Middle East Today,
https://doi.org/10.1007/978-3-030-25229-8_8

163

problems and challenges that created the space in which Daesh has thrived. This includes dealing effectively with the cumulative effect of almost half a century of insecurity, sectarian and ethnic fragmentation, weak governance and economic mismanagement.[2]

As part of the Global Coalition Against Daesh (GCAD), the United Arab Emirates (UAE) has been actively supporting international efforts to stabilise and rebuild Iraq, co-chairing with Germany (as well as, more recently, with the United States) the Coalition's Working Group on Stabilisation (WGS). In the wake of the Saudi-Iraq rapprochement, the UAE authorities have also indicated an interest in developing a new relationship with Baghdad and progressively try to (re)gain a measure of influence in Iraqi politics. Playing to what they see as their main strengths, they have focused on economic engagement and sought to build relationships across ethnic and confessional lines, prioritising initiatives that could foster long-term reconstruction and state consolidation objectives.

In this context, the UAE's commitment to post-Daesh efforts in Iraq has become increasingly intertwined with broader foreign policy objectives. In particular, the renewed interest in Iraq's reconstruction and state-building agenda appears to overtly derive from a desire to counter Iran's influence. Indeed, in helping Iraq rebuild, the UAE is advocating for the development of a stronger, physically and institutionally rebuilt Iraq that would not only prove more resilient to violent extremism and terrorism, but also able to mitigate the impact of foreign interference in Iraq by its neighbours. As such, whereas in most areas of regional unrest the UAE authorities have been inclined in recent years to adopt a narrower understanding of stability, framed as the absence of acute crises or large-scale violence, in the case of Iraq, they have instead chosen to promote a transformative agenda predicated on the idea that building a more inclusive, viable and unified state represents the best way to both foster long-term stability and regain a degree of influence in a complex and divided society that cannot simply or easily be controlled.

As the UAE's involvement in post-Daesh Iraq illustrates, notions of both stabilisation (as a process) and stability (as an objective of stabilisation efforts) remains remarkably elastic in the MENA context. As such, while there has been a distinct trend in Western countries towards a more realistic, less ambitious approach to stabilisation, the impact of the regionalisation of the stabilisation agenda in the MENA region remains uncertain, with regional countries with an interest in advancing stability recurrently adapting both the nature of the task and the goals to be achieved to contrasting, and sometimes rapidly evolving, regional dynamics and realities.

Against this backdrop, this chapter assesses the support provided by the UAE to post-Daesh stabilisation and reconstruction efforts in Iraq from 2014 to 2018. It first reviews the role of the WGS of the GCAD in helping the government of Iraq promote and coordinate stabilisation activities. With the scope of transitional stabilisation projects being progressively broadened to include wider reconstruction and development efforts, it then examines the UAE's approach to stability in Iraq. In doing so, this chapter analyses the main challenges facing the UAE in helping Baghdad implement a transformative agenda through economic engagement, cross-confessional outreach and support to security sector reform.

From Stabilisation to Reconstruction: The Role of the Global Coalition Against Daesh

In Iraq, the military campaign to disrupt, degrade and ultimately defeat Daesh has been accompanied by stabilisation activities aimed at providing governance, security and basic services to liberated communities. Since 2015, these efforts have included facilitating the return of displaced Iraqis, clearing mines and remnants of wars, restoring basic municipal services like electricity, water, education and health, along with setting conditions for longer-term recovery and reconstruction. Moving away from a mid-conflict practice akin to counter-insurgency, stabilisation practices became increasingly viewed as a set of post-conflict activities needed in the intersection between humanitarian and development efforts.

Through the Global Coalition Against Daesh, the international community has played a key role in stabilising areas liberated from Daesh's control. Established in September 2014, the GCAD consists of 79 international partners (75 countries and 4 international organisations). Beyond its military actions in Iraq and Syria, the GCAD has also positioned itself as a key mobilising and coordinating mechanism through focused activities and interest groups aimed at achieving 'a full and enduring defeat of Daesh as a global threat'.[3] In total, it has provided more than US$22 billion in stabilisation, humanitarian assistance and economic support in Syria and Iraq.[4] In particular, the WGS has been active in helping coalition partners and the government of Iraq mobilise resources and plan stabilisation activities.[5] It has also facilitated coalition efforts aimed at re-establishing governing capacity and public services in liberated areas.

At the invitation of the Government of Iraq, the WGS set up, in June 2015, the UNDP-administered *Funding Facility for Immediate Stabilisation* (FFIS), which became the primary vehicle for stabilisation activities supported by the international community in Iraq.[6] FFIS's work is overseen by a Steering Committee chaired by the Secretary General of Iraq's Council of Ministers. A number of donors to FFIS are 'sitting members, and relevant governors are also invited'.[7] In principle, stabilisation priorities are set by the central Iraqi government, through command and coordination cells at the governorate level, with Iraqi subnational governments also responsible for deciding on specific projects to be implemented.[8] Yet, in practice, the task of laying out the stabilisation response has been primarily carried out by the UNDP and the Office of United Nations Resident Coordinator and Humanitarian Coordinator for Iraq, headed between 2014 and 2018 by Lisa Grande. UNDP's prominent role was also endorsed by leading members of the WGS, including the UAE, which kept a low profile with regard to project selection and oversight during the stabilisation phase in Iraq.[9]

The FFIS established four categories—described in UNDP documents as four 'windows'—under which stabilisation projects must fall: (1) Public Works and Light Infrastructure Rehabilitation, which finance light repairs of key public infrastructure such as clinics, schools, water facilities, power grids, government buildings, access roads, etc.; (2) Livelihoods activities, which aim to jump-start the economy and generate income for local households, particularly families returning to their homes; (3) Capacity Support, which provides technical support for local governments, boosting their immediate response capacity to cope with the challenges arising during stabilisation, and; (4) Community Reconciliation Projects, aimed to help local leaders and community groups promote social cohesion and dialogue with special attention to local women's groups, and start a restorative justice process.[10]

Initially, the UNDP-led fund was designed for projects of short-term duration (six months or less). When the FFIS was established it was expected, indeed, that as soon as international actors would leave a city or a district, longer-term stabilisation and reconstruction projects would be undertaken by the Iraqi government using public revenues.[11] However, this sequencing has not materialised, in part due to the drastic drop in oil revenue in 2014–2015.[12] Therefore, in order to bridge the FFIS and longer-term recovery, a follow-on programme was initiated in the Spring of 2016—the *Funding Facility for Extended Stabilisation* (FFES)—

covering up to two years. In particular, the FFES has been intended to fund medium-scale projects that generate large numbers of jobs, incentivise mass returns, and help consolidate corridors between stabilised cities and districts.[13] Management, implementation, and oversight of the FFIS and FFES are, however, the same, as is the project selection process. As of December 2017, both funds had received US$563 million in funding, from twenty-five donor countries and the European Union, including US$53 million from the United Arab Emirates and US$2 million from Kuwait.[14] In total, more than 350 stabilisation projects in 28 different areas in Iraq have been either initiated or completed since mid-2015.[15] In other areas liberated from Daesh, the UNDP has also supported quick-impact projects through the Iraq Crisis Response and Resilience Programme (ICRRP), a sister instrument for early recovery and resilience.[16]

Today, international stabilisation efforts in Iraq revolved around two main lines of action. The first one is centred on the need to muster additional financial support for the finalisation of the stabilisation phase. For the WGS, this in particular involves finding ways to cover the FFIS/FFES' funding gap, currently estimated at US$560 million,[17] for ongoing programmes in five key areas across Iraq that still require intensive stabilisation support: (1) Western Nineveh; (2) Baiji-Hatra Corridor; (3) Western Anbar; (4) Mosul; and (5) broader Hawija. Another key task for the WGS is to integrate Explosive Remnants of War (EWR) clearance into broader stabilisation efforts, while building the capacity of local authorities to manage clearance operations, in particular in residential areas and on agricultural land.

The second line of action is to broaden the scope of transitional stabilisation projects to wider reconstruction and development efforts. Indeed, as stabilisation work in Iraq begins to conclude, the WGS is also gradually assisting the Government of Iraq in longer-term development activities aimed to reorient the country's trajectory towards structural stability and economic prosperity.[18] This objective was clarified in the 'Guiding Principles from the Global Coalition to Defeat Daesh', endorsed by the GCAD members in February 2018. In the short term, this means adapting to mechanisms necessary to bring in the private sector, as well as ensuring greater support for police training, including through the establishment of a centralised training facility for the Iraqi federal and local police.[19] In parallel, the Iraqi authorities have also striven to ensure that the international community would remain strongly committed to its long-term reconstruction agenda, at a moment when the focus of the coalition is seen as progressively shifting to Syria. Within this context, the February 2018 Conference for the Reconstruction of Iraq was organised to garner reconstruction support from the international community. The Conference saw foreign ministers and principals of the GCAD's 79 members convene to discuss financing for the post-Daesh reconstruction phase. It also drew participants from 51 development funds and financial institutions, and 107 local, regional and international non-governmental organisations, as well as 1850 private sector representatives.[20] Discussions highlighted priorities shared by the international community and the Iraqi authorities with regard to both the physical and human dimensions of reconstruction (infrastructure, private investment, societal issues, good governance and accountability).

In the end, however, the three-day event mobilised less than US$30 billion of additional international support, a far cry from the US$88 billion the Iraqi government says it would need to finance its 10-year reconstruction plan, unveiled in June 2017.[21] The United States, which spent more than US$1.7 billion in humanitarian and stabilisation action in Iraq in the 2014–2017 fiscal years, did not promise any aid at the conference, vowing instead to offer around US$3 billion in loans, loan guarantees and insurance funds to American firms investing in Iraq, while nudging other countries to increase their contribution.[22] Germany pledged 500 million euros (US$617 million) and the European Union 400 million euros (US$494 million). Overall, the biggest pledges made during the conference came from the Arab Gulf States and Turkey. The latter announced US$5 billion in loan funds and credit easing, while the Islamic Development Bank announced a contribution of US$500 million. For their part, the Arab Gulf States pledged more than US$10 billion dollars: the host of the event, Kuwait, allocated US$1 billion in loans and another US$1 billion in investments, while the UAE pledged US$500 million, in addition to US$5.5 billion in private sector investments.[23] Saudi Arabia promised US$1.5 billion and Qatar announced it would contribute US$1 billion.

As pointed out by observers, reconstruction support from Arab Gulf States falls within the realm of a recent diplomatic push initiated by Saudi Arabia in 2014 and aimed to rebuild ties with Baghdad and gain influence over Iraq's future trajectory, either through direct support or multilateral channels.[24] For the UAE in particular, the willingness to play a role in longer-term rebuilding efforts stems from the conviction that structural changes in Iraq could not only help build stability in the long term, but also give a new momentum to projects to regain a measure of influence in Iraqi politics. As such, whereas the immediate post-Daesh stabilisation efforts in Iraq were mainly regarded by UAE authorities as essentially apolitical, technical activities best carried out by specialised agencies,[25] reconstruction funding is promoted with clear foreign policy objectives in mind.

THE UAE'S APPROACH TO STABILITY IN IRAQ

Over the last decade, the Middle Eastern regional security complex has undergone a profound internal transformation driven by territorial disputes, power and status rivalries, wars and regime transitions, ideological competitions, and ethnic, cultural and sectarian divisions.[26] Faced with multiple security challenges, the UAE has responded to these new conditions with an increasingly assertive and interventionist regional policy, energetically trying to shape dynamics and influence political developments in most areas of regional unrest. As Khaled Al Mezaini puts it: 'Regime transition in Egypt, Tunisia, and Libya, the growth of movements of political Islam, and the rise of extremism and sectarianism all required significant change in the UAE's external behaviour. Leaders in the UAE [...] realised that the changing dynamics in the region required a change in foreign policy'.[27]

In the MENA region, the shift in UAE foreign policy has been primarily associated with a greater emphasis put on regional stability, today formally identified as one of the key strategic objectives of its external action.[28] As Anwar Gargash, the UAE Minister of State for Foreign Affairs and International Cooperation, described it: 'We (the UAE) work very hard to what I call return to stability [...] after almost a decade of chaos and a decade of challenges [...]'.[29] This shift in foreign policy has also been reflected in the authorities' support for projects intended to 'rejuvenate and create credibility for the Arab nation-state', perceived as the best way to defeat extremism and counter Iran's disruptive role in the Middle East and beyond.[30]

Yet, in recent years, these two objectives have remained largely disconnected, with efforts to build stability mainly conceived as an urgent effort to defuse acute crises and ensure order in conflict-affected countries. From Egypt, Libya, Bahrain, to, arguably, Yemen, the military, diplomatic, and economic tools used to bring back stability were not primarily expected to build lasting peace and prosperity but rather establish basic but effective security and governing systems that would prove resilient to external shocks, changing distributions of power, and shifting domestic demands.

As pointed out by Rotmann, 'a resilient country may still be deeply fragile, with unrepresentative, broadly illegitimate and sometimes violent politics, lack of respect for human rights and the rule of law, minimal levels of basic security and livelihood, and for most, few if any opportunities for advancement'.[31] In this regard, the UAE's renewed engagement with Iraq and support for its long-term reconstruction agenda stands in sharp contrast with other recent foreign policy initiatives it has promoted. Indeed, as mentioned, the authorities in the UAE have been increasingly eager to promote a transformative agenda in Iraq, providing support to Baghdad's stated readiness to tackle structural sources of conflict and state fragility through the promotion of responsive institutions, good governance, rule of law, accountable security forces and broad-based social and economic development, in part to ensure long-term stability and in part to limit Iran's influence in Iraq.

For the UAE, this represents not only an important challenge, but also an exceptionally delicate exercise in bilateral diplomacy. For most of the past 15 years, Abu Dhabi has been reluctant to engage directly and actively with the main political forces operating in Baghdad, seen mainly as impossible partners closely aligned with Iran. This was particularly visible during Nouri Al Maliki's eight years as Iraqi prime minister (May 2006–September 2014), during which the UAE sharply reduced its engagement.[32] Among other things, the UAE's disengagement was illustrated by the sharp decline in the country's foreign assistance to Iraq during this period: from around US$20 million in 2006 and 2007, it fell to less than US$5 million in 2008, US$4.9 million in 2009, US$1.1 million in 2010, US$6.7 million in 2011, US$5.3 million in 2012, and US$6.2 million in 2013 (Fig. 8.1). Also, whereas the Iraqi government was recipient of about 40–60% of the UAE foreign aid disbursement to the country before 2008, foreign assistance programs during the subsequent years were exclusively directed at and implemented by non-state entities that were operating outside Baghdad's control.

As such, the resignation of Prime Minister Maliki, following Daesh's swift capture of vast swathes of Iraqi territory in 2014, provided a new opportunity for re-engagement. Along with other Arab Gulf countries, the UAE publicly expressed congratulations to the new designated Prime Minister Haidar Al Abadi, indicating an 'interest in developing a new relationship with him and Iraq'.[33] This prompted a number of major political and diplomatic initiatives aimed at restoring Iraq-Arab Gulf Countries relations. After years of relative disengagement, Saudi Arabia, in particular,

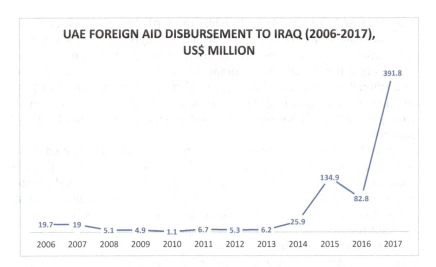

Fig. 8.1 UAE foreign aid disbursement to Iraq (2006–2017) US$ million

sought actively to re-establish its diplomatic presence in Iraq, appointing in June 2015 its first resident ambassador to Iraq in 25 years.[34] This was followed in February 2017 by the visit of the Saudi Foreign Minister, Adel Al Jubeir, to Baghdad—the first such visit since 1990. A few months later, in June 2017, Prime Minister Al Abadi made an official visit to Riyadh as part of a Gulf regional tour that also brought him to Kuwait and Iran, before returning to Saudi Arabia, in October 2017, to inaugurate a new Saudi-Iraqi Coordination Council.

Crucially, these high-level diplomatic initiatives promoted by Saudi Arabia were interpreted in Abu Dhabi as a signal allowing other Arab Gulf States to re-engage themselves with Baghdad. After a period of hesitation, the UAE authorities explored the possibility of building better relations with Iraq. As a result, diplomatic relations between the two countries progressively improved after 2014, along with the bilateral trade which doubled between 2010 and 2017.[35] The amount of UAE foreign aid received by the Iraqi state also went back to pre-Maliki levels, reaching US$25.9 million in 2014, before jumping to US$134.9 million in 2015, US$82.8 million in 2016, and US$391.8 million in 2017 (Fig. 8.1).

In parallel, the UAE became more open to (re)building ties across ethnic and confessional lines of the Iraqi society and elites, including

Iraqi Shia Arab leaders. As such, while the UAE has, at times, preferred to avoid state channels to channel its aid through individuals and non-governmental organisations in Iraq, mostly from the Arab Sunni community, its recent political and economic re-entry in Iraq has taken a more institutional approach, capitalising on what has been perceived as positive domestic trends in Baghdad—namely growing anti-Iranian sentiments among a number of Iraqi Shia leaders and an appetite for balanced regional relations.

Overall, however, it seems clear that the UAE has only limited leverage to influence Iraqi politics and policy. While some have argued that this could be a 'blessing in disguise', allowing for greater flexibility and a better alignment with Baghdad's own desire to create a balance of allies, Emirati authorities will nonetheless be required to show strategic patience in order to build the influence they seek and help the Iraqi leadership move past cycles of failure and address the structural problems that have perpetuated state weaknesses.[36] These long-term challenges include establishing representative and responsive state institutions, enhancing relations between the central government and regional authorities, tackling endemic corruption, reforming the security sector, and fostering reconciliation and trust among Iraqi communities. In this context, the UAE authorities have opted to prioritise what they see as their main strengths, focusing on economic engagement as the main tactical avenue to help support these long-term objectives. They have also identified security sector reform and cross-confessional outreach as other potential ways to pursue engagement and stronger relations with Iraq.

Promoting a Transformative Agenda in Iraq: Opportunities and Challenges

In recent years, economic engagement has been perceived by the authorities in the UAE as the least controversial way to regain a degree of influence in Iraq. More generally, it is also the one area where Arab Gulf countries believe they could have an advantage over Iran, in spite of Tehran's head start since 2003. The electricity sector is an example. In recent years, Iraqis have witnessed a constant deterioration in most basic services—including electricity. Surveys carried out by the Iraqi Ministry of Planning's Knowledge Network showed that in 2015 the average household received just 7.6 hours of electricity from the national grid each day, with 79% of those surveyed rating electricity services delivery as 'bad' or 'very bad'.[37] In this context, both Saudi and Emirati companies have expressed interest in working to improve Iraq's power system. In early 2018, Arab Gulf officials met with their Iraqi counterparts to discuss linking the Iraqi and GCC electric grids.[38] Saudi Arabia went a step further when it offered, in July 2018, to build a solar power plant and sell electricity to Iraq at a steep discount,[39] following the decision of Iran to cut its electricity supply to Iraq's southern provinces of Ziqar and Meysan.[40] The Iranian decision sparked a wave of protests against corruption and poor government services, during which the Iranian Consulate in Basra was also attacked.

With Arab Gulf Countries, in particular Saudi Arabia, already investing heavily in power generation, investment in power infrastructure in Iraq thus has the potential to achieve both objectives of assisting the Iraqi government in improving basic service delivery to the population and countering Iranian influence. As Langenhahn puts it: 'The Islamic Republic understands that its influence over Iraq's power sector is a major geopolitical coup and that any changes would have implications for its control over Baghdad as well as regional power dynamics. In the short term, (Arab Gulf Countries) may only be able to offer Iraq band-aid fixes such as fuel or portable generators. However, in the medium to long term, the two countries together have the resources to provide Iraq with the electricity it requires, diminishing Iranian control over Iraq's economy, depriving Iran of hard currency, and bolstering political stability through economic development'.[41] The UAE and Iraq also established, in September 2017, a joint business council with the objective of enhancing investment and trade between the two countries and identifying related priorities in vital sectors of Iraq.[42] Dubai-based property developer Emaar has also expressed interest in the US$10 billion Al-Rashid City real estate development project in Baghdad.[43]

That being said, the weakness of the regulatory framework for investment in Iraq has proven to be a strong deterrent against Emirati investment in Iraq. After the Kuwait Conference, UAE officials described a host of obstacles to seeing their pledge materialise. These included, in particular, the lack of guarantees to ensure payment in case investment defaults, as well as visible attempts to curb corruption.[44] Arab Gulf investors have also expressed concerns about not being paid on time or that their assets be seized or reallocated, in addition to the lack of skilled labour and lengthy contract review process.

To mitigate these concerns, UAE investors seem to have increasingly chosen to rely on local sovereign development funds and charities to allocate funding to projects, paying contractors or, in some cases, carrying out projects directly.[45] As an Emirati official, quoted by the ICG, explained: 'I see this as a new approach to foreign aid, to link it to institutions such as the Abu Dhabi Fund that have their very specific criteria. What it does is to fix the cash problem of corruption. With the Abu Dhabi Fund, the [Iraqi] government provides us with projects, [the Fund] does a technical assessment, and instead of just giving cash, which could disappear, we build relationship with local institutions'.[46] Overall, however, it remains unclear whether the UAE is ready to play the long game in Iraq: despite the current commitment to the longer-term goal of Iraqi reconstruction, it is still too early to tell whether both the UAE public and private investors will be ready to tolerate low or negative returns on investment in the short term and resist withdrawing or scaling back their activities if they encounter resistance or political setbacks.[47]

The prospect of early disengagement is even more likely in areas of cooperation where Abu Dhabi is starting from a low base. In the security sector, for instance, periodical attempts since 2014 at strengthening existing pockets of efficiency in the Iraqi military have failed to morph into long-term support for broader reform of security sector institutions. The current hesitations may be primarily linked to what Abu Dhabi appears to see as a lack of both willingness and capability of the Iraqi central government to get to grips with the broad set of problems that have plagued the post-Saddam Iraqi forces.[48] In fact, post-2003 Iraqi elites have repeatedly failed to create a cohesive, professional and integrated national force capable of providing security, under the rule of law across all communities in Iraq.[49] Instead, what has emerged is a weak and hollow force, riven by cronyism, poor leadership and sectarian splits.[50]

Certainly, the challenge of reforming the Iraqi security forces is daunting—with many key elements of their structural fragility being symptomatic of the broader sources of weaknesses facing the Iraqi state as a whole. First, widespread corruption has crippled the Iraqi military's capabilities and combat-effective resources, also provoking a sharp decline in quality and morale.[51] For instance, a 2014 government audit revealed that more than half of the army's forces were 'ghost soldiers', existing on paper only and defrauding an estimated 25% of the Ministry of Defence's annual budget. During the military campaign against Daesh, funds earmarked for soldiers' food and fuel were also embezzled, with reports suggesting that soldiers in Mosul had to buy their own supplies from local markets and cook the food themselves. Beyond corruption, the Iraqi army has also suffered from political constraints on professionalism and military effectiveness. Former Prime Minister Maliki, in particular, strived to insulate his regime from the potential for a military coup, staffing his security forces with loyalists, separating key army units from the military chain of command, and building up forces under the Interior Ministry to counterbalance the army. Political competition with rival groups also led him to appoint many commanders on a temporary basis to bypass parliamentary review and confirmation.[52]

In addition, the problem of state control over militias has resurfaced in recent years. In its fight against Daesh, the security apparatus fragmented into groups under, parallel to, and apart from the state of which the Popular Mobilisation Forces (PMF or al-Hashd al-Shaabi), an umbrella organisation made up of some 60 militias groups with about 60,000 fighters in total, became the most significant one. These groups, many of which emerged in the post-2003 security vacuum, gained a fresh impulse from the Daesh takeover of Mosul in June 2014, when Prime Minister Maliki and his allies 'established the Hashd Commission and then used an emergency call by Ayatollah Sistani to enlist young men in these pre-existing units'.[53]

While the volunteers have also included Iraqi Christians, Shia Turkmen, as well as tribal sheikhs from the Al-Anbar province, the main beneficiaries of this popular mobilisation have been the Shia religious parties.[54] In particular, the most powerful of these units have been trained and advised by the Iranian security apparatus, especially the Quds Force of the Iranian Revolutionary Guard Corps (IRGC), and remain closely affiliated with Ayatollah Khamenei.[55] In recent months, the Iraqi government has announced its intention to fully integrate the PMF groups into the formal state institutions, with the former Prime Minister Al Abadi (2014–2018) promising to devote a significant part of the post-Daesh rebuilding efforts to reforming the disjointed security sector. Yet, the authorities in Baghdad have yet to articulate, let alone implement, a coherent plan for the PMF's future in the overall security architecture.[56] As a result, these groups have been able to maintain a large degree of autonomy vis-à-vis the Iraqi state, thus undermining 'its legitimacy by acting in the security, political and economic spheres outside the chain of command and the formal security apparatus'.

For the UAE, the influence that the pro-Iranian groups exert over the Iraqi security sector continues to represent a major obstacle for closer defence ties with Baghdad.[57] In fact, recent attempts by the UAE to provide the Iraqi military with additional capacity have shown that unwelcome practical concessions to pro-Iranian groups are all but unavoidable. For instance, materials supplied to the Iraqi army during the military campaign against Daesh were seized by pro-Iranian PMF units. For similar reasons, the UAE, and more broadly the Arab Gulf countries, have been reluctant to take part in joint exercises and expand military cooperation with Iraq.[58] Within the WGS, Abu Dhabi has also adopted a discreet posture towards 'blue training' support provided by the WGS' Police Training Sub Group as part of the current transition from stabilisation to sustainable reconstruction.

As such, while the UAE authorities have well understood the importance of strengthening the role of Iraqi central institutions, including in the security sector, the current Iraqi predicament—as well as the regional and local dynamics that buttress it—have compelled them to adopt more indirect approaches. In post-Daesh Iraq, this has meant working with international partners and institutions that share a common vision of the Iraqi security sector's future to ensure that top SSR activities will receive the necessary diplomatic, technical and financial support. In the end, however, the gap between long-term needs in a vital sector of state consolidation and the limited capacity of the UAE to support and facilitate the formulation of a tailored roadmap for security sector reform underlines the challenges facing the UAE in promoting a transformative agenda in Iraq.

Finally, the UAE has provided a clear support for the recent push by Baghdad to de-emphasise sectarian rhetoric, while striving to rebuild ties across confessional lines of the Iraqi society and elites, including from the Iraqi Shia community. Indeed, as it tries to regain a foothold in Iraq, Abu Dhabi appears to be betting on the idea that the vast majority of Shiites would prefer to place their national (Iraqi) or ethnic (Arab) identities above the confessional (Shia) one. The UAE authorities, in particular, have showed their readiness to work closer with Iraqi nationalist trends and engage with a range of Shia political leaders who have pushed for a non-sectarian agenda, such as Haidar Al Abadi and Muqtada Al Sadr, both of whom travelled to Abu Dhabi in 2017.[59] They have also underscored the importance of cross-confessional engagement as a way to show Iraqis—from all constituencies—that they 'stand to benefit from a more independent national policy that restore Iraq's standing in the Arab world and gains a measure of distance from Iran'.[60]

Outreach to Shia community in Iraq aligns with the UAE foreign policy priority to de-escalate regional sectarian tensions, defeat extremism on both sides—Sunni and Shia—and foster stability. As Minister of State Gargash pointed out: 'we do not really see ourselves necessarily as a Sunni state, we see ourselves as a national state, and I think this is important for us as we move forward. It is extremely important if we are really looking for stability to try and replace the sectarian rhetoric, whether it is Sunni or Shia, which has dominated a lot of the fringe and sometimes perhaps centres of political debate in the region'.[61] As such, outreach to political Shia elites in Iraq has been accompanied by investment in projects that carry high symbolic weights in (predominantly Sunni) areas liberated from Daesh. The UAE, for instance, announced in April 2018 that it would fund the US$50.4 million reconstruction of Mosul's Grand al-Nouri Mosque, whose 800-year-old minaret was blown up by Daesh.[62] Yet, anti-sectarian messages seem unlikely to succeed unless they also contribute to fostering the Iraqi state's ability to harness and sustain an inclusive national identity. On many occasions, the UAE has highlighted the necessity to strengthen the Iraqi central government and political institutions around patriotic appeals of Iraqi-ness as the best approach to foster long-term stability and roll-back Iranian influence.[63] As underlined by UAE authorities: 'Much of the rhetoric coming out of Iraq is staunchly opposed to Iran's influence in the country, indicating a strengthening Iraqi identity that can cut through sectarian divides'.[64]

The paradox, however, is that recognising and working closer with nationalist trends within the Shia community has been increasingly perceived as a zero-sum game, played at the expense of Iraq's Arab Sunnis. This is particularly salient with regards to the reconstruction agenda. Iraqi Sunni leaders have expected the UAE—and more largely the Arab Gulf States—to support post-Daesh reconstruction of their cities. Yet, so far, the vast majority of investor interest has been in the 'Shiite-dominated south, the location of Iraq's main oilfields, and where the Iraqi National Investment commission is seeking to direct the bulk of foreign investment in oil, gas, and petrochemicals'.[65] As a result, some leaders of the Iraqi Sunni community have complained that they are being disregarded in the renewed Gulf States' outreach and have been urging them to shift their financial focus towards improving local economic conditions that the government and the international community have prioritised for reconstruction—including through projects advertised during the Kuwait Conference. More broadly, leaders from the Sunni community expect that Gulf States will push for Sunni specific demands, including political reforms, to address the problem of disenfranchisement of the Sunni Arab population and pursue a broader national reconciliation process, including through the abolishment of specific de-baathification measures that have proven largely counterproductive. As it tries to rewrite the narrative of its past engagement with Iraq, the UAE is thus confronted with the necessity to ensure that its efforts to rebuild trust and court public opinion across confessional lines fit into the broader political and economic context in which they take place. And, this will undoubtedly require a public diplomacy strategy, aimed at supporting reconciliation among Iraqi parties and communities, that is yet to be publicly articulated by the UAE authorities.

CONCLUSION

In Iraq, the path out of fragility has been framed as a demanding integrated exercise that requires significant levels of diplomatic, development, military and police cooperation, as well as foreign investment and technical assistance, over sustained periods of time. As the stabilisation phase begins to conclude, the Iraqi government is trying to secure the long-term support of the international community for its reconstruction agenda. With most western countries, in particular the United States,[66] increasingly reticent to sponsor and bear the cost of transformative projects aimed at building structural stability overseas, this support has primarily come from regional countries, in particular from the Arab Gulf States. Indeed, while most recent regional efforts to advance stability have been conceived as an essentially conservative endeavour, focused on immediate attempts to move on from situations of acute crises, Arab Gulf capitals have showed an increased willingness to play a useful role in helping the Iraqi authorities address current issues of state failure, as part of a recent attempt to re-engage with Baghdad. For the UAE, it seems that the promotion of a transformative agenda in Iraq is directly connected with foreign policy stances that prioritise regional stability. The UAE's interest in re-engaging with Iraq also derives from a desire to mitigate Iranian influence in Iraqi domestic affairs, leading to the development of a broader and highly politicised conception of both immediate stabilisation and longer-term reconstruction efforts.

Through its regionalisation, the stabilisation agenda thus remains remarkably elastic both in form and content, with both narrow and broader conceptions of stabilisation used interchangeably and adapted as regional and local circumstances change. In this context, what is meant by stabilisation, as well as the nature of the task and its objectives, remains uncertain, further complicating regional actors' ability to prepare for, design, execute and evaluate attempts to address the complex realities of state fragility in the Middle East and North Africa region.

NOTES

1. See Culbertson et al. (2017) and Mansour (2018).
2. See Cordesman (2017).
3. See The Global Coalition Against Daesh Website, http://theglobalcoalition.org/en/mission-en/. Accessed in May 2018.
4. Ibid.
5. The Working Group on Stabilisation is one of five coalition working groups that are coordinating specific coalition activities, including military support, counter-finance, counter-messaging, and efforts to stem the flow of foreign fighters. It includes representatives from 34 countries and international organisations: the Arab League, Australia, Austria, Belgium, Canada, Czech Republic, Denmark, EU, Egypt, France, Greece, Iceland, Iraq, Italy, Jordan, Kuwait, Latvia, Lebanon, Luxemburg, Morocco, Netherlands, Norway, Poland, Qatar, Romania, Republic of Korea, Saudi Arabia, Spain, Sweden, Turkey, the United Kingdom, and the United States. The latter is also currently co-chairing the meetings of the Working Group, along with Germany and the UAE. Ibid.
6. See UNDP (2016, 2017a, b).
7. See UNDP (2016, p. 9).
8. Ibid.
9. As such, whereas the UAE has been a very active member of the Syria Recovery Trust Fund (SRTF), assiduously vetting financial and material supports provided to Syrian opposition groups and individuals, representatives of the UAE have appeared more lenient towards the various stabilisation activities discussed during the meetings of the Working Group. Overall, as one observer pointed out: "the primary role of the Working Group on stabilisation has been to fund raising; during WGS meetings, participants were essentially told to go back home, talk to their capitals and get funding for the UNDP projects." Personal Interview, Abu Dhabi, August 2018
10. Funds have been primarily expended in the first two categories. Also, in early 2017, 'Window' four was closed.
11. See UNDP (2016, p. 10).
12. Ibid.
13. Ibid.
14. See UNDP (2017b, p. 75). Only five of these donor countries are not members of the WGS: Estonia, Finland, Japan, New Zealand, and Slovakia.
15. See http://www.iq.undp.org/content/iraq/en/home/operation/projects/crisis_prevention_and_recovery/ICRRP.html. Accessed in July 2018.
16. Among Arab Gulf States, only Saudi Arabia and Kuwait provided funding for the ICRRP—US$7.96 million and US$1.25 million, respectively.
17. "Meeting Summary: Working Group on Stabilization," 11 April 2018, Berlin, Germany (unpublished).

18. Structural stability is defined by the UK Government's Stabilisation Unit as "political systems which are representative and legitimate, capable of managing conflict and change peacefully, and societies in which human rights and rule of law are respected, basic needs are met, security established and opportunities for social and economic development are open to all." See UK Stabilisation Unit (2014, p. 1).
19. "Meeting Summary: Working Group on Stabilization," op. cit.
20. See Sattar (2018).
21. In the short term, US$23 billion is required for basic stabilisation and rebuilding, with US$65 billion needed over the medium term. See Laub (2017).
22. "Kuwait Summit Promises US$30 Billion in Iraq Reconstruction Aid," *DW*, 14 February 2018. On the evolving US approach to stabilisation and reconstruction under the Trump administration, see Parello-Plesner (2018).
23. At the Conference, Anwar Gargash, UAE Minister of State for Foreign Affairs and International Cooperation, explained that the pledge of US$500 million includes US$250 million via the Abu Dhabi Fund for Development for infrastructure projects, US$100 million to help UAE electricity companies fund projects in Iraq, US$100 million to support and promote UAE exports. "UAE Offers $500m to Support Reconstruction of Iraq," *Arabian Business*, 14 February 2018.
24. See Ibish (2018, p. 1).
25. Again, this comes in sharp contrast to the country's position with regard to post-Daesh stabilisation activities in Syria.
26. See Gervais (2017).
27. See Almezaini (2017, p. 197).
28. See UAE Ministry of Foreign Affairs and International Cooperation, https://www.mofa.gov.ae/EN/TheMinistry/Pages/Our-Strategy.aspx. Accessed in October 2018.
29. Dr. Anwar Gargash, UAE Minister of State for Foreign Affairs and International Cooperation, The IISS Manama Dialogue 2017, Second Plenary Session, 9 December 2017, https://www.iiss.org/events/manama-dialogue/manama-dialogue-2017. Accessed in July 2018.
30. Ibid.
31. See Rotmann (2016, p. 6).
32. As such, during this period, UAE support was largely limited to various individuals and organisations from the Iraqi Sunni community.
33. "VP, Mohamed bin Zayed Wish Success for Iraqi New Prime Minister-Designate," *WAM*, 14 August 2014; See Ibish (2018, p. 11).
34. In September 2015, the Iraqi government reciprocated and sent its own ambassador to Riyadh. According to many observers, Saudi's re-engagement with Iraq primarily stems from a broader reassessment of its

foreign policy vis-à-vis Iran. It has been argued that when King Salam bin Abdulaziz Al Saud ascended to the throne in 2015, he and his son, then Deputy Crown Prince Mohammed bin Salman assessed that the Saudi policy towards Tehran was too reactive and inefficient and set about formulating a new, more assertive foreign policy towards its regional rival. As one expert described it: "Saudi leaders undertook the strategic equivalent of triage: they decided which theatres could still be saved from Iranian domination and focused on those." In particular, while there was a sense that with Syria and Lebanon, it was too late, the leadership in Saudi Arabia felt that in "Iraq and Jordan there (was) a scope to keep Iran out." See International Crisis Group (2018a, p. 2).

35. http://www.economy.gov.ae/english/Knowledge-Section/TradeRelations/Pages/Trade-Relation.aspx. Accessed in September 2018.

36. Ibid.

37. Iraq is also facing a significant electricity theft problem: in 2015, the Ministry of Electricity collected payments for just 12% of the electricity it produced. See Iraq Knowledge Network (2011).

38. See Langenhahn (2018).

39. Under this agreement, Iraq will buy the electricity for US$21 per megawatt-hour, or a quarter of what it paid Iran for the imports, according to Iraq's Ministry of Electricity spokesman Mussab Serri. "Iraq Says Saudi to Sell Power at a Fraction of Iran's Price. The Deal Includes Building a 3,000-Megawatt Plant in Saudi Arabia," See *The National* (2018). This was later was denied by the Iraqi government spokesperson later on Iranian state television. See Langenhahn (2018).

40. It is estimated that Iranian electricity supply amounts to one-third of the total electricity in Basra. Ibid.

41. Ibid.

42. According to the UAE Ministry of Economy, the main UAE companies operating in Iraq include: Union Cement Company (UCC), Emaar Properties, Al Awael Holding, Julphar Gulf Pharmaceutical Industries, Al Rawabi Dairy Company, Fire & Safety UAE, National Fire Fighting Manufacturing Company NAFFCO, ALFAHIM Group, Al Maabar Investments International Investment, Abraaj Capital, Galfar Engineering & Contracting, Globalpharma, DAMAC Properties, Dana Gas, Dubai Investments, Rotana Hotels and Resorts, Crescent Petroleum, Gulftainer Limited, Al Aqili Group, Abu Dhabi Islamic Bank, and Neopharma, http://www.economy.gov.ae/english/Knowledge-Section/TradeRelations/Pages/default.aspx. Accessed in September 2018.

43. Similarly, Saudi Arabia is reportedly considering investment in the Akkas gas field in Anbar governorate, west of Iraq, following the signature of 18

memoranda of understanding on energy Issues between Saudi Arabia and Iraq in December 2017. International Crisis Group (2018a, p. 8).

44. Ibid.
45. Ibid.
46. Ibid.
47. See Ibish (2018).
48. See Dodge (2014).
49. See Beal (2016).
50. This was clearly illustrated in the Summer of 2014, when the army quickly disintegrated during the first phases of the military campaign against Daesh.
51. See "The Military Balance" (2016, p. 331); see also Dodge (2014).
52. See De Bruin (2014).
53. See Abouaoun et al. (2018). Throughout the military campaign against Daesh, the PMF provided the Iraqi military with much needed capabilities and enabled the advance to retake the cities of Ramadi in October 2015, Fallujah in June 2016 and Mosul in July 2017—even though the PMF's role was reduced in the more recent battles.
54. Before the 2018 parliamentary elections, Shia-dominated militias within the PMF were mainly see as divided into three, sometimes competing, camps based on their respective allegiances to ayatollahs Khamenei and Sistani, and Muqtada al-Sadr. The pro-Khamenei camp includes in its leadership former Prime Minister Maliki, the Badr organisation's Hadi al-Ameri, Asaib Ahl al-Haq's Qais Khazali, and Abu Mahdi Al Muhandis. See Jabar and Mansour (2017).
55. See International Crisis Group (2018a). These units include the Badr Organisation (founded in Iran in 1982 as the armed wing of the Supreme Council for the Islamic Revolution, SCIRI), Asaib Ahl al-Haq (2006), Kataeb Hezbollah (2007), Kataeb Sayed al-Shuhada (2013), Harakat Hezbollah al-Nujaba (2013), and Kataeb Jund al-Imam, a fighting unit formed during the uprising against Saddam Hussein's regime in 1991 and reactivated after 2003. See International Crisis Group (2018b).
56. Within this context any attempt to increase state control over the PMF is likely to require extensive and prolonged negotiations with all parties involved. Indeed, past experiences (for instance in Afghanistan and Somalia) suggest that such organised forces with significant foreign support will not disband or integrate without a political bargain of some sort, irrespective of any laws or executive directives that are put in place.
57. See International Crisis Group (2018b).
58. See Gervais (2018).
59. "Iraq cleric Muqtada Al Sadr Meets with Sheikh Mohammed bin Zayed," *The National*, 13 August 2017.
60. See Ibish (2018, p. 1). With Najaf as point of reference for most Arab Shai populations in the Gulf, the UAE has also a clear security interest

in de-emphasising the sectarian rhetoric and building ties with the more prominent Shia religious leaders and families of Iraq.

61. Dr. Anwar Mohammed Gargash, IISS Manama Dialogue 2017 Second Plenary Session "Political and Military Responses to Extremism in the Middle East," 9 December 2017.
62. "UAE Rebuilding of Mosul Mosque 'Defeats Extremism'," *The National*, 9 July 2018.
63. "UAE Says Iraq Election Shows Waning Iranian Influence," *Reuters*, 7 June 2018.
64. Ibid.
65. See National Investment Commission (2017) and International Crisis Group (2018a, p. 17).
66. See Parello-Plesner (2018).

Bibliography

Abouaoun, Elie, Hamasaeed, Sahrhang, and Garrett, Nada. *As Iraq Prepares for Elections, Iran's Influence Looms Large: How Iran's Role in Iraq Has Evolved Since the Toppling of Saddam Hussein*. Washington, DC: United States Institute of Peace, 2018.

Almezaini, Khaled. "The Transformation of UAE Foreign Policy Since 2011." In Kristian Coates Ulrichsen (ed.), *The Changing Security Dynamics of the Persian Gulf*. Oxford: Oxford University Press, 2017.

Beal, James S. *Mission Accomplished? Rebuilding the Iraqi and Afghan Armies*. Thesis. Monterrey: Naval Post Graduate School, 2016.

Cordesman, Anthony H. *After ISIS: Creating Strategic Stability in Iraq*. Washington, DC: Center for Strategic and International Studies, 2017.

Culbertson, Shelly, and Robinson, Linda. *Making Victory Count After Defeating ISIS. Stabilization and Challenges in Mosul and Beyond*. Santa Monica: Rand, 2017.

De Bruin, Erica. "Coup-Proofing for Dummies: The Benefits of Following the Maliki Playbook." *Foreign Affairs*, 27 July 2014.

Dodge, Toby. "Can Iraq Be Saved?" *Survival*, vol. 56, no. 5 (October–November 2014): 7–20.

Gervais, Victor. "The Changing Security Dynamic in the Middle East and Its Impact on Smaller GCC States' Alliance Choices and Policies." In Khalid S. Almezaini and Jean-Marc Rickli (eds.), *The Small Gulf States: Foreign and Security Policies Before and After the Arab Spring*. London: Routledge, 2017.

———. *Consolidating the Iraqi State: Challenge and Opportunities*. Abu Dhabi: Emirates Diplomatic Academy, 2018.

Ibish, Hussein. *The Power of Positive Diplomacy: Saudi Outreach in Iraq Since 2014*. Washington, DC: The Arab Gulf States Institute in Washington, 2018.

International Crisis Group. "Iraq's Paramilitary Groups: The Challenge of Rebuilding a Functioning State." *Middle East Report No. 188*, 30 July 2018a.

———. "Saudi Arabia: Back to Baghdad." *Middle East Report No. 186*, 22 May 2018b.

International Institute for Strategic Studies. *The Military Balance 2016*. London: The International Institute for Strategic Studies, 2016.

Iraq Knowledge Network. *Central Statistic Office, Government of Iraq*, 2011: 45.

Jabar, Faleh A., and Mansour, Renad, *The Popular Mobilization Forces and Iraq's Future*. Beirut: Carnegie Middle East Center, 2017.

Langenhahn, Eva. "For Saudi Arabia, an Electric Opportunity in Iraq." *War on the Rocks*, 30 August 2018.

Laub, Zachary. "What to Watch in Post-ISIS Iraq and Syria." *Council on Foreign Relations*, 19 October 2017.

Mansour, Renad. *Rebuilding the Iraqi State: Stabilisation, Governance and Reconciliation*. Brussels: Directorate-General for External Policies, 2018.

National Investment Commission. *Iraq Investment Map 2017*, 2017.

Parello-Plesner, Jonas. *Post-ISIS Challenges for Stabilization: Iraq, Syria and the U.S. Approach*. Washington, DC: Hudson Institute, 2018.

Rotmann, Phillipp. "Towards a Realistic and Responsible Idea of Stabilisation." *Stability: International Journal of Security and Development*, vol. 5, no. 1 (2016): 1–14.

Sattar, Omar. "Conference for Iraq Draws Investors Instead of Donors." *Al-Monitor*, 23 February 2018.

The National. "Iraq Says Saudi to Sell Power at a Fraction of Iran's Price," 30 July 2018.

UNDP. *Funding Facility for Stabilization. Annual Report*, United Nations, 2016.

———. *Funding Facility for Stabilization. Q3 Report*, United Nations, 2017a.

———. *Funding Facility for Stabilization. Q4 Report*, United Nations, 2017b.

UK Stabilisation Unit. *The UK Government's Approach to Stabilisation*. UK Government, 2014.

CHAPTER 9

Economic Stabilisation of the MENA Region: 'Old' vs. 'New' Actors

Saskia van Genugten, with Neil Quilliam

INTRODUCTION

Conflicts in the MENA region tend to end up in the history books as struggles fought between groups representing different political, ethnic and often religious backgrounds. This also seems to become the fate of the conflicts that engulfed the region in the first part of the twenty-first century, most notably in Afghanistan, Iraq, Egypt, Tunisia, Libya, Yemen and Syria. Reporters and experts have predominantly analysed these conflicts through the lenses of clashing political views and growing hatred between ethnicities and religious denominations. The lifting of the authoritarian straitjacket provided by the former Tunisian President Zine Abidine Ben Ali, or by Muhammed al-Qaddafi in Libya, allowed for a myriad of underlying tensions to come to the surface. The conflict in Libya that led to the fall of the Qaddafi regime was first analysed as one between Qaddafi-

S. van Genugten (✉)
Ministry of Defence, The Hague, The Netherlands

N. Quilliam
Chatham House, London, UK

© The Author(s) 2020   185
V. Gervais and S. van Genugten (eds.), *Stabilising the Contemporary Middle East and North Africa*, Middle East Today,
https://doi.org/10.1007/978-3-030-25229-8_9

loyalists (implied to be anti-democratic in their political preferences) and anti-Qaddafi rebels (implied to be more liberal and charmed by the tenets of Western democracies). After the fall of the forty-plus-year old rule of the Qaddafi's and their key allied tribes, the analysis morphed into this being a struggle between Islamists and moderates, between those in 'Tripolitania' and those in 'Cyrenaica'. Similar lenses have dominated reporting on developments in Egypt, Tunisia and Syria. In Yemen, the emphasis was on the authoritarianism of Ali Abdullah Saleh, and in Bahrain, the religious roots of the uproar have been centre stage, playing out through the uprising of a Shi'ite majority against a repressive Sunni regime.

In a similar fashion, those security exporters that for decades, if not centuries, have been involved in efforts to contain and address a range of traditional and non-traditional threats in the MENA region, have in recent times emphasised non-economic objectives and have deployed mainly non-economic instruments to reach their political goals: they have focused on military interventions aimed at eradicating, or at least uprooting, extremists and militant groups and have put time and effort in bringing opponents together in political forums, including UN-facilitated peace processes. An economic 'Marshall Plan' for the Middle East has been mentioned by a few individuals, but has never been seriously considered by those traditional, Western actors engaged with the region. For them, the economic side of the stabilisation equation is mostly covered by relatively modest development programmes, generally with a focus on job creation and advocacy for dignified livelihoods. Considering the massive economic problems the region deals with, in virtually all cases, the actual impact of these programmes remains limited and given the demographics, the region is likely to continue to suffer from structural economic weaknesses in decades to come.

At the same time, the twenty-first century has seen the emergence of a number of new actors in the region, including China and actors from the Gulf States. These newcomers seem much more favourable of an economics-led approach to stability and have dedicated substantial financial resources to the bulging budget deficits of conflict-ridden Arab countries and, in some cases, have even engaged in the construction of entire new neighbourhoods or cities under the umbrella term of stabilisation. This chapter zooms in on this economic dimension of stabilisation. It does so for two reasons: first of all, while identity politics are undoubtedly a key factor of instability in the MENA region—as Steven Cook aptly points out elsewhere in this volume—it is often the economic patterns underlying these clashing identities that constitute the true root causes of tension, rather than ethnicity, religion or political world views. For example, it could be argued that the different tribes in Yemen or in Libya do not primarily fight each other because they truly, inherently dislike each other's identities, but because they have been part of an unfair system of redistribution of economic wealth. In Bahrain, the uprising was not necessarily about the different Islamic sects, but about who receives the economic benefits and opportunities. In Tunisia, the unprivileged youth was sick and tired of the economic growth of the country being channelled into businesses and families depending on how close they are to the established elites. In Egypt, the uprisings started as 'bread riots' and in Libya, the struggle quickly became one about who will control the vast oil resources of the country. Thus, as much as the Arab uprisings were about enhancing liberty and dignity, they were about curbing corruption, subsidy reform and economic hardship.[1] Secondly, this chapter focuses on this particular dimension because it is in this realm that the differentiation between 'traditional' and 'new' international security exporters active in the broader MENA region might come most clearly to the fore. It is also in the deployment of economic instruments of stabilisation that the long-standing international actors in this field, including the US, the UK, France and the EU, increasingly seem to get eclipsed by those 'new' actors.

ECONOMIC DRIVERS OF CONFLICT IN THE MENA REGION

In order to stabilise the complex nature of the MENA region, it is evident that one needs to have a good understanding of what elements of the region actually are causing the instability. Arguably, many of the key drivers of conflict are economic in nature. The region is home to several of the richest oil and gas producers of the world, as well as some of the poorest states on the globe. As such, the region is characterised by large economic inequality, not only between states, but also, and arguably more important, within states. In a 2015 report, the World Bank stated that the MENA region (still) represented a puzzle. Judging from their own stated goals and the progress made on the Bank's performance indicators, the countries in the region were on a progressive path to better times. With Yemen being the exception, they were all showcasing economic growth, a reduction of poverty and an increased access to infrastructure—including to the Internet.[2] Still, even as the GDP per capita on average seemed to increase, the general population got ever more frustrated, also reflecting a structural problem of economic governance. Inequality, politicised redistribution, unfairness, corruption and the inability to change the system through the system itself were indeed left uncaptured by the indicators these international institutions used to try to monitor a country's well-being. As a consequence, these standard development data points failed to see the 2011 outburst of popular anger coming. Arguably, these measurements did not only miss the good number of 'vertical inequalities' the MENA region displayed, meaning those between the elites and the general population, but also many of the 'horizontal inequalities'—the inequalities between groups. In the scholarly literature, such inequalities have long been indicated as powerful drivers of civil wars.[3]

In the first two decades of the twenty-first century, the MENA region saw an intensification of conflict driven by a mix of territorial disputes, power and status rivalries, ideological, ethnic and sectarian competition, exacerbated by international interventions such as in Afghanistan and Iraq and the above-mentioned inequalities. Regardless of what was the actual trigger to the respective conflicts, these states one by one dealt with a good number of difficult-to-solve structural problems that had formed a fertile context for conflict to emerge. To name a few: pretty much all states deal with relative unproductivity of the workforce and high unemployment numbers. Millions of young individuals in the region keep transitioning into adulthood with little chance of a dignified livelihood. While official youth unemployment rates in the smaller Gulf States are hovering around 14%, official rates reached 49% in Libya, 42% in Egypt and 29% in Jordan in 2014.[4] A quick glance at the population pyramids of, for example, Jordan, Egypt and Yemen should suffice to illustrate that the situation is likely to get worse before it gets better.[5] Youth unemployment in the region is indeed forecasted to remain the world's highest for the time to come, and suboptimal education systems are producing graduates that are not well-qualified for the labour market, while wages remain uncompetitive in global terms.[6] Partly as a way of keeping domestic stability, public sectors absorbed substantial parts of the active labour force. Within the region, government jobs are often preferred and respected more than private sector positions due to the overall prestige and security, but also the relatively lower workload, the higher number of holidays and other additional benefits. The caveat is that getting those more desirable government jobs often depends on family connections and status.

Another structural problem includes the dependency on subsidies, which has also become institutionalised in the region partly to avoid domestic instability. Many states in the region have a fiscal system heavy on subsidies for fuel, electricity and food. [7]

On the one hand, this led to unnecessarily high state expenses and macroeconomic problems. On the other hand, these market distortions have created smuggling opportunities between neighbouring states that did not have such purchasing incentives in place—the smuggle routes between Libya and Tunisia being a good case in point. These structural difficulties have been subsequently exacerbated by a significant politicisation of the economy. Unfair redistribution, nepotism and corruption are rampant in the region. And while this is a well-known issue slowing productivity and growth, governments have decided, to a large extent, not to act on it. For example, assessing the situation in Egypt, the OECD concluded that much more can and should be done with regard to political will, legal provisions and institutional arrangements to fight corruption, whereas 'the Egyptian government is of the view that its legislative and institutional framework is adequate for detecting, investigating, and prosecuting corruption offences'.[8] In sum, in the MENA region, economic polarisation has in many places been solidly aligned with social and political polarisation.[9]

CONFLICT, ECONOMIC PROBLEMS AND THEIR IMPACT ON STABILISATION EFFORTS

The conflicts that the MENA region has endured over the past two decades have exacerbated the economic context in which stabilisation efforts are being deployed. A key consequence is that conflict-affected countries are often incapable to pay themselves for stabilisation and reconstruction of the hard and soft infrastructures damaged during the fighting. Another key issue that external 'stabilisers' need to find solutions for is the institutionalisation of 'war economy' dynamics during a protracted conflict.

The cost of waging war or escalating conflicts through military and other means can be staggering. Combat is likely to leave its toll on infrastructure and the risk of damage, combined with the prevailing uncertainty, has in many places affected investors' and consumers' confidence, thereby increasing the risk premium on direct foreign investments. Given these costs and the related loss of income, the macroeconomic fundamentals of a country in conflict tend to deteriorate. Iraq, for example, experienced an unprecedented economic shock caused by a sharp rise in spending on security, while the low oil prices exacerbated the deficit spending.[10] As a result, since

2013, Iraq has suffered an estimated US$42 billion decrease in GDP.[11] In Tunisia and Egypt, unrest and acts of terrorism caused significant drops in tourism revenue. In Libya, the conflict led to a sharp drop in oil production, the main source of state income. This meant a massive decrease in the disposable income of the Libyan population. To illustrate, in 2017, the GDP was expected to rise by 25.6%, but this still meant that income per capita only reached 65% of its pre-conflict (2010) levels.[12] After the toppling of the Qaddafi regime, the decision was made to add anyone who could qualify as a revolutionary fighter to the state payroll, which further inflated the already bulging public sector wage payments budget line of the national budget. Worse, it created a perverse situation in which, when different anti-Qaddafi groups turned against each other, both sides were paid salaries by the state. Other conflict-related macroeconomic problems included rampant inflation and further rising unemployment rates.

As a result of these financial difficulties, the states affected were often in no position to pay for stabilisation and reconstruction. The international community tends to showcase efforts to help financing through large mediatised conferences, such as the Supporting Syria and the Region conference that was co-hosted by the UK, Germany, Kuwait, Norway and the UN in London in 2016, or the 2018 international conference on Iraq reconstruction held in Kuwait, or the 2018 International Conference for the Reconstruction of Benghazi, or for example the 2015 Egypt Economic Development Conference. Most of these conferences are partly aimed at starting to deal with the damage brought to infrastructure, including damage to 'hard' infrastructure assets such as roads, bridges and ports as well as to 'soft' infrastructure, including governance, economic and social institutions. The devastation of both types of infrastructure has been large in many parts of the region that witnessed fighting, but cities where the anti-Daesh coalition has taken on extremists have arguably taken the biggest toll, including Mosul and Fallujah. Prior to the February 2018 Kuwait Conference, the Iraqi government estimated the total reconstruction costs at US$88 billion, based only on the damage to hard infrastructure assets. The details of this amount were never published and according to the calculations of Frank R. Gunter, the actual amount lies closer to US$198 billion.[13] Conflicts can also erect unexpected economic barriers, such as the one caused by the 200 vessels sunk in or nearby Iraq's primary port of Umm Qasr North to Basrah back in 2004.[14] Another example is the damage done to sections of the interconnected transmission system in Libya, which caused blackouts in several cities. Infrastructure reconstruction is thus a common theme within stabilisation approaches but it tends to be hampered by a lack of finance, a lack of skilled workers, bureaucratic inefficiencies and corruption and, according to the West, the dominance of state-owned enterprise and regulatory hostility towards private business within the region. As we will discuss in the third section of this chapter, this is however a point on which the Western actors of stabilisation are increasingly challenged by the newcomers.

Conflicts also tend to alter the economy and increase illicit activities and those trades and industries related to sustaining the conflict, often in a decentralised way as illustrated in the case of Libya.[15] The protracted nature of the conflicts in the contemporary MENA region has also caused an institutionalisation of activities that are considered part of a 'war economy'.[16] Having a good view on the dynamics of these activities is of importance to plan the implementation of stabilisation efforts as well as to be able to do a reality check that manages expectations. In the past decades, the Balkans, Afghanistan and Iraq have for example shown how vulnerable conflict and post-conflict areas are to becoming playgrounds of organised crime. The local dynamics can have costly implications for international actors running programmes on the ground, both in financial and in political terms. Jonathan Goodhand, assessing the Afghan war economy, identified three types of subcategories within the 'war economy': the 'combat economy', which includes the production, mobilisation and allocation of economic resources to sustain conflict and economic strategies of war; the 'shadow economy' that operates outside state-regulated frameworks; and the 'coping economy', referring to economic survival strategies of populations whose livelihoods are affected by the war.[17] Within all three categories, the space for illicit activities is substantial and manifests itself in, for example, an increase in armed protection services for properties, business interests and flows of (illicit) goods.[18] The range of illicit activities can be large. In an assessment of the illicit economy of Iraq, Phil Williams notes the increase of oil-related criminal activities, such as the theft and smuggling of oil and gas, which he stated 'became almost a national pastime in Iraq, while funding much of the violence'.[19] Kidnapping, both for economic and political purposes, is another activity that became more prevalent in Iraq, but also constituted a daily reality in Libya. Other illicit activities, including extortion, drug trafficking and the smuggling of goods and people, have all been able to feed on the disorder, the lack of governance, the insecurity of travel and the loss of economic livelihoods. Complicating the matter in several places has been the breakdown of central governance and the fragmentation that has followed, meaning that economic dynamics can be different from one spot and locality to the other. This is in particular true in those places where a split has occurred in economic governance structures, such as in Libya and in Yemen.

Thus, any attempt to successfully rebuild Iraq or other countries or regions will need to see attempts at combatting organised crime integrated into the stabilisation efforts in the region.[20] As Barnett Rubin noted: 'Ending war in Afghanistan might transform the criminalised war economy into an even faster-expanding criminalised peace economy. Whoever rules Afghanistan, the incentives for misgovernment are nearly irresistible'.[21] In Iraq, the US objectives for reconstruction and development were severely hampered by organised crime. Illicit activities strengthened the insurgency and funded sectarian conflict as different groups desired to control the same criminal markets. Organised crime was also seen as the main spoiler in the oil industry, which external security exporters had labelled as the driver for growth and progress in post-Ba'athist Iraq.[22] Ideally, combatting these undermining dynamics would be integrated into peace processes, which then can take into account for example the creation of institutions or checks and balances for accountability over economic and political decision making. A key question in this regard for stabilisation efforts remains how to convince war profiteers to change their professional focus to peaceful and licit activities.

Relatedly, those that ambition increased stability in the region will need to understand and be able to interrupt the linkages between illicit economic activities and insurgents or terrorist groupings. In Afghanistan, the Taliban generated revenues from the narcotics business, extortion and the illegal exploitation of national resources. As Collin Clarke pointed out during a congressional testimony in September 2018, the fact that Daesh was able to acquire US$6 billion in financial reserves demonstrates that, despite the progress made on countering financing of terrorism and money-laundering, the international community is still very much learning how to crack down on the economic model of such groups.[23] Interesting to add is that Clarke also argues that Daesh' ability 'to raise money through criminal activities provides it with an opportunity to survive and even make a comeback in Iraq and Syria over the next several years'.[24] All in all, these predatory economic dynamics have a significant impact on the likelihood of success of stabilisation activities, in particular in humanitarian and developmental projects, but also where it involves peace processes, military efforts and infrastructure reconstruction, which are known to be a major source of corruption.

ENTER THE 'NEW' ACTORS: MORE EMPHASIS ON THE ECONOMIC DIMENSION

In this volume, we have defined stabilisation as an inherently political concept. International actors use a variety of military and non-military instruments to reach a level of stability. Local leaders in turn can then rebuild their country along the lines those external stabilisers would like them to. We also argue that as a result of the political nature, there is no clear definition of the end goal ('stability') and that there is no common understanding of the sequencing of activities. What does seem clear is that, with the emergence of new actors in the field of stabilisation, the range of approaches has increased, complicating the discussion around the concept even further. In particular in this economic dimension, the difference in approach is visible between the more traditional Western actors in the MENA region and those that more recently have raised their profiles, including China and the Gulf countries. In general, traditional actors tend to focus first and foremost on military and political instruments of stabilisation, with the economic issues mainly addressed as part of humanitarian and developmental aid. In the West, the rationale is one in which one first creates a stable security environment, and based on that stability, businesses and investors will take the country forward. In a slightly different rationale, China tends to put almost all its emphasis on economic instruments, with the idea that economics in many ways can shape politics, thereby partly reflecting their own foreign policy objectives and strategies. The Gulf countries are somewhere in the middle: they use political, military, development and economic instruments in their approach, but still tend to put more weight on the economic aspects of stabilisation than most Western actors do. Both with regard to China and the Gulf countries, it can be argued that these countries can outdo the West in terms of budget support and strategic investments in the MENA region, given their economic clout and the fact that businesses are significantly more state-led than in the West, which can make strategic investments more targeted. The increased competition that has emerged has also highlighted that the West might have neglected this particular instrument of the stabilisation toolbox in the past decades.

The guiding principles of USIP, with regard to stabilisation, can be considered illustrative for the broadest possible 'Western' view on economic stabilisation. USIP lists four main economic objectives: macro-economic stabilisation; control over the illicit economy and economic-based threats to peace; employment generation; and market economy sustainability.[25] Western governments have a tendency to leave economic stabilisation to development agencies and to multilateral institutions, with little actorness for private businesses, which are seen as more objective and neutral forces that have a general interest in the resolution of conflict. Following their donors' objectives, development agencies active in the region tend to focus on job creation and stimulation of private sector dynamics. They also often provide advisory and training services on how to achieve fiscal sustainability, with the United States Agency for International Development's (USAID) project supporting the Afghan Ministry of Finance efforts in public financial management as a good illustration. The provision of substantial loans is often considered the domain of multilateral organisations such as the World Bank and the International Monetary Funds, in order to create a certain detachment from the political objectives of individual states involved. 'Tasked with this role in stabilisation efforts', the World Bank Group has made fragile and conflict-affected states into an important focus for assistance in recent years. But while the role of these institutions over the decades has changed, the emphasis remains on institutional and regulatory frameworks to deal with fiscal and external balances and debts. As such, their policy approach tends to reflect a certain Western bias. As a result, these institutions are often accused of being part of the problem, for example in Jordan, where income tax regulations as part of the IMF package were a trigger for protests.

Of course, economic considerations do play a role in the way traditional actors have tried to solve the ongoing conflicts in the region, but the argument is that politics tend to have taken central stage. The approach to the conflict in Libya is telling in this regard. For years, the international community had focused predominantly on the Libyan *Political* Agreement, with the World Bank playing a role in trying to keep the economic governance institutions as depoliticised as possible. But since 2017, the emphasis has shifted considerably to the Libyan *Economic* Dialogue, which by January 2019 was in its ninth session of what was in essence a US-led initiative. The shift partly reflected an acknowledgement that agreeing on practical and concrete economic conditions during peace negotiations is crucial. Something that actually has repeatedly been voiced among others by Nobel Prize laureate Martti Ahtisaari.[26] Nonetheless, this economics-first focus remains a challenge for mediators, as it requires a different kind of thinking with regard to the design of a peace process.

Turning to the new actors in stabilisation in the contemporary MENA region, a different, less piecemeal approach towards economic instruments emerges. While the focus is mostly on the Gulf States' expanding financial clout in the MENA region, China seems to operate in the region with a similar goal and approach, but has been able to keep its strategic rationale under the radar as it has kept itself as much as possible away from military or political adventures in the region. China did not send any troops and stressed its long-standing foreign policy notion of non-interference in other states' domestic affairs. Instead, it almost entirely relied on economic instruments, and patience, to work towards its strategic objectives. The actual amounts of money that China is providing to the broader MENA region remains unclear as it does not publish any aggregate numbers. Nonetheless, an interesting research project from 2017 came to the conclusion that China poured as much economic aid into the rest of the world as the US does. The difference is that only about a fifth of that can be considered traditional aid, while most of the money comes in the form of commercial loans with interests payable to Beijing.[27] Still, different from the loans and grants multilateral institutions tend to provide, these come as—initially— no-strings-attached financial packages.

Afghanistan can potentially be an illustrative case about the way China operates in areas that are a focus of stabilisation missions. There, since the beginning of the post-9/11 war, China long avoided becoming part of the multilateral efforts. As mentioned by Zhao Huasheng, unlike the Western powers, China had no interest in rebuilding Afghanistan politically or in altering its 'political structures, social patterns or ideological orientations'.[28] Instead, China provided massive economic assistance and maintained close ties with the Afghan government, which in 2016 led to the signing of the Treaty of Friendship, Cooperation and Good Neighbourly Relations with Kabul. China subsequently won the bid for Afghanistan's US$3 billion Aynak copper mines project, making it the largest foreign investor in the war-torn country.[29] While that investment has not gone well in commercial terms as corruption and the poor security have prevented the project from truly taking off, China has managed to use its economic position in the country to create political leverage. This has for example led to the facilitation of talks between the Afghan government and the Taliban.[30] Leaving the non-interference principle aside, in 2018, China was talking about setting up a training camp for Afghan soldiers, to which it would also send its own soldiers.[31] Sceptics see in this the establishment of a military base abroad, but so far China has rejected that assessment.

The Afghan case illustrates China's behaviour in the MENA region. In 2016, China had become the leading investor in that region,[32] and according to the Investment Climate Report in 2017, around a third of all foreign investment into the region came from China, with an amount that was three times higher than that of US investments.[33] Western traditional security actors would probably not consider such investments as part of a stabilisation package, but in the view of Beijing, economic development is an instrument to mitigate security problems. China's economic instruments are very much intertwined with the strategic and political objectives of the Chinese state, and as such, in 2018, Chinese President Xi Jinping pledged US$20 billion in loans to MENA countries to facilitate economic and industrial reconstruction in the Middle East.[34]

Thus, China is using economic instruments and financial mechanisms to 'buy' itself a role in the crowded geopolitical landscape of the MENA region. More than in the West, these economic instruments tend to be aligned with political objectives. Initially, China tends to claim a non-political role and stresses the difference with the intentions of former Western colonial powers. Chinese investments in the region are underpinned by the China-Arab States Cooperation Forum (CASCF) and the Belt and Road Initiative (BRI). This framing into a broader economy-based, global approach helps in creating and sustaining a non-politicised image. At the same time, the conditions tied to Chinese investments are non-transparent and China has not provided details on when or how the money for the MENA region will be dispersed and on what (long term) conditions. What Beijing is clear about is that by 2020, it aims to reach a US$600 billion trade aggregate with the Middle East. Even in Syria, the Chinese are trying to build up momentum. Chinese-Syrian negotiations over trade and investment have already led to commitments of close to US$2 billion in reconstruction projects and to the 2018 Syria Reconstruction Project Symposium, which was hosted by the Chinese-Arab Exchange Association and the Syrian Embassy in Beijing.[35] Given the precedents elsewhere in the world, it lies in the line of logic that at some point in time, these new dependencies on Chinese money will start having their impact in the political realm.

Turning to the Gulf actors, it can be argued that they started to get involved in stabilisation activities after the Arab uprisings of 2011, as Timo Behr elsewhere in this volume sets out. Gulf actors are by now deploying a good variety of stabilisation instruments and do so more and more in a coherent way. However, given the strengths and their own experiences with economic development, they also tend to emphasise the economic instruments much more than the traditional Western 'security exporters' do. Indeed, the speed with which they offered massive sums through a variety of economic instruments, including grants, hard-currency deposits, fuel products, loans and investments dwarfed the economic aid from other external actors.[36]

Saudi Arabia, the UAE and Qatar quickly became the biggest foreign aid donors to North Africa.[37] Their eagerness to seek stabilisation of the region seems to be a key factor in determining the destination of development assistance funds post-2011. Most of the aid went to Egypt, which is also a good case study to illustrate the divergence in the type of political stability the different Gulf States tend to promote. The UAE, Qatar and Saudi Arabia started off on the same foot, providing an estimated US\$17 billion to the post-Mubarak military regime. But when Mohamed Morsi of the Muslim Brotherhood was elected to the presidency, only Qatar continued to provide financial aid. In contrast, with the regime change back to semi-military rule under Abdel Fattah el-Sisi, Saudi Arabia and the UAE decided to step up the assistance once again, in particular by betting on increased stability through big economic projects and a steady inflow of foreign investments. In the two years that followed, Gulf States allegedly provided over US\$23 billion in assistance.[38] During Egypt's 2015 Economic Development Conference, an additional US\$12 billion was pledged by Saudi Arabia, the UAE, Kuwait and Oman.[39]

The Gulf actors also bring their economic diplomacy to other fragile regions, in particular the Horn of Africa. With stabilisation efforts stretching to conflict preventive measures, it is worth zooming into the situation in the Horn. Learning from past experiences, the Saudi government has become more effective at supporting projects in-country through the deployment of capital into key sectors, rather than simply distributing aid to support budgets or offset debt. While precise data on Gulf investment portfolios is hard to come by, the main areas of Gulf economic engagement in the region include extractive industries, real estate, private investment and banking, retail, tourism and education.[40] The roles played by a combination of agencies, including the Saudi Arabian Monetary Agency (SAMA), prominent business families closely aligned with the state, Jeddah-based Organisation of Islamic Cooperation (OIC), Saudi Fund for Development and charity organisations and private foundations, such as Sultan bin Abdulaziz Al Saud Foundation, have been instrumental in underpinning stability in the Horn of Africa. The total value of the investments for Saudi Arabia in the Horn of Africa is estimated at around US$4.9 billion.[41] An important economic instrument of Saudi Arabia to exert influence in the Horn of Africa has indeed been SAMA, which has not just provided monetary stability at home, but also engaged in central bank to central bank support to its Red Sea partners. For example, SAMA made a series of critical monetary transfers to Sudan in order to help arrest the depreciation of the Sudanese pound following the secession of South Sudan, which took with it three-quarters of Khartoum's oil reserves. SAMA deposited US$1 billion in Sudan's central bank in August 2016 aimed at shoring up Sudan's foreign reserves.[42] SAMA's intervention enabled the Sudanese government to manage public unrest following a series of food price hikes[43] and proved essential in helping Omar al-Bashir stay in power. The Saudis are also reported to have provided the Sudanese with US$5 billion in military aid.[44] SAMA also gave direct support to Eritrea's Central Bank in 2015, after the government granted Saudi Arabia and the UAE permission to use its southern port of Assab in the war with the Houthi-led coalition in Yemen.[45]

It is difficult to know to what extent Saudi investors co-ordinate their investment decisions in conjunction with the government—directly or indirectly, but given the relationship between the state and the private sector, it would be difficult to imagine that there was no close coordination. Saudi Arabia and Sudan began a series of talks in May 2018 that resulted in an agreement, which means that Riyadh will supply Sudan's energy needs on credit for the next five years. Saudi Arabia is now committed to provide 1.8 million tonnes of oil a year to Sudan, which has helped Khartoum overcome a sharp foreign currency crisis and an acute fuel shortage.[46] Saudi's support to Sudan, such as providing billions in concessional loans and bank deposits, has been instrumental to securing the continued engagement of Sudanese troops in Yemen and Sudan's breaking off ties with Iran in the wake of the Saudi execution of Shia cleric Sheikh Nimr al-Nimr.[47]

Similarly to Saudi Arabia, the UAE has complemented its diplomatic and military presence in the Horn of Africa through the careful deployment of capital. The UAE has significantly increased investments in infrastructure, real estate, hospitality, transportation and telecommunications. Nevertheless, the UAE financial support in the Horn of Africa differs from Saudi Arabia's as UAE investments in the Horn of Africa are intended to help stabilise the sub-region, as long as they support its ambition of building and operating ports throughout the Red Sea region and give it basing rights.

DP World was formed when Dubai Ports Authority and Dubai Ports International merged in 2005 and has, by and large, acted as an instrument of UAE foreign policy. DP World has won concessions to manage a string of ports in the hands of national and subnational governments—Djibouti, Bosaso (Puntland), Kismayo (Jubaland Interim Authority) and Barawe (southern Somalia, South-Western state).[48] These concessions, as noted above, serve the UAE's foreign policy and its projection of power in the Red Sea and the Indian Ocean. For example, following the deal reached between DP World and Somaliland government, or the management of Berbera Port (2016), which was followed by establishment of DP Berbera joint venture,[49] the UAE was granted the rights to establish a military base in the region.[50] It was no surprise that an Emirati company won the US$90 million contract to build the naval base which includes a 300-metre inland berthing port with a depth of 7 metres 'to support the military airport', accommodating naval vessels to patrol the Gulf of Aden.[51] Subsequently, Shafa Al Nahda Contracting, a partner of DP World, has won the contract for the port expansion that will be carried out with an investment of US$101 million.[52]

UAE state-owned enterprises have also made a series of significant investments in Sudan. The single largest Gulf Arab Investment in the Horn (US$3 billion), for example, is a UAE capital outlay for the manufacturing of sugar in Ethiopia.[53] UAE businesses have also invested in various sectors in Sudan including industry, transportation, energy, water and irrigation in Sudan. The total value of UAE investments in Sudan amount to more than US$7.6 billion.[54] While the UAE has lent direct financial support to Egypt to shore up the regime, it has not intervened in quite the same manner as in the Horn of Africa. It did however deposit US$1.4 billion in Sudan's Central Bank in March 2018 to bolster its foreign exchange reserves.[55]

These developments in the Horn of Africa can also be read as part of strategic competition between the different Gulf States. Saudi and Emirati investments in the ports of Berbera (Somaliland), Doraleh (Djibouti), Bosaso (Somalia) and Assab (Eritrea), the ongoing Saudi support for Sudan's ambitious Dam Programme and promises of billions of Qatari riyals for agriculture and light manufacturing and social services in Darfur can all be understood in the context of escalating rivalries between Middle Eastern states.[56]

Conclusion

The economic dimension of stabilisation should not be underestimated, not in the least because better economic prospects are likely to be the only way for the region to truly find some form of sustainable stability. For the moment, the economic outlook in conflict and post-conflict areas remains precarious. Conflict has led to the destruction of infrastructure, the development of vested interests in a war economy and in the illicit trade in goods and services. As such, calls for economic stabilisation and economic reform are at the centre of current policy debates, and at the minimum, those practicing stabilisation need to take into account that there are those benefitting from the war, and that, to divert their economic activities away from disruptive and undermining activities, the right incentives or punishments need to be developed and applied. Not in the least to ensure that its own stabilisation activities stand some chance to succeed.

Traditional security exporters have long been used to reacting to these economic contexts with pledges of limited funds for development projects and by leaving it up to multilateral institutions such as the World Bank and the IMF to provide larger loans, with conditionality. Instead, Western actors predominantly have tried to create the right political and governance conditions for a private sector to flourish and economic growth to happen—not necessarily with significant results. That static approach is currently being challenged, as new actors, in particular China and Gulf actors, are putting a lot more emphasis on the economic instruments of stabilisation and are not shy to massively invest with their state-led enterprises and investment vehicles. China in particular is putting most of its weight on economic instruments, stating it is not interested in getting involved in the region with political or military means. Given the precedents elsewhere in the world, at some point in the future, these new dependencies on Chinese money will have their impact in the political and social realm. The Gulf actors tend to take a position between these two 'extremes': they blend economic, military, political and humanitarian instruments, though still emphasise the economic aspects of stabilisation much more than the 'traditional' actors do. The different approaches have their advantages and disadvantages for the states that are subjected to them, and finding a healthy way of combining what the different external actors have to offer might be a step into the direction of increasing stability.

Notes

1. Malik and Awaddalah (2011).
2. World Bank Group (2015).
3. Stewart (2008).
4. ILO figures.
5. Van Genugten (2016).
6. World Bank Group (2016).
7. El-Katiri and Fattouh (2017).
8. OECD (2009).
9. See Talani (2014).
10. Gunter (2015).
11. IMF, Iraq second review of the three year standby agreement.
12. World Bank Economic Outlook.
13. Gunter (2015).
14. *Financial Times* (2004).
15. Eaton (2018).
16. See Keen (1998).
17. Goodhand (2004).
18. Skaperdas (2001).
19. Williams (2009).
20. Al Mahmoud (2015).
21. Rubin (2000).
22. Williams (2009).
23. Clarke (2018).
24. Ibid.
25. USIP guiding principles.
26. Berdal and Wennmann (2010).
27. Hatton (2017).
28. Huasheng (2012).
29. Bukhari (2012).
30. Ramachandran (2018).
31. Reuters (2018a).
32. Han and Rossi (2018).
33. Middle East Monitor (2017).
34. Reuters (2018b)
35. Marks (2018).
36. Isaac (2011).
37. Watanabe (2017).
38. Ibid.
39. Georgy and Kallin (2015).
40. Economist Intelligence Unit (2014).
41. Meester et al. (2018).

42. *The Guardian* (2016).
43. Abo Alabass (2015).
44. Sudan Tribune (2016).
45. Plaut (2016).
46. Reuters (2018c).
47. Abo Alabass (2015).
48. Kantack (2017).
49. World Maritime News (2016). The agreement included an automatic 10-year extension for the management and development of a multi-purpose port project at Berbera. DP World, accordingly, set up a joint venture with 65% control together with the government of Somaliland to manage and invest in the port ( ). In March 2018, Ethiopia concluded an agreement with DP World and Somaliland Port Authority which granted it a 19% stake in the Port of Berbera, see also Gulf News (2018).
50. *The Economist* (2017).
51. Manek (2018).
52. Mitchell (2018).
53. Meester et al. (2018).
54. *The Gulf Today* (2018).
55. Reuters (2018d).
56. Meester et al. (2018).

BIBLIOGRAPHY

Abo Alabass, Mohammed Bassem. "Gulf States Lend Sudan US$2 Billion to Boost Foreign Reserves." *Bloomberg*, 20 July 2015.

Al-Mahmoud, Hamoud. "The War Economy in the Syrian Conflict: The Government's Hands-Off Tactics." *Carnegie Endowment for International Peace*. December 2015.

Berdal, Mats, and Achim Wennmann (eds.). *Ending Wars, Consolidating Peace: Economic Perspectives*. IISS, 2010.

Bukhari, Syed Waqas Haider. "The Role of China in Economic Stabilisation and Reconstruction of Afghanistan." *Margalla Papers*, 2012.

Clarke, Colin P. "An Overview of Current Trends in Terrorism and Illicit Finance: Lessons from the Islamic State in Iraq and Syria and Other Emerging Threats." Testimony Before the Committee on Financial Services Subcommittee on Terrorism and Illicit Finance, *United States House of Representatives*, 7 September 2018.

Eaton, Tim. "Libya's War Economy: Predation, Profiteering and State Weakness." *Chatham House*, April 2018.

El-Katiri, Laura, and Bassam Fattouh. "A Brief Political Economy of Energy Subsidies in the Middle East and North Africa." *International Development Policy*, vol. 1, (2017).

Economist Intelligence Unit. *GCC Trade and Investment Flows*, 2014.

Financial Times. "Hundreds of Sunken Ships in Iraq Waters," 5 October 2004.

Georgy, Michael, and Stephan Kallin. "Gulf Arab Allies Pledge $12 Billion to Egypt at Summit." *Reuters*, 13 March 2015.

Goodhand, Jonathan. "From War Economy to Peace Economy? Reconstruction and State Building in Afghanistan." *Journal of International Affairs*, vol. 58, no. 1 (2004).

Gulf News. "Ethiopia Acquires 19% Stake in DP World Berbera Port," 1 March 2018.

Gunter, Frank R. "Iraq's Perfect Storm." *Foreign Policy Research Institute* (2015).

Han, Aisha, and Rachel Rossi. "What Are the Implications of Expanded Chinese Investment in the MENA Region?" *Atlantic Council*, 10 August 2018.

Hatton, Celia. "China's Secret Aid Empire Uncovered." *BBC News*, 11 October 2017.

Huasheng, Zhao. "China and Afghanistan: China's Interests, Stances and Perspectives." CSIS, March 2012.

Isaac, Sally Khalifa. "Gulf Assistance Funds Post-2011: Allocation, Motivation and Influence." IEMED, 2015.

Kantack, Jacqulyn Meyer. "The Gulf Contest for the Horn of Africa." *Critical Threats*, 26 September 2017.

Keen, David. "The Economic Functions of Violence in Civil Wars." Adelphi Paper No. 319. International Institute for Strategic Studies. Oxford University Press, Oxford, 1998.

Malik, Adeel, and Bassem Awadallah. "The Economics of the Arab Spring." CSAE Working Paper WPS/2011–23, Oxford and Jeddah, December 2011.

Manek, Nizar. "U.A.E. Military Base in Breakaway Somaliland Seen Open by June." *Bloomberg*, 6 November 2018.

Marks, Jesse. "In the Competition over Syria's Reconstruction, China Is the Likely Winner." *Defense One*, 2 March 2018.

Meester, Jos, Willem van den Berg, and Harry Verhoeven. "Riyal Politik: The Political Economy of Gulf Investments in the Horn of Africa." *Netherlands Institute of International Relations "Clingendael"*, April 2018.

Middle East Monitor. "China Is Largest Foreign Investor in Middle East," 24 July 2017.

Mitchell, Charlie. "DP World Launches $442m Port Expansion in Somaliland." *The National*, 11 October 2018.

OECD. "Egypt: Anti-corruption." *Business Climate Development Strategy*, December 2009.

Plaut, Martin. 2016. *Understanding Eritrea: Inside Africa's Most Repressive State*. New York: Oxford University Press.

Ramachandran, Sudha. "Is China Bringing Peace to Afghanistan?" *The Diplomat*, 20 June 2018.

Reuters. "China Denies Planning Military Base in Afghanistan," 29 August 2018a.

Reuters. "China's Xi Pledges $20 Billion in Loans to Revive Middle East," 10 July 2018b.

Reuters. "UPDATE 1-Sudan in Talks with Saudi Arabia on Five-year Oil Aid Agreement." 7 May 2018c.

Reuters. "Sudan Central Bank Receives $1.4 bln Deposit from UAE-SUNA," 13 March 2018d.

Rubin, Barnett R. "The Political Economy of War and Peace in Afghanistan." *World Development,* vol. 28, no. 10 (2000): 1789–1803.

Skaperdas, Stergios. "The Political Economy of Organized Crime: Providing Protection When the State Does Not," 2001.

Stewart, Frances (ed.). *Horizontal Inequalities and Conflict: Understanding Group Violence in Multiethnic Societies.* New York: Palgrave Macmillan, 2008.

Sudan Tribune. "Saudi Arabia Gives Sudan US$5 Billion in Military Aid," *Sudan Tribune,* 23 February 2016.

Talani, Leila. *The Arab Spring in the Global Political Economy.* Basingstoke: Palgrave Macmillan, 2014.

The Economist. "The Ambitious United Arab Emirates," 6 April 2017.

The Guardian. "Why Has Sudan Ditched Iran in Favour of Saudi Arabia?" *The Guardian,* 12 January 2016.

The Gulf Today. "UAE Plays Key Role in Sudan Economy," 14 March 2018.

Van Genugten, Saskia. "The MENA Youth Conundrum: Generating Productivity, Preventing Disillusionment." *Emirates Diplomatic Academy Insight,* September 2016.

Watanabe, L. "Gulf States' Engagement in North Africa: The Role of Foreign Aid." In Khalid S. Almezaini and Jean-Marc Rickli (eds.), *The Small Gulf States: Foreign and Security Policies Before and After the Arab Spring,* 168–181. New York: Routledge, 2017.

Williams, Phil. "Criminals, Militias, and Insurgents: Organized Crime in Iraq." *Strategic Studies Institute,* 2009.

World Bank Group. "Inequality, Uprisings, and Conflict in the Arab World." *MENA Economic Monitor,* October 2015.

World Bank Group. "Middle East and North Africa: Public Employment and Governance in MENA," May 2016.

World Maritime News. "DP World Wins 30-Year Concession for Somaliland Port." *World Maritime News,* 5 September 2016.

PART III

Emerging Issues

CHAPTER 10

Urban Warfare: Stabilisation of Cities

Virginia Comolli

INTRODUCTION

Conflict in the twenty-first-century Middle East and North Africa (MENA) is becoming increasingly urbanised: the destruction suffered by the cities of Raqqa and Aleppo, to mention two of the most severe instances, is evidence of this trend. So is the fact that 40% of Syrian internally displaced persons (IDP) are in cities (rather than camps) and they are among the approximately 12 million people displaced by the conflict (equal to 50% of Syria's pre-war population).[1] In the light of the magnitude of this crisis, it comes as no surprise that there is a growing need for developing effective stabilisation operations that take into account specific pressures felt by cities such as rising populations, migration patterns, ethnic tensions, weakening of urban services and infrastructure, institutional deterioration, and the presence and role of non-state (armed) groups, among other factors.

There are some urban-specific factors—which are interconnected and will be discussed in more detail in the ensuing pages—that set cities and towns apart from rural environments. First, evidence indicates that cities have taken the brunt of most by-products of war in terms of both human

V. Comolli (✉)
International Institute for Strategic Studies, London, UK

© The Author(s) 2020
V. Gervais and S. van Genugten (eds.), *Stabilising the Contemporary Middle East and North Africa*, Middle East Today,
https://doi.org/10.1007/978-3-030-25229-8_10

207

and physical loss. Second, cities are usually the economic engine of their countries as the largest revenue-generators, hence they often have greater strategic importance compared to the countryside. Third, more than in rural settings, economic activities are dependent on the existence and integrity of infrastructure, hence without infrastructural reconstruction such as rebuilding roads that are used to take produce from the countryside to city markets, re-starting the economy is virtually impossible, making speedy reconstruction essential. Additionally, it further increases the onus on the military to do its utmost to avoid infrastructure and service disruption or destruction, which would negatively affect citizens. Fourth, cities are sensitive and often symbolic places in the eyes of state institutions, civilians and armed groups. The stakes are higher when it is about winning control over a strategic hub or centre. Fifth, the higher density of civilian population and infrastructure results in multiple challenges, including: distinguishing the enemy from the civilian population; a three-dimensional man-made environment where it is more challenging for the military to launch assaults and protect themselves from high-ground (and sometimes subterranean) attacks by armed groups[2]; deploying soldiers among civilians and ensuring the law of armed conflict and international humanitarian law are respected while civilians are effectively in the middle of the battleground (more civilians and infrastructure equate to higher risk of collateral damage and, among other considerations, the need to rethink the type of weapons to be used). Finally, cities are not only economic hubs for licit economic activities, they are also magnets for criminal networks because of the 'business' opportunities they offer and because of the conducive environment represented by poorly controlled slums which are a trademark of cities in developing and fragile countries.

Classic military and counter-insurgency literature has traditionally focused on insurgencies and guerrilla activities in rural areas and, as a result, responses have been tailored to those theatres of operation. However, at present conflict manifests itself primarily in urban settings with this trend unlikely to see a reversal in the future. This realisation, and the urban-specific factors mentioned above, translates into specific challenges for stabilisation efforts. In this context, it is key to highlight that, in cities, the human terrain is more fragmented than in rural settings, with several different—and sometimes rival—communities and groups split along ethnic, religious and political lines. Additionally, stabilisation efforts are faced by the *systemic* character of cities, which is something that fundamentally differentiates them from rural areas (in fact, this might be the very nature of cities) and relates to the way that one public service or piece of infrastructure is connected to the functioning of several others. For instance, the suspension of service provision of basic needs such as clean water or electricity causes the gradual deterioration of other services and businesses and can even prompt emigration from the city and labour shortages. Another example of the uniquely systemic character of urban stability is that of Baghdad shortly after the US invasion in 2003: the delay in re-establishing electricity and other basic services impacted people's ability to access their jobs, income and food and had a severe impact on the population's views towards the new political leadership.[3]

With these considerations in mind and in order to develop effective responses resulting in lasting gains, it is key to first move away from the state-centric bias that usually accompanies interventions in conflict and post-conflict settings in favour of initiatives at sub-national (municipal) level. Second, the concept of stabilisation, which in some circles carries predominantly security connotations, needs to be significantly broadened to include, alongside military and law enforcement actors, also humanitarian, aid, development, urban planning and reconstruction components. This approach differs from traditional security-centred short-term interventions in so far that it sets the basis for longer-term efforts that arguably have higher chances of producing enduring stability and of increasing cities' resilience to shocks—including to the risk of a possible return to instability and conflict.

Setting the Context

The MENA region has witnessed a fivefold population increase since the 1950s, reaching 569 million people in 2017. Egypt and Iraq have become the key demographic hubs in the region and the former is expected to remain the most populous country until at least 2050.[4] Significantly, by 2100 MENA's population is expected to be bigger than China's and double Europe's. Furthermore, and notwithstanding a decline in fertility and the fact that the so-called youth bulge appears to have already hit its peak (in the 1970s and 1990s in North Africa and the Middle East respectively), youth numbers are high. According to the United Nations Development Programme (UNDP), 60% of Arabs in 2015 were under the age of 30 and almost 50% of the population was younger than 24.[5] Growth has been accompanied by increased concentration in urban centres and today, approximately 55% of the world's population reside in urban centres—a percentage that is projected to grow for the foreseeable future. In the MENA region, since the 1990s, the urban population has overtaken the rural one, and by 2050 nearly 90% of population growth will happen in cities, according to UN projections.[6] In Saudi Arabia, for instance 83% of people already live in cities.[7] In Jordan, the 2016 census showed that the population had increased by nearly 87% in the preceding decade, and Amman's population had nearly doubled.[8] A study published in 2016 indicated that Tehran's population had exceeded the city's capacity by 70%.[9]

Urbanisation tends to lead to economic and social benefits. Karachi, to mention one example, is home to 12% of the total population of Pakistan, and alone it generates over 50% of the country's tax revenue. However, urbanisation also has a number of negative implications. Local municipal authorities are often unable to meet the needs of new urban dwellers who converge in cities in large numbers seeking employment, better prospects and security. The result is the establishment of informal settlements or slums. At present, in low-income as well as in fragile and conflict countries, over 60% of the urban population ends up living in slums in which the state has limited presence. Informal governance and illicit or grey economies become the norm, and non-state armed groups such as criminal gangs and often violent extremists thrive.[10] This is evidenced by now infamous slums such as Kibera in Nairobi (Kenya) and Orangi Town in Karachi (Pakistan). The latter counts approximately 2.4 million inhabitants and is home to criminal gangs, mafia-style networks and even jihadi elements.[11] In a 2014 study, UN-Habitat warned about 'autonomous and "no-go" zones such as slums and other informal settlements, that effectively lie outside local and central government control'.[12]

These implications are very visible across MENA as millions of young people flock to large towns and cities in search of economic prospects. Here, the limited capacity of many of the regional countries to generate sufficient educational and employment opportunities for their young citizens—alongside the added complication presented by large numbers of refugees in countries neighbouring Syria and Iraq—is a socio-economic as well as a security concern. The unemployed are likely to be drawn to informal and even illicit economic activities, and their discontent has the potential for fuelling social tensions, civil unrest and even conflict. A stark example of these linkages is represented by the wave of unrest known as the Arab Spring in which key contributing factors where large youth bulges and unemployment.

The violence afflicting Raqqa, Aleppo, Hodeida and Benghazi, among other cities, is a reminder that conflict is becoming intrinsically urbanised. Indeed, images of widespread physical destruction of cities and towns, alongside severe loss of life, are a permanent feature of war reporting. They highlight the extent to which combat is impacted by the urban terrain and, at the same time, how badly the fighting is impacting urban infrastructure, the continuation of day-to-day economic and social activities in a given city or town, the provision of services, and long-term plans for reconstruction once hostilities eventually come to an end. To put things into perspective, in 2017 the United Nations estimated that US$1 billion would be needed to rebuild Mosul's infrastructure. Around 90% of the Old City had been destroyed in the battle for Mosul and, as they retreated, Daesh fighters had sabotaged key sites such as the airport and oil refineries.[13]

Notably, MENA cities had also witnessed some of the most notable instances of urban conflict of the second half of the twentieth century: the Battle of Algiers (1956–1957); Beirut during the Lebanese Civil War (1975–1990); Hafez Al Assad's siege of Aleppo (1980); and the Algerian Civil War (1991–2002) which was fought across a number of cities where armed groups had their main support bases. These prominent examples should not feed a belief that this problem only pertains to the MENA region. Approximately 50 million people around the world were estimated to be affected by armed conflict in cities in 2015, according to a study conducted by the International Committee of the Red Cross (ICRC), including, for example, in countries as diverse as Mexico and Somalia.[14]

Reinforcing the interplay between conflict and cities, a 2004 study on the effects of conflict in Afghanistan and Pakistan's Tribal Areas on Kabul and Karachi concluded that 'the "classic" rural warlord seems to morph gradually into a modern urban one'.[15] Indeed, insurgencies and other types of non-state conflict in rural or border areas have the ability to spill over into cities in the form of weapons flows and militant activity, exacerbating political tensions and fuelling criminal economies. Some experts have even taken a step further in highlighting the role of violent non-state actors, arguing that is indeed the prominence of such armed groups in modern conflict that has contributed to urbanising war: cities are the places where irregular fighters have a chance to prevail against conventional forces.[16]

Academics and practitioners working in the field of strategic studies have long focused on urban warfare as an all-out struggle in densely built areas and, for that reason, a difficult and unforgiving sub-type of operation. Indeed, the term 'Stalingrad syndrome' has been coined to indicate the arguable belief that all wars will be as destructive as one of the most important and bloodiest battles of the Second World War—The Battle of Stalingrad (August 1942–February 1943). There, Germany suffered a catastrophic defeat at the hands of the Soviet Army. For instance, the 2017 battle to liberate Mosul from Daesh has been likened, by some senior military officers, to Stalingrad. It took nine months for 90,000 coalitions troops to defeat 5000 Daesh fighters in an environment in which low-technology, brutal on-the-ground battle, largely became the only viable option.[17] Notwithstanding the magnitude of battles such as the one in Mosul, one could argue that the parallel with Stalingrad only accurately reflects a select number of contemporary battles.

The understanding of urban environments as battlefields has resulted in silos when trying to think about urban security policies. Urbanists, development practitioners and institutions such as UN-Habitat have been left to work with a limited policy toolbox. To better understand how the changing character of conflict affects cities, it is helpful to think more strategically about security in cities beyond the concept of urban warfare. Additionally, even when the latter is concerned, in order to appreciate the uniqueness of the urban environment some military thinkers have put forward the idea that cities should be treated like human bodies reliant on 'metabolic' inflows such as food, fuel, money, information, producing waste outflows, and sometimes suffering from serious cancer-like diseases such as conflict which require treatment from multiple medical practitioners. Like a body, cities and towns have their core and appendices and are adaptive and complex.[18]

The need for a multi-disciplinary approach in cities has even been recognised by senior military figures. In 1999, US General Charles Krulak coined a highly influential concept: the three-block war.[19] State forces deployed to unstable urban environments have to combat non-state foes in one block, conduct peacekeeping in the next block and deliver humanitarian aid in the next one. This approach rests on the realisation that conflict has become hybrid and protracted and non-state actors had become the protagonists. These new aspects of conflict put existing response mechanisms to the test. This was clear in the conflict that erupted in eastern Ukraine in 2014 and that prompted extensive examinations of the concept of 'hybrid war' consisting of a combination of tactics used simultaneously by both states and a variety of non-state actors, primarily in cities.[20]

These complex problems are well known in Gaza's urban centres. Hamas has used multiple weapons systems and complex ambushes, and it has fully exploited the complexities of densely populated urban environments in its fight against Israeli forces.[21] In the 2000s, authorities in the Colombian city of Medellín had to improvise a number of policing, military and architectural solutions in order to stabilise *comunas* (slums) controlled by a combination of left-wing guerrillas and powerful criminal groups. These lessons were also painfully learned by US Special Forces deployed to Mogadishu, Somalia in 1993, as part of a humanitarian support operation that ended in one of the landmark urban battles of recent decades.[22]

Adopting Different Approaches to Conflict and Post-conflict Cities

Given the multifaceted challenges presented by conflict and post-conflict scenarios, and as emphasised in the many cases mentioned in this paper, what is needed is much more than military or security interventions. The concept of stabilisation lacks a universally agreed definition.[23] In some countries, and in spite of cross-departmental cooperation, experts have argued that ministries of defence tend to dominate stabilisation.[24] Instead, stabilisation, especially when designed to address the complexities of urban environments, would benefit from being significantly broadened to include, alongside military and law enforcement actors, also humanitarian, aid, development, urban planning and reconstruction components. Along similar lines, longer-term efforts have higher chances of producing enduring stability and of increasing cities' resilience to shocks—including to the risk of a possible return to instability and conflict. The US Army itself, cognisant of the unique challenges presented by the urban environment, has stressed the growing role and influence of non-military organisations (and civilians) in urban stabilisation operations. Indeed, it sees the military as only 'a tool' in a broader multi-agency civilian-led effort which could take years before the desired outcome is achieved.[25] One of the many benefits of military-civilian integration was evident in 2004 in Fallujah where integration of US Marines and civilian organisations (e.g. Civilian Affairs personnel) from the planning to the execution phases of the operation ensured that messaging such as warning of upcoming offensives would reach the population effectively.[26]

A number of scholars have contributed to this debate, providing valuable recommendations. Writing for the Clingendael Conflict Research Unit, Leontine Specker has argued for greater integration of socio-economic recovery programmes into post-conflict stabilisation. This approach, albeit relevant to most post-conflict scenarios, is particularly pertinent to urban theatres owing, among other aspects, to their systemic nature. In fact, as mentioned earlier, cities often drive countries' economies hence they become crucial in bringing economies shattered by conflict back on their feet. In Benghazi, Libya's second largest city, an expansion of commercial and construction activities in recent years has helped the re-birth of the city—notwithstanding a security situation that remains volatile—and pointed to the beneficial impact of encouraging investments and economic activities.[27] In spite of differences, Specker highlights four recurrent similarities in post-conflict scenarios: economic regression, deterioration of infrastructure, social decay and weak governance.[28] Based on these factors, she recommended; first, that socio-economic recovery be systematically integrated into peacebuilding and stabilisation programmes; Second, that local, including informal, investors were to be allowed room to play a key role in the early recovery phase rather than focusing disproportionally on attracting foreign investors; third, that a mix of short-term flexible programmes (such as temporary employment for former combatants) should accompany long-term initiatives.[29]

Sultan Barakat and Shipra Narang-Suri have made a case for urban planning in conflict-affected cities.[30] They lamented that a short-term approach adopted by many international actors that favoured emergency relief and early recovery was detrimental to the chances of successfully implementing initiatives and planning that would promote sustainable development and foster community reconciliation in the post-conflict era. Indeed, they argued, urban planning could become a 'vital ingredient in the process of national recovery after wars'.[31] Specifically, conflict cities would benefit from 'area-based' approaches. Area-based approaches have increasingly been adopted by an array of research centres and other organisations working on conflict and post-conflict challenges. This moves away from individuals or households towards a larger scale focus has been described as a 'paradigm shift' in urban areas.[32] Area-based responses to conflict involve targeted actions and aid delivery to promote the recovery of specific areas. For instance, this can consist of building public services in a given neighbourhood (and monitoring progress as time goes by). Another important aspect of this approach is greater participation by local communities in defining priorities and strategies. This, in turn, ensures that assistance and recovery efforts target specific challenges. Additionally, this approach differs from more traditional ones which tended to be focused on short-term emergency strategies in which public services and infrastructure were more or less afterthoughts.[33]

The area-based approach and any other strategy that involves long-term urban recovery require tight cooperation among various policy actors, the military, the humanitarian sector, and even non-state armed groups in order to face the interconnected challenges that are peculiar to urban centres. Many contemporary cases show that cities affected by conflict are unlikely to quickly transition to peace. Somalia's capital Mogadishu, for instance, continues to suffer from attacks years after local and international troops formally liberated the city from al-Shabaab militants. Similar stories can be seen in Baghdad, Kabul and Haiti's Port-au-Prince. Protracted armed conflicts have, as indicated by the ICRC, a 'cumulative impact on three key components of the urban system': people (with their unique skills), hardware (buildings, infrastructure) and consumables (water, fuel, medicine).[34] Working on even one of these items requires dialogue across sectors, including militaries and non-state groups that exert de facto territorial control over some urban peripheries or slums. Furthermore, the area-based approach can help armed forces in their ever-more-challenging quest to consolidate security after large-scale military operations in urban theatres.

The 2016 Chilcot Report, a major independent review of British military failures in Iraq, strongly argued that the long delays in the re-establishment of essential services and basic urban security to protect civilians from looting and other rampant crimes that followed the overthrow of Saddam Hussein in 2003, were key factors leading to the post-invasion chaos.[35] Additionally, among the lessons the US military has drawn from the experience on Mosul was that 're-establishing governance in the city, with an eye towards basic human services will be essential in maintaining popular support'.[36] With these reflections in mind, it is evident that both armed forces and humanitarian actors have an interest in well-functioning urban services.

Additionally, the *conduct* of military operations, in protracted and low-intensity conflicts that often follow major wars, is particularly relevant to the urban discussion. The respect for international law on the conduct of hostilities is, as always, crucial. Disregarding such regulations has specific impacts on cities including the deterioration of services and infrastructure that are essential for millions of lives. Legal experts have highlighted how urban warfare presents one of the most challenging contexts for the application of international humanitarian law. Civilians are in fact at the centre of the battlefield when it comes to urban stabilisation operations which require armies to use restraint and proportionality in the use of force to limit civilian fatalities and collateral damage as well as to build their own legitimacy in the eye of the population and eventually secure its support.

Yet, non-state armed groups have the propensity to hide among civilians making the distinction between combatants and non-combatants often hard to establish.[37] Israel's Operation Protective Edge (2014) was an example of this trend, with Hamas accused of often resorting to using civilian facilities to shield their operations mindful of the fact that Israeli military retaliation would have resulted in international condemnation.[38] With this in mind, operations such as the battle of Baghdad in March–April 2003 exemplified the need for, and effectiveness of, precision fire (in this case by the Americans) to limit collateral damage while inflicting devastating damage to the enemy. Gathering real-time situational awareness through the use of UAVs had also contributed to more precise targeting hence reduced civilian fatalities and infrastructural damage.[39]

At this stage, it is worth reflecting on the nature of the various actors involved in urban stabilisation operations, whether they be foreign troops from a militarily stronger partner country, multinational contingents, local troops, police or paramilitary forces. These different security actors have different levels of professionalism and training; have access to more or less sophisticated weaponry; and enjoy different degrees of legitimacy and acceptance among civilians (would external actors be seen as foreign 'invaders'? Would local troops be feared?). In addition, of course, there would be differences between military actors and civilian law enforcement ones.

Impossible to separate from the discussion on cities and conflict in the MENA region is the issue of refugee flows. The crises in Syria and Iraq have produced extremely large numbers of refugees and IDPs seeking safety away from conflict areas. The vast majority of refugees and IDPs live in cities.[40] Zaatari (Jordan), the Middle East's largest refugee camp, is 'home' to approximately 80,000 Syrians concentrated in an area of just over five square kilometres.[41] This makes it Jordan's fourth largest *city*. Yet, around 80% of all Syrian refugees currently in Jordan live *outside* camps, usually in cities and town, working in the informal or illegal sector and likely to be exploited by unscrupulous employers and landlords.[42] The sudden arrival of new dwellers poses significant strains on the receiving communities, infrastructure and services. In Jordan for instance, refugees amount to 30% of the population. The influx of refugees has prompted an increase in rental prices and made the already limited amount of affordable housing even more scarce.[43] In addition, it has presented a challenge to cities' identities. Locals, even those well-disposed towards receiving conflict-displaced civilians, sometimes lament having to share often already limited resources with the newcomers who are at times seen as receiving preferential treatment. This presents an ethical and practical challenge and raises questions as to whether it is sensible to distinguish between IDPs and refugees in fragile settings where the infrastructure is weak or failing.[44] In addition, some of the receiving cities might still be struggling with their own challenges related to post-conflict reconstruction. This is the case of Beirut in which the reconstructions efforts following the civil war of the 1970s and 1980s had fuelled divisions and hindered the chances of uniting the city through a common pluralistic vision.[45] An effective way of addressing problems affecting a given city or neighbourhood could entail the involvement of displaced civilians in the decision-making process which leads to the design of solutions. This in turn would contribute to the creation of a shared identity and avoid the distinction between 'us, the locals' and 'them, the IDPs or refugees'. Yet, there have been cases in which locals have blocked the arrival of migrants and were yet to come to terms with the reality that, owing to the dire situation in the countries of origin, migrants were likely to remain in the receiving cities and towns for the long term, thus altering the local demographic landscape.[46]

The Many Challenges of Post-conflict Stabilisation in Urban Theatres

As already alluded to in the preceding discussion, as conflicts become more protracted, the lines between conflict and post-conflict (and even peace, at times) are blurred.[47] Conflict recidivism is common and some researchers estimate that 40% of countries emerging from a civil war are likely to relapse into conflict within a decade of the end of the hostilities.[48] The US military has underscored these trends by arguing for a 'more fluid, non-linear concept of conflict' and, as a stabilisation officer aptly put it, 'it's not post-conflict when you're getting shot at'.[49]

With these premises in mind, it goes without saying that *post-conflict stabilisation* can be particularly daunting. Every post-conflict situation, in both urban and rural settings, presents an array of challenges for peacebuilding and stabilisation that include, among others, disarmament, demobilisation and reintegration (DDR) of armed groups, Security Sector Reform (SSR), reconstruction, and socio-economic recovery. Crucially, the integration of all of the above, the combination of military and civilian efforts, and the need for tackling both immediate priorities such as restoring security and governance in a given area and setting the basis for economic growth in the longer term, become additional challenges in their own right. Additionally, every post-conflict theatre will have its own peculiarities impacting what changes and actions need to be prioritised.

This chapter has been able to draw from the experiences of, and literature around, a number of settings contending with the challenges of cities transitioning to peace, e.g. Belfast and Baghdad, or witnessing situations of instability, e.g. Johannesburg and Karachi. The existence of multiple studies is not surprising given that cities appear to be bearing the brunt of most of the by-products of war, whether the physical destruction or the influx of refugees and IDPs. As such, the ability of cities to adapt to post-conflict requirements through effective urban management and development to complement security efforts is crucial to build resilience to future challenges. Through this approach, the aim should also be to resolve any long-standing grievances that might have driven the conflict so that history does not repeat itself. The housing shortage in Kigali, for instance, has been deemed as fuelling the growing social gap that contributed to the Rwandan genocide in 1994.[50]

There exist substantial differences related to specific conflict circumstances, community capacity and the strength and organisation of local institutions. As such, it would be unrealistic to claim that a one-size-fits-all model of post-conflict stabilisation, transformation and urban management exists. Nevertheless, there is value in drawing lessons that could inform interventions in cities in different regions. Importantly, the examples discussed below highlight the complexity of dealing with short-term as well as long-term issues, that is, stabilising a city first and then ensuring it remains stable in the long run.

One of the many challenges of post-conflict situations is the rebuilding of relations between the public and authorities. Above all, the relationship between the people and the police (and other security forces) is crucial. Importantly, whereas it is non-state armed groups such as rebels, jihadists and criminals, that are commonly identified as the main drivers of insecurity, in a number of settings state authorities such as the military and the police have been perpetrating violence by adopting repressive and heavy-handed responses to security challenges or through their direct involvement in criminal activities. It is in such cases that reform is most needed to restore authorities' legitimacy in the eyes of the civilian population. Against this backdrop, Alice Hills' in-depth study of post-conflict policing argues that order, rather than security, is what is truly meaningful for people's lives and is a more significant issue in post-conflict cities. Indeed, security is merely a means to an end, that is, order. In her work, that includes cities as varied as Basra, Kabul, Freetown, Juba, Sarajevo and many others, she concludes that notwithstanding case-specific differences, all post-conflict cities share ineffective police forces and 'the fragmented, localised and temporary nature of security provision'.[51] She concluded that the re-emergence of order after a conflict reflects the power relations and patterns of subjugation that are by-products of insecurity.[52]

As such, other experts have argued that the promotion of legitimate security has to be prioritised. To achieve that, policymakers should ensure that security programmes require cooperation between the police and the public with the community being in the driver's seat when it comes to defining the direction and nature of efforts.[53] Additionally, it has been noted that police forces can only be as effective as the institutions behind them, namely courts, prisons and the judicial system as a whole. Lessons from Afghanistan and Iraq have indeed strengthened this argument and emphasised the fact that in the aftermath of conflict local law enforcement is likely to be unable to resume its role effectively, hence the deployment of international police advisors becomes needed.[54] A contemporary example is Italy's contribution to the stabilisation of Iraq, under the auspices of the Global Coalition against Daesh, which centres around the Carabinieri Task Force training of police units, ranging from police techniques courses to counter IEDs; from community policing to cultural heritage control, from crowd and riot control to crime scene investigation.[55]

The importance of reforming police forces is further highlighted by the nexus between conflict and crime, which is particularly evident in conflict-affected and post-conflict cities and produces pernicious effects. Although evidence shows that transnational organised crime, illegal trafficking and illicit economies impact the nature and duration of conflict; it can be argued that conflict may itself be 'criminogenic'—that is, it generates crime.[56] The same can be said of post-conflict scenarios. Activities such as drug trafficking, money laundering, arms trafficking and extortion are inherently drawn to cities due to their international connections and widespread availability of vulnerable areas and populations that armed groups can exploit. A number of cases from around the world highlight the importance of taking into consideration criminal agendas in the context of peace negotiations—an approach that has often been discarded with detrimental effects, such as in Sierra Leone and Haiti in the 1990s and in Iraq following 2003, when the rapid demobilisation of Iraqi forces translated into the formation of violent criminal gangs.[57] Additionally, post-conflict criminality (including street crime) and criminality-driven corruption—recurrent features of urban environments—also run the risk of deterring foreign investors from entering the licit market, which undermines prospects for economic development and growth and for reducing fragility. There are further economic repercussions from laundering criminal proceeds into the legal economy. In the case of real estate, for instance, this can result in inflated prices, reduced purchasing power for the local population, and increased inequality and economic marginalisation.[58]

Iraq after 2003 is a typical example of the challenges that a post-conflict situation presents. Above all is the fact that whereas formal conflict might be over, violence and instability are likely to continue and to move along a continuum that, one hopes, would eventually (but not always) lead to actual peace. Iraqis have been in and out of conflict ever since 2003, with even the transition phases being characterised by high vulnerability to shocks and crisis.[59] A study by Shaymaa Alkhalefy, Poorang Piroozfar and Andrew Church discusses the tensions between centralised and local level decision-making. It recalls how Iraqi urban planning had always followed a top-down approach, failing to engage with local authorities, the private sector and civil society, and resulting in tensions born out of the failure of social integration and the inability to meet the true needs of local communities.[60] On the contrary, the interests of higher levels of government were the ones prioritised in local urban planning.[61] A key lesson from the Iraqi experience was the importance of decentralising decision-making at the provincial and municipal level and delegating sufficient authority to local development agencies and municipal councils—hence producing a more participatory model of urban management. Furthermore, this approach implies the building of a common vision for the city with stakeholders aligned around it and working in close cooperation. In this context, Cities Alliance noted that positive outcomes had resulted from allowing urban systems to self-organise once appropriate common visions and policy frameworks had been set up.[62]

There is broad agreement around the assumption that community participation in post-conflict reconstruction helps increase cities' resilience to future shocks. Such participation can be fostered through housing interventions.[63] An assessment of cities with significant levels of instability including Karachi, Kigali, Managua, Medellín, Mexico City, Nairobi, and São Paolo and conducted by Diane Davis at Harvard University, conceptualised resilience as individuals' or communities' ability to resist 'through strategies that help them establish relatively autonomous control over the activities, spaces, and social or economic forces and conditions that comprise their daily lives'.[64] A further layer to this is the role of personal identity and the ability to identify with a certain neighbourhood hence becoming truly invested in its development. In the absence of that feeling of belonging, meaningful social networks are hard to build, as exemplified by the case of Diesloot in Johannesburg, hence weakening urban resilience.[65] Community participation can take multiple forms. In Mexico City, for instance, through the involvement in participatory budgeting programmes, citizens were able to engage in a dialogue with the authorities around priorities and investments and could then offer their input so that interventions would be better targeted.[66]

Following the end of the Troubles, the ethno-nationalistic conflict that plagued Northern Ireland for most of the second half of the twentieth century, the city of Belfast changed dramatically and with that the economy. Notably, the post-conflict economy in the city grew unevenly, depending on the specific sector and space, with entire areas—especially those in the west and north of the city that had suffered the most during the conflict—being left behind. This led to further segregation (and discontent) and exclusion from the economic dynamism experienced in the south. Brendan Murtagh's analysis of the Belfast case study highlights the importance of promoting mobility to ensure as many people as possible avoid being trapped in depressed neighbourhoods from which they become unable to access employment opportunities.[67] This assessment underpins the need for two fundamental policy responses to foster greater urban inclusiveness. First, in order to address segregation, it is key to understand what would be the most-needed and efficient modes of public transport that would help those living in the poorest areas reach industrial and commercial areas. In addition, albeit more expensive, it would be beneficial to introduce flexibility of routes in the design of public transport networks that adapt to the changing environment and urban dynamics, such as for instance the building of new markets or other economic centres people would need to access.[68] A second form of needed policy initiative highlighted by the Belfast case concerns investments in the labour market that are particularly targeted to the requirements of the youth in areas at risk. In Belfast, they are represented by interface areas, i.e. parts of the city where nationalists and unionists share a physical boundary and are known for being the sites of greater social deprivation and sectarian violence.[69] Support, funding and training for targeted projects, instead of traditional skill-based approaches that are unlikely to attract marginalised groups, have proved successful.[70]

Admittedly, the above recommendations speak to *longer-term* interventions to foster greater urban inclusiveness beyond the immediate-term requirements of stabilisation. Yet, one could argue that the experience of Belfast reinforces the need for designing approaches to stabilisation that address immediate concerns by, for example, creating immediate and/or temporary employment opportunities (as indicated earlier in this chapter) but that are also mindful of possible future requirements for which stabilisation operations can provide solid bases. For instance, this could amount to offering jobs to former combatants in a way that both avoids their stigmatisation and takes into account security concerns and respects expectations of the broader community. The latter, in fact, is likely to resent former combatants so it is crucial that no section of society is excluded from economic activities in order to avoid inequalities towards certain groups, including women.[71]

For lessons for stabilisation, Rwanda's capital Kigali is a case study worth considering: following the 1994 conflict, it went from 'urban catastrophe to model city' praised internationally, including by UN-Habitat, for its rapid and peaceful development.[72] Kigali's model was implemented on three bases: first, highly centralised policy-making driven by the consolidation of the Rwandan Patriotic Front (RPF) at the national and city-level; second, an elite-driven approach aimed at turning Kigali into a regional financial, ICT and logistics hub; and third, the de-prioritisation, albeit not officially, of creating new economic opportunities for the poor either in the cities or in rural areas—something that international donors also lamented.[73] The question remains as to whether this is a truly sustainable model. In the short term, the approach adopted in Kigali proved effective in stabilising the city and setting the foundations for reconstruction and future economic growth but, arguably, it did so at the expense of the poorer sections of society. City authorities did not shy away from large-scale expropriations of informal settlements and the relocation of their inhabitants outside the city. By doing so, they effectively promoted social segregation between the Rwandan elite and expats living in highly securitised neighbourhoods featuring upscale properties and amenities, and the low-earners for whom living in Kigali was no longer feasible. This exclusionary approach, especially in the light of demographic and urban growth trends and the resulting increasing demand for economic and employment opportunities, points to its limited sustainability on the longer term, including as it creates the potential for discontent and unrest.[74]

The issue of segregation is well known to the inhabitants of several Middle Eastern cities. Somehow reminiscent of the Kigali experience, the reconstruction of Beirut's city centre has been accused of having a heavily commercial character which, albeit intended as a way of portraying neutrality, eventually resulted in accentuating the divide between those who could afford some of the expensive goods sold in the new modern establishments, such as Starbucks, and those unable to do so.[75] These examples further reinforce the need for regional actors involved in urban stabilisation to plan and implement reconstruction projects that, first, are not built on Western standards—featuring upmarket shopping centres that most locals won't be able to afford—and second, are mindful not only of the needs of local elites but also, and more importantly, would benefit the most vulnerable sections of society rather than further marginalise them.

Concluding Discussion

The preceding pages have brought to the fore the intersection between, on the one hand, demographic and urbanisation trends and, on the other, conflict. Urbanisation itself is not a source of instability. On the contrary, cities often are the main propellers of a country's economic growth. Yet, they can become the stage of multiple forms of instability. In some cases, violence is generated from *within* the city and, more precisely, in informal settlements or slums that become home to non-state armed groups. Elsewhere, in places such as Syria, it is full-blown conflict that has made its way into towns and cities increasing the onus on the military to rethink the use of explosive weapons and focus on increasing precision targeting to limit collateral damage as much as possible—a true challenge in densely populated areas such as cities. Across the world, there are also many cities that experience a mix of these first two categories which is typical of lower-level conflict that usually follows war and is often fuelled by the interrelationship between conflict/post-conflict dynamics and crime. Finally, there are cases, common in South Asian megacities for instance, in which the by-products of near-by conflict such as the dislodgment of armed groups who then seek refuge in cities, endogenous criminality and other stresses such as inflows of refugees contribute to a volatile mix, sometimes requiring the deployment of military and paramilitary troops to sedate violence.

Because of the peculiarities presented by cities, new and more cross-sectoral approaches to stabilisation have better chances of producing long-term stability and fostering resilience to shocks, crises and indeed future conflict. Notwithstanding the important role played by international actors in the form of military, development or humanitarian assistance and by national level authorities, local engagement and cooperation are paramount. Indeed, there is great value in redressing the existing state-centric bias in favour of moving towards initiatives at the subnational level. In this regard, and as exemplified by the earlier discussion about post-2013 Iraqi cities, engaging local communities fosters a feeling of local ownership and is more likely to guarantee sustainability of new approaches in cities. In addition, a population-centric approach in urban stabilisation operations allows for building legitimacy for the international actors which, among other benefits, improves public opinion and facilitates the collection of human intelligence (HUMINT). The growing consensus around this approach became apparent in the course of a recent IISS-ICRC project. Too many interventions supported by international organisations and governments are channelled through national agencies without the involvement of municipal and other local authorities. The latter are likely to have a better understanding of local needs, dynamics and priorities and can support an area-based approach, that is, one that is tailored to a specific environment. In addition, responses need to feature non-governmental organisations and the expert community. Equally, approaches ought to be multi-sectoral to include developmental, humanitarian, security and urban planning elements. Experts have begun to argue that development and emergency responses are converging and that development efforts should start while a conflict is still ongoing, for example, by helping set up water-supply systems rather than by distributing bottled water. In other words, development becomes part of the response to conflict in cities.[76]

Moreover, whereas armed forces, especially Western ones, have been forecasting and preparing for *intensive* fighting in urban areas aimed at defeating an opponent, a number of examples mentioned in this chapter show that low-intensity armed opposition can remain a persistent problem in the absence of fully fledged conflict (or beyond the formal end of a conflict). The security forces involved initially would have objectives not hugely different from those in rural settings: to establish the rule of law and deter armed spoilers, primarily to pave the way for further political and economic strengthening. However, they would need to be accompanied by a range of technical and political actors able to engage with local communities, power brokers and physical infrastructure that are more numerous and interconnected in the urban system. Therefore, security forces would need to be complemented by urban planning, social engagement in marginalised areas, political power brokering with a variety of influential local leaders and sectarian groups, engineering expertise for rebuilding and 'quick-win' solutions as well as economic and business development in order to offer employment in areas likely to be deprived and fragile.

Undeniably, cooperation among multiple actors brings challenges vis-à-vis the sequencing of responses; the availability of resources and sustainability of efforts; competition among different agencies; and sustaining efforts in the light of changing political priorities on both the donor and recipient sides. The presence of several international organisations also runs the risk of fragmenting local communities. Developing mutual understanding and trust in peacetime among various agencies and especially between military and non-military actors is fundamental to increase chances of better cooperation once a crisis erupts. One recommendation would be for military forces to have 'sockets' where humanitarian organisations can be 'plugged in' easily during conflict situations. Multi-agency joint training for the conduct of operations in urban settings would support and complement this approach.[77] Urban planners and architects deserve a final mention. Their role should move beyond coordinating service supply. Instead, their designs and planning can contribute to creating and shaping a common sociopolitical identity in a given city that would increase social cohesion and make a city less vulnerable to shocks such as violence or full-blown conflict. As such, they should be involved in stabilisation efforts in cities.

Notes

1. IDMC, *Syria*, Internal Displacement Monitoring Center, 2018. http://www.internal-displacement.org/countries/syria. Accessed November 2018.
2. See Gerwehr and Glen (2000, pp. 7–8, 12–14).
3. See *The Report of the Iraq Inquiry: Executive Summary* (2016, pp. 93–94).
4. See McKee et al. (2017).
5. See UNDP (2016).
6. McKee et al. (2017, pp. 17–18).
7. See, *Population of Cities in Saudi Arabia*, World Population Review (2018). http://worldpopulationreview.com/countries/saudi-arabia-population/cities/. Accessed November 2018.

8. Obeidat, Omar, "Population Grew by 87% Over a Decade—Census," *The Jordan Times*, 22 February 2016. http://www.jordantimes.com/news/local/population-grew-87-over-decade-%E2%80%94-census.
9. "70% of Tehran Population Beyond Optimum Level," *Financial Tribune*, 19 June 2016. https://financialtribune.com/articles/economy-domestic-economy/43937/70-of-tehran-population-beyond-optimum-level.
10. World Bank, *World Development Indicators*. http://databank.worldbank.org/data/reports.aspx?source=2&series=EN.POP.SLUM.UR.ZS&country=LIC. Accessed July 2018.
11. Author's field research, Karachi, April 2017.
12. See UN-Habitat (2015, p. 35).
13. See *The IISS Armed Conflict Survey 2018* (2018, pp. 100–101).
14. See ICRC (2015, p. 7).
15. See Esser (2004, p. 37).
16. Sassen, Saskia, "Welcome to a New Kind of War: The Rise of Endless Urban Conflict," *The Guardian*, 30 January 2018. https://www.theguardian.com/cities/2018/jan/30/new-war-rise-endless-urban-conflict-saskia-sassen.
17. Nicholls, Dominic. "Future War Will Result in Destruction 'Beyond Our Comprehension', Says US General," *Telegraph*, 20 August 2018. https://www.telegraph.co.uk/news/2018/08/20/future-war-will-result-destruction-beyond-comprehension-says/.
18. See Spence and Amble (2017).
19. See Krulak (1999).
20. See Reisinger and Golts (2014).
21. Asymmetric Warfare Group, *Modern Urban Operations. Lessons Learned from Urban Operations from 1980 to the Present*, 31 November 2016. https://info.publicintelligence.net/AWG-UrbanWarfare.pdf.
22. See IISS (2017, p. 55).
23. One of the available definitions is the one designed by the British government which I include here as an example: "Stabilisation is one of the approaches used in situations of violent conflict which is designed to protect and promote legitimate political authority, using a combination of integrated civilian and military actions to reduce violence, re-establish security and prepare for longer-term recovery by building an enabling environment for structural stability." See Stabilisation Unit (2014).
24. See Rotmann (2016).
25. See US Army, *Field Manual No. 3-06 (FM 90-10)* (2006).
26. Asymmetric Warfare Group, *Modern Urban Operations*, 2016, p. 24.
27. Fitzgerald, Mary, "Benghazi Economy Flourishes Amid Precarious Security," *Financial Times*, 6 May 2014.
28. See Specker (2008).
29. Ibid.

30. See Barakat and Narang-Suri (2009, p. 106).
31. Ibid., p. 123.
32. See Garcia et al. (2017).
33. See International Institute for Strategic Studies (2018).
34. See ICRC (2015, p. 7).
35. See *The Iraq Inquiry* (2016, pp. 93–94).
36. Asymmetric Warfare Group, *Modern Urban Operations*, 2016, p. 34.
37. International Humanitarian Law Research Initiative, "Conduct of Military Operations in Urban Areas," *Monitoring International Humanitarian Law in Iraq*, May 2004. https://reliefweb.int/sites/reliefweb.int/files/resources/D633328DB1E855D5C1256FAA0034DA79-Military_Urban_Areas_Harvard_May_2004.pdf.
38. Asymmetric Warfare Group, *Modern Urban Operations*, 2016, p. 30.
39. Ibid., p. 22.
40. Khokhar, Tariq, "Chart: Most Refugees Don't Live in Camps," *The Data Blog*, The World Bank, 2016. https://blogs.worldbank.org/opendata/chart-most-refugees-dont-live-camps.
41. UNHCR, "Zaatari Refugee Camp - Factsheet, February 2018," *Reliefweb*, 14 February 2018. https://reliefweb.int/report/jordan/zaatari-refugee-camp-factsheet-february-2018.
42. Jordan INGO Forum, *Syrian Refugees in Jordan. A Protection Overview* 3, 2018, p. 6. https://reliefweb.int/sites/reliefweb.int/files/resources/JIF-ProtectionBrief-2017-Final.pdf.
43. Ibid., p. 4.
44. See IISS (2018, p. 5).
45. See Randall (2014).
46. See IISS (2018, p. 5).
47. FAO, *Protracted Crises and Conflicts*. http://www.fao.org/in-action/kore/protracted-crises-and-conflicts/en/. Accessed July 2018.
48. See Caplan and Hoeffler (2017, pp. 133–134).
49. See Binnendijk and Johnson (2004, p. 90).
50. Fernando Murillo and Eudes Kayumba, *Refugee Dwelling Project in Kigali (Rwanda): Utopia of Reintegration?* 2003. https://www.academia.edu/5787245/Refugee_Dwelling_Project_in_Kigali_Rwanda_Utopia_of_Reintegration. Accessed July 2018.
51. See Hills (2009).
52. Ibid., p. 202.
53. See Davis (2012, p. 11).
54. See Caan (2005).
55. Global Coalition against Daesh, *How Italy Supports the Lobal Coalition Against Daesh*. http://theglobalcoalition.org/en/how-italy-supports-the-global-coalition-against-daesh/. Accessed November 2018.
56. See Comolli (2017).

57. See Berdal (2009).
58. See Dininio and Lawson (2013).
59. See Brown et al. (2011, p. 4).
60. See Alkhalefy et al. (2016, p. 4).
61. Graham Tipple, *The State of Iraq Cities Report: Cities in Transition. Report for Republic of Iraq-Ministry of Municipalities* (Newcastle upon Tyne: Global Urban Research Unit, 2007), unpublished, cited in Alkhalefy, Poorang, and Church, *Resilience Through Urban Management of Reconstruction in Post-conflict Setting*, op. cit.
62. See Cities Alliance (2006).
63. See Barakat (2003).
64. See Davis (2012, p. 7).
65. Ibid.
66. Ibid.
67. See Murtagh (2008, p. 22).
68. Ibid., p. 23.
69. See Cumming et al. (2016).
70. See Murtagh (2008, p. 23).
71. See ILO (2009).
72. See Goodfellow and Smith (2013).
73. Ibid., pp. 16–17.
74. Freedom House, "Rwanda Profile. Freedom in the World 2017." https://freedomhouse.org/report/freedom-world/2017/rwanda. Accessed September 2018.
75. Urban Polarisation, *Beirut. The Urban Environment: Mirror and Mediator of Radicalization?* http://urbanpolarisation.glazprom.org/index.php?option=com_content&view=section&layout=blog&id=9&Itemid=82&lang=en. Accessed November 2018.
76. See IISS (2018).
77. Ibid.

Bibliography

Alkhalefy, Shaymaa, Piroozfar, Poorang, and Church, Andrew. *Resilience Through Urban Management of Reconstruction in Post-conflict Settings: A Focus on Housing Interventions in the Case of Iraq*. Brighton: University of Brighton, 2016.

Barakat, Sultan. "Housing Reconstruction After Conflict and Disaster." Network Paper no. 43, *Humanitarian Practice Network*, 2003.

Barakat, Sultan, and Narang-Suri, Shipra. "War, Cities and Planning: Making a Case for Urban Planning in Conflict-Affected Cities." In Dennis Day, Annette Grindsted, Brigitte Piquard, and David Zammit (eds.), *Cities and Crisis*. Bilbao: Universidad de Deusto, 2009.

10 URBAN WARFARE: STABILISATION OF CITIES   229

Berdal, Mats. *Building Peace After War*. Oxon, UK: Routledge, 2009.

Binnendijk, Hans, and Johnson, Stuart E. (eds.). *Transforming for Stabilization and Reconstruction Operations*. Washington, DC: Center for Technology and National Security Policy National Defense University, 2004.

Brown, Graham, Langer, Arnim, and Stewart, Frances. "A Typology of Post-conflict Environments." Working Paper for Centre for Research on Peace and Development, *University of Leuven*, 2011.

Caan, Christina. "Post-conflict Stabilization and Reconstruction: What Have We Learned from Iraq and Afghanistan." Peace Brief. Washington, DC: USIP, 2005.

Caplan, Richard, and Hoeffler, Anke. "Why Peace Endures: An Analysis of Post-conflict Stabilisation." *European Journal of International Security*, vol. 2, no. 2 (2017): 133–512.

Caplan, Richard, Hoeffler, Anke, and Brinkman, Henk-Jan. An analysis of post-conflict stabilization. *European Journal of International Security*, vol. 2, no. 2 (2017): 133–152.

Cities Alliance. *Guide to City Development Strategies: Improving Urban Performance*. Washington, DC: CA, 2006.

Comolli, Virginia. "Transnational Organized Crime and Conflict." In *Pathways for Peace: Inclusive Approaches to Preventing Violent Conflict*. Washington, DC: World Bank, 2017.

Cumming, Mark, et al. *Growing Up on an Interface Findings and Implications for the Social Needs, Mental Health and Lifetime Opportunities of Belfast Youth*. Belfast: OFMDFM, 2016.

Davis, Diane. *A Toolkit for Urban Resilience in Situations of Chronic Violence*. Report for the United States Agency for International Development (USAID). Cambridge: Center for International Studies, Massachusetts Institute of Technology, 2012.

Desjardins, Jeff. "These Will Be the World's Megacities in 2030." *World Economic Forum*, 28 October 2018.

Dininio, Phyllis, and Stearns Lawson, Brooke. *The Development Response to Drug Trafficking in Africa: A Programming Guide*. Washington, DC: USAID, 2013.

Esser, Daniel. "The City as Arena, Hub and Prey: Patterns of Violence in Kabul and Karachi." *Environment and Urbanization*, vol. 16, no. 2 (2004): 31–38.

Garcia, David, et al. *Thinking Bigger: Area-Based and Urban Planning Approaches to Humanitarian Crises*. London: The International Institute for Environment and Development, 2017.

Gerwehr, Scott, and Glen, Russell W. *The Art of Darkness: Deception and Urban Operations*. Santa Monica, CA: RAND, 2000.

Goodfellow, Tom, and Smith, Alyson. "From Urban Catastrophe to 'Model' City?: Politics, Security and Development in Post-conflict Kigali." *Urban Studies*, vol. 50, no. 15 (2013): 3185–3202.

Hills, Alice. *Policing Post-conflict Cities*. London: Zed Books, 2009.

ICRC. *Urban Services During Protracted Armed Conflict*. Geneva: International Committee of the Red Cross, 2015.

ILO. *United Nations Policy for Post-conflict Employment Creation, Income Generation and Reintegration*. Geneva: United Nations, 2009.

International Institute for Strategic Studies. *Strategic Survey. The Annual Assessment of Geopolitics*. Oxon: Routledge, 2017.

―――. *The IISS Armed Conflict Survey 2018*. Oxon: Routledge, 2018.

Krulak, Charles C. "The Strategic Corporal: Leadership in the Three Block War." *Marine Corps Gazette*, vol. 83, no. 1 (1999): 18–22.

McKee, Musa, et al. "Demographic and Economic Material Factors in the MENA Region." MENARA Working Papers 3, Menara Project, October 2017.

Murtagh, Brendan. "New Spaces and Old in 'Post-conflict' Belfast." Conflict in Cities and the Contested States Working Paper 5, *King's College London*, 2008.

NATO, Analysis and Simulation Panel Study Group SAS-030. "Urban Operations in the Year 2020." RTO Technical Report 71, 2003.

Randall, Edward. "Reconstruction and Fragmentation in Beirut." Conflict in Cities and the Contested State Working Paper 29, *King's College London*, 2014.

Reisinger, Heidi, and Golts, Aleksandr. "Russia's Hybrid Warfare. Waging War Below the Radar of Traditional Collective Defence." NATO Research Paper 105. Rome: Nato Defense College, 2014.

Rotmann, Phillipp. "Towards a Realistic and Responsible Idea of Stabilisation." *Stability: International Journal of Security and Development*, vol. 5, no. 1 (2016): 1–14.

Sampaio, Antonio. "This Is How Megacities Are Being Held Back by Violence." *World Economic Forum*, 30 June 2015.

―――. "The New Frontlines Are in the Slums." *Foreign Policy*, 3 July 2018.

Savage, Kevin, and Muggah, Robert. "Urban Violence and Humanitarian Action: Engaging the Fragile City." *The Journal of Humanitarian Assistance*, 19 January 2012.

Specker, Leontine. "Integrating Socio-Economic Recovery into Post-conflict Stabilization Programmes." CRU Policy Brief 7(23), *Clingendael Conflict Research Unit*, 2008.

Spence, John, and Amble, John. *A Better Approach to Urban Operations: Treat Cities Like Human Bodies*. West Point: Modern War Institute, 2017.

The Report of the Iraq Inquiry: Executive Summary. London: UK Government, 2016.

UK Stabilisation Unit. *The UK Government's Approach to Stabilisation*. UK Government, 2014.

UN DESA. *World Population Prospects: 2015 Revision*. United Nations, 2015.

―――. *World Population Prospects: 2017 Revision*. United Nations, 2017.

UNDP. *Arab Human Development Report 2016. Youth and the Prospects for Human Development in a Changing Reality*. United Nations, 2016.

UN-Habitat. *State of African Cities 2014: Re-imagining Sustainable Urban Transitions*. United Nations, 2015.

———. *The World's Cities in 2016*. United Nations, 2016.

US Army. *Field Manual No. 3-06 (FM 90-10)*. *Urban Operations*. Washington, DC: Department of the Army, 2006.

CHAPTER 11

Redrawing the Lines in the Sand? Quests for Decentralisation, Regional Autonomy and Independence Among Syrian Kurds and South Yemeni Separatists

Leo Kwarten

INTRODUCTION

In August 2014, at the height of its power, Daesh was keen to show to the world that the borders that have kept the Middle Eastern countries divided were sacred no longer. As a bulldozer brought down the fence that had once been the border between Syria and Iraq but was now a mere relic in the recently established 'Caliphate', a Daesh fighter proudly proclaimed on video: 'We don't believe in the Sykes-Picot Agreement'.[1] Of course, he was referring to the 1916 agreement between Great Britain and France which carved the Ottoman Empire up into British and French spheres of influence. Based on their imperial interests at the time, the 'lines in the sand' drawn by Sykes-Picot became the blueprint for the current borders in the Levant. Despite routinely being criticised by Islamists, minorities and

---

L. Kwarten (✉)
Clingendael Institute, The Hague, The Netherlands

© The Author(s) 2020
V. Gervais and S. van Genugten (eds.), *Stabilising the Contemporary Middle East and North Africa*, Middle East Today,
https://doi.org/10.1007/978-3-030-25229-8_11

233

Arab nationalists alike as the main cause of many present-day evils in the Middle East, such as religious division and incompetency to unanimously engage regional crises, the 'lines in the sand' have never been redrawn. On the contrary, when challenged, Middle Eastern countries are able to act with unusual unanimity to defend these borders as was the case with Iraq's annexation of Kuwait in 1990. At the time, in a highly unconventional coalition, soldiers from the Arab Gulf States, Syria and Egypt among other states, fought shoulder by shoulder with US forces to liberate Kuwait from Saddam Hussein's army. A quarter of a century later, Daesh could never have been dismantled—and Sykes-Picot 'restored' if you like—if there had not been a shared interest to do so by unusual bedfellows such as the US, Russia, Iran, Syria, Iraq and local Kurdish fighters in both Syria and Iraq.

Nevertheless, borders in the Middle East are increasingly being challenged today by local actors striving for decentralisation of state powers, far-reaching autonomy or independence. The Arab revolts that flooded the Middle East in 2011 have destabilised political orders once considered unshakable. Some of the old regimes, like in Libya, crumbled under mounting popular pressure and post-Qaddafi elite infighting. This effectively split the country into several regions with self-styled governments and militia-based armies. This not only upset the existing political, economic and social balance that the former autocratic regime had so meticulously constructed in order to remain on top, but it also awakened dormant desires in hitherto neglected regions for a radical re-division of power.

Despite the fact that the warring parties in Libya in a UN-led initiative agreed to the formation of a Government of National Accord (GNA), which was installed in Tripoli in March 2016, this did not prevent Libya from continuing being a playground for centrifugal forces. Some of them are ethnic minorities, such as the Amazigh (Berbers), Tubu and Tuareg who seek to reclaim their language, culture or sometimes even their civilian rights, for which there was no place in Qaddafi's highly centralised and oppressive state structure. Other forces, such as the Barqa movement in Cyrenaica, strive to introduce a federal system in Libya with its own parliament, police force and courts while foreign policy and the armed forces would remain with the central government. Other regimes, like Assad's in Syria, desperately fought back and countered the opposition by the use of excessive force. In the process, social cohesion disintegrated as religious and ethnic groups were played off against each other by the regime in an attempt to survive. This resulted in civil strife and foreign intervention. In the turmoil, opportunities unexpectedly arose for regions and political actors inside Syria that had long been marginalised or oppressed by the central state. Suddenly, they gained importance because of the weakening of state authority, shifting power balances, support by foreign powers yearning to buy influence or simply because the opportunity presented itself. In doing so, they threw a direct challenge to concepts of stabilisation and centralisation of state power. These developments pose formidable challenges for both international and regional players. In the cases of Libya, Syria and Yemen, the UN has appointed special envoys tasked with bringing stability by consulting the warring parties and starting up a peace process. Unfortunately, these efforts have mostly failed, for various reasons. In Libya, an internationally recognised unity government has indeed been installed but it turned out to be incapable of establishing its authority on the ground. In Syria, UN-sponsored peace negotiations got nowhere as the opposition is hopelessly divided while the regime preferred to rely on foreign backers Russia and Iran to attain a military victory. In Yemen, the civil war is caught up in the wider regional struggle between Saudi Arabia, the UAE and Iran. With regional powers being deeply involved, centrifugal forces being plentiful and interests being divergent, international efforts to bring stability are thrown back and forth between wish and reality. Through reconciliation talks, international efforts focus on strengthening state authority, but on the ground progressive decentralisation is a reality not to be ignored.

The so-called Arab spring and its chaotic aftermath have unavoidably triggered a debate on whether the current borders in the Middle East are still tenable now that civil wars in Syria, Iraq, Yemen and Libya seem to have irreparably damaged relations between minorities, tribes and regions which not so long ago lived relatively peacefully together. For example, Barak Mendelsohn argued in *Foreign Affairs* in November 2015—Daesh still ruled vast territories in Syria and Iraq at the time—that 'attachment to the artificial Sykes-Picot borders no longer makes sense'. He advocated an independent Sunni state that would link Sunni-dominated territories on both sides of the border.[2] In hindsight, Mendelsohn badly miscalculated international and regional resolve to fight any party that wants to redraw the borders of the Middle East. Other observers have been more reflective. For example, Sholto Byrnes criticised Mendelsohn's argument at the time for implying 'that states can only be stable and have a sense of internal coherence if they are based on a single ethnicity or culture'.[3] Indeed, if this were the criterion for a successful state, most states in the world would not be able to function properly. The fact is that minorities in the Middle East have lived peacefully together for centuries. Moreover, the ethnic or religious dismemberment of multicultural states—Byrnes mentions the divided Bosnia that is the result of the Dayton Peace Accords in 1995—is not necessarily a success story either. In Bosnia, federalism was imposed by outside forces in an ultimate effort to end the conflict. But Dayton saddled the former Yugoslav republic with a complicated government system consisting of two entities and a central government in an effort to appease all warring parties, meaning Serbs, Croats and Bosniaks. It was an ugly framework, a 'construction of necessity',[4] although it turned out to be highly successful in putting an end to the fighting and endorsing stability in the Balkans as a whole. On the other hand, Dayton did not bring reconciliation in the long-term. The root causes of the conflict were not addressed. A costly international stabilisation mission remains necessary to oversee forced separation and there is no guarantee that tensions will not flare up again as soon as the mission withdraws.

A similar situation was created in Iraq where Kurdish autonomy was imposed on the Iraqi state by outside forces. In 1991, the US, Britain and France established a no-fly zone in Northern Iraq to protect the Iraqi Kurds from persecution by the Iraqi regime, thereby creating de facto Kurdish autonomy. In 2005, two years after the US invasion of Iraq, Kurdish regional government was legalised in the new Iraqi constitution. However, despite Kurdish autonomy being embedded in a legal framework, territorial and financial disputes between Baghdad and Erbil re-emerge time and again, as are Kurdish threats to totally dissociate Iraqi Kurdistan from the Iraqi state, indicating that long-term stability has not been attained if that ever will be the case.

Hence, in the context of international stabilisation efforts, one should have a hard look at the attempts of some political groups in the Middle East to make use of the civil wars in their country to redraw the borders or rewrite the constitution in a way that decentralises the state's power or grants them autonomy. In this chapter, two cases will be examined: Syrian Kurdistan and South Yemen. In Syria, like in Iraq, the Kurds were admittedly threatened by the rise of Daesh in 2014. However, it also presented them with a golden opportunity to prove themselves to the US and Europe as indispensable allies in the global fight against terrorism by participating in the Global Coalition against Daesh. Building on international appreciation of their courageous role in the fight against the jihadists, while smartly adjusting their narrative to fit with those international actors that work for stabilisation in the Middle East, they articulated their political aspirations by unilaterally seeking regional autonomy. However, Kurdish autonomy in Syria is vehemently contested by both the central state and virtually all powers in the region.

In Yemen, the capture by the Iranian-backed Houthi rebels of the capital Sanaa in 2015 immensely bolstered the separatist movement in the south. Since South Yemeni separatists lost their war of independence in 1994, southern resentment against what they perceive as domination by the central government never ceased. Originally civilian but growing more militant as the civil war drew close, the separatists gained importance after they successfully fought off the Houthi onslaught on Aden in 2015. Their success on the battlefield prevented Yemen from being completely drawn into Iran's sphere of influence. Militarily and financially supported by the Arab coalition that intervened in March 2015, the separatists have been able to recapture large swathes of what used to be South Yemen while preparing for a separate administrative infrastructure. Unlike the Syrian Kurds, Yemeni separatists may have tacit regional support for their political ambitions. However, in the UN-led peace negotiations to stabilise Yemen the separatists have been largely marginalised. This has contributed to their efforts to pursue a 'go-it-alone' strategy.

This chapter examines the circumstances in which Syrian Kurds and Yemeni separatists were encouraged to accelerate their struggle for regional autonomy or independence. Taking local factors, regional involvement and international reactions into account, what is the impact of these decentralisation efforts on international stabilisation efforts in the region which often tend to be largely focused on state-level negotiations? Are these decentralising forces likely to subdue if a 'national' solution is found? And if not, what then?

SYRIAN KURDISTAN: SOUTH OF THE RAILWAY LINE

Currently numbering around 40 million, the Kurds are generally considered to be the main victims of Sykes-Picot. After the defeat of the Ottoman Empire during the First World War, their ancestral grounds became divided between Turkey, Iran, Iraq and Syria. At the Conference of San Remo, in April 1920, the victorious allied powers determined the League of Nations mandates for the administration of the former Ottoman vilayets. The French had been allotted 'Syria', although its boundaries were still subject to negotiations. In the Treaty of Sèvres, which was concluded in August 1920, the border between French Syria and the Ottoman Empire was put much further north than it is today. In this area, Sèvres provided for an autonomous territory for the Kurds under French patronage. It is often referred to by Kurdish nationalists as the Kurdish state they claim to have had a right to from the start. As a matter of fact, it was a truncated Kurdistan, located in today's Turkey and leaving out the areas of Kurdish settlement in what we now know as Iran, Iraq and Syria. However, it was the best the Kurds would ever get from Sykes-Picot. Unfortunately, the idea was short-lived. Under pressure from the Turkish war of independence, led by Kemal Atatürk, the allied powers were soon forced to return to the negotiating table. In 1923, at the Conference of Lausanne, the Syrian—Turkish border was redrawn further south following the Berlin–Baghdad railway line. It left Arabic-speaking communities on the Turkish side and Kurdish-speaking communities on the Syrian side. South of the railway, Syrian Kurdistan was born as 'a waste product of the colonial division of the Middle East', as the German cultural anthropologist Thomas Schmidinger elegantly described it.[5]

The idea of Kurdish political autonomy developed much slower in Syria than in Iraq, Iran and Turkey. It was partly a matter of numbers: the Kurds in Syria make up a minority of only 10%, much less than in neighbouring countries.[6] At the time, political autonomy was an idea mainly entertained by intellectuals but hardly shared by the population at large. The newly created state of Syria was dominated by Sunni Arabs, whereas the distant north was a patchwork of Kurds, Arabs, Christian denominations, Turkmen and Chechens who were connected through complex structures to local aghas and sheikhs. They traditionally harboured a dislike of the central state and resisted its attempts to curtail the *local* autonomy they had enjoyed for centuries. However, *political* autonomy remained an alien concept to them. The Syrian Kurds became politicised as the result of a mix of domestic and regional factors. In the years following independence in 1946, Syrian political life became increasingly dominated by Arab nationalism. This translated into repression of non-Arab minorities, especially the Kurds. In 1958, when Syria entered an ill-fated union with the Egypt of Gamal Abdel Nasser, the great leader of pan-Arabism, this was accompanied by a crackdown on Kurdish political activists. Matters became even worse after the coup by the ultra-nationalistic Baath party in 1963. For Kurds, it was safest to be considered as Arabs by assimilating themselves culturally and linguistically, unless they wished to be seen as a danger to Syrian national integrity.[7] The 'Syrian Republic' became the 'Syrian Arab Republic'. Arabisation policies dictated that education was in Arabic only. The use of the Kurdish language and Kurdish cultural manifestations were discouraged. Hafez Al-Assad, who seized power in 1970, slightly shifted this rigid approach by introducing a policy of co-optation. Kurds were granted positions in the government and religious establishment provided they remained on the proper side of the invisible red line: renounce your Kurdish identity and any reverence to 'Kurdistan'.

Ironically, it was Assad who unintentionally provoked Kurdish nationalism in Syria when he started to militarily support the Kurdistan Workers' Party (PKK) in Turkey. In 1978, the PKK was founded by Abdullah Öcalan. Mixing leftist ideologies with Kurdish nationalism, it struggled to establish an independent Kurdish state in Turkey. For Assad, always the Machiavellian, it was simply a matter of geopolitics. By supporting the PKK, he could put pressure on Turkey at a time it threatened to reduce the supply of water to Syria by building a series of dams in the Euphrates and the Tigris. In exchange for allowing Öcalan to direct the Kurdish struggle in Turkey from Damascus, the PKK promised to refrain from political activity among the Kurds in Syria itself. However, due to 20 years of PKK presence in Syria and the Kurdish struggle raging just north of the railway line, the regime could not prevent the emergence of a new political awareness among its own Kurds. The Syrian Kurds were similarly affected by developments in neighbouring Iraq. In April 1991, the US, France and Britain established a no-fly zone in Northern Iraq to protect the Iraqi Kurds from persecution by the Iraqi regime. By doing so, they created de facto Kurdish autonomy within the Iraqi state. Only in 1998, under military pressure from Turkey, did Assad decide to ditch the PKK. Öcalan was expelled from Syria and has been incarcerated in Turkey since. Repression of Kurdish activists in Syria resumed and even accelerated after current President Bashar Al-Assad succeeded his father in 2000. However, even then most of them refrained from using violence and hardly anyone demanded autonomy.

In 2003, a Syrian affiliate of the PKK was founded, the Democratic Union Party (PYD).[8] It developed into becoming the most powerful political party in Syria's Kurdish areas today. Traditionally, the Kurdish political landscape is scattered into many parties. Some parties, like the Kurdistan Democratic Party of Syria (PDKS) which has strong links with Iraq, have split over relations with mutually competing Iraqi Kurdish parties. Other splits were cleverly staged by Syrian intelligence. Schmidinger concludes that political or ideological differences cannot explain this diversity though. Mostly, it had to do with personal rivalries and the extent to which one was co-opted by the regime.[9] So when the Syrian revolution started in 2011, the Kurdish parties were divided, weakly organised and poorly prepared.

KURDISH FEDERALISM AND MILITARY COOPERATION WITH THE US

Although there were demonstrations against the regime by grass-roots organisations in the Kurdish-dominated areas like elsewhere in Syria, the prevailing mood among the Kurdish political parties was to wait and see. As was to be expected, they failed to unite on one common platform. Only one party, the Kurdish Future Movement, joined the Syrian National Council (SNC), the umbrella organisation of the Syrian opposition based in Istanbul which was largely supported by the US, the EU and Turkey. Sixteen other parties, mainly stemming from the PDKS, were united in the Kurdish National Council (KNC). It was closely aligned with President Masoud Barzani of the Kurdish Regional Government of Iraq. From the start, relations between the KNC and the SNC were tense. The former sought the political decentralisation of Syria, meaning formal autonomy, but the latter only wanted to discuss 'administrative decentralisation'.[10] It fed suspicions within the KNC with regard to Turkey, which was close to Barzani at the time, of pressuring the Syrian opposition not to give into demands for Kurdish autonomy. Obviously, Turkey rejects the idea of Kurdish autonomy in Syria. It fears the effect this may have on the aspirations of its own Kurdish citizens. Similarly, Turkey's ruling AK-party is close to the Syrian Muslim Brotherhood which dominated the SNC and opposes federalism in Syria as well.[11] Although the KNC later joined the Syrian National Coalition, this controversy re-emerged again and again.

The PYD refused to join the KNC. It took a most controversial decision by colluding with the Syrian regime. Although the specifics of the secret talks that presumably took place between the PYD and regime officials are unknown, the fact is that in July 2012 regime forces suddenly withdrew from most parts of Al-Jezira, Kobane and Efrin leaving the emerging power vacuum to be filled by the PYD militias, the People's Protection Units (YPG). By doing so, the PYD was able to firmly establish its political, security and administrative presence, that is, de facto autonomy. Although Assad must have withdrawn from the remote areas in order to unleash the bulk of his army on the rebels in Syria's heartland, it most certainly was a temporary decision and by no means recognition of Kurdish autonomy. The PYD's collusion with the Syrian regime stirred bad blood with the Syrian opposition. It does not recognise the PYD administration which it considers as a step towards separatism. They refuse to accept the Kurds as a separate people or nation but consider them as Syrian citizens.[12] When the PYD unilaterally announced the Democratic Federation of Northern Syria on 17 March 2016, commonly known as 'Rojava', it was rejected by the regime, opposition and international community alike. It is not even accepted by the KNC, which strives for autonomy as well but maintains that a federalist system should be established following discussions with the Syrian Arab opposition. The KNC does not participate in the federal administration and accuses the PYD of authoritarianism. Acting unilaterally and ignoring the objections of not only the Syrian opposition but also the majority of the other Kurdish parties, let alone of the Syrian regime and Turkey, one may wonder if the PYD project might ever have stood a chance of succeeding for long.[13] However, similar to the case of the separatists in Southern Yemen, the dynamics of the civil war in Syria inflated the importance of the PYD. The Yemeni separatists were instrumental in averting the Houthi onslaught and were able to augment their political footprint in the process, the same was true for the YPG-militias in the fight against Daesh. They simply happened to be the only boots on the ground available for the US-led coalition.

For the time being, the US and its partners chose to ignore the political implications of this mutually beneficial cooperation. The short-term objective of defeating Daesh by arming, training and politically bolstering a decentralising power such as the PYD/YPG completely overruled efforts by UN Special Envoy Staffan de Mistura to stabilise the situation in Syria by dragging the Assad regime and the opposition to the negotiating table in Geneva in order to find a solution based on 'the territorial integrity, unity and the sovereignty' of the Syrian state.[14] Little helpful was that the UN's approach in Syria focused on negotiations between the regime and the official Syrian opposition only, while disregarding the political demands of the Syrian Kurds. The same mistake was made in Yemen where UN-led negotiations between the legitimate government and the Houthi rebels left the southern separatists out in the cold. This encouraged both Syrian Kurds and Yemeni separatists to pursue a 'go-it-alone' policy seeking the help of foreign backers, turning their back on the central state and thereby frustrating international stabilisation efforts. Turkey, a member of NATO, vehemently opposed US military assistance to a PKK affiliate-based along its border. To placate the Turkish government, the US needed to apply some political cosmetics.[15] Hence, an entity named the 'Syrian Democratic Forces (SDF)' was founded in October 2015 as an ethnically and religiously multifaceted umbrella of forces fighting Daesh. The SDF is made up of Assyrian, Turkmen, Armenian, Circassian, Chechen and Arab militias including factions of the Free Syrian Army (FSA), although its main body consists of the Kurdish YPG and the Women's Protection Units (YPJ). As long as the fight against Daesh continued, the Turks reluctantly accepted this arrangement, although President Erdoğan kept referring to the YPG as 'terrorists' and put them on a par with the so-called Islamic State. As Turkey saw it, US efforts in Northern Syria amounted to the unravelling of the Sykes-Picot borders. This would endanger the integrity of the Turkish state itself as it would encourage the PKK in its struggle for Kurdish self-determination.

Military cooperation with the US highly influenced the way 'Rojava' took shape. After the collapse of the 'Caliphate' in the course of 2017, in which the SDF played a decisive role, the PYD effectively controlled 20% of Syrian territory. That included the oil and gas fields near the city of Deir Ezzor, but also huge areas with a majority of Arabs who were wary of Kurdish dominance. Securing the area north of the Euphrates, in compliance with the coalition's demands, was at the expense of conquering the corridor connecting the autonomous regions of Kobane and Efrin. Arrangements between the US and Russia, in which the latter accepted the presence of US troops northeast of the Euphrates and the former Russia's dominance in the rest of Syria, led to Russian President Putin giving tacit approval to Erdoğan to invade Efrin in January 2018 and effectively killing Kurdish autonomy there.

Assad's Resurrection and the Future of Federalism

Until 2015, Assad's position looked increasingly untenable. The common view was that whatever the outcome of the civil war in Syria, it would not be a return to the old days of authoritarian rule. However, since Russia and Iran militarily intervened on Assad's side, the ugly face of his regime has resurfaced in a whole string of former opposition strongholds, from Aleppo via Ghouta to Deraa. Most of the areas were evacuated through 'reconciliation' agreements (*musalaha*), a euphemism for negotiated surrender. The regime's only concession to the rebels and their families being trapped in their surrounded neighbourhoods was giving them the choice between being bussed to rebel-held areas in the north or accepting 'shelter' by the government in camps where they would go through an uncertain process of security clearance.[16] Local reconciliation agreements have been given priority over serious negotiations on the future of their country between all parties involved in Syria. Since 2014, peace talks have been taking place between the regime and the opposition in Geneva, under the auspices of the UN, and in Astana/Sochi, under the auspices of Russia, Turkey and Iran. However, none of them have yielded any results in terms of a re-division of power. Only once, the issue of federalism was formally brought up. At the peace talks in Astana, in January 2017, the Russians unexpectedly floated the idea of federalism when they circulated a draft for a new Syrian constitution among the attendees. In their proposal, the Russians suggested that the word 'Arab' be deleted from the country's official name (Syrian Arab Republic). It specifically mentioned the 'Kurdish cultural self-ruling systems' which would use the Arabic and Kurdish languages equally. It proposed Syria's decentralisation into a federation of administrative regions. A bicameral legislature would be introduced, meaning an elected National Assembly and an Assembly of Territories. To preserve the territorial integrity of Syria, state borders could be modified by a general referendum only. All in all, it looked like something the Syrian Kurds could live with.[17] The Russian initiative took the regime and the rest of the international community by surprise. An advisor to President Assad commented that the regime is against any kind of federalism: 'The Russian proposal does not work in Syria. It puts a bomb under every article in our current constitution (…). You cannot take Arabism out of our constitution. It is our culture, our identity, not just for Arab Syrians but for all Syrians'.[18] Eventually, the regime did not seem to take the Russian proposal very seriously. It was interpreted as a way for the Russians to court the Syrian Kurds, who are the US' closest ally, while at the same time pressuring Turkey by openly flirting with the idea of federalism.[19] Even if the Russian initiative was genuine, then it was ill-prepared. Not even Russia's Iranian and Turkish partners in Astana, let alone the UN knew about it, so it attributed nothing to international efforts to bring stability to Syria.

The above illustrates that after the demise of Daesh, Syria has become even more a boxing ring for regional and international actors and their proxies. The future of Syria as a state, what its constitution should look like and how the grievances of the Syrian opposition will be addressed—all this has been made subordinate to the interests of these states. In this respect, not much has changed since Sykes-Picot a hundred years ago. It does not bode well for the prospect of Kurdish autonomy, especially because the common denominator of virtually all players in Syria is opposition to Kurdish autonomy because it would upset the regional balance. This balance is based on keeping the current borders as they are, promoting a strong central state that asserts its authority throughout its territory and disencouraging autonomy for minorities and regions as they would be vulnerable to exploitation by foreign powers and incite like-minded regions and minorities across the border laying the seed for future conflicts.

By openly seeking autonomy, the Syrian Kurds have embarked on a highly uncertain project. Any illusion they may have had about the US supporting Kurdish political ambitions was dealt a blow on 19 December 2018 when President Trump suddenly announced the withdrawal of the American troops from Syria. Feeling abandoned and facing the formidable Turkish army which stood ready to invade Syria and eradicate Kurdish autonomy, the architects of 'Rojava' now only had Assad to turn to. That was bad prospect indeed.

Unless the PYD could hammer out a deal with the Assad regime in which the Kurdish regions would be granted certain rights (although they will remain a far cry from autonomy), Assad would remain resolved to restore full authority over the entire Syrian territory by all means. With his adversaries defeated and no alternative to his leadership around, Assad currently represents the only option for having a strong central state in Damascus. This reality has by now hit home with all stability seeking powers both within the Middle East and outside. Another challenge is the local administration by the PYD. Although the para-state structures set up by the autonomy government have created a sense of normality,[20] they are not politically comprehensible. Indeed, non-Kurdish minorities are represented at the highest levels but that is not the case for Kurdish parties opposing the PYD, for example, the KNC. The already existing tensions between rival Kurdish parties could be further exploited by several regional players, such as Turkey, Syria and Iran, who are set on destroying Kurdish autonomy.

SOUTH YEMEN: AN EXAMPLE OF FAILED INTEGRATION

On 22 May 1990, the leaders of the Yemen Arab Republic and the People's Democratic Republic of Yemen commonly referred to as North Yemen and South Yemen signed a unification agreement. At the time, the agreement had the support of most citizens in both North Yemen and South Yemen, although it had been hastily drafted, poorly thought out and it was, as one observer described, 'shorter than a marriage contract'.[21] On both sides, opportunistic reasons prevailed. North Yemen had been ruled by President Ali Abdullah Saleh since 1978 along populist and Arab nationalist lines while exploiting tribal alliances to consolidate power in an extremely personal way. With a larger population, 12 million at the time against 2.6 million in the South, it was the stronger partner in the marriage who was to benefit most from the oil reserves that had recently been discovered across the ill-defined and contested borders between the two states. South Yemen, on the other hand, had been the Arab world's first and last truly Communist state. While tribalism, conservatism and Islamic law dominated in the north, the south had been ruled along secular lines while heavily relying on Soviet support. However, at the same time, the comrades in the political bureau tacitly still relied on their tribal power bases. This became apparent when in 1986 fierce infighting erupted within the ranks of the ruling Yemen Socialist Party (YSP) triggering a brief but bloody civil war which severely weakened the party. There is no doubt that these events, in addition to the collapse of the Soviet Union and the economic ruin that followed, pushed southern leaders towards unification with North Yemen. However, unification would not resolve their internal differences.[22]

The newly created Republic of Yemen did not bring the benefits southern leaders had been hoping for. In 1993, Ali Salim Al-Beidh, the former leader of South Yemen who had moved to Sanaa to become vice-president under Saleh, withdrew to Aden protesting what he perceived as the economic marginalisation of the south. He soon withdrew his support for the unified state. In 1994, war broke out. Saleh's army helped by tribal militias from the north and supporters of rival southern leaders reunited Yemen by force. The southern military collapsed and the secessionists fled into exile, despite being financially and politically supported by most members of the GCC, including Saudi Arabia and the UAE. These states were wary of a united Yemen under Saleh who only recently had supported Iraq's invasion of Kuwait.[23] However, for the south their support was too little too late. After the war, the government in Sanaa proceeded with the total integration of North and South Yemen. Although the unification agreement of 1990 had stipulated that free and fair elections be held, President Saleh was not the kind of leader who genuinely believed in democracy as a power-sharing instrument. The southern leaders who signed the deal in 1990 had badly miscalculated Saleh's intentions. The YSP, once the uncontested ruling party in South Yemen, was marginalised after the 1993 elections now holding only 56 seats in the 301-seat unified Yemeni parliament. In the unification process, the south, being the minor partner, was simply swallowed up by the north. In hindsight, it is fair to say that the 'democratic approach' to integrate the two Yemens, while keeping the central government in Sanaa and leaving existing state institutions mostly intact, stimulated southern separatism even before union was realised.

After the secession attempt, the south was being treated by Saleh as a potentially rebellious area whose inhabitants were not to be trusted. It became a regional backwater in the united Republic of Yemen that was both neglected and exploited. It would only be a matter of time for a political organisation to emerge and challenge the political situation. In 2007, Al-Hirak Al-Janubi (the Southern Movement) was established as a political organisation to protest discrimination of southerners in the police, army and government apparatus and general economic neglect. In the security field, Saleh had dismantled the security structure of former South Yemen replacing it with his own people from the north.[24] Al-Hirak was, and still is, an umbrella movement containing leftist, secular, tribal, conservative and even salafist elements. The government's approach to its mostly peaceful demonstrations was heavy-handed which geared southern demands swiftly towards secession and a return to the former independent state of South Yemen. With regard to the international response, one may see a parallel between the security situation in Yemen in the 1990s and that in Iraq and Afghanistan a decade later. Donor countries, notably the US, tend to prioritise their own immediate security concerns over the objective of long-term stability. In the case of Yemen, the US priority number one was combatting Al-Qaeda (AQAP). As long as Saleh cooperated, Washington would turn a blind eye to the fact that Yemen's president considered the power institutions of the unity state as his personal domain thereby heavily relying on the northern tribes loyal to him.

Interviews with leaders from Al-Hirak reveal a deeply rooted mistrust of northern politicians. They not only point to former President Saleh who expropriated large plots of privately owned land in the south to reward his political cronies, but also to the Islamist Al-Islah party which had sided with Saleh during the 1994 war. Al-Islah is generally considered as being responsible for the subsequent Islamisation of southern society despite it being thoroughly secularised by more than 150 years of British and Communist rule. Al-Hirak leaders perceive a wide cultural gap with the north. One of them disdainfully remarked: 'It is telling that the north introduced two new laws immediately after they captured Aden in 1994. They lifted the ban on chewing qat. And it became legal to marry more than one wife'.[25]

FOREIGN INTERVENTION AS OPPORTUNITY TO REGAIN INDEPENDENCE

When President Saleh was forced out of power in 2012 as the result of large-scale street protests and mediation by the GCC, this did not translate into tangible results for the southern separatists. Saleh's successor, Vice-president Abd Rabbu Mansour Hadi, was admittedly a southerner from Abyan province. However, he was considered a 'traitor' by many of the separatists after he had sided with Saleh in the 1994 war. Although Hadi is frequently referred to as weak, corrupt and totally dependent on Saudi support, he remains a formidable adversary to those dreaming of an independent South Yemen. After all, Hadi came to power legitimately as the president of a united Yemen and is recognised as such by the international community. This is emphasised in several UN Security Council resolutions that were adopted since 2011 starting with endorsing the GCC-initiative that paved the way for Hadi's election in February 2012[26] and later on condemning the way the Houthis dissolved parliament and forced Hadi from power in January 2015.[27] For the same reason, Hadi has the support of powerful defenders of Yemeni unification like Al-Islah and the tribal confederations loyal to General Ali Mohsen Al-Ahmar.[28]

The GCC-plan of 2011 that saw the departure of Saleh also provided for a National Dialogue Conference (NDC) to prepare for political transition in Yemen. Reconciliation was one of the tools for realising stability in Yemen mentioned in the GCC-initiative and endorsed by the UN Security Council. Other tools mentioned in UNSC-resolution 2051[29] are restructuring of security and armed forces, supporting transitional justice and calls on the international community to face the humanitarian and economic challenges in Yemen. The conference was held in 2013 in Sanaa, under the auspices of Hadi and the UN special envoy to Yemen, Jamal Benomar. Although it had a working group on the 'southern issue', the NDC was boycotted by most southern leaders from the start. One of them described the conference as a 'smokescreen pulled up by Saudi Arabia to let the traditional northern parties supported by Riyadh, consolidate their power over the whole of Yemen'.[30] The final document called for a fifty-fifty representation of northerners and southerners in the parliament and the shura council, but was unable to come up with plans for a new political system that would appease the south. The NDC members recommended the transformation of Yemen into a six regions federal state, to be included in the new constitution. The former South Yemen was to be divided into two regions, Hadhramaut and Aden. However, the boundaries between the regions were not clearly demarcated nor was the problem of the management of natural resources and the allocation of their revenues settled.[31] The federal system as discussed by the NDC, and later adopted by a presidential panel headed by President Hadi, was rejected by Al-Hirak. It was also rejected by the Houthi rebels who in 2014 captured Sanaa and ousted Hadi. This makes the federal system as suggested by the NDC a bone of contention rather than a comfortable basis for a negotiated solution to the war in Yemen, although others cling to some form of federalism as the only solution for Yemen.[32] As a Yemeni diplomat currently serving the Hadi government privately admitted: 'A new national dialogue is necessary to decide on a federation, a co-federation of north and south or even two independent states'.[33]

For Al-Hirak, the Saudi Arabian-led intervention in the Yemen civil war in March 2015 was like a gift from heaven. In March 2015, Houthi militias and Yemen Army units loyal to Saleh, who after his removal from power had sided with his former Houthi enemies, entered Aden. In response, a military intervention was launched by Saudi Arabia, the UAE and seven other countries in order to stop Yemen from totally falling under the control of the Houthis. For Saudi Arabia and the UAE, the Iranian-backed Houthi's were completely unacceptable as the masters of both north and south Yemen. There was this perception of becoming surrounded by the Iranians who, after having 'occupied' Baghdad, Damascus and Beirut, now 'gained a foothold' on the Arab peninsula. In the process, supporters of Al-Hirak were hastily armed by the coalition in an effort to defend Aden, 'their capital', from the Houthi-Saleh onslaught, and they were successful. However, the question arises if the boosting of the southern separatists does bode well for the survival of Yemen as a unified state. There is a parallel to be drawn with US support for the Syrian Kurds in which the short-term objective of defeating Daesh, or in Yemen's case stopping the perceived 'Iranian advance', jeopardises the long-term international objective of stabilising the situation in the state as a whole. Whereas the Syrian Kurds coordinated their military strategy with the regime in Damascus to a certain extent, the same cannot be said of Yemen's southern separatists. On several occasions, they actually fought against the legitimate government of Hadi in Aden and they did everything to undermine his authority, at least in the south.

For years, southern separatism had been a sideshow in Yemen's multiple conflicts. Since 2004, both the Sanaa government and Saudi Arabia as the traditional power broker in Yemen had been completely occupied by the Houthi insurgency in the north. This was followed by the revolution of 2011, Saleh's departure and the National Dialogue which had brought southern separatists next to nothing. Then in 2015, they were suddenly propelled into being a major force on the ground for the coalition to save Yemen from being absorbed into Iran's orbit. Ironically, some leaders of Al-Hirak, like Al-Beidh, had just ended their flirtation with the Islamic Republic after they felt that the Iranians had done nothing to prevent the Houthis from attacking the south. Moreover, the southerners were unwilling to snub the Saudis. At the same time, the separatists are uncomfortable with Saudi Arabia and especially some of its allies in Yemen, like the Hadi government and Al-Islah. In 2015, they suddenly found themselves in the same trench with forces that wrested southern independence from them in 1994. Almost by nature, they are drawn to the other major coalition partner, the UAE, which is a relatively new kid on the block in Yemen but one with distinctly different strategic objectives than its Saudi partner. One of them is reducing the influence of political Islam, especially the Muslim Brotherhood, to the extent that the Emiratis cannot stomach Al-Islah as allies. It sits more comfortable with Al-Hirak, which is a hodgepodge of secular and conservative elements, although it has salafists within its ranks as well. Furthermore, the UAE concentrates its military activities in Yemen in the provinces bordering the Gulf of Aden, Bab Al-Mandab and the Red Sea. It has been argued that it wants to secure these waterways as a guarantee for the safe passage of its oil tankers to export markets. The current narrative in the UAE is that 'Bab Al-Mandab is more important to us than the Strait of Hormuz, and we do not accept that the Muslim Brotherhood or Iran control these waterways'.[34] In this respect, it should be noted that the UAE has built a string of ports it has access to in Somalia and Eritrea.[35] On a national level, this sits well with the interests of many separatists who look forward to the prospect of Emirati protection and investment in the ports of Aden and Mukalla. However, others fear Emirati meddling in southern affairs.[36] On an international level, these developments are followed with interest as one of the most important reasons for the international community to bring stability to Yemen is to secure these waterways through which 15% of the international trade passes. Relatively new players as the Saudi Arabia, UAE, Turkey and Egypt may bring in a new perspective in a domain in which security is usually guaranteed by non-Arab actors such as the US, France, China and Japan. That makes it all the more important that national, regional and international interests are to be taken into account when trying to stabilise Yemen.

How Feasible Is Southern Independence?

When the coalition started to arm southern separatist forces in 2015, this was done out of necessity to stop the Houthi advance. Subsequently, these forces were useful in terms of bringing stability when they started to police recaptured areas in the south and to defend them against attacks by Al-Qaeda. Seen from the separatist perspective, one may obviously consider them as the nucleus of the power institutions needed for the establishment of a viable independent southern state in the future. This may be wishful thinking, but their embolstered presence on the ground is a reality that has to be taken into account by any international task force promoting stability in Yemen. The longer the war in Yemen lasts, the more visible the political impact of these militias becomes. On 11 May 2017, the secessionist Southern Transitional Council (STC) was formed by a majority of Al-Hirak factions. In its 'Historic Aden Declaration' of 4 May 2017, the STC says that it strives for 'realising the aspirations of the people of the south to be the masters over their territory and to build their national, federal, democratic and free state'.[37] The STC stems from a conflict between the separatists and the Hadi government over appointments and the latter's inclination towards Al-Islah. During street battles with Hadi's forces in January 2018, the STC gained control over virtually the entirety of Aden. In doing so, they seriously undermined the authority of the legitimate government.

Seen from the perspective of international stabilisation efforts, one may consider the southern separatist movement as a potential 'party spoiler'. Admittedly, it is a force that was indispensable for stopping the Houthi advance on Aden in 2015, but by boosting separatist forces in the process the Arab coalition might have laid a bomb under the future of Yemen as a unified state. Again a parallel can be drawn with US support for Syrian Kurdish separatists in the fight against Daesh. It obviously stabilised the situation in Northeast Syria for the time being, but it also sowed the seeds for future conflicts with regional repercussions. The weakness in terms of international stabilisation efforts in both the Syrian and Yemeni cases is that important local forces were largely left out in the cold during subsequent peace negotiations organised by the UN or, in Syria's case, Russia, Turkey and Iran. As these efforts tend to focus on talks between 'government' and 'opposition' only, which is a task that is challenging enough in itself, these empowerment seeking local players were simply not invited, or they were only indirectly involved or were merely granted a seat as observer. Consequently, already existing feelings of marginalisation are strengthened and the urge to militarily attain what cannot be realised at the negotiation table becomes irresistible.

CONCLUSION

What conclusions can be drawn from the recent experiences in Syrian Kurdistan and South Yemen with regard to local actors striving for autonomy or separation? Or to put it into the perspective of international stabilisation efforts, how should we deal with forces prone to redrawing borders or decentralising the national state while simultaneously relying on them to deal with urgent matters such as keeping the legitimate government in power (Yemen), fighting global terrorism (Syria, Iraq and Libya) or stemming illegal migration to Europe (Libya)? How do we engage autonomy or secession seeking communities such as Kurds, Amazigh, Tuareg and Cyrenaican nationalists who seek to amend constitutions or old colonial borders which may not be ideal but which most regional and international powers have chosen to respect? Of course, there does not exist a uniform approach to deal with these matters. Looking at Syrian Kurdistan and South Yemen, there obviously are both similarities and differences between the two regions. Both the Kurds and the Yemeni separatists operate in an environment in which the central state vehemently fights to asserts its authority over the whole state's territory, which it is entitled to according to international law, despite the fact that the civil war has torn it apart into local entities it will not be able to control for the time being. In both Syria and Yemen, the civil war has attracted regional powers to intervene in the war supporting one party or the other. They do so proactively in an attempt to influence the course of the battle in order to minimise the effect of the war on their own societies or to pursue geopolitical objectives.

In doing so, state actors doggedly cling to the current borders. Despite the fact that the colonial borders in the Middle East are far from ideal, they offer a rare point of reference which is based on international law. Discussing current state borders in order to find a solution to civil wars or empowering minorities is unanimously rejected as it would open another Pandora's box which would probably affect the domestic situation in the neighbouring countries much more than letting the civil war muddle through. In this way, Syria and Yemen have become arenas in which regional powers compete through proxies. They often even act according to unwritten rules. Hence, those who want to fumble at the international borders are considered as party spoilers and dealt with accordingly. As a result, both the PYD/YPG and the separatists in South Yemen have very little if any regional and international backing for their cause. The only reason that their cause gained prominence, but hardly recognition, is the course the civil war has taken and their close cooperation with powers from the outside. This enabled them to amplify their political demands. Both have an uneasy relationship with the legitimate government. Where the PYD has decided to put its eggs in different baskets by both colluding with the Assad regime and acting as the US militia in Syria, the southern separatists of the STC are more or less at war with President Hadi although it keeps on paying lip service to the legitimacy of his government. On the other hand, the Syrian Kurds are surrounded by more regional opponents to their project than the STC.

Both the PYD and the southern separatists have not been very active in the peace process. Both are convinced that the format is unsympathetic to their political demands. So, the PYD never collaborated with the 'Arab' opposition of the SNC, while the Yemeni separatists barely participated in the 'Saudi dominated' National Dialogue in 2013. Detached from the main opposition, both groups have sought to create facts on the ground by unilaterally declaring autonomy (Syrian Kurds) or forcibly trying to take over government institutions (southern separatists). Such one-sided and not internationally supported measures are usually not very productive. This was illustrated by the Iraqi Kurdish referendum on independence in September 2017 which immediately provoked countermeasures by the neighbouring countries. In Syria and Yemen, such steps are more or less ignored by international backers for the moment, for the sake of attaining stability or geopolitical goals, until the situation dictates otherwise.

In both Syria and Yemen, 'national dialogue' has often been suggested as the panacea to solve the problems that led to the civil war. However, circumstances in both countries for the use of national dialogue as a tool to stabilise the situation are entirely different. In Syria, the Kurds are confronted with a resurging regime. The Assad regime admittedly promotes 'national dialogue', but if it ever takes place it will do so on the regime's conditions and without any supervision by an international body like the UN or the Arab League. Both are deeply mistrusted by the Syrian regime. The only international support for the Kurds should have come from the US, but Trump's sudden decision to withdraw US troops from Syria proved how skin-deep their opportunistic alliance with the Americans actually was. In other words, the Syrian Kurds will have to strike a separate deal with the regime which may grant them certain rights as a reward for them acting as a kind of 'loyal' opposition during the war. After all, they never sought the overthrow of the regime like the SNC did. On the contrary, the YPG/SDF coordinated with the Syrian army on the battlefield. However, what they will receive from Damascus will be far short from the kind of autonomy they presently enjoy.

From the viewpoint of promoting stability in Assad's post-war Syria and the Kurdish position therein, it is recommended that the international community works towards embedding certain Kurdish cultural rights in the Syrian constitution as to prevent old grievances lingering on into the future threatening stability, such as allowing for the use of the Kurdish language in public education and the right to publicly express Kurdish cultural identity. Complete repair of the damage done by the 1962 census in terms of lost nationality and citizens' rights will be another step welcomed by the Syrian Kurdish community as a whole. It should also not dissociate Kurdish rights from urgent humanitarian aspects concerning Syria that need to be attended to in order to promote stability in both Syria and the neighbouring countries. One should think of guarantees by the Assad regime for the safe return of the millions of Syrian refugees from Turkey, Lebanon and Jordan, rebuilding houses and infrastructure and the amendment by the Syrian government of Law 10 (2 April 2018) which calls on Syrians to register their private properties with the Ministry of Local Administration within a specific period or risk seeing their properties relinquished to the state.[38] In addition, channels of communication with the regime in Damascus, which were cut off by the US and most European countries, should be rebuilt. However, one should stop short of full restoration of diplomatic relations or of removing Syrian officials and entities from the US and EU sanctions lists. The rational behind this is that Assad's staying in power is a reality the international community will have to cope with if it wants the regime to cooperate with measures for increasing stability as mentioned above. Upgrading of diplomatic relations (partial) removal of individuals and entities from the sanctions lists and providing the necessary funding for the rebuilding of Syria should be used as an instrument of leverage on the regime. Finally, external actors should promote democracy in the current para-state structures set up by the autonomy government in Rojava as they are not politically comprehensive. This should be done to prevent a situation in which the PYD negotiates with the Syrian regime acting as if they are representing all citizens living in the areas they control, which is not the case.

In Yemen, a new national dialogue should be included in any peace agreement as so many Yemeni, regional and international parties are involved. So far, the UN-sponsored peace negotiations have concentrated on finding common ground between the two main enemies only, i.e. the legitimate government and the Houthis. However, the conflict in Yemen is too complex and the adversaries too many and too diverse for the negotiations to fall within such a simple framework. Future negotiations will need to include a wider range of parties, including the STC, as called for by Yemenis across the political spectrum.[39] This may work as an incentive for the separatists to tie the future of South Yemen to a solution for Yemen as a whole and to refrain from taking unilateral steps. From the viewpoint of promoting peace and future stability in Yemen and the question of southern separatism, it is recommended that the international community does the utmost to reach a lasting and endurable ceasefire in Yemen and continues promoting peace negotiations through the UN, but change the format in a way that allows participation of other parties involved, especially potential 'party spoilers' like the STC who could frustrate any agreement they were not party to. In this redefined format, the STC should have the same status of participation as the Houthi rebels. Regional stakeholders such as Saudi Arabia, the UAE and Iran should be invited as well as other international and regional players. As a model of reference, one could look at the Madrid Conference of 1991 in which the international community tried to revive the Israeli-Palestinian peace process. Although the Madrid conference did not directly yield major accomplishments, its format to a certain extent contributed to the concluding of the Oslo Accords between Israel and the Palestinians in 1993 and the peace treaty between Israel and Jordan in 1994. The unique feature of Madrid was that it was inclusive. It allowed for two tracks of negotiations, bilateral and multilateral, and for regional players to be involved as it concerned a conflict that could not be solved without regional backing, as is the case with Yemen. As a reference to future research, one could explore if the Madrid format is applicable to the situation in Yemen.

In both South Yemen and Syrian Kurdistan, political activists tend to romanticise the political future they dream of and fight for. However, there are lessons that need to be learned. After South Sudan had voted for independence in January 2011, and seceded from Sudan, internal differences came out in the open once again and the young country slipped into a devastating new civil war of its own making. Both Syrian Kurds and Yemeni separatists should never forget the schisms within their own ranks. These won't disappear even after the lines in the sand have been redrawn. Only genuine democratic reform will prevent these internal differences to be exploited by the world outside. Because the civil war may end but interference by interest seeking nations never will.

NOTES

1. "Bulldozing the Border Between Iraq and Syria: Daesh (Part 5)," *VICE News*, 13 August 2014.
2. See Mendelsohn (2015).
3. Sholto Byrnes, "Will Drawing New Borders Create and Sustain Peace?" *The National* (UAE), 8 December 2015.
4. See Keane (2001, p. 61).
5. See Schmidinger (2018, p. 38).
6. According to the CIA Factbook the Kurdish minority in Iraq is 15–20%, in Turkey 19%.
7. See Schmidinger (2018, pp. 56–57).
8. "The Kurdish Democratic Union Party," Beirut: Carnegie Middle East Center, 1 March 2012.
9. See Schmidinger (2018, pp. 79–85).
10. Interviews with SNC-leaders in Istanbul, January 2012.
11. "The Kurdish National Council in Syria," Beirut: Carnegie Middle East Center, 15 February 2012.
12. "The Kurdish National Movement in Syria: Political Goals, Controversy and Dynamic," Interview with Joseph Daher, Syria Freedom Forever website, 1 November 2016.
13. "Hukumat Suriya wa-mu'aridun laha yarfudun 'I'lan Akrad "ta'sis nizam federali" shamali al-bilad," *BBC*, 17 March 2016.
14. All UN Security Council resolutions adopted since 2012 stress that the political solution to the Syrian conflict should be based on the sovereignty, independence, unity and territorial integrity of the Syrian state. See https://www.un.org/press/en/2015/sc12008.doc.htm.
15. Schmidinger (2018, p. 113)
16. "How a Victorious Assad Is Changing Syria," *The Economist*, 28 June 2018.
17. "Russian Draft Proposal for a New Syrian Constitution," *MEMRI*, 9 February 2017.
18. Interview with Bassam Abu Abdullah, Damascus, March 2017.
19. Interviews with Syrian minister and Syrian political analyst on basis of anonymity, Damascus, March 2017.
20. See Schmidinger (2018, p. 139).

21. See Al-Muslimi (2015).
22. Gamal Gasim, "What Is Going on in Southern Yemen?" *Al-Jazeera*, 29 January 2018.
23. See Al-Muslimi (2016).
24. Interview with former Yemeni government official, February 2018.
25. Interviews with Al-Hirak leaders in January and February 2018.
26. UNSC-Resolution 2014, 21 October 2011.
27. UNSC-Resolution 2201, 15 February 2015.
28. Interview with Baraa Shiban, Yemeni activist and participant to the National Dialogue Conference in 2013–2014, London, January 2018.
29. Adopted by the Security Council at its 6784th meeting, on 12 June 2012.
30. Interview with a leader from the Southern Transitional Council, February 2018.
31. See Al-Akhali (2014).
32. Faisal Ali, "Al-Yaman … al-federaliyya tariq al-khalas," *Al-Jazeera*, 12 December 2016.
33. Interview with Yemeni diplomat, February 2018.
34. Interview with Emirati defence expert, February 2018.
35. Van Genugten (2017).
36. See, e.g., interview with dissident Al-Hirak leader Fadi Baoum in Aden Al-Yawm on 26 September 2017. "Ba 'um: Istabdalna al-Muhtall al-Yamani bi-Muhtall Imarati bi-Daraja Asasiyya."
37. Translated by the author from the Arabic text on the STC-website. http://stcaden.com/pages/3.
38. Full text of Law 10 (Arabic). https://www.sana.sy/?p=733959.
39. See Delozier (2018).

BIBLIOGRAPHY

Al-Akhali, Rafat. *The Challenge of Federalism in Yemen.* Washington: Rafik Hariri Center for the Middle East, The Atlantic Council, May 2014.

Al-Muslimi, Farea. "The Southern Question: Yemen's War Inside the War." Beirut: Carnegie Middle East Center, 8 July 2015.

———. "A History of Missed Opportunities: Yemen and the GCC." Beirut: Carnegie Middle East Center, 5 January 2016.

Delozier, Elana. *Framing Yemen Peace Negotiations.* Washington: The Washington Institute for Near East Policy, 31 May 2018.

Keane, Rory. *Reconstructing sovereignty. Post-Dayton Bosnia Uncovered.* London: Ashgate, 2001.

Mendelsohn, Barak. "Divide and Conquer in Syria and Iraq: Why the West Should Plan for a Partition." *Foreign Affairs*, 29 November 2015.

Schmidinger, Tomas. *Rojava—Revolution, War and the Future of Syria's Kurds.* London: Pluto Press, 2018.

"The Kurdish Democratic Union Party." Beirut: Carnegie Middle East Center, 1 March 2012.

"The Kurdish National Council in Syria." Beirut: Carnegie Middle East Center, 15 February 2012.

Van Genugten, Saskia. *External Powers in the Horn of Africa: The Case of Iran*. Abu Dhabi: Emirates Diplomatic Academy, February 2017.

CHAPTER 12

Egypt and Turkey: Identity as a Source of Instability

Steven A. Cook

INTRODUCTION

For policymakers and officials in the United States, Europe and the Gulf, Egypt and Turkey are 'strategic partners' that are critically important to regional security. It is hard not to understand why. Egypt is the largest Arab country with the region's largest military and controls the Suez Canal, through which ten per cent of global trade passes. The country has also been at peace with Israel for almost forty years. Leaders in Saudi Arabia, the UAE, Bahrain and other countries regard Egypt as their 'strategic depth' in the confrontation with Iran. For its part, Turkey's position at the centre of some of the most pressing policy concerns of the West and Middle Eastern countries has, for many policymakers and analysts, rendered the country an asset to the West. For the Arab world and Israel, Ankara is an influential player in the Eastern Mediterranean, the Levant, the Gulf and even the Red Sea. In the mid-2000s, the Turks positioned themselves as problem-solvers in Lebanon, the Gaza Strip and between Israelis and Syrians. Since

S. A. Cook (✉)
Council on Foreign Relations (CFR), New York, NY, USA

© The Author(s) 2020
V. Gervais and S. van Genugten (eds.), *Stabilising the Contemporary Middle East and North Africa*, Middle East Today,
https://doi.org/10.1007/978-3-030-25229-8_12

259

that time, however, the Turkish government has contributed to instability around the region, especially in Syria and Iraq. As was the case a decade ago, Turkey's policies are driven in large part by the domestic political calculations of President Recep Tayyip Erdogan, which have changed considerably during this time and accounts for Ankara's swing from regional peacemaker to a source of instability.

Central to the idea that Egypt and Turkey are important partners of the West is the fact that policymakers in the West tend to regard both countries as sources of regional stability. For example, there can be no regional Arab-Israel war without Egypt. The Egyptians have also been an important interlocutor with the Palestinians and a critical actor in the Gaza Strip. As Egyptian diplomats never tire of telling their interlocutors, Israelis, Palestinians, Americans, Jordanians and others in the region recognise that Cairo is indispensable in managing the periodic crises in Gaza. After the dissolution of the Soviet Union, policymakers in the West believed that Turkey could be an important partner in the stability of the Eastern Mediterranean, an interlocutor that could help secure Arab-Israeli peace, and a 'model' for countries seeking more democratic and prosperous futures after the Arab uprisings.[1] In the early years after the Justice and Development Party (AKP) came to power, the Turks sought to end the conflict in Cyprus, used their good offices to nudge Israelis and Syrians to negotiations, and seemingly resolved a central problem of politics in many Arab countries—the accumulation of Islamist political power. This dynamic attracted the interest of Arabs across the political spectrum. Turkey's significant economic growth during the first decade of the twenty-first century also gave rise to the idea that Turkey as a 'trading state' could forge a more stable and prosperous region through economic statecraft. Finally, Turkey's Cooperation and Coordination Agency has invested considerable resources in North Africa, sub-Saharan Africa, the Balkans and Central and East Asia to share Turkey's development experience.

For all that Egypt and Turkey have done to support peace and development in the Middle East and beyond, in recent years they themselves have become unstable. This has contributed to a chaotic and violent dynamic that is gripping the Middle East. Domestic dramas in both countries have spilled across national borders, making it difficult for other actors to stabilise places like Libya, the Gaza Strip, Syria and Iraq. Although their political, social and economic contexts are quite different in details, at a level of abstraction, both countries are confronting a mix of factors that have conspired to accentuate economic challenges, intensify polarisation and, in particular, deepen already intense debates over national identity. This has, in turn, led analysts to suggest that leaders use all manners of coercion in the effort to establish control, which has only further undermined stability, creating a feedback loop of force, violence and additional polarisation.[2] This chapter argues that although analysts and officials in the United States, Europe and the Middle East have long considered Egypt and Turkey to be stable and stabilising actors, a critical reading of their political trajectories suggests otherwise. It further examines the common and divergent social, economic and political dynamics in these countries that are driving instability. Finally, the chapter critically examines the drivers of instability in Egypt and Turkey separately, though it highlights a common feature in both settings: identity. This is an issue that is understudied in previous analyses of instability and stabilisation.

EGYPT: MORE CONTINUITY THAN CHANGE

Contrary to the idea that Egyptians are innately non-rebellious, they have been openly revolting against their rulers at regular intervals since the Orabi uprising in 1882. The next convulsion came in 1919 with the 'Nationalist Revolution' followed by three decades of political instability until the Free Officers' coup of July 1952 promised reform and change. In February and November 1968, Egyptians students turned out *en masse* to protest the light jail sentences handed down to military officers deemed negligent and thus responsible for Egypt's defeat in the June 1967 War. Demonstrators assailed Egypt's leaders for the heavy hand of the security services, demanded political and personal freedoms and called for parliamentary reforms. Popular anger erupted again in 1972 and once again centred around universities, where students were outraged over what they regarded as Anwar el Sadat's reluctance to take on Israel despite his public commitments to restore Egyptian sovereignty over the Sinai Peninsula. The students, along with the large numbers of Egyptians who joined them in protest, also demanded a more open and equitable political system.[3] In January 1977, the Egyptian armed forces were called into the streets to extinguish an uprising over a plan to slowly reduce subsidies on basic foodstuffs. Large-scale demonstrations remained largely absent from Egyptian politics. The lack of protests throughout the 1980s and the 1990s did not mean that Egyptians had acquiesced to President Hosni Mubarak's rule, however. There was considerable political ferment throughout this period that exploded in protest in March 2003. Organised (and approved by Egypt's Ministry of Interior) ostensibly to express anger at the American invasion of Iraq, the protest in Tahrir Square of approximately 25,000 people turned into a demonstration against Mubarak and his family. This event kicked off almost a decade in which popular resistance became a common feature of Egyptian politics, culminating with the 25 January 2011 uprising that brought down Mubarak after almost thirty years in power.

The transition from Mubarak to the Muslim Brotherhood's Mohamed Morsi in June 2012 was a period of unrest and violence. The first five months of President Morsi's term were generally calm, but after he issued decrees consolidating his power, Egyptians once again took to the streets and remained there almost continuously until the Supreme Council of the Armed Forces (SCAF) overthrew the Egyptian leader with the help of millions of Egyptians who protested against Morsi and the Brothers in late June and early July 2013. The much hoped for prosperity, stability and democratic governance that former Defence Minister and now President Sisi promised Egyptians has not materialised. After a brief period of euphoria—much of it state manufactured—Egyptians are now confronted with the economic pain that IMF-approved structural adjustment requires, a tenacious terrorist threat, and a predatory state that is more repressive than under either Mubarak or Morsi. In order to establish political control, the Egyptian authorities have applied overwhelming force against those who have at times dared to organise on Egyptians streets. The most well-known and bloodiest of these efforts was the massacre of about 800 people in Rabaa Square in August 2013.[4] Since then, the Egyptian state has employed mass arrests of those suspected of harbouring anti-regime sentiments. This has cast a wide net that includes not only terrorists, but also students, journalists, academics and a variety of others. The authorities have institutionalised this repression through legislation that a politically pliant parliament easily approved. These include rules, regulations and laws that on everything from terrorism to civil society and the press that are broadly interpreted to punish dissent.[5] The July 2013 coup d'état and the ongoing effort on the part of the state to close off channels of opposition are part of a broad effort to reset Egyptian politics in a way that precludes the possibility of another uprising.[6] Although the authorities have emphasised that the measures the state has undertaken are necessary for stability, these efforts may ultimately prove to be drivers of instability. This is a function of the 'repression-radicalisation dynamic' in which individuals who were previously committed to pursuing their political agendas through the established rules of the game determine that with each successive round of state repression this strategy is unsustainable and thus take up arms as to seek redress for their grievances.[7] Western analysts too often downplay the role ideology plays in political violence, but there is no denying that coercive efforts aimed at ensuring stability can produce the opposite outcome.

CHALLENGES TO GOVERNANCE IN EGYPT

Egypt confronts a complex set of economic, demographic, environmental and social problems, the cumulative effects of which could be mitigated, but for lack of good governance. The country's massive bureaucracy—6.5 million strong—has never efficiently delivered services. Basic competencies in routine areas of public administration and public safety are sorely lacking. For example, in 2017 Egypt ranked 120 out of 190 countries in ease of doing business, a marginal improvement, but still rather low.[8] Since 2004, the Egyptian government declared its intention to improve the country's business environment. When it comes to corruption—an issue that was at the forefront of the January 2011 uprising—Egypt ranks 117 out of 180 countries.[9] These illustrative examples are a direct reflection of the inefficiencies of a bureaucracy that remains largely autonomous unto itself.[10] In the years prior to the uprising against Mubarak, there were a string of natural and manmade disasters, from collapsing hillsides and building fires to train accidents and ferry disasters that killed well over 1000 people. Many of these incidents were preventable, but for the corruption and indifference among individuals charged with serving the public.[11] This situation has not improved in the years since Mubarak fell. Egyptians remain at risk from both the shortcomings of their country's infrastructure and the bureaucracy, which is charged with ensuring that regulations are met. Egypt's unresponsive state is not a new development, but as Egypt's multi-faceted challenges become more acute as a result of demographics, climate change, economic underdevelopment and other factors, the problem of governance is in and of itself a driver of instability.

The state of Egypt's bureaucracy is in part a function of the way in which the political system works that the Free Officers built after coming to power in 1952. Initially self-identified reformists, the officers quickly discovered that the best way to consolidate their power was to forge an entirely new set of political institutions.[12] Within this order is an informal linkage between the presidency, the fulcrum of Egypt's political system and the armed forces, which conspires against Egyptians.[13] No doubt Egypt's senior officer corps consists of people with good intentions and the best interests of Egypt at heart, yet the crises and problems that have strained Egyptian public life over six decades are directly connected to the military's position as the locus of power, prestige and authority in the political system. Instead of preparing the country for democracy as the SCAF claimed in the 18-month transition from Mubarak to Morsi, the senior command was working assiduously to ensure that the agglomeration of activists known as 'the revolution' did not succeed in its efforts to forge a more democratic political system. At the same time, in their effort to prevent the Muslim Brotherhood from realising the group's (also anti-democratic) vision for Egypt, they carved out special exceptions to presidential powers, effectively undermining Morsi's authority in national security and defence, broadly defined. The result did not merely constrain the new Egyptian leader, but contributed to the political polarisation of the country. Morsi responded to what he and his supporters considered to be the provocations of the military with both uncompromising rhetoric intended to mobilise his supporters and an accumulation of powers that the military had not specifically appropriated. In November 2012, Morsi issued decrees that rendered his decisions and those of the Constituent Assembly writing a new constitution, beyond the review of the courts.

This action-reaction dynamic in which the SCAF sought to salvage the political system that its predecessors had set up and in response the Muslim Brotherhood's efforts to protect their own political project, culminated in the military's intervention on 3 July 2013. The toppling of Morsi and the violent aftermath of the coup d'état altered the military's role in the political, social and economic life of the country. Previously content 'to rule, but not govern', the officers have asserted their authority in virtually every sphere of governance in an effort to ensure the continuity of the political order.[14] The stunning irony is that in their effort to reset the system the officers have done much to radicalise and destabilise the political arena. This includes mass arrests—some estimates indicate that Egypt has 40,000 political prisoners—forced disappearances, the detention of large numbers of journalists, an information blackout on the fight against extremists in the Sinai Peninsula, a radical re-writing of Egyptian nationalism, intimidation of the business community and the expansion of the military's already well-developed economic interests. This approach to pacifying the country and returning Egypt to the 'normal course' of politics stems from a narrative—purposefully nurtured by the military establishment—that places the armed forces at the centre of the country's development and implicitly casts disdain upon civilian leaders for their alleged incompetence.[15] The officers have long held these ideas, but they were reinforced during Egypt's turbulent politics during the transition from Mubarak. The SCAF desperately wanted to relieve itself of the burden of administering the country, but found that civilian politicians were, from its perspective, unwilling to place the national interest above narrow parochial concerns. Thus, the officers have become more open and aggressive in the political arena than in previous decades.

This is not to suggest that Egypt's current tribulations are solely the fault of the military establishment. Other powerful actors such as the General Intelligence Directorate, the Judiciary, and, in particular, the Ministry of Interior have shaped Egyptian politics through their internecine struggle and pursuit of parochial interests. Throughout the transition from Mubarak to Morsi and throughout the latter's short tenure, the officers of the Ministry of Interior sought to reinforce their autonomy. In order to forestall a purge of the ministry and subsequent prosecution of officials involved in human rights violations, the Ministry either pulled back from the streets or applied significant force to control public spaces in an effort to convince Egypt's leaders that they could not live without the police. This resulting violence and polarisation had negative consequences for Egypt's stability.

The problem of governance in Egypt extends to the economy. Egypt's chronic economic underdevelopment is a function of poor governance. The fact that 10% of the population lives in slums, 26% of Egyptians live in poverty, the inflation rate is 30 and 12% are officially unemployed (though it is likely significantly higher) contributes to an environment in which anger, protest and potentially violence are more likely.[16] This is particularly so because the Egyptian government's narrative that broad-based economic development and growth is benefitting the people is at odds with objective reality. The difference between the two played a role in mobilising protests during the 2011 demonstrations against Mubarak. There is evidence that Egyptian officials have long been aware of this problem and sought to address it through neoliberal reforms. Since the late 1990s, the Egyptian government has claimed that transformation from a centrally controlled economy to a market economy was largely complete. This was not entirely true, however. Anwar el Sadat's 1974 *infitah* created a commercial economy without the formal institutions of a market economy. Thus, even though the private sector was given ever-increasing latitude and visibility within the economy, much of what business did—especially the larger concerns—was based on its owners' proximity to the state. There were exceptions to this situation, but generally Egypt's informal politics have provided advantages to certain groups within the business community that demonstrated a loyalty to the Executive.

The importance of linkages between the private sector and Egypt's power structure was brought into sharp relief during the late Mubarak period with the rise of business titans whose fortunes increased with their proximity to Gamal Mubarak and his Policies Secretariat of the ruling National Democratic Party. The result helped further distort the development of Egypt's private sector and precluded the development of a regulatory framework that could level the playing field for those entrepreneurs without *wasta* or connections. A set of formal institutions further reinforced the disadvantage to those who were not members of a rarefied elite. It was during this period that Egypt marked considerable economic growth, but the benefits were perceived to be unevenly distributed in favour of those at the nexus of business and politics who leveraged neoliberal reforms to their advantage. Thus for much of the late Mubarak era, employees within the state-owned sector were in open revolt.

IDENTITY AS A SOURCE OF STABILITY

Many of the issues outlined above are well known, but identity is an issue that is consistently overlooked in the context of regional instability. The 2011 uprising gave new voice and urgency to this old theme in the struggle for Egypt. Gamal Abdel Nasser's nationalisation of the Suez Canal in July 1956 was the ultimate expression of the rallying cry 'Egypt for the Egyptians' that first began to appear in the 1880s. Intentional or not, Nasser articulated a vision of what Egypt was and what it meant to be Egyptian. This was critical in a country with problematic sovereignty and whose citizens demanded social justice, more representative government, and dignity over at least the previous seventy years. With the nationalisation, Nasser was essentially promising Egyptians that from that moment on, the country's resources would be used to realise economic development, social mobility and national power.

One of the reasons Abdel Fatah el Sisi consciously connected himself to Nasser after coming to power in 2013 was the enduring idea among many Egyptians—though not necessarily economic elites—that the Nasser era was the last time Egypt was successful. They are not wrong. In the eleven years between nationalisation of the Suez Canal and the June 1967 defeat, the economy grew (albeit at a modest rate), there was unprecedented social mobility in the form of free education and promise of employment, elites were brought to heel through the nationalisation of their assets, and Nasser established Egypt as an influential actor in global politics—whether through the Non-Aligned Movement, its status as the leading voice of Arab nationalism, the country's partnership with the Soviet Union, or, of course, Egypt's confrontation with Israel. After Nasser's death in 1970, Anwar el Sadat sought to establish, in his words, a 'state of institutions', to reorient Egypt's state-dominated economy and to align Egyptian foreign policy with the United States and the West. His ostensibly reform-minded agenda obscured his real intention, which was to destroy the power centres in Egyptian politics that were legacies of the Nasser era and thus a threat to the new leader.[17] In this, Sadat was successful, but in an entirely different way his changes were a failure because they did not make sense to the vast majority of people. They had enjoyed a modicum of economic progress and social mobility during the Nasser years, which had been accomplished through the machinery of the state. Never mind that state-directed development had run its course, the idea of permitting private interest greater latitude in the economy ran against everything that Egyptians had been told about themselves and their country over the previous two decades. In addition, these changes included a rapprochement with the United States, the inheritor of Great Britain's position in the Middle East. The powerful ideas about what Egypt stood for and what it meant to be an Egyptian that Nasser had articulated and nurtured clearly endured, but were no longer consistent with state policy. This gap destabilised Egyptian politics and contributed to significant challenges to Egypt's security, including the January 1977 Bread Riots, the large-scale crackdown in the summer of 1981, and finally Sadat's assassination in October 1981.

Hosni Mubarak, having been a young air force officer during the Nasser era and then as Sadat's vice-president, had first-hand knowledge of the two profoundly different visions. Nasserism and Sadat's 'Corrective Revolution' roiled the political arena in large part because these ideas were linked to questions about Egyptian identity. Consequently, during his almost thirty-year tenure, Mubarak sought a middle way and avoided sweeping ideological affirmations about Egyptian society. He maintained critical aspects of his immediate predecessor's policies—peace with Israel, greater room for the private sector, and a strategic alliance with the United States. Yet in an implicit acknowledgement of a regime founded on an uncompromising nationalism, the centrality of the state and the promise of Egypt, Mubarak never defended the accommodation with Israel or the ties with Washington and was profoundly ambivalent about neoliberal economic reforms. Mubarak stood for 'stability for the sake of development', which was his slogan for the 1999 presidential referendum. From his perspective, it may have seemed pragmatic to convey to the Egyptian people that material benefits would come if they were just patient. Yet those benefits never arrived for enough people, and lacking an emotionally appealing vision of the future, Mubarak relied on coercion and force to remain in power. It worked until it did not, and on the heels of eighteen days of protests, the military command determined that Mubarak was a threat to social cohesion and was told he was no longer needed.

Morsi experienced the same problem as Mubarak and Sadat before him. Although Western analysts had long believed that the Muslim Brothers articulated a vision for Egypt that made it the most prominent, influential and prestigious opposition group in the country, Morsi was unable to appeal to enough Egyptians to realise the Brotherhood's goals. Egypt's elites certainly did much to ensure his failure, but had Morsi been able to appeal to a broader set of Egyptians, he could have prevailed in the struggle with the military, judiciary, ministry of interior and intelligence services. Yet too many Egyptians rejected the Brotherhood's moralising mission, which they regarded as an assault on Egypt's identity, and were thus willing to throw their support behind the military and help Sisi force Morsi from the presidency. In their effort to reset Egyptian politics, the officers promised Egyptians security, prosperity and representation. Before trying to achieve these goals, they presided over a radical reinterpretation of Egyptian nationalism and identity that expunged the Brotherhood's role in the development of both. They have also sought to re-engineer the institutions of the state in an effort to ensure that the period between 25 January 2011 and 3 July 2013 can never happen again.[18] However, an important challenge facing the Egyptian leadership remains the necessity of articulating a materially and emotionally appealing narrative about the future, without which—and without the promised prosperity, security and representative government—it is likely to be forced to rely on coercion in order to establish and maintain control. This is an indication of potential instability given that coercion is the least efficient and most expensive means of establishing political control. Once some citizens demonstrate that the costs of opposing the government are not as steep as previously believed, it is likely that others will join them. This leaves a leader the choice of applying more force or succumbing to the demands of their opponent, neither of which necessarily result in stability.

Turkey's Problematic Stability

Like Egypt, Turkey has a longer history of instability than commonly assumed. In the late 1970s, Left–Right violence took the lives of almost 5000 Turks. The street violence of the 1970s coincided with a number of ineffective coalition governments that were unable to manage Turkey's mounting economic problems. The situation became so unstable that on 12 September 1980, the Turkish military stepped in, brought down the government, undertook a widespread crackdown and oversaw economic restructuring. After the ratification of a new constitution in 1982, the officers handed the country back to civilian leaders. Turkey enjoyed stability for the remainder of the decade, but political and economic problems returned in the mid-1990s when the Islamist *Refah* (Welfare) party won the most votes in the 1995 general elections. Initially, then-Turkish president, Suleyman Demirel, tapped two rival right-of-centre parties to form a blocking coalition, but that government faltered on the personality differences between the party leaders. Demirel then asked the leader of Welfare to form a government, which lasted until June 1997 when the military forced its dissolution in what Turks refer to as the 'blank coup'. The name derives from the fact that the General Staff accomplished its goals not through the deployment of tanks and troops into the streets, but rather through political pressure and an information campaign designed to heighten public anxiety in officially secular Turkey about the Welfare party's agenda. The end of Turkey's first experience in Islamist-led government gave way to a number of Right–Left coalition governments that struggled to provide coherent leadership and confidence in the economy. Divided ideologically; under pressure over serious allegations that various ministers were corrupt; and intimidated by a military leadership that demonstrated a sense of purpose, unity of command and thinly veiled disdain for civilians, Turkey's civilian leadership was paralysed and the country drifted. Turks then experienced two painful financial crises in 2000 and 2001 as a result of massive corruption in the banking sector and personal differences between the president and prime minister over how to handle the crisis. In the midst of this wrenching financial contraction, Turks turned out in the streets to protest the anaemic response from their leaders. In one poignant moment, a florist threw his empty cash register at Prime Minister Bulent Ecevit who floundered as Turkish banks teetered under the weight of bad loans, prompting fears that the Turkish government would default on its own debt as foreign investors fled the country.

270 S. A. COOK

Against the backdrop of all of these destabilising problems, Turkey was fighting an insurgency. In 1984, a Marxist-Leninist group under the leadership of a Kurdish graduate of Ankara University named Abdullah Ocalan launched a terrorist campaign against the Turkish government, attacking Turks and Turkish interests both at home and abroad. The conflict has waxed and waned over thirty-five years, but never ended and has continued to be a critical destabilising factor in Turkish politics (discussed below).

THE RISE OF THE AKP

The 2002 electoral victory of the AKP, which a group of young reformists carved out of Turkey's Islamist movement 18 months earlier, brought government stability and economic growth back to Turkey. At the same time, the government undertook wide-ranging political reforms that were enough for the European Commission to recommend that Brussels begin EU membership negotiations with Ankara. These successes translated into 47% of the popular vote in the August 2007 elections. In the five years after its first electoral victory, the AKP garnered an additional 11% of the popular vote and widened its base to include cosmopolitan liberals, big business and a larger number of average Turks, in addition to its core constituency of pious Turks, including Kurds. Yet the political stability that the AKP provided began coming undone at exactly the same time as this electoral triumph. And just as in Egypt, this slide towards polarisation and political instability began with the armed forces.

In May 2007, Recep Tayyip Erdogan and the party leadership determined that they would nominate Abdullah Gul—the foreign minister who also served as prime minister for a short time—to be the country's 11th president. The Turkish General Staff objected. The officers, educated and enculturated in the secular values and institutions of the Turkish republic, feared that Gul, a founder of the AKP, would enable the AKP's Islamist-inspired agenda. The 1982 constitution, written at the behest of the military, gave the Turkish president the power to approve or reject all legislation. Thus, the presidency was a firewall against what the senior command regarded to be the excesses of its civilian politicians. The officers feared that a Gul presidency would facilitate the Islamisation of society and the country's political institutions. Erdogan ignored the commanders and called snap elections. The AKP's success in the August elections forced the military on the defensive and Gul became president. At the same time as the showdown between Erdogan and the General Staff over the next president, Turkish police discovered a cache of weaponry in the basement of an apartment building in Istanbul. The subsequent investigation allegedly revealed a plot by the so-called Deep State—military officers, intelligence operatives, politicians, organised crime figures, journalists, university professors and others—to create instability in the country to provoke a coup and bring an end to the AKP government. What became known as the Ergenekon case became a conspiracy within a conspiracy in which the ruling party and its then partners, followers of the cleric Fethullah Gulen, used the original allegations to harass and arrest critics of the government. They also manufactured evidence against large numbers of military officers. Then in March 2008, Turkey's prosecutor general filed a case against the AKP with the Constitutional Court, charging the party with being a 'center of anti-secular activity'. The court found the AKP guilty, but—by dint of a reform that the party had pushed through parliament in 2003—the justices fell one vote short of closing the AKP and instead fined the party $20 million.

In each of these cases, the AKP and its leaders prevailed, but they also reinforced the belief that the Turkish establishment would go to any length to prevent Erdogan from governing and realising his controversial vision for Turkey emphasising religious values. Consequently, Erdogan abandoned the consensus-building approach that marked much of AKP's first five years in favour of a strategy of polarisation, as he sought to pulverise his opposition. This deepened existing rifts between the rising class of people who were AKP's core constituency and those who had long held political and economic power. There was increased pressure on journalists, media companies, big established business concerns and especially the armed forces. In one dramatic moment in July 2011, the entire senior command of the military resigned *en masse*, stating they could no longer protect their officers from zealous civilian prosecutors. Erdogan and the AKP had made progress subordinating the General Staff to the institutions of the state, but now went about cultivating loyal cadres within the officer corps, undermining decades in which the Turkish military remained above politics even as its leaders regarded it as their scared duty to police and protect the political system.

As the AKP accumulated power and became more insular, it abandoned its legacy as a party of good, clean governance in favour of patronage and crony capitalism. Anger over this state of affairs resulted in the Gezi Park protests in the summer of 2013 where anywhere from hundreds of thousands to about two million Turks gathered in public spaces around the country to protest the redevelopment of the small park on the edge of Istanbul's Taksim Square into a mall.[19] The loss of valuable and increasingly endangered green space in central Istanbul to a shopping centre designed to look like Ottoman-era military barracks was the proximate cause of the demonstrations, but the Turks who took to the streets also voiced their frustration at the corruption, arrogance of power and brutality of the government and its security forces. These were not people who were some type of 'fringe' as deputy Prime Minister Bulent Arinc averred, but rather citizens who the AKP had marginalised in its effort to institutionalise its power at the expense of other political forces in the country.

On the heels of the Gezi Park protests came the break between the AKP and its Gulenist allies. In late 2013 and early 2014, a series of tape recordings were released to the Turkish media in which ministers, members of Erdogan's family, the prime minister and others were heard discussing ill-gotten gains. This was the latest in a tit-for-tat conflict that had been brewing for much of the previous year that had developed over Erdogan's efforts to reach an accommodation with the PKK. Although the *Hizmet*— as Gulen's movement is called—projects a liberal and progressive agenda to its international interlocutors, it has often behaved in the opposite manner in Turkey. Erdogan called the revelations of corruption an attempted coup, saw to it that the AKP buried the allegations in a parliamentary investigation and began a massive purge of Gulen's followers from the bureaucracy—including the police and public prosecutors—universities and media outlets. It was in this environment of political polarisation and fear that elements of the Turkish armed forces sought to overthrow the government and kill President Erdogan.

The attempted coup which took place on 15 July 2016 failed. Outside of Turkey, there has been considerable speculation about how the failed putsch took place and who was behind it. Various explanations have been offered, but they remain (educated) guesses because the Turkish leadership immediately determined that Fethullah Gulen and his followers were responsible. This may be the case, but there was no independent investigation into the plot and given that the vast majority of the Turkish media is in the hands of owners and editors friendly to the AKP, Turkish journalists echoed the government's narrative. For all the time and attention Western analysts have devoted to trying to understand how the coup unfolded, the political effects of the failed effort are far more important, especially for Turkey's political trajectory and stability. The failed takeover, which President Erdogan referred to as a 'gift from God', provided an opportunity for the government to accelerate the purge that was already underway. Since July 2016, more than 200,000 people have been either detained, arrested or terminated from their jobs. Typically those who have been caught up in this expansive crackdown are accused of being a member of a terrorist organisation—either followers of Fethullah Gulen or members of the Kurdistan Workers' Party or PKK. As a result, Turkey is now among the most repressive countries in the region.

There is no evidence that the Gulenists have been radicalised as a result of the purge, but the logic of the repression-radicalisation dynamic—a problem in Egypt—may yet manifest itself. The Gulenists have proven themselves capable of taking extraordinary measures—surreptitiously recording adversaries, forging evidence, and taking part in the failed coup—that it is not inconceivable that followers resort to violence. As far as the Kurds are concerned, the narrowing of political space for the one legal Kurdish-based party in Turkey, whose leadership is in jail, also increases the potential for violence.

Ethno-Nationalism and Turkey's Stability

Like Egypt, the issue of identity adds complexity to Turkey's already demanding political challenges. The polarisation and radicalisation of Turkey's political arena has unfolded against the backdrop of Syria's civil war. The inflow of refugees from that conflict, numbering about 3.5 million, the development of extremist infrastructure—the result of Turkey's own dubious policy choices in an effort to bring down the Assad regime—and the way the conflict in Syria propelled Kurdish nationalism has proven to be destabilising. It is the latter challenge, however, deeply rooted in the history, politics and political culture of the Turkish Republic, that has shaken the country to its core. This should not be surprising because the conflict with the Kurds is most importantly about identity.

When analysts (erroneously) invoke the idea that countries in the Middle East are 'artificial'—the product of the imagination and machinations of colonial officials—they never include Turkey. There is, of course, good reason for this as Turkey was never a subject of a colonial power, but it is a country that was essentially conjured in the mind of one man, Mustafa Kemal or Ataturk. Despite the awesome legacy of the Ottoman Empire, the Republic of Turkey's history is not that much longer than other countries in the Middle East. Its founding in 1923 was what political scientists—borrowing from evolutionary biologists—might call a 'punctuated equilibrium', in which a short, dramatic period of change demarcates one era from another.[20] In order for Ataturk to resist the predations of the French, Greeks and Italians who sought to carve up Anatolia, build a new country and secure it, he needed to alter the loyalties of the people in Anatolia. Thus, he undercut the prestige of the sovereign, who was both Sultan and Caliph, by disestablishing religion. In the 1920s, the Caliphate was abolished, the constitutional article identifying Islam as the state religion was deleted, and the office of Sheikh ul-Islam was disbanded. In another critical move, in place of a multicultural, multi-ethnic, multi-religious empire, Ataturk conjured an ethno-national state based first and foremost on 'Turkishness' and secondarily on a distinctly Western conception of modernity. These were radical changes that required significant reforms of Turkish society that were often implemented through coercion. For example, in the effort to build the new Turkish man and woman, there was no room for the Kurdish man and woman. As a result, Kurdish identity was officially obliterated. Kurds became 'mountain Turks' and were prohibited from engaging in cultural rituals and education in their own language. It is true, of course, that pious Turks have been able to accumulate political and economic power, and many Kurds have become well integrated into the social, economic and political life of the country, but Ataturk's reforms have become 'structural', and as a result have continued to haunt Turkey along both religious and ethnic dimensions. The stunning irony of Turkey's current tribulations is that Erdogan and the AKP had a positive vision for the future that for a time captured the collective imagination of a large enough number of Turks that he and the party could have mitigated, if not resolved, the struggle over identity in Turkey. Erdogan's conception of Turkish society emphasised religious values—though not *sharia*—at the expense of ethnic identity. This held out the twin promise that the pious Turks could accumulate political and economic power without threatening those who wanted to lead a secular lifestyle and softening the hard edge of ethnicity that had been central to the republic's founding ethos and myths. In this way, religious values would be the ties that bind citizens of the republic, thereby reducing nationalist/separatist/culturally autonomous impulses among many Kurds that sowed so much distrust among ethnic Turks and rendered twenty per cent of the population a potential security threat.

The politics of Turkish and Kurdish nationalism have, however, proven too potent (and tempting to politicians) to overcome. In 2008, Erdogan announced that his government would invest $12 billion—including a TV station that would broadcast in Kurmanji—in the predominantly Kurdish southeast, but this opening to the Kurds and Erdogan's later effort to negotiate an end to the decades-long war with the PKK came to naught.[21] Turks and Western observers differ on the reasons for these failures, but they are the result of: Turkey's 2014 local elections in which the AKP ceded votes—without losing a mayoralty—to the Nationalist Movement Party (MHP); Turkish inaction at the siege of Kobani in the fall of 2014; the AKP's loss of its parliamentary majority in the June 2015 elections; the murder of two Turkish policemen at the hands of Kurdish terrorists; the American alliance with the Syrian Kurdish People's Protection Units (YPG)—which are directly linked to the PKK—in the fight against the Islamic State; and the YPG's territorial gains along the Turkish frontier in northern Syria. All of these developments combined to create a set of incentives for Erdogan to reverse his previous efforts to seek accommodation with the Kurds and align himself with hardcore nationalists. It also gave an upper hand to Kurds who have sought to process their grievances through violence, rather than those who have sought the same through the legal political process. The result was a return of a hot war between Turkey and the PKK in the southeast and northern Iraq and two Turkish invasions of Syria.

CONCLUSION

There are problems in both Egypt and Turkey currently contributing to instability that could be mitigated or even resolved through better policy decisions. Both cases indicate that in a variety of ways, economics contributes to—if not always causes—political instability. It thus stands to reason that improved management of the economy, including, but not limited to, rooting out and prosecuting corrupt actors, reforming social safety nets, passing laws and regulations to prevent crony capitalism and insulating economic policymakers from political pressures would help ease societal tensions, especially in economies like Turkey's that have experienced high growth rates. Overall, the possibility of good governance is more likely in Turkey, where as recently as the early and mid-2000s the government has expanded services, infrastructure, transportation and health care, than in Egypt. There the political system that the Free Officers discovered in the 1950s has proven over and over again to produce benefits for the military and their civilian partners with suboptimal outcomes for society. Still, there is always the possibility that Egypt's political system will evolve to become more responsive to the needs of its citizens. This was the dream of many who took part in the 25 January 2011 uprising, and even many of those who supported Abdel Fatah el Sisi's coup d'état in 2013.

The more difficult problem, and the one that is likely to continue to produce cycles of instability and violence, is identity. Among the many justifications for their support for the military intervention that toppled Mohamed Morsi, Egyptians declared that they wanted to 'protect the heart and soul' of their country. This was another way of saying that the moralising vision for Egypt that Morsi and the Muslim Brotherhood harbour contradicted a collective sense of what it meant to be Egyptian. That does not necessarily mean that the disparate groups across the political spectrum that opposed Morsi agree on exactly what that means. Indeed, the question of identity has been the central drama of Egyptian politics since the late 1800s. As noted, the armed forces and their civilian allies have now gone about restructuring Egyptian history, nationalism and identity in a way that delegitimises the Brotherhood and obscures its role in twentieth-century Egyptian politics, but without themselves articulating a vision of Egypt that conceives of identity in a way that makes sense to large numbers of Egyptians. The predictable result is a contested political arena in which different actors—Islamists, extremists, liberals, nationalists of all stripes, socialist revolutionaries and many others—are vying with each other and the defenders of the state to define Egypt. Having no answer themselves, the military establishment and the presidency have used force, or the threat of force, to establish political control. For now, the potential for regime-threatening popular protest seems to have ebbed because of Sisi's unfettered deployment of violence and arrests, but that has hardly solved the problem. Until a political figure emerges who can articulate a vision that appeals to most Egyptians, a dynamic of authoritarianism and instability will continue to undermine the governability of Egypt.

Turkey's circumstances are somewhat different, but are equally if not more vexing. Whereas the tribulations of Egypt's identity are wrapped around competing ideas, the Turks have the added volatile element of ethnicity. The tragedy of the AKP era is the missed opportunity to ease the 'Kurdish problem' that coincides with the arc of the state-building project in the Turkish Republic. With its emphasis on religious values and concomitant resentment towards the values of Kemalism, the AKP worldview could thus accommodate the idea that because Kurds in Anatolia were Muslims, the ethnic divisions between them and Turks could be bridged. As a result, the AKP invested heavily in courting religious Kurds—a reliable constituency—poured economic resources into Turkey's southeast, and even supported negotiations with the PKK. Yet even as adroit a politician as Recep Tayyip Erdogan could not overcome the hard realities and irreconcilable difference between Turkish and Kurdish nationalism. Erdogan and the AKP failed, and beginning with the 2014 local elections when the party ceded votes, if not mayoralties, to the MHP, the Turkish leadership has sought to capture its constituency. With the help of PKK violence and side deals with the MHP leadership, Erdogan has largely succeeded. This may serve him well electorally, but it has deepened the divide between Turks and Kurds, which will destabilise Turkish politics for the foreseeable future.

NOTES

1. See, for example, Alterman and Malka (2012), Altunisik and Cuhadar (2010), Taspinar (2012), Habibi and Walker (2011), and Kemal Kirisci, "The Rise and Fall of Turkey as a Model for the Arab World." https://www.brookings.edu/opinions/the-rise-and-fall-of-turkey-as-a-model-for-the-arab-world/.
2. See Cook (2017, Chapters 4 and 6).
3. See Abdalla (2008).
4. See Holmes (2014).
5. See Ferguson (2016) and Sonia Farid, "Egypt's New Anti-Terror Law: An In-Depth Read," MENASource (Blog), The Atlantic Council of the United States, 10 July 2015.
6. See Heydemann (2007) and Cook (2007). Egyptian leaders and their supporter often argue vehemently that the military's intervention on 3 July 2013 to topple President Mohamed Morsi was not a coup d'état. They argue that because there were millions—perhaps as many as 30 million— who demonstrated against Morsi in the days leading up to his ouster, the military was carrying out the will of the people in what amounts to a 'second revolution'. One can both understand these sentiments given the exigency of infusing the new leaders, especially then-Defense Minister Abdel Fatah el Sisi, legitimacy and recognise that the idea that the military's actions do not constitute a coup are entirely inaccurate. Civil-military relations theorists have long recognised that a coalition of military officers *and* civilians are, among a variety of factors, that make a coup d'état successful. The Egyptian coup follows a pattern of successful coups in other countries such as Brazil (1945, 1954, 1964) and Turkey in 1980 and 1997 in which civilians and military officers collaborated to bring elected leaders down. For a complete discussion of this phenomenon, see Alfred Stepan, *The Military in Politics: Changing Patterns in Brazil* (Princeton: Princeton University

278 S. A. COOK

Press, 1971), 93–97 and Claude E. Welch Jr. and Arthur K. Smith, *Military Role and Rule: Perspective on Civil-Military Relations* (North Scituate, MA: Duxbury Press, 1974), Chapter 1.

7. See Anonymous (2017), Hamid (2010), and Sullivan and Abed-Kotob (1999, Chapter 4).
8. Trading Economics, Ease of Doing Business in Egypt. https://tradingeconomics.com/egypt/ease-of-doing-business.
9. Corruption Perceptions Index 2017, Egypt. https://www.transparency.org/country/EGY.
10. Nashat Hamdy and Ahmed Aboulenein, "Egyptian Parliament Approves Civil Service Law After Rare Defiance of Sisi," Reuters, 4 October 2016; "Taking on Egypt's Big Bureaucracy," Middle East Institute, October 2015. http://www.mei.edu/publications/taking-egypts-big-bureaucracy.
11. See Cook (2011, pp. 180–184).
12. See Gordon (1996, Chapter 5).
13. See Cook (2007, pp. 39–40).
14. Ibid.
15. Ibid.
16. Arab Republic of Egypt. https://data.worldbank.org/country/egypt-arab-rep.
17. See Beattie (2000), Hinnebusch (1988), and Vatikiotis (1991).
18. See Heydemann (2007).
19. "Turkey at a Crossroads: What Do the Gezi Park Protests Mean for Democracy in the Region," *Hearing Before the Subcommittee on Europe, Eurasia, and Emerging Threats, Committee on Foreign Affairs*, U.S. House of Representatives, 113th Congress, 26 June 2013; "Gezi Park Protests: Brutal Denial of the Right to Peaceful Assembly in Turkey," *Amnesty International*, October 2013.
20. See Krasner (2009, pp. 3–4).
21. See Tavernise (2008).

BIBLIOGRAPHY

Abdalla, Ahmed. *The Student Movement and National Politics in Egypt 1923–1973*. Cairo: The American University in Cairo Press, 2008.
Alterman, Jon, and Malka, Haim. "Shifting Eastern Mediterranean Geometry." *The Washington Quarterly*, vol. 35, no. 3 (2012): 111–125.
Altunisik, Meliha, and Cuhadar, Esra. "Turkey's Search for a Third Party Role in Arab–Israeli Conflicts: A Neutral Facilitator or a Principal Power Mediator?" *Mediterranean Politics*, vol. 15, no. 3 (2010): 371–392.
Anonymous. "Regime Repression and Youth Radicalization in Egypt." Policy Brief 2, Egypt-Radicalization. Berlin: Heinrich-Böll Stiftung, February 2017.

Beattie, Kirk J. *Egypt During the Sadat Years*. New York: Palgrave Macmillan, 2000.

Cook, Steven A. *False Dawn: Protest, Democracy, and Violence in the New Middle East*. Oxford: Oxford University Press, 2017.

———. *Ruling but Not Governing: The Military and Political Development in Egypt, Algeria, and Turkey*. Baltimore: The Johns Hopkins University Press, 2007.

———. *The Struggle for Egypt: From Nasser to Tahrir Square*. Oxford: Oxford University Press, 2011.

Daragahi, Borzou. "Egyptians Become Victims of Soaring Crime Rate." *Financial Times*, 1 May 2013. https://www.ft.com/content/7ffac226-adab-11e2-a2c7-00144feabdc0.

Ferguson, David. "Silencing the Arab Spring with Co-opted Counterterrorism." *Berkeley Journal of Middle East and Islamic Law*, vol. 7, no. 1 (2016): 1–33.

Gordon, Joel. *Nasser's Blessed Movement: Egypt's Free Officers and the July Revolution*. Cairo: The American University in Cairo Press, 1996.

Habibi, Nader, and Walker, Joshua W. "What Is Driving Turkey's Re-engagement with the Arab World?" Middle East Brief 49, *Crown Center for Middle East Studies*, April 2011.

Hamid, Shadi. "The Islamist Response to Repression: Are Mainstream Islamist Groups Radicalizing?" Policy Briefing, *Brookings Doha Center*, August 2010.

Heydemann, Steven. "Upgrading Authoritarianism in the Arab World." Analysis Paper No. 13, *Saban Centre for Middle East Policy*. Washington, DC: Brookings Institution Press, October 2007.

Hinnebusch, Raymond A., Jr. *Egyptian Politics Under Sadat: The Post-populist Development of an Authoritarian-Modernizing State*. Boulder: Lynne Rienner Publishers, 1988.

Holmes, Amy Austin. "Why Egypt's Military Orchestrated a Massacre." *Washington Post*, 22 August 2014.

Huntington, Samuel P. *Political Order in Changing Societies*. New Haven: Yale University Press, 1968.

Krasner, Stephen D. *Power, the State, and Sovereignty: Essays on International Relations*. London: Routledge, 2009.

Kuran, Timur. "Now Out of Never: The Element of Surprise in the East European Revolution of 1989." *World Politics*, vol. 44, no. 1 (October 1997): 7–48.

Magdy, Samy. "PM Says Ethiopia Will Not Cut Egypt's Share of Nile Waters." *Washington Post*, 10 June 2018.

Nouihed, Lin. "Egyptians Losing Patience with Sisi as Economy Deteriorate." Reuters, 23 October 2016.

Olson, Mancur, Jr. "Rapid Growth as a Destabilizing Force." *Journal of Economic History*, vol. 23, no. 4 (December 1963): 532–536.

Phelps, Timothy. "Egypt Uprising Has Its Roots in a Mill Town." *Los Angeles Times*, 9 February 2011.

Raghavan, Sudarsan, and Mahfouz, Heba Farouk. "Egypt's Powerful President Is Facing Unusual Dissent Over Rapidly Rising Prices." *Washington Post*, 18 July 2018.

Stepan, Alfred. *The Military in Politics: Changing Patterns in Brazil*. Princeton: Princeton University Press, 1971.

Sullivan, Denis J., and Abed-Kotob, Sana. *Islam in Contemporary Egypt: Civil Society vs. the State*. Boulder, CO: Lynne Rienner, 1999.

Taspinar, Omer. "Turkey: The New Model?" In Robin Wright (ed.), *The Islamists Are Coming: Who They Really Are*. Washington, DC: Woodrow Wilson Center for International Scholars and the U.S. Institute of Peace, 2012.

Tavernise, Sabrina. "Turkey Plans $12 Billion Infusion for Kurdish Region." *New York Times*, 11 March 2008.

Underwood, Alexia. "Sisi Won Egypt's Election. That Doesn't Mean He Is Safe." Vox.com, 3 April 2018.

United States Institute of Peace and the United States Army Peacekeeping and Stability Operations Institute. *Guiding Principles of Stabilization and Reconstruction*. Washington, DC: United States Institute of Peace Press, 2009.

U.S. House of Representatives, Committee on Foreign Affairs. "Turkey at a Crossroads: What Do the Gezi Park Protests Mean for Democracy in the Region." *Hearing Before the Subcommittee on Europe, Eurasia, and Emerging Threats*, 113th Congress, 26 June 2013.

Vatikiotis, P. J. *The History of Modern Egypt: From Muhammad Ali to Mubarak*, 4th edition. Baltimore: The Johns Hopkins University Press, 1991.

Wahish, Naveen. "Alarm on the Census." *Al Ahram Weekly*, 5–11 October 2017.

Welch, Claude E., Jr., and Smith, Arthur K. *Military Role and Rule: Perspective on Civil-Military Relations*. North Scituate, MA: Duxbury Press, 1974.

Wittfogel, Karl A. *Oriental Despotism: A Comparative Study of Total Power*. New Haven: Yale University Press, 1957.

CHAPTER 13

Distributing Justice: Transitional Justice and Stabilisation in North Africa

Zinaida Miller

INTRODUCTION

In 2013, two contentious years after Egyptian President Mubarak was toppled by popular protest, Egypt's interim president created a Ministry of Transitional Justice and National Reconciliation.[1] Not long after he was appointed, the founding Minister of Transitional Justice declared that the time was not yet ripe for transitional justice in Egypt.[2] In Tunisia, the post-revolution government passed a Transitional Justice Law, following the establishment of a Ministry of Human Rights and Transitional Justice. In Libya, the post-Qadhafi government fought a pitched battle with the Interdnational Criminal Court (ICC) over the government's capacity and willingness to prosecute members of the deposed regime. At the Security Council, the Swiss Mission delivered a letter on behalf of over 50 states calling for a referral of the situation in Syria to the ICC.[3]

Z. Miller (✉)
Seton Hall University, South Orange, USA

© The Author(s) 2020　　　　　　　　　　　　　　　　　　281
V. Gervais and S. van Genugten (eds.), *Stabilising the Contemporary Middle East and North Africa*, Middle East Today,
https://doi.org/10.1007/978-3-030-25229-8_13

A few short years later, the Egyptian Ministry of Transitional Justice had been effectively abolished, collapsed into the Ministry of Legal and Parliamentary Affairs. Egypt, it appeared, had moved in two years from not being ready for, to no longer needing, transitional justice.[4] In Tunisia, a widely heralded truth commission continued its work even as high-level government officials attempted to pass a law to limit investigation of economic mal-distribution and corruption. At The Hague, the ICC found Libya's government unable to try Saif Al-Islam Qadhafi, implicitly questioning the state's coherence and sovereign control. In New York, China and Russia blocked a referral of Syria's situation to the International Criminal Court.

These developments took place against the backdrop of contested elections, continuing assertions of military power, constitutional struggles, regional conflagration, international intervention, economic deprivation, protests and war. More importantly, they took place *in concert with* those factors and events. The choice to do 'justice' and how justice is defined, the manner in which it is done, the language in which it is denigrated or advanced, the actors who control its institutional manifestation, all contribute to the distribution of human, material and symbolic resources. Moreover, they shape a narrative of countries as stable or unstable, sovereign or not, transitional or regressive and successful or failed.

The centrality of transitional justice to conflict and political change today gives that enterprise a significant—but unpredictable—role in the allocation and distribution of resources and political power and thus in the establishment of sustainable peace. Accountability, justice, truth and reconciliation are often seen as necessary fellow travellers of peace and political change, but justice can be an unsettling force in negotiation just as much as a contributing factor to political settlement. Particularly in situations of contested and unsettled transitions, calls for justice might be the slogan of the government, the political opposition or popular resistance—or all three at the same time. In some situations, transitional justice may function as a 'preservative' force, one 'which concededly sacrifices the aims of ideal justice for the more limited ones of assuring peace and stability'.[5] In others, calls for justice might be the driving force not only in an initial transition but for ongoing resistance when seemingly radical change has turned out to be more conservative in practice. The tension between preservative practices of justice and justice discourses that continually challenge powerful actors has been an essential aspect of politics and law in the post-2011 Middle East and North Africa.

This chapter identifies ways in which transitional justice in the MENA region has affected (or effected) stability, shaped change and allocated power.[6] In doing so, it argues for a view of justice projects as distributional and political—and thus as critical sites of social contestation—rather than inherently stabilising or destabilising. In certain circumstances, transitional justice can generate a persistent confrontation with a violent past as well as a space to challenge an unequal present. It can also, however, be instrumentalised on behalf of the powerful, deployed against the weak, or defanged and delegitimised in any number of ways. As a result, no clear linear or causal relationship exists between stabilisation and transitional justice.[7]

The chapter is structured around four examples of the political and distributive nature of transitional justice, exemplified by three North African countries in which both the discourse and institutionalisation of transitional justice post-2011 have been particularly prominent: Egypt, Tunisia and Libya.[8] Section "Beginning Justice", outlines the critical role of the conditions of transition, particularly in areas where supporters of a past regime retain some power or where a return to violent conflict seems likely. Using the cases of Egypt and Tunisia, it reveals the ways in which contestations over justice both reflect and contribute to struggles over political power and thus to the possibility of a stable transition. Section "Practicing Justice", analyses the politics of practicing justice through specific mechanisms, particularly the tensions between expectations of prosecution and the endemic limitations of the form. Prosecutions can serve the transitional function of holding past leaders responsible and stabilising a new regime, but they can also be inadequate, politicised and restricted by time and subject matter. Moreover, the choice of both prosecutions and jurisdiction may itself become wrapped up in political struggle. In Libya, a battle over International Criminal Court jurisdiction served as a proxy for asserting sovereignty against a backdrop of national fragmentation. Section "Economising Transitional Justice", takes up the challenge of justice for economic violence, corruption and inequality.[9] Attention to the economic causes and consequences of resistance and revolution can represent a partial fulfilment or a dilution of revolutionary demands; likewise, it can be championed or quashed by key actors depending on the threat they perceive in according some measure of economic accountability. The final section "Memorialising Justice", highlights the importance of time for forms of justice that vaunt memory and history as tools of reconciliation and sustainably stable politics. This is by no means an exhaustive list, but rather an exemplary one, demonstrating through select examples how transitional justice functions as a site of struggle and distribution.

The concerns raised in each section overlap and reappear, since each implicates others. For example, the choice of mechanisms influences which types of violence are addressed: trials, which focus on individual guilt and narrow ambits of crimes, offer anaemic sites for assessing long-standing socio-economic inequality. The conditions of transition may affect the mechanisms chosen, since the degree of stability or consensus during times of political change will make certain practices appear preferable over others. The design of mechanisms both produces and relies upon particular interpretations of past violence and abuse, inevitably privileging some claims, histories and memories over others. Thus, while the categories identified here offer a useful heuristic, the separation of these concerns into four discrete areas should not be taken as a practical division among them.

Transitional justice practices assert themselves in moments of instability to ensure that a violent past will not continue to haunt and subsequently obstruct a peaceful future. Yet their primary objective may not always be stability itself. Justice practices in moments of radical political change seek a series of complementary and conflicting goals, including retribution, restoration, reconciliation and reparation. They claim the capacity to call perpetrators to account and to fulfil the needs and desires of victims. They construct a precarious balance between local needs and international demands that sometimes conflict. And while some might hope for a practice of law that can operate outside politics, transitional justice exposes the simultaneous collusion and contradiction between the two. Justice and politics are intimately intertwined, but that has never guaranteed a happy marriage between their plural objectives. By definition, revolution and political change unbalance existing distributions of power and resources. As those forces founder, continue, surge or return, transitional justice provides a consistent site for enduring contestations over identity and community as well as human and material resources.

Beginning Justice

Transitional justice has the peculiar distinction of being both a product of and constitutive of transition itself. Without some sort of political change, the practices of justice would be part of the normal operations of a state. Yet without transitional justice, the contours of the transition remain unclear. A seemingly settled transition (such as the fleeing of a deposed dictator followed by a democratic election or the end of a war through total victory) may make the implementation of justice smoother, but it can also open the door for a new regime to use the process to consolidate power and punish long-standing opponents. A chaotic and fragile transition makes justice seem riskier but can also offer more openings for diverse actors to benefit. As leaders became embattled during the Arab uprisings, some believed that the MENA region's transitions would most closely resemble the Latin American post-authoritarian transitional paradigm.[10] Diverse national trajectories, however, have challenged any large-scale regional comparisons. Moreover, regional dynamics and ongoing conflicts raise questions about how to do justice after, or even during, active conflict. The conditions of a transition inevitably influence the distributional outcomes of justice processes and the sustainability of peace.

At its inception, transitional justice mechanisms were established in countries that were presumed to be in transition from violent authoritarian rule to democracy, a stage that seemed to demand a special type of justice—one that could respond to political transformation.[11] As the Cold War came to a close, increasing civil wars prompted a shift in focus to a larger post-conflict agenda for assisting states and societies in recovering from variety of abuses and atrocities. Transitional justice increasingly became linked to peacebuilding along with, or sometimes instead of, democracy promotion.[12] Although hardly viewed as conflict resolution mechanisms themselves, transitional justice mechanisms were intended to contribute to the stability and consolidation of peaceful governance, through their role in preventing repetition of harms as well as in coordination with disarmament and other initiatives.[13]

In the MENA region, political change has meant everything from competitive elections to open warfare. In many countries, elements of old regimes have retained power or re-emerged over time, leading to questions about not just the functioning but the deployment of transitional justice in both discourse and practice by various, often opposing, parties. In Libya, administrative purges, contested prosecutions and ongoing rights violations intersected with violent destabilisation. In other countries, calls for justice came from protesters seeking to question governments that even in the midst of, or directly after, transition failed to recognise or redress past abuses or current violations.

The Egyptian case exemplifies the ways in which the conditions of transition shape not only the field of justice but also the contributions of the practice and discourse of justice to the allocation of power and resources.

A contested, plural, arguably failed transition featured rapid shifts in power between different leaders, the Supreme Council for the Armed Forces (SCAF), and the Muslim Brotherhood. The initial successes of revolutionary protest crumbled under the weight of an entrenched state structure. Prosecutions were both partial and political; successive rulers were implicated in violence—and also called for justice. Efforts to pursue accountability were both significant and significantly limited, leading to an impoverished approach to transitional justice and belying early hopes that it would play an important role in stabilising political change and opening up a long-closed government.[14]

As in Tunisia, the 2011 protests in Egypt were revolutionary rather than reformist in nature; demands were articulated not as a call for elite pacts or partial restructuring but for popular overthrow and structural change.[15] Yet the end of Mubarak's rule, while momentous, did not shake the foundations of military control and the 'deep state'. Despite the sometimes lacklustre nature of political change and thus of the transition, however, both the discourse and practices of transitional justice remained at the forefront of politics and law. Throughout the rapid succession of rulers—Mubarak, SCAF, Morsi, Mansour and El Sisi—public calls for justice and accountability remained pervasive, as did violence and violation. Some commissions of inquiry were established and prosecutions conducted during what might be called the first and second transitions,[16] but they never constituted a comprehensive response to protestors' calls for social justice nor to decades of unaccountable violence and corruption.

By limiting successive prosecutions to a narrow set of individuals and a restricted temporal scope (essentially the protests and transition itself), any link between transitional prosecutions and the transformative potential of justice largely dissolved. Moreover, the perception that accountability remained elusive prompted further demonstrations at key points.[17] Prosecutions that did take up more long-standing crimes such as corruption seemed aimed at limiting human rights prosecutions and focusing on particular high-level cases rather than a systemic history of human rights violations. After several waves of protest, former President Mubarak, his two sons and other former government officials were charged with corruption and human rights violations.[18] Mubarak was found innocent in 2017 of killing protestors during the uprising; he and his sons were found guilty of embezzlement but released upon appeal.[19] The trials of Mubarak's successor, Mohamed Morsi, were tagged alternately as victor's justice, transitional justice, political retribution, a flawed but necessary accountability process—

or some combination thereof.[20] These alternating characterisations reveal the ways in which justice practices during political upheaval in particular become not just about indictment and trial but about the narrative and perception of the event itself. At stake is the legitimacy of not just a particular case but of the parties and leaders that claim the mantle of political change.

A contested transition may be further limited or obstructed by an entrenched judiciary comprised of those who served the prior regime.[21] Judges find themselves balancing the demands of past and future, sometimes interpreted as a competition between stability and political-legal innovation. In a context like Egypt—where the country was already riven by opposing revolutionary claims and suspicion between Muslim Brotherhood supporters and other opposition groups—justice processes may become less engine of change than a brake on transformation.[22] Divisions among opposition groups made it difficult to unify around a particular vision of justice.[23] Nonetheless, transitional justice efforts can potentially play a role in foregrounding popular grievances and giving voice to any independent voices of the judiciary and resurgent civil society. In circumstances of ongoing military control, calls for transitional justice can reflect popular resistance. In this context, Aboueldahab argues, transitional justice should be understood as a '*process*, as opposed to a definitive outcome'.[24]

In Tunisia, where regime change and competitive elections initially suggested a paradigmatic transition, the justice landscape nonetheless offered a battleground for contesting and consolidating political arrangements, allocating power and resources and debating the nature of the transition itself.[25] In a last attempt to maintain power before he fled the country, President Ben Ali announced 'a fair and transparent investigation on crimes committed by security forces against demonstrators'; limited commissions were established to investigate state abuses under the regime and violence during the uprising.[26] After Ben Ali fled, an Amnesty Law was passed releasing political prisoners arrested under the Ben Ali regime and establishing a reparations programme aimed at financial compensation and the public reintegration of political prisoners. At the same time, hundreds of corruption-related lawsuits were filed against a number of individuals, including Ben Ali and his family.[27] Although many, including Ben Ali, were charged and sentenced in absentia, others were acquitted, resulting in anger among victims, who sought to overturn the decisions.[28]

The establishment of a Ministry for Human Rights and Transitional Justice and the 2013 passage of the Transitional Justice Law raised hopes for an evolving, sustainable form of justice, but many of the processes became targets of suspicion and dissension among competing political parties and their supporters. Efforts to distribute reparations were seen by some as inequitable awards to supporters of particular parties.[29] The Truth and Dignity Commission (L'Instance Verité et Dignité, or IVD), created in 2014 with a broad mandate to address violations between 1955 and 2013, became over time an instrument and symbol of political division.[30] The association of the IVD with an earlier era of post-Ben Ali governance reflected the difficulty of adapting an ongoing justice process to a political climate subject to rapid shifts in alliances and power. Tunisia represents a significant example of the sometime-recursive nature of transitional justice: not only do transitional states engage in battles over the legitimacy of justice, but justice itself can become a primary 'site of contestation for post-revolutionary legitimacy'.[31]

PRACTICING JUSTICE

The conditions under which transition has taken place not only elevate particular groups and individuals to power but make certain approaches to justice more plausible than others. Although in theory the list of tools used to pursue justice in transition could be infinite, in practice transitional justice has been tied to a common list of institutional approaches: truth commissions or other commissions of inquiry, criminal prosecutions, administrative purges or vetting schemes, reparations and related compensation programmes. Constitutional reforms, transformations of the education system and curricula, contextually specific practices, and memorialisation projects have also been associated with transitional justice in a variety of sites.[32] In each context, the new government or regime has been faced with the question of how to simultaneously confront the violence and violations of the past while avoiding a return to conflict or authoritarianism in the near future. Depending on the nature of the transition, the interests of the parties who retain or gain power in transition or war, and the level of international attention, the choice of particular approaches to justice can embolden certain groups, appeal to or anger victims, privilege some claims and harms over others, and mitigate or exacerbate societal fear and rage.

From the perspective of stability, the choice among mechanisms can have unpredictable effects.[33] Commissions that result in little material change can seem 'merely' symbolic, leading to renewed frustration and anger. Prosecutions that address only limited individuals or crimes may similarly seem unsatisfactory in a situation of ongoing political change; moreover, if judicial action at the criminal or constitutional level reflects continuity with a past regime rather than a break with past politics, the judiciary can become a flashpoint for popular anger.[34] Vetting regimes (in which government and security officials of the prior regime are either completely or partially barred from office) appear to offer a clear institutional break with a corrupt past but may all too often be utilised as weapons in an ongoing contestation between old and new forces. The determination of which institutions to implement and what their mandate will be not only reflects the balance of power in transition but can itself become a field of struggle over whose claims and voices will be privileged, which time period will be addressed, whether perpetrators or victims will be foregrounded, and how local practices will intersect with international legal and political priorities.

Within the common list of institutional practices associated with transitional justice, prosecutions have occupied an increasingly special place, including in the MENA region. High-level prosecutions of deposed leaders or war criminals have been embraced by scholars and activists alike as not only legally necessary but performatively and symbolically central to transition and reconstruction.[35] Such trials often serve the purpose of demonstrating the new government's deference to the rule of law and thus help to consolidate a new, stable post-authoritarian or post-conflict reality. Yet the pursuit of prosecutions, particularly as the primary or singular tool of justice, can be both destabilising and limited in practice. Depending on whether prosecutions take place at an international tribunal or in national courts, they may feel overly removed from local context or become enmeshed in local politics.[36] The accused or their allies may destabilise society in their efforts to avoid trial; moreover, the search for 'accountability may serve to hamper reconciliation, and help to reify divides in society'.[37] If transitional justice institutions are viewed as illegitimate, externally imposed, lacking in popular participation or motivated by self-interest, both the sustainability of the institution and its stabilising effect may be imperilled.

An edited collection published relatively soon after the uprisings commented that 'transitional justice debates [in the MENA region] have mainly revolved around how best to promote retributive justice' rather than debating the merits of different forms and conceptions of justice.[38] Yet it has not only been the choice of mechanisms but the justice pursued within them that has been limited; for example, the relatively few 'transitional' trials conducted in Egypt and Tunisia were primarily limited to crimes committed during the transition rather than past harms, raising questions about the objectives and scope of retributive justice in this context.[39] Limitations in capacity or due to politics can lead to trials addressing only some of the wide cast of characters involved in perpetrating war crimes or sustaining a brutal regime.[40] Even in ideal circumstances, criminal justice is by definition arranged to establish individual guilt and generally addresses a narrow set of crimes rather than a broader panoply of harms. In Tunisia, prosecutions were largely de-linked from a coherent transitional justice agenda and thus for the most part ineffective at creating a broader sense of accountability.[41] In Egypt, many protesters focused on calls for retributive justice, viewing it as a necessary antidote to years of authoritarian impunity.[42] Prosecutions can be significant and empowering for victims—but they may also be disappointing and traumatic.[43] It was in large part due to mass protests over several months in 2011 that the Supreme Council of Armed Forces (SCAF) finally arrested (deposed President) Mubarak and eventually brought him to trial, albeit for a relatively minimal list of crimes.[44] Yet Egyptian prosecutions were selective in scope and limited in effect. In Egypt, transitional justice generally and trials in particular became signal flashpoints among the SCAF, new political forces and a broad swath of civil society and popular protesters, each of whom had a competing interest in preventing, slowing or promoting transitional justice.[45]

In Libya, both the decision to implement particular processes and the modes of their implementation became sites of contestation over power and sovereignty among local actors and between national and international players. The 2013 Political Isolation Law, a vetting regime, became a tool for excluding not just those who had wholeheartedly supported Qadhafi but those who had led the uprising, due to their prior positions in the government.[46] As a result, individuals who might otherwise have played a role in facilitating Libya's transition towards political stability, particularly the judiciary, were unable to participate in governance.[47] The Political Isolation Law also permitted groups within Libya to embrace transitional agendas focused on excluding political enemies rather than (potentially) reconciling with them, making it look to some like victor's justice.[48]

Operating in parallel, retributive justice became not only an arena for political battle among local actors but a site of intense negotiation and conflict between the divided Libyan leadership and international institutions. In February 2011, the Security Council passed a resolution referring the situation in Libya to the International Criminal Court, which subsequently issued arrest warrants for Muammar Qadhafi, his son Saif al-Islam Qadhafi and his director of military intelligence Abdullah El Senussi.[49] The resolution referring the situation to the ICC barely preceded the authorisation for the use of force in Resolution 1973 which permitted NATO troops to intervene militarily, resulting in the overthrow of the Qadhafi regime.[50] As a result, international criminal justice, military intervention and sovereign control have been directly interwoven from the beginning of the Libyan transition. While the ICC's statements with regard to Libya focused on fighting impunity and pursuing justice, the Court's actions were entangled in the complex politics of multiple international interventions in Libyan politics, law and governance. That tangle grew more complex when the post-Qadhafi government challenged the ICC's jurisdiction on complementarity grounds, claiming that it had both the capacity and the right to try Saif al-Islam Qadhafi and Abdullah El Senussi itself.

The complementarity challenge represented an assertion of sovereignty by the Libyan government against both national and international challengers.[51] Directed to the ICC was a claim of Libyan ownership: the post-Qadhafi government wanted to conduct their own trials and find their own justice. At the same time, it deployed admissibility as an instrument for asserting its legitimacy even in the absence of full territorial and population control. The government was, in other words, using one area of international law (ICC admissibility) to mitigate its weaknesses in another (sovereignty). The Court's rejection of the admissibility challenge underlined the same weaknesses, however, finding that the Tripoli government had insufficient control of the area in which Saif al-Islam Qadhafi was being held (Zintan, a town in western Libya under militia control) and thus could not carry out his arrest and prosecution.[52] The struggle over jurisdiction— The Hague or Tripoli—exposed both the internal struggles of post-Qadhafi Libya and the tensions in an international complementarity doctrine that centred on claims by a (fragile, fragmented and deteriorating) post-conflict regime to ownership over its own justice processes. It also revealed the ways in which a particular practice of justice (prosecution) could become a battlefield for those vying for control of the state and its resources in the aftermath of political change.

Economising Transitional Justice

Not only the conditions and practices of transition but the causes that provoked the initial political change play a significant role in the allocation of power and resources. This is particularly acute in the case of economic crimes and inequality. Many of the 2011 uprisings in the MENA region were sparked directly and explicitly by anger over poverty, economic and regional inequalities, unemployment and corruption. The centrality of these concerns to the protests made clear the need to integrate economic considerations into any institutions meant to account for the past or sustain peace in the future. Political dissatisfaction with repressive leadership played an important, provocative role in the uprisings, but anger over radical inequality and deprivation were in many places inextricable from anti-authoritarian sentiment.[53]

Even prior to the uprisings, it had become increasingly clear that inequality and deprivation played a significant role in conflict and social dissension globally and thus affected the shape of justice. For more than a decade, transitional justice activists and advocates have struggled with the question of how much and how fully the institutions can attend to the legacies of unequal economic distribution, economic rights violations, corruption and land dispossession.[54] Transitional justice processes, including in Kenya, Sierra Leone, the Philippines and Liberia, have grappled explicitly with these issues.[55] The relationship to stability, however, remains difficult to parse or predict. Some argue that when political change is driven by the daily lived experience of deprivation in the face of governmental corruption or of economic inequality overlaid on clear regional or racial lines, only the recognition, reparation and resolution of those harms will stabilise state and society.[56] Others suggest that economic change is better left to experts in something other than justice and law or that processes that foreground economic redistribution is more destabilising than sustaining.[57] Just as the choice of justice institutions can have the effect of privileging certain actors or harms, discourse around the inclusion or exclusion of economic violence and its relation to stability can itself become a way to empower particular groups or claims.

In Egypt and Tunisia, important tensions arose between revolutionary calls during the uprisings and more conservative paths taken during the transitions, particularly in the realm of economic harms. Moreover, different groups vying for power used arguments about the relationships among justice, stability and economic distribution to amass further power to themselves. The Egyptian uprising was sparked and driven by anger over—among other things—economic deprivation and inequality. Corruption trials did take place, but they were limited in both targets and subject matter. They also had larger consequences for accountability. Trials that did focus on corruption in Egypt—an area often neglected in transitional justice for being linked too closely to structural considerations—created a 'means to shroud the neglected of accountability for widespread torture, killings, and other civil and political rights abuses committed for decades'.[58] In other words, to the degree that corruption trials took place, they served the function of evading confrontation with both a long history of violent human rights violations and a deep structure of unequal power and resources.

Tunisia's tensions between revolution and preservation manifested somewhat later in the process, particularly when government officials began to use stability as an alibi for limiting economic justice. Ben Ali's rule in Tunisia was characterised not only by violations such as arbitrary arrest and imprisonment, torture and repression of political dissent, but by socio-economic rights violations, corruption, unfair extraction practices and a differentiated regional economy.[59] Combined with growing unemployment and economic crisis, anger over deprivation, inequality and poverty helped spark the 2011 revolution. In response, the Tunisian transitional justice process paid unusually close attention to economic harms. The earliest of these processes represented placatory efforts towards the resistance; directly before stepping down, Ben Ali himself called for the establishment of commissions to address, among other issues, corruption.[60] Once formed, the commission heard testimony and took complaints from victims; unlike a broadly conceived truth commission, it was devoted solely to economic crimes and remained limited in scope.[61]

With increasing international and domestic input, the Tunisian transitional justice processes expanded to include a plethora of issues, including economic violence. Some civil society activists associated transitional justice with practices that could more fundamentally alter economic relations and regional inequities rather than focusing solely on the truth-telling and retributive objectives of many transitional justice processes.[62] The 2013 Transitional Justice Law, which established the Truth and Dignity Commission's (IVD), includes in its purview investigation of the misuse of public funds as well as recommendations for economic reform (among others). The Law called on the Commission to propose suggestions for the reform of institutions that participated in corruption and granted to it a number of quasi-prosecutorial powers, such as the ability to utilise both regular and specially constituted courts to investigate a variety of rights violations, including economic rights, the capacity to summon witnesses, protect them and order forensic work.[63] The IVD included a financial arbitration process, which successfully oversaw an agreement by former President Ben Ali's son-in-law to return looted assets along with cases involving Ben Ali's family members[64]; thousands of claims were filed, mainly regarding financial crimes.[65]

Although Tunisia's transitional justice process represented one of the more robust engagements with the legacy of economic harm, it also became an apt example of the distributional politics of justice. The IVD became part of the contestation over power between the ruling political parties as well as between the government and parts of civil society over the nature and character of justice. In September 2017, the Tunisian parliament crippled the IVD's work—partly in the name of stability—by passing the Administrative Reconciliation Law (initially named the Economic Reconciliation Act). The bill effectively ended ongoing or future prosecutions of civil servants involved in corruption and embezzlement who did not personally benefit from their corrupt acts. Although the law technically distinguished between personal enrichment and corrupt acts committed essentially under orders (and thus without personal benefit), there was little or no way to distinguish between the two.[66] As a result, the effort to investigate economic crimes and understand the wider corruption of the Ben Ali regime was compromised.[67] While the bill's supporters argued that the bill was intended to support economic development by minimising instability, critics suggested that it served primarily to insulate former members of the Ben Ali regime who were well-represented in the government. From its first draft, the Administration Reconciliation Law provoked vehement protests by civil society activists who viewed it as a betrayal of both the revolution and the promise of transitional justice.[68] More broadly, dissatisfaction among Tunisians about the rate and scale of economic change prompted new protests against the regime in January 2018, suggesting that any hopes that the IVD could ameliorate resentment based on economic deprivation and rights violations were outweighed by immediate concerns about the state of the national economy, ongoing corruption and unemployment.[69]

Corruption and unequal distribution were endemic to the governments in Egypt and Tunisia, making social and economic justice key to the protests and thus to the transitional negotiation over the nature of justice. As the justice processes developed, however, the politics of economic justice came into sharp relief. Attention to an economically unjust past could be a way to avoid dealing with other forms of past violence or a way for newly empowered parties to tar transitional justice with the charge of instability.

Memorialising Justice

Tropes of 'never again' abound in transitional justice, often bound up in the explicit or implicit embrace of history and memory as a baseline for reconciliation and non-repetition. Truth commissions tend to rely on the significance of official memory and public history: greater knowledge about a violent past (of repression, of torture, of the brutality of a regime that made people silently disappear) will ensure that the abuses will not be repeated. Trials of former leaders can not only establish the rule of law but retell a history that leaders have managed to suppress. Both truth commissions and criminal trials often find themselves freighted with the responsibility of retelling the history of a particular conflict, creating space for survivors to testify and remember harms done to them and making possible broadscale social reconciliation. The outcomes of these efforts, however, have been conflicted at best, not least because reconciliation is difficult to define and history can be a divisive source of violence just as much as a productive site for social reconciliation.[70]

In this arena, there can easily be a mismatch between form and function. The courtroom, for example, can be a problematic place to establish history; truth commissions may write narrow histories.[71] Moreover, archival preservation and survivor testimony require dedicated resources and expertise. In addition, the preoccupation with the past as a source for the future can sometimes obscure how much mandates or policy decisions have limited the timeline for justice in advance. To view transitional justice as a confrontation with an unjust past does not in itself reveal *which* unjust past will be addressed. In countries with long histories of violence, beginning with colonial harms, the horizon can be long. Yet transitional justice processes rarely address more than recent events. The result is—as in the choice of institution or the decision to include economic harms—to highlight some groups, violations and experiences as the paradigmatic victims of a particular past. To put it differently: to remember is also to classify. Just as the determination of reparations identifies only some individuals or groups as recipients of material or symbolic assistance, the structure of mechanisms based on seeking truth or preserving memory can create a hierarchy of victimhood that reflects or exacerbates potent societal divisions.[72]

Most of the governments subject to protest and overthrow in the MENA region were run by long-standing leaders who had instituted strong central authority, themselves following colonial systems that operated through violence and dispossession. Systematic discrimination against minority groups was rampant, as was unjust enrichment of elites and regional favouritism.[73] As a result, examining, accounting for and interrogating earlier periods raises questions not just about recent memory and history but much longer timescales of abuse, division and exploitation. Many of the trials that have taken place in the region have focused on a narrow time frame, trying crimes only related to a particular uprising rather than extending the timeline back to include the abuses of the prior leadership. As a result, the processes may highlight change while showing fealty to some continuity. In Egypt, prosecutions mainly focused on abuses during the uprising were paired with trials for earlier corruption. The effect was to separate one past (of recent physical violence and civil and political violation) from another (one of corruption, detached from political change). The temporal choice created a particular narrative about the 'exceptional' nature of human rights abuses rather than 'the culmination of decades of human rights violations leading up to it'.[74]

Earlier abuses and the memory of them still wend their way into transitional processes—sometimes directly and sometimes implicitly—but the narrowed time frame of justice short-circuits attempts at establishing history or preserving memories. Rather than an evaluation of the legacy of long-term harms perpetrated by brutal regimes, justice is reframed as a narrow technical tool to address immediate violence. As a result, it serves leaders who seek to legitimise themselves by calling for an accounting of recent action while eliding their own connections to earlier abuses.[75] Recent memory too can become polarised and reshaped in the process—as has happened in Egypt, where widely divergent narratives of events since the 2011 protests have emerged.[76]

The Tunisian truth commission was granted a longer temporal mandate, permitting a deeper inquiry into past abuse. The IVD had the capacity to recognise those who suffered under the prior regime and rewrite Tunisian history, in addition to potentially preventing future violence 'driven by the deepening economic, social and identity divides between the country's north and south'.[77] Yet Tunisia's memory politics are also intertwined with competitions over victimhood, violation and recognition. Abuses took place over decades and under both the Bourguiba and Ben Ali regimes; to 'remember' them is also to identify particular groups (such as leftists or An-Nahda members) as victims—and, conceivably, as perpetrators or bystanders of abuses against others. A fundamental rift opened between those who believed a preoccupation with the past would inherently destabilise and those who viewed the IVD and associated measures as the only path towards sustainable peace and democratic rule.[78] The privileging of particular victims or specific forms of reparation allow for 'a different story about the past [to be] told, and, thereby, a different form of political project...is served'.[79]

The preservation of the past becomes all the more fraught when the present is dominated by conflict rather than transition. Yet just as the conditions of transition shape plausible versions of justice, so too does a long-term continued conflict raise questions about the documentation of ongoing violations. Trapped in one of the more entrenched and bloody conflicts in the region, Syria has become a focal point of discussions about the possible contributions of transitional justice to peace. Aboueldahab argues that the ongoing nature of the conflict along with the efforts by local actors to create archives and documentation of current abuses suggests that 'the documentation of violence should be considered as both a stand-alone mechanism of transitional justice and as a means to lay the foundation for a variety of future post-conflict justice goals'.[80] In other words, documentation may itself constitute transitional justice, in addition to facilitating the establishment of other institutions and mechanisms in the future. Moreover, activists are documenting not just physical integrity abuses such as torture and killing but large-scale displacement and land seizures in order to facilitate both accountability and also return.[81] This suggests a fruitful intersection with other considerations: it is not only about the creation of an archive that can create a basis for future justice processes but the parameters of that archive that will shape what sort of justice is done.

CONCLUSION

In situations of radical injustice, stability itself can be counter-revolutionary. The uprisings of 2011 were, by definition, destabilising; they sought dramatic change in the face of long-standing socio-economic deprivation and inequality, lack of accountability and brutal violence. In the aftermath of conflict or successful changes in leadership, however, the effort to stabilise state and society can potentially represent part of the project of building a peaceful and just future. Justice was one of the calls of the 2011 protests; it was also one of the promises of the post-2011 arrangements. The commonality of the call—by international actors, protests, government officials, opposition parties—suggests a united front for transitional justice. In practice, however, struggles over the form, character and content of justice become part of transitions themselves—not least because transitional justice can serve as a rallying cry for protest or as a form of regime legitimation. The plasticity of transitional justice offers a platform for diverse actors with opposing interests to compete over control of new governments and politics. As a result, no linear relationship exists between stabilisation—which often implies consolidated governmental control—and justice, which could conceivably either support or disrupt that power. At the most granular level, these struggles should be understood as fragments of, rather than separate from, contestations over power, resources and violence.

Tunisia, Libya and Egypt are hardly anomalous in their imbrication of law and politics, but they do provide important examples for how justice processes, particularly in moments of radical change or possibility, are inextricably linked with specific local and regional distributional dynamics. Such links can potentially strengthen justice practices by imbuing them with legitimacy, strengthening their relevance for local claims and establishing a foundation for political upheaval. Where regressive forces maintain strong claims to power, however, including when the judiciary remains at least partially tied to the past leadership, and where insecurity remains prevalent, justice and accountability measures have less capacity to strengthen redistributive programmes or establish meaningful reparation to victims of past harm. As institutions that bear responsibility for holding individuals and governments to account for past violence, trials and commissions often raise expectations that cannot be fulfilled within the existing political climate. The disappointment of those expectations can fuel further frustration and eventual unrest. Moreover, delimiting the temporal or substantive scope of investigation, inquiry or prosecution immediately narrows the horizon of justice. The result may be to reignite recent anger in the face of continuities in repression or deprivation, to establish a new stability premised on a return to military rule, or, most dramatically, to devolve into armed conflict.

Justice processes struggle to mediate among opposing parties while seeking to present justice itself as residing outside political conflict. Given the impossibility of separating law or justice from politics, we should focus instead on pragmatically and contextually understanding the costs and benefits of particular processes and practices. In its highest order, transitional justice could offer not a short-term fix to long-term social problems but an ongoing confrontation with the past and reinvention of the present. Perhaps the most important lesson for stability is to understand justice as a distributional process, one which contributes to the allocation of power, legitimacy and resources to any number of groups and as a result remains inevitably interwoven with the continual formation and reformulation of state and society.

NOTES

1. See Omar (2014).
2. Shalakany (2014, p. 373).
3. Permanent Mission of Switzerland to the United Nations (2013).
4. See Miller (2015).
5. See Teitel (2002, p. 898).
6. I do not explicitly discuss here the meeting points of religion and justice. See, e.g., Khatib (2014). By definition, however, political Islam is critical to many of the processes I discuss in the chapter, most prominently in the election and then deposing and prosecution of Mohamed Morsi in Egypt and in the rise of An-Nahda in Tunisia.
7. See Sriram (2007).
8. The radically different experiences and effects of transitional justice in these three geographically proximate states serves implicitly to highlight a baseline challenge for the transitional justice field: despite its genuine commitment to local context and participation, the temptation to generalise by region or by mechanism is strong. While the chapter does reference the region and offers some comparative points, it attempts primarily to focus on the specific dynamics in which the calls for, and institutionalisation of, justice have played an important role—and to use that to extrapolate not a toolkit or common approach but an analysis of the different ways in which justice can operate to preserve or challenge political and legal order.
9. On the terminology of "economic violence", see Sharp (2014).
10. See, for example, Diamond (2011) and Fisher and Stewart (2014).
11. See Teitel (2000).
12. See Sriram (2007).
13. *Guidance Note of the Secretary-General* (2010).
14. See Omar (2014).
15. As Abou-El-Fadl points out, the slogan in Egypt, as in Tunisia, was "'The People Want the Fall of the Regime,' where the Arabic word for 'regime', al-nizam, also connotes 'order' or 'system'." See Abou-El-Fadl (2012, p. 320).
16. The International Crisis Group uses the terminology of the 'second transition' in *Marching in Circles* (2013b).
17. Omar (2014).
18. See Lesch (2014).
19. See Mourad and Ahmed (2017).
20. Morsi was tried for escaping prison, inciting violence, murder, treason, conspiracy, and collaboration, among other charges and in several trials taking place over several years. There were numerous sentences and several cases that were overturned on appeal. For a succinct summary of the numerous legal proceedings involving Morsi, see Bernard-Maugiron (2018, p. 224).

For discussion of the trials and their characterisation, see, for example, Youssef (2017), Al-Arian (2015), and Hellyer (2013).

21. See Aziz (2016b).
22. See Sultany (2017, p. 160).
23. Aziz argues that revolutionary groups wanted to substantively transform the legal system while liberal opposition groups wanted merely procedural protections. See Aziz (2016b, p. 211).
24. Ibid.
25. See Mullin and Rouabah (2014).
26. See Andrieu (2016, p. 269).
27. See Mullin and Rouabah (2014, p. 4).
28. See Sultany (2017, p. 179).
29. See Andrieu (2016, pp. 271–272, 281); International Crisis Group, *Transitional Justice and the Fight Against Corruption* (2016).
30. Organic Law on Establishing and Organizing Transitional Justice (Unofficial Translation by ICTJ).
31. See Lamont (2016, p. 100).
32. Report of the Secretary General, "The Rule of Law and Transitional Justice in Conflict and Post-conflict Societies" (2004); see also International Center of Transitional Justice, "What Is Transitional Justice".
33. See Sriram (2017, p. 61).
34. See Sultany (2017).
35. Karen Engle discusses critically the increasing use of criminal law and rejection of amnesties Engle. Kathryn Sikkink offers a much more positive take on the same trend Sikkink.
36. See, for example, Peskin (2005) and Subotic (2009).
37. See Sriram (2007, p. 587).
38. See Fisher and Stewart (2014, p. 4).
39. Aboueldahab (2017a, p. 4).
40. See, for example, Mamdani (2014).
41. See Andrieu (2016, pp. 275–277).
42. See Aboueldahab (2017a, p. 42).
43. See Varney et al. (2017).
44. Email correspondence with Issandr El Amrani, North Africa Project Director, International Crisis Group (13 October 2018). Mubarak was eventually convicted of embezzlement, an important but also extraordinarily narrow finding given the legacy of abuse under his thirty year reign. Reuters (2015).
45. Email correspondence with Issandr El Amrani, North Africa Project Director, International Crisis Group (13 October 2018).
46. Boduszyński and Wierda (2016, p. 142).
47. Judges and prosecutors saw the law as an instrument for removing them from office and further destabilising the judicial system Salah (2014).
48. See Boduszyński and Wierda (2016, p. 158).

49. UN Security Council Resolution 1970 (26 February 2011).
50. UN Security Council Resolution 1973 (17 March 2011).
51. See Kersten (2014).
52. ICC Pre-Trial Chamber I (2013a). The El Senussi admissibility challenge was accepted on the grounds that the same case was proceeding concurrently in Libya and that the authorities were neither unwilling nor unable to carry it out. Ibid.
53. See Cammett and Diwan (2014, p. 2).
54. See, e.g., Sharp (2014), Miller (2008), and Arbour (2007).
55. See, e.g., Slye (2017), Carranza (2008, p. 324), *Witness to Truth: Report of the Sierra Leone Truth and Reconciliation Commission*, vol. III, Ch. 1, para. 143–149 (2004), and Liberian Truth and Reconciliation Commission, *Consolidated Final Report* (2009, sec. 9.9.1).
56. See, for example, Nichols (2014). For a useful taxonomy of the arguments for and against including economic violence in transitional justice generally—including with regard to sustainable peace and stability, see Sharp (2014).
57. On not over-stretching the field, see Waldorf (2012) and McAuliffe (2017).
58. See Aboueldahab (2017a, p. 43).
59. See Andrieu (2016, p. 268).
60. See Lamont (2016, p. 85).
61. See Andrieu (2016, p. 270).
62. International Crisis Group, *Transitional Justice and the Fight Against Corruption* (2016, p. 8).
63. Organic Law, Art. 43 (2013).
64. See El Malki (2017).
65. International Crisis Group, *Transitional Justice and the Fight Against Corruption* (2016) and El Malki (2017).
66. See Guellali (2017).
67. Human Rights Watch, *Tunisia: Parliament Shouldn't Undercut Transitional Justice* (2018).
68. See Lincoln (2017).
69. See Aydogan and Yildirim (2018).
70. See Sriram (2016, p. 27).
71. On history in the courtroom, see Arendt (1963) and Simpson (2007). On the limits of truth commission history, see Posel (2008).
72. On the relationship between reparations and victimhood, see Miller (2008, pp. 284–287). On the construction, politics and effects of victimhood in transitional justice, see Weinstein (2016).
73. See Hanieh (2013).
74. See Aboueldahab (2017a, p. 24). Memorialisation does not, of course, happen only or even primarily through trials or other official activities.
75. See Turner (2016).

302   Z. MILLER

76. Email correspondence with Issandr El Amrani (October 14, 2018).
77. *Tunisia: Transitional Justice and the Fight Against Corruption* (2016, p. 17).
78. *Tunisia: Transitional Justice and the Fight Against Corruption* (2016, pp. 13–17).
79. See Andrieu (2016, p. 264).
80. See Aboueldahab (2018).
81. Ibid., 13.

BIBLIOGRAPHY

Aboueldahab, N. "Transitional Justice Policy in Authoritarian Contexts: The Case of Egypt." *Brookings Doha Center Publications,* 19 October 2017a.

———. *Transitional Justice and the Prosecution of Political Leaders in the Arab Region.* Oxford: Hart Publishing, 2017b.

———. *Writing Atrocities: Syrian Civil Society and Transitional Justice.* Brookings Doha Center Publication, 7 May 2018.

Abou-El-Fadl, R. "Beyond Conventional Transitional Justice: Egypt's 2011 Revolution and the Absence of Political Will." *International Journal of Transitional Justice,* vol. 6, no. 2 (2012).

Al-Arian, A. "The Many Trials of Mohamed Morsi." *Al-Jazeera,* 2 May 2015.

Amnesty International. *'We Want an End to the Fear': Abuses Under Tunisia's State of Emergency,* 2017a.

———. *Setting the Scene for Elections: Two Decades of Silencing Dissent in Rwanda,* 2017b.

Andrieu, K. "Confronting the Dictatorial Past in Tunisia: Human Rights and the Politics of Victimhood in Transitional Justice Discourses Since 2011." *Human Rights Quarterly,* vol. 38, no. 2 (2016).

Arbour, L. "Economic and Social Justice for Societies in Transition." *New York University Journal of International Law & Politics,* vol. 40, no. 1 (2007).

Arendt, H. Eichmann in Jerusalem: A Report on the Banality of Evil. New York: The Viking Press, 1963.

Aydogan, A., and Yildirim, A.K. *The Economic and Political Dissatisfaction Behind Tunisia's Protests.* Carnegie Endowment for International Peace, 23 January 2018.

Ayed, O. "Prolongation de l'IVD en Tunisie: 'Un geste d'apaisement du gouvernement'." *France 24,* 29 May 2018.

Aziz, S. "Theater or Transitional Justice: Reforming the Judiciary in Egypt." In C.L. Sriram (ed.), *Transitional Justice in the Middle East and North Africa.* New York: Oxford University Press, 2016a.

———. "Independence Without Accountability: The Judicial Paradox of Egypt's Failed Transition to Democracy." *Penn State Law Review*, vol. 120, no. 3 (2016b).

Bernard-Maugiron, N. "Transitional Justice in Post-revolutionary Egypt." In Stéphane Lacroix and Jean-Pierre Filiu (eds.), *Revisiting the Arab Uprisings: The Politics of a Revolutionary Moment*. New York: Oxford University Press, 2018.

Boduszyński M., and Wierda, M. "Political Exclusion and Transitional Justice: Study of Libya." In C.L. Sriram (ed.), *Transitional Justice in the Middle East and North Africa*. New York: Oxford University Press, 2016.

Borer, T.A. "Reconciling South Africa or South Africans? Cautionary Notes from the TRC." *African Studies Quarterly*, vol. 8, no. 1 (2004).

Cammett, M., and Diwan, I. *The Political Economy of the Arab Uprisings*. New York: Routledge, 2014.

Carranza, R. "Plunder and Pain: Should Transitional Justice Engage with Corruption and Economic Crimes." *International Journal of Transitional Justice* (2008).

Commission on Human Rights. *Promotion and Protection of Human Rights: Study on the Right to the Truth*, E/CN.4/2006/91, 8 February, 2006.

Diamond, L. "A Fourth Wave or a False Start? Democracy After the Arab Spring." *Foreign Affairs*, 22 May 2011.

El Amrani, I., and Lindsey, U. "Tunisia Moves to the Next State." *Middle East Research and Information Report*, 8 November 2011.

El Malki, F., *Tunisia's Partisan Path to Transitional Justice* (Carnegie Endowment for International Peace), 7 March 2017.

Engle, K., Miller, Z., and Davis, D.M., *Anti-impunity and the Human Rights Agenda*. New York: Cambridge University Press, 2016.

Fisher, K.J., and Stewart, R., *Transitional Justice and the Arab Spring*. New York: Routledge Press, 2014.

Guellali, A. "New Reconciliation Law Threatens Tunisia's Democracy." *World Policy Blog*, 2 October 2017.

Guidance Note of the Secretary-General: United Nations Approach to Transitional Justice (2010).

Hanieh, A. *Lineages of Revolt: Issues of Contemporary Capitalism in the Middle East*. Chicago: Haymarket Books, 2013.

Hellyer, H.A. "The Trial of the Muslim Brotherhood." Brookings, 12 November 2013.

Human Rights Watch. *Libya: Flawed Trial of Gaddafi Officials*, 28 July 2015.

———. *Tunisia: Parliament Shouldn't Undercut Transitional Justice*, 23 March 2018.

International Center for Transitional Justice. "What Is Transitional Justice." Available at https://www.ictj.org/about/transitional-justice.

International Criminal Court Pre-Trial Chamber I, Decision on the Admissibility of the Case Against Abdullah Al-Senussi, ICC-01/11-01/11.

International Crisis Group. *Trial by Error: Justice in Post-Qadhafi Libya*, 17 April 2013a.

———. *Marching in Circles: Egypt's Dangerous Second Transition*, 7 August 2013b.

———. *Tunisia: Transitional Justice and the Fight Against Corruption*, 3 May 2016.

Kersten, M. "Justice After the War: The International Criminal Court and Post-Gaddafi Libya." In Kirsten Fisher and Robert Stewart (eds.), *Transitional Justice and the Arab Spring*. New York: Routledge, 2014.

Khatib, L. "Challenges of Representation and Inclusion: A Case Study of Islamist Groups in Transitional Justice". In Kirsten Fisher and Robert Stewart (eds.), *Transitional Justice and the Arab Spring*. New York: Routledge, 2014.

Lamont, C.K. "The Scope and Boundaries of Transitional Justice in the Arab Spring." In C.L. Chandra Lekha Sriram (eds.), *Transitional Justice in the Middle East and North Africa*. New York: Oxford University Press, 2016.

Lesch, A.M. "Troubled Political Transitions: Tunisia, Egypt, and Libya." *Middle East Policy*, vol. 21, no. 1 (2014): 62–74.

Lincoln, J. "Manich Msamah and the Face of Continued Protest in Tunisia." *Jadaliyya*, August 24, 2017.

Mamdani, M. "The Truth According to the TRC." In Ifi Amadiume and Abdullahi An-Na'im (eds.), *The Politics of Memory: Truth, Healing and Social Justice*. London: Zed Books, 2000.

McAuliffe, P. *Transformative Transitional Justice and the Malleability of Post-conflict States*. Northampton: Edward Elgar, 2017.

Mégret, F., and Samson, M.G., "Holding the Line on Complementarity in Libya: The Case for Tolerating Flawed Domestic Trials." *Journal of International Criminal Justice* 11 (2013): 571–598.

Miller, E. "A Close Look at the Changes to Egypt's Ministries." Atlantic Council, 1 October 2015.

Miller, Z. "Effects of Invisibility: In Search of the 'Economic' in Transitional Justice." *The International Journal of Transitional Justice*, vol. 2, no. 2 (2008): 266–291.

Mourad, M., and Ahmed, H. "In Final Ruling, Egypt Court Finds Mubarak Innocent in Killing of Protestors." Reuters, 2 March 2017.

Mullin, C., and Rouabah, B. "Requiem for Tunisia's Transition?" *Jadaliyya*, 22 December 2014.

Mullin, C., and Patel, I. "Contesting Transitional Justice as Liberal Governance in Revolutionary Tunisia." *Conflict and Society*, vol. 2, no. 1 (2016): 104–124.

Nichols, S. "Reimagining Transitional Justice for an Enduring Peace: Accounting for Natural Resources in Conflict". In Dustin Sharp (ed.), *Justice and Economic Violence in Transition*. New York: Springer, 2014.

Omar, R. "The Delay of Transitional Justice in Egypt." *Middle East Institute*, 12 February 2014.

Organic Law on Establishing and Organizing Transitional Justice (Unofficial Translation by ICTJ) (2013).

Permanent Mission of Switzerland to the United Nations (2013).

Peskin, V. "Beyond Victor's Justice? The Challenge of Prosecuting the Winners at the International Criminal Tribunals for the Former Yugoslavia and Rwanda." *Journal of Human Rights*, vol. 4, no. 2 (2005): 213–231.

Posel, D. "History as Confession: The Case of the South African Truth and Reconciliation Commission." *Public Culture*, vol. 20, no. 1 (2008): 119–141.

Quinn, J.R., and Freeman, M., "Lessons Learned: Practical Lessons Gleaned from Inside the Truth Commissions of Guatemala and South Africa." *Human Rights Quarterly*, vol. 25 (2003).

Report of the Secretary-General, "The Rule of Law and Transitional Justice in Conflict and Post-conflict Societies." S/2004/616, 23 August 2004.

Republic of Liberia Truth and Reconciliation Commission Final Report (2009).

Reuters. "Mubarak Sentenced to Three Years in Jail for Corruption." 9 May 2015.

Rome Statute of the International Criminal Court (2002).

Rowen, J. *Searching for Truth in the Transitional Justice Movement*. New York: Cambridge University Press, 2017.

Salah, H. "Libya's Justice Pandemonium." *Human Rights Watch*, 14 April 2014.

Shalakany, A. "The Day the Graffiti Died." *London Review of International Law*, vol. 2, no. 2 (2014): 357–378.

Sharp, D. (ed.). *Justice and Economic Violence in Transition*. New York: Springer, 2014.

Simpson, G. *Law, War, and Crime: War Crimes, Trials and the Reinvention of International Law*. Cambridge: Polity, 2007.

Slye, R. "Putting the J into the TRC: Kenya's Truth Justice and Reconciliation Commission." In Mia Swart and Karin van Marle (eds.), *The Limits of Transition: The South African Truth and Reconciliation Commission Twenty Years On*, 2017.

South Africa Truth and Reconciliation Commission (1998).

Sriram, C.L. "Justice as Peace Liberal Peacebuilding and Strategies of Transitional Justice." *Global Society*, vol. 21, no. 4 (2007): 579–591.

———. "Transitional Justice in Comparative Perspective: Lessons for the Middle East." In C.L. Chandra Lekha Sriram (ed.), *Transitional Justice in the Middle East and North Africa*. Oxford University Press, 2016.

———. "Beyond Transitional Justice: Peace, Governance and Rule of Law." *International Studies Review*, vol. 19 (2017).

Subotic, J. *Hijacked Justice: Dealing with the Past in the Balkans*. Ithaca: Cornell University Press, 2009.

Sultany, N., *Law and Revolution: Legitimacy and Constitutionalism After the Arab Spring*. Oxford: Oxford University Press, 2017.

Teitel, R. *Transitional Justice*. New York: Oxford University Press, 2000.

Teitel, Ruti G. "Transitional Justice in a New Era." *Fordham International Law Journal*, vol. 26, no. 4, art. 2 (2002): 893.

———. *Globalizing Transitional Justice: Contemporary Essays*. New York: Oxford University Press, 2014.

Turner, C. *Transitional Justice in Egypt: A Challenge and Opportunity*. The Tahrir Institute for Middle East Policy, 14 May 2016.

United Nations Security Council Resolution 1970, 26 February 2011.

United Nations Security Council Resolution 1973, 17 March 2011.

Varney, H., Zduńczyk, K., and Gaudard, M. *The Role of Victims in Criminal Proceedings*. New York: International Center for Transitional Justice, 2017.

Waldorf, L. "Anticipating the Past: Transitional Justice and Socio-Economic Wrongs." *Social and Legal Studies*, vol. 21 (2012).

Weinstein, H.M. "Victims, Transitional Justice and Social Reconstruction: Who Is Setting the Agenda?" In Inge Vanfraechem et al. (eds.), *Justice for Victims: Perspectives on Rights, Transition and Reconciliation*. London: Routledge, 2016.

Witness to Truth: Report of the Sierra Leone Truth and Reconciliation Commission, 2004.

Youssef, Adham. "Former Egypt President Mohamed Morsi Found Guilty of Insulting Judiciary." *The Guardian*, 30 December 2017.

CHAPTER 14

The Soldier and the Curator: The Challenges of Defending Cultural Property in Conflict Areas

Jean-Gabriel Leturcq and Jean-Loup Samaan

INTRODUCTION

In late 2012, Islamist insurgents in Mali seized control of huge parts of the northern regions of the country. Along with their territorial conquest, terrorist organisations such as Ansar al Din, started targeting monuments such as mausoleums, mosques and cemeteries in Timbuktu—a centre of Islamic civilisation from the thirteenth to the seventeenth centuries. The leader of the group, Abu Dardar, then declared 'not a single mausoleum will remain in Timbuktu'.[1] A year later, Daesh launched its own campaign of devastation across Iraq and Syria. In the Iraqi city of Mosul, the mosque of Nabi Yunus and the shrine of Imam Awn al Din were destroyed among many

---

J.-G. Leturcq (✉)
Musée Du Louvre, Abu Dhabi, United Arab Emirates

J.-L. Samaan
National Defense College,
Abu Dhabi, United Arab Emirates

© The Author(s) 2020   307
V. Gervais and S. van Genugten (eds.), *Stabilising the Contemporary Middle East and North Africa*, Middle East Today,
https://doi.org/10.1007/978-3-030-25229-8_14

other monuments. Similarly, churches and Sufi shrines were systemically targeted by militants. In Syria, soon the ancient city of Palmyra became the victim of Daesh attacks, with the demolition of many statues and temples. The destruction of Palmyra, the 'irreplaceable treasure' as French historian Paul Veyne called it, provoked awe and uproar in the international community.[2] Timbuktu, Mosul, Palmyra had been part of our universal heritage, relics of a distant past that in some cases are now gone. UNESCO's then Director-General Irina Bokova depicted the destructions as 'a form of cultural cleansing'. These waves of attacks raised the level of awareness within the international diplomatic community, and as a result, on March 24, 2017, the UN Security Council released its first-ever resolution dedicated to the protection of cultural heritage.[3]

This latest wave of terrorist attacks against cultural property, or 'tangible heritage' to use UNESCO's terminology,[4] put the defence of cultural heritage decisively on the diplomatic agenda. In the eyes of decision-makers, these destructions demonstrated that heritage was not a collateral damage of war but one of its ostentatious targets. Furthermore, these attacks were perpetrated by non-state armed groups, which posed a new challenge for policy and lawmakers as the efforts conducted until then had primarily focused on cases involving states or state-backed actors. This triggered a momentum on the international stage to launch new policy initiatives. In particular, France and the UAE jointly pushed in 2017 for the creation of an International Alliance for the Protection of Heritage in Conflict Areas (ALIPH)—summarised by the acronym ALIPH. As a result, the protection of cultural property was now to be considered as a factor in the planning of both stabilisation operations and post-stabilisation efforts.

It follows the logic of the concept of stabilisation itself understood as an approach blending military means with humanitarian, developmental and other tools. Over the last decade, the stabilisation debate that derived from the Iraqi and the Afghan experiences has tended to look primarily at the reconstruction of infrastructure and national institutions to restore security and revive the economy.[5] These are essential components of state-building but they address only the technical functioning of a society, not its cultural cohesion. Cultural property plays a direct role in cementing ties between individuals belonging to the same community: in other words, monuments are the physical translation of an 'imagined community', to use Benedict Anderson's concept.[6] If the contemporary policy agenda has shed light on the necessity to prevent cultural destruction, the phenomenon is by no means unprecedented as monuments have been targeted throughout history: Erostrate set on fire Artemis' temple in Ephesus in 356 BC and more recently, the infamous book burning ceremonies organised by the Nazi regime in the 1930s served a similar purpose as Daesh's tactics. This is why practitioners should not underestimate the importance of defending, or restoring, cultural property, as it is these monuments that shape the identity of the local population, and by extension pave the way for the stabilisation of that society. But adding the defence of cultural property to the stabilisation enterprise has several implications for policymakers: the need for third parties to undertake intervention to directly protect property in situ; the need for guidance for militaries undertaking stabilisation operations to avoid unintentional destruction of cultural property; non-military engagement to guide armed fighters in achieving their aims without harming cultural property; intervention to remove property from the state; and finally, rebuilding or rehousing cultural property in a post-conflict context.

In this perspective, this chapter aims to bring to light these numerous initiatives of international actors to defend cultural property before, during or after conflicts. It starts by retracing the issue of protecting cultural property in times of war in modern history. The review demonstrates how the topic is not entirely new, as evidenced by the relocation of Spanish artworks to Switzerland during the civil war and the famous task force of the Monuments Men during the Second World War.[7] If protecting cultural property predated the contemporary stabilisation agenda, we underline that the threat posed by extremist non-state actors such as Boko Haram and Daesh has jeopardised much of the framework provided by international humanitarian law and therefore call for a new policy response. The second part of the chapter analyses more closely these recent developments and more specifically how they paved the way for the creation in 2017 of an ALIPH. This Alliance constitutes a valuable case study to reflect on the diplomatic instruments that can be deployed against the destruction of cultural heritage in conflict zones. We then discuss the priorities, and challenges, of this new initiative. Finally, the third part highlights some of the most significant issues policymakers will need to address in the near future: the governance of multiple initiatives involving intergovernmental organisations as well as NGOs; the traditional clash between armed forces and cultural communities; the uncertainties regarding the legal framework relating to the ongoing conflicts; and finally, the practical challenge of establishing 'safe havens' for cultural property.

The Origins of Cultural Property Protection

To understand how protecting cultural heritage has become an important policy consideration when it comes to stabilisation efforts in conflict areas, we need to go back to the origins of the concept of cultural heritage itself, and how cultural property protection turned into a parameter of a return to social order. In fact, the issue of defending monuments and sacred sites preceded the contemporary debate on stabilisation efforts in conflict areas. It can be traced back to the aftermath of the French Revolution, when intellectuals and politicians emphasised the importance of preventing the destruction of monuments and the looting of libraries by the revolutionary crowds. In that respect, the famous paper by Abbé Grégoire, the 'Report on the destructions perpetrated by vandalism and the means to suppress it' (*Rapport sur les destructions opérées par le vandalisme, et sur les moyens de le réprimer*),[8] issued in 1794, constitutes the conceptual blueprint of public policies for the protection of cultural heritage. The author called on the parliament to pass and implement laws protecting cultural heritage. Protecting the artefacts while punishing the offenders was his core message. Victor Hugo's *War on demolishers!* (1825) used the same pattern of opposition to denounce the impunity of those demolishing monuments and the lack of enforcement of laws protecting heritage. Altogether, these writings coined the concept of protection of cultural property as a collective moral duty.

This sense of moral duty eventually resurfaced at the level of the international community in 1907, when the second Hague Convention of 1907 on Laws and Customs of War on Land was issued. For the first time, an international agreement mentioned the protection of cultural property during wartime and forbade the destruction of the enemy's cultural property.[9] Specifically, Article 56 stated that 'all seizure of, destruction or wilful damage done to institutions of [historical, charitable, educational, artistic, scientific] character, historic monuments, works of arts and science, is forbidden, and should be made a matter of legal proceedings'.[10]

The first half of the twentieth century saw an increasing demand for preserving cultural property during wartime. The peace treaties of that era usually included clauses on reparations for the destruction or plunder of cultural property. Noticeably, the Treaty of Versailles in 1919 stated that 'Germany undertakes to furnish to the University of Louvain, within three months after a request made by it and transmitted through the intervention of the Reparation Commission, manuscripts, incunabula, printed books, maps and objects of collection corresponding in number and value to those destroyed in the burning by Germany of the Library of Louvain'.[11] In 1935, another treaty on the 'protection of artistic and scientific institutions and historical monuments' was adopted in Washington by the USA and Pan American states only. But as the international system of the interwar period was on the brink of collapse, the treaty had barely any chance to become embedded in practice. The absence of concrete measures made impossible the implementation of these texts.[12] In the aftermath of the Second World War, the International Military Tribunal at Nuremberg convicted several German officials for their implication in the destruction of cultural heritage.[13] The years following the Second World War brought a new momentum. Specifically, the United Nations Educational, Scientific and Cultural Organization (UNESCO) was created in 1946. UNESCO's core mission was to promote peace through the promotion of education, science and culture, including protection and cultivation of cultural property. It was meant to build a dialogue among different civilisations in this specific field. The organisation quickly promoted an intergovernmental conference that paved the way for the drafting of the 1954 Hague Convention for the Protection of Cultural Property in the Event of Armed Conflict.

The Hague Convention was the first universal treaty protecting cultural heritage in the context of armed conflicts. Until today, it remains the bedrock of all actions in this regard. The preamble of the document states that 'damage to cultural property belonging to any people whatsoever means damage to the cultural heritage of all mankind, since each people makes its contribution to the culture of the world'.[14] For the first time, an international document with legal implications provided a detailed, extensive list of cultural property, both immovable (building, sites and monuments) and movable (works of art, artefacts and books). According to the document, the parties were requested to safeguard heritage in time of peace 'against the foreseeable effects of an armed conflict' (Article 3). This implied taking all measures to efficiently protect heritage, such as preparing inventories, documentation and protected storage facilities. In the event of a conflict, State parties were requested to refrain from exposing cultural property to damage and destruction and must stop looting and theft in their country and in other states.

A new step was reached in the 1970s, first with the Convention for the Protection of Cultural Property and Preventing the Illicit Import, Export, and Transfer of Ownership of Cultural Property. The document complemented the 1954 Convention by enjoining the states to create infrastructure dedicated to the conservation of heritage. Then, in 1972, a Convention Concerning the Protection of World Cultural Heritage and Natural Heritage was adopted. The document substantially reinforced the responsibility of the international community with regard to the protection of cultural heritage. It established a World Heritage List that bound member states to implement and provide means for the protection of international cultural property. The geopolitical context mattered: the 1972 Convention was a direct result of the International Campaign to Save the Monuments of Nubia, launched by UNESCO in 1960. The campaign had succeeded in raising the awareness of governments regarding the necessity to formally include cultural property as elements to defend against the risk of war. Unfortunately, all these conventions faced immense challenges when it came to their application. Taken together, the 1954 Hague Convention and its two protocols established a comprehensive set of rules governing armed conflict and ensuring the safety of cultural property during a war. As pointed out by the International Committee of the Blue Shield (ICBS),[15] these legal instruments have built an international regime for cultural property that serve two functions: first, they are prohibitive, as in the case of International Humanitarian Law, by setting out prohibitions that parties are obliged not to violate, and by criminalising such violations.[16] Second, they are 'protective and pre-emptive, by obliging States Parties to take measures which protect cultural property during times of peace, in order to ensure its safety from attack, looting, and other damaging effects of war'.[17]

In parallel, the success of the World Heritage List stimulated a global interest in cultural heritage in the 1980s and 1990s. Cultural property was assigned social and economic values and became a tool for peace-making and economic development, contributing to the reconstruction of social fabric and economic structures. But ultimately, it is only in the 1990s that the defence of cultural property became a component of what would be called today the stabilisation agenda. If until then culture had been largely seen as a victim of conventional conflicts between two states, the international community came to the realisation that state collapse and civil war could equally lead cultural heritage to be targeted by one group with the clear intent to destroy a population and its identity. The breakup of Yugoslavia during that period and the multiple conflicts between its ethnic communities triggered this realisation. Following the Balkan wars, the first protocol of the 1954 Convention corresponding to conventional warfare was amended with a second protocol in 1999, adapted to the scenarios of non-conventional conflicts, meaning intra-state conflicts or conflicts involving non-state belligerents. However, these provisions would soon prove insufficient, as revealed by the multiple assaults on cultural property in the subsequent years.

THE DEFENCE OF CULTURAL PROPERTY AS A STABILISATION EFFORT: THE EMERGENCE OF ALIPH

In the last decade, a shift occurred in the way policymakers looked at the issue of protecting cultural property. For terrorist organisations, destroying the traces of cultural heritage progressively became a very powerful means of communication to seek international exposure. In the 2000s and 2010s, a pattern emerged where such attacks were turned into a systematic tactic of these groups in conflict zones. The destruction of the Buddha statues in Bamyan, Afghanistan in 2001, the bombing of al-Askari Mosque in Iraq in 2006, and the wave of destructions caused by armed groups in Mali in 2012, Iraq or Syria in 2014 and 2015, all exposed the weakness of legal instruments and the incapacity of international organisations to prevent those destructions. Mass media coverage of these destructions led the international community to react. As a result, the UN Security Council adopted on March 24, 2017 Resolution 2347. Pushed by France and Italy, the document was heavily influenced by the events in Syria and Iraq. It was the first UN Security Council resolution to focus exclusively on cultural heritage, condemning the destruction of cultural property as well as its looting and illegal trafficking, particularly by non-state armed groups. The wording of the document is worth considering: the resolution stated that the destructions were an 'attempt to deny historical roots and cultural diversity in this context can fuel and exacerbate conflict and hamper post-conflict national reconciliation, thereby undermining the security, stability, governance, social, economic and cultural development of affected States'.[18] The resolution reinforced the 1954 Convention and the two protocols by encouraging states to ratify the legal instruments and implement them by training, inventorying, documenting cultural property, and taking protective measures in time of peace and enforcing them by further criminalising offenses to cultural property. In addition, the resolution encouraged member states 'to provide financial contributions to support preventive and emergency operations, fight against the illicit trafficking of cultural property, as well as undertake all appropriate efforts for the recovery of cultural heritage'.[19]

The fight against the illicit trafficking of cultural property constitutes another illustration of how protecting cultural heritage has become a component of stabilisation efforts. This campaign involves local law enforcement organisations as well as international organisations such as the International Council of Museums (ICOM). For instance, in July 2017, UNESCO launched in Dakar a programme dedicated to this mission for the Sahel region. Along with police forces, border control agencies, representatives of Interpol and UN agencies, the UNESCO initiative also involves the directors of national museums of Mali, Mauritania, Niger and Senegal.[20]

But even prior to the UN Security Council resolution, a new organisation was born out of the moral shock triggered by Daesh's destructions in Syria and Iraq. In early 2015, a new initiative to tackle this challenge emerged. The story of this initiative is revealing as it sheds light on the major issues surrounding the topic of protecting cultural property. It started with two countries at its forefront: the United Arab Emirates and France. Both countries had been active for years in the two separate fields of cultural diplomacy and counterterrorism, and they were now joining forces to raise the global awareness on the defence of cultural heritage across the world. This initiative is a telling case study to help better comprehend the policy implications of protecting cultural heritage in conflict zones. At the Ise-Shima G7 Summit in Japan in May 2016, the principles of the French-Emirati initiative were announced by the president-director of the Musée du Louvre, Jean-Luc Martinez. Martinez had been mandated by the then president of France, Francois Hollande, to propose fifty initiatives to protect world heritage, among which was an international conference on safeguarding endangered cultural heritage.[21] The conference was convened before the end of the same year, and the creation of an international fund to sponsor specific programs was also announced.[22] These two objectives were driving the efforts of Paris and Abu Dhabi: better safeguarding cultural property under the threat from belligerents and preserving the cultural diversity which is systematically targeted by terrorist groups.

The initiative positioned the protection of cultural heritage at the intersection between post-conflict reconstruction and the struggle against extremism. In that perspective, it served a coherent goal for a country such as the UAE that was already playing a key role in the field of countering the ideological support to terrorist propaganda as it hosts the headquarters of Hedayah, an international centre for expertise to counter violent extremism. Similarly, the location of Abu Dhabi for the French-Emirati conference was emblematic: the city that was hosting the Louvre-Abu Dhabi—a universal museum dedicated to the exchange between artworks and sculptures from around the globe—was an obvious symbol of the spirit of the conference. France and the UAE appointed two personal representatives of their Heads of State to prepare the coming conference: Jack Lang, president of the Paris-based Institut du Monde Arabe and Mohamed Al Mubarak, chairman of Abu Dhabi Department of Culture and Tourism. The first phase of the project was conducted at a fast pace: in only a few months, the team organised what became the Abu Dhabi Conference on Safeguarding Endangered Cultural Heritage that took place on the 2nd and 3rd of December 2016 with forty participating states. In the Abu Dhabi Declaration signed at the end of the conference, all heads of states declared their 'common determination to safeguard the endangered cultural heritage of all peoples, against its destruction and illicit trafficking'.[23]

Following the conference, the second phase, involving an effort to create a new international entity, was more complicated. The new organisation was named the ALIPH. Geneva was soon selected as the location for its headquarters.[24] As the drivers of the initiative, France and the UAE were the biggest donors: in the donors' conference at the Louvre in March 2017, they, respectively, pledged donations of US$30 million and US$15 million dollars. Additionally, Saudi Arabia offered US$20 million, Kuwait US$5 million, Luxembourg US€3 million, Morocco US$1.5 million and the American entrepreneur and philanthropist Thomas Kaplan US$1 million.[25] Other contributors were later announced, states such as China, private donors such as Jean-Claude Gandur (Switzerland), institutions such as Mellon Foundation. Kaplan was appointed as the first president of ALIPH in 2017. The following year, an executive team, directed by Valery Freland, started functioning, and in November 2018, ALIPH announced US$77.5 million in pledges.[26] The fund aims to support programmes that cover the 'entire heritage chain': prevention by training and implementing emergency safeguarding plans; emergency protection during the conflicts; and conservation and restoration of artworks following conflicts. Italy has also offered its expertise to train police, curators and restorers.[27] At the same time, the French-Emirati initiative sees itself as creating a complex and ambitious international network of safe havens for endangered cultural property. The idea is to build temporary safe havens for emergency transfers of cultural goods if a country considers that it is under immediate threat. Such actions already occurred in past conflicts.[28] China later announced in response to the Abu Dhabi Declaration that it would be the first Asian country to offer its support by making the China National Museum a safe haven, able to host temporarily material culture threatened by an ongoing conflict.

In January 2019, ALIPH issued its first annual call for projects and an opened call for emergency relief grants.[29] ALIPH announced the funding its first rehabilitation projects, for instance with the Mosul Museum, a project carried out by a consortium of international museums led by the Louvre and the Smithsonian Institution. Other initiatives include the rehabilitation of the Tomb of Askia in Gao (Mali), as well as the rehabilitation of Mar Behnam monastery in Khidr (Nineveh plain, Iraq). ALIPH also funded a capacity building programme, Earthen Architecture Conservation Course (Getty Conservation Institute) and supported the Institut du Monde Arabe's exhibition *Cités Millénaires*, raising public awareness on the conservation of endangered cultural heritage. But if this French-Emirati initiative evidenced a new momentum on the international stage, it did not solve several key challenges with regard to the concrete implementation of a policy to protect cultural property during armed conflicts. The following section looks specifically at the most salient ones.

The Policy Ramifications of Protecting Cultural Artefacts in Conflict Zones

This final section looks at four of the most pressing issues facing policymakers and stakeholders: the governance issue, the cultural clash between curatorial and military communities, the applicability of the legal framework in the current security environment, and finally, the operational complexity of defending artefacts in conflict zones.

The Issue of International Governance

Over recent decades, numerous actors have emerged, with sometimes a rather similar mandate. The primary organisation remains until today UNESCO. The 1954 Hague Convention for the Protection of Cultural Property in the Event of Armed Conflict posits that the UN agency is mandated to provide 'technical assistance in organising the protection of their cultural property, or in connection with any other problem arising out of the application of the present Convention or the Regulations for its execution'.[30] UNESCO's work in the field goes beyond The Hague Convention and includes other initiatives. It operates an Emergency Preparedness and Response Unit which monitors ongoing conflicts—like typical crisis management cells in ministries of foreign affairs or defence. In 2015, UNESCO also launched the Heritage Emergency Fund that aims to provide financial assistance in immediate crises. In addition to these programmes, the organisation also initiated in 1999 the establishment of a Committee for the Protection of Cultural Property in the Event of Armed Conflict. Composed of twelve States Parties that adhered to The Hague Convention and its second protocol, the committee offers guidance at political level in all major matters—for instance international assistance to Mali or Libya. Nevertheless, UNESCO's role during crises is a modest one that concentrates on advocacy and public awareness campaigns rather than practical intervention.[31] Its Emergency Preparedness and Response Unit has very limited resources: with only five permanent members, it does not play an operational role but focuses instead on the coordination of UNESCO's relations with other organisations involved in a crisis. Likewise, its Committee for the Protection of Cultural Property in the Event of Armed Conflict allows the organisation to maintain its centrality in the governance of issues related to the protection of cultural property but like other initiatives, it has limited capacities of its own and relies mostly on coordination with other entities.

This leads us to consider the significant role played by non-governmental organisations. In 2016, the International Committee of the Red Cross (ICRC) signed a memorandum of understanding with UNESCO which states that the ICRC 'may assist in rescuing specific cultural property at imminent risk, for example by facilitating the evacuation of collections and/or providing supplies and equipment needed to undertake emergency safeguarding measures'.[32] Among other NGOs, we discussed above the role of the ICBS which may be one of the most active ones. Whereas the ICRC mostly plays an operational role, the ICBS focuses on education and training programmes in order to prepare the personnel of cultural organisations to respond to emergency situations or to plan post-crisis reconstruction. It is also worth mentioning that the NGO Geneva Call, which specialises in the protection of civilians in the event of armed conflict, has put cultural heritage on the list of its priorities.[33] In contrast to other actors, Geneva Call has historically maintained dialogues with non-state actors involved in wars, in order to prevent the destruction of monuments.

This overview underlines the myriad entities involved in the protection of cultural sites. However, there is no clear governing principle behind the mandates of each of them. Although UNESCO seems an obvious centralising body, it remains a UN agency that can only coordinate between all other stakeholders without commanding them. It is also worth remembering the diplomatic context behind UNESCO. The organisation has been under tremendous financial pressures following its decision in 2011 to admit the Palestinian territories as an independent member state. This led to the decision from the US government to cut off American funding for its annual budget—which amounted to 22%, followed ultimately by the announcement by the Trump administration of the US withdrawal from UNESCO in 2018.[34] In other words, UNESCO has today neither the political capital nor the financial resources to act as the centralising body. Furthermore, the existence of several parallel initiatives at the level of fundraising—such as ALIPH—call into question the risk of unnecessary redundancies and financial waste. As mentioned above, ALIPH was conceived as a small entity to avoid the traditional problems plaguing international organisations. This directly reflected the underlying concerns regarding the capacity of UNESCO to fulfil this part of its mission and the explicit intent of ALIPH founders not to follow that path. Nevertheless, the decision to add a new actor to the international landscape did not prevent unwarranted competition between these stakeholders.

Finally, this complex landscape may reflect the many efforts and initiatives launched by international organisations and NGOs but *a contrario*, it shows a rather limited role for military organisations. At the national level, armed forces usually do not dedicate a specific team or unit to these matters. Concretely, legal departments of ministries of defence may be asked to address the issue while preparing the framework for an imminent intervention and reviewing the details of the rules of engagement—which indirectly will contain elements on the protection of cultural property. The legal advisors (the 'legad' in the military jargon) will then coordinate with the operations unit, the J-2, which is responsible for the conduct of the war effort. At the regional level, there is no specific process for organisations such as NATO or the EU to deal with the issue of protecting cultural property during a military intervention. More specifically, NATO standards posit that establishing measures to protect cultural property such as a no-strike list is the responsibility of its member states. In 2011, during the planning process of operation Odyssey Dawn and Unified Protector in Libya, it was indeed the allies, rather than NATO as a whole, that assembled that list, to preserve cultural sites.[35] More generally, this quasi-absence of military organisations from the governance environment epitomises a more profound issue here: the one of a cultural clash.

The Cultural Clash Between Soldiers and Curators

Defending cultural property requires a dialogue between armed forces and cultural communities in the planning of military intervention (to prevent destruction), stabilisation operations (to relocate artefacts) or post-stabilisation efforts (to ensure their long-term safety). But although a dialogue is needed, it would be an understatement to say that soldiers and curators live in two different worlds. They come from contrasting educational and professional backgrounds that rarely, if ever, cross. When facing crises, both will behave differently. Officers and their troops assess a conflict environment in terms of threats and challenges. They then define a strategy of ways and means to degrade or destroy these identified dangers. As a result, they may look at cultural sites as topographical details of a battlefield—potentially obstacles or outposts—but not as a direct priority. Because armed forces follow very strict procedures with regard to the chain of command and the conduct of operations, they usually perceive the intervention of civilians such as UN personnel or NGOs as unnecessary interference that may confuse the prioritisation of objectives and eventually compromise the military strategy. On the other side, the personnel of cultural sites have a different background and different priorities. They may want to coordinate and exchange information with armed forces to prevent the destruction of historical monuments but at the same time, they may fear that this consultation may turn into collusion, if not complicity. Curators on the battlefield merely try to survive and protect the artefacts on their site. To that aim, they may desire to remain neutral and avoid getting trapped into the political logic of the ongoing conflict. Again, the cultural community is rarely at ease when talking with the armed forces about the above-mentioned 'no-target list' which details a number of cultural sites (and their GPS coordinates) to be protected from military strikes.

In some ways, the cultural clash between these two communities may echo the clash between the armed forces and humanitarian NGOs but the rift in the former case is even deeper. Humanitarian workers and soldiers may not share the same culture but they are both accustomed to see each other in a conflict zone. Years of peacekeeping and peace-making operations have helped to build a sense of understanding between them and although the humanitarian-military relations are far from perfect, there is at least a legacy of exchanges that has grown over the last decades.[36] This link simply does not exist in the field of protecting cultural property. One way to address this issue could be to reinforce the dialogue between organisations in charge of protecting cultural heritage sites and armed forces through common preparatory training initiatives, rather than only during emergency situations.

When the UK, in 2017, finally ratified the 1954 Convention, a Military Cultural Property Protection Unit within the Armed Forces was created to better educate British armed forces about this dimension of stabilisation operations. Along with the creation of the unit, the Cultural Protection Fund, a £30 million fund was established for the period 2016–2020. The fund administered by the British Council in partnership with the Department for Digital, Culture, Media and Sport, is financed from the UK Government's Official Development Assistance. It is dedicated to the safeguard and promotion of cultural property in conflict-affected areas by providing financial support to organisations on the ground (grants below £100,000 for emergency relief and, large grants up to £2 million). Its initial focus is on the Middle East and North Africa where 12 target countries (Egypt, Jordan, Lebanon, Libya, Iraq, the Palestinian Territories, Syria, Tunisia, Turkey, Yemen, Sudan and Afghanistan) are expected to be the primary recipients.[37] In August 2018, the Fund had been or was engaged in 34 projects for £17.7 million. The organisation might be contemplating the possibility to continue operating after 2020 with a prospect of adapting its scope to needs on the ground and to the priorities of the UK international political agenda.[38] Similarly, institutions such as the Smithsonian Institution in Washington DC, a US federal cultural body, contribute to training armed forces in the preservation of cultural property prior to being deployed on the ground. Bridges between the army and curatorship exist as evidenced by some cases such as the one of Corine Wegener, the director of the Smithsonian Cultural Rescue Initiative, a programme dedicated to the preservation of cultural heritage in crisis situations. Wegener served in the US Army Reserve for 21 years. In that capacity, she was deployed in 2003 to Iraq and assigned to assist after the looting of the Iraqi National Museum.[39] Such a combination of training and education in both military affairs and art history is obviously rare but should be encouraged. Both communities could exchange past experiences and define 'lessons learned' to build a framework of understanding. Ultimately, raising awareness on both sides with regard to their respective missions and common goals could help overcome this cultural clash.

More broadly, this cultural clash between soldiers and curators relates to one of the fundamental challenges of today's stabilisation agenda. The contemporary philosophy of stability operations relies on the principle of a whole-of-government approach. In this view, stabilisation involves the mobilisation of a combination of military, political, development and humanitarian resources and actors. Like for the soldier and the curator, the key challenge of this holistic approach is therefore to manage different, sometimes contradictory, rationales for intervention in fragile states which inevitably generate tensions between the proponents of provision of humanitarian assistance—a neutral endeavour by its nature—and those that support political and military objectives.

The Legal Conundrum

As discussed in the first section of this chapter, there are plenty of legal documents applicable for the protection of cultural property. They include the 1949 Geneva Conventions, the 1954 Hague Convention, the World Heritage Convention, the 1970 UNESCO Convention as well as international human rights law that directly applies to this situation. In other words, the sources of international rules to protect heritage are numerous but unfortunately, they tend to be designed for scenarios that are not entirely relevant in today's environment. Based on the history of the Spanish civil war and the Second World War, this international legal framework was designed to cover conventional conflicts between two or more states. The list of criminal cases on the protection of cultural property in armed conflict reflects this phenomenon: most of the cases have in fact been prosecuted by the International Criminal Tribunal for the former Yugoslavia.[40] But as the contemporary conflicts in Mali and Syria evidence, today's biggest threats actually come from non-state actors, terrorist organisations that simply dismiss international norms, which limits the deterrence effect of international law.

There is however one important case, the Al Mahdi case, that may pave the way for change. In August 2017, the International Criminal Court (ICC) found Ahmad Al Faqi Al Mahdi responsible for 'intentionally attacking protected cultural and religious sites'.[41] Al Mahdi was a commander of Ansar al Din who conducted the destruction of ten religious and historic monuments in Timbuktu in 2012. Noticeably, the ICC charged Al Mahdi only with this count and no mention was made of civilian casualties, making it the first case ever of an individual being prosecuted by the ICC for a war crime against cultural property.[42] The Al Mahdi case provoked a significant controversy among legal experts. Some have praised the short and effective prosecution as a way to restore the credibility of the ICC. In the context of global outrage regarding the atrocities perpetrated in Mali, it underlined the ability of international law to make non-state actors such as terrorist or insurgent groups accountable for the destruction of cultural property. Others have been more sceptical and argued that the case was merely political scenery and reflected an improper use of the ICC. The scale of the attack—targeting ten monuments—was obviously insignificant when compared to the human victims of armed groups in Mali during that same period. Moreover, it has been suggested that Al Mahdi was unlikely to be the sole person responsible for the attacks and therefore was only one individual in a loose chain of command that organised these crimes. As this discussion evolves among experts, the future legal implications of the Al Mahdi case remain to be seen. But even if it was to lead to a strengthening of the ICC and the ability of the international community to hold insurgents and terrorists accountable for such acts, it is still doubtful that this could effectively deter radicalised individuals in future scenarios.

The Operational Implications

The most complex challenge of protecting cultural artefacts during conflicts is undoubtedly the operational translation of this goal. For years now, armed forces engaged in humanitarian interventions have been incorporating this parameter in their operations planning process. This follows one of the provisions of the 1954 Hague Convention which stipulates that states should 'plan or establish in peace-time, within their armed forces, services or specialist personnel whose purpose will be to secure respect for cultural property and to co-operate with the civilian authorities responsible for safeguarding it'.[43] This starts in the ministries of defence with education and training programs for soldiers. Several countries such as France, Austria, Belgium, Netherlands, the US or Italy, have designed specific handbooks and courses for their officers to raise their awareness of the importance of defending cultural property during operations.[44] The publication in 2016 of the UNESCO Military Manual demonstrated the growing importance of formalising standards in this field. The document was meant to serve as a practical guide to the implementation by military forces of the rules of international law for the protection of cultural property in armed conflict'.[45] Before entering a battlefield, military commanders need to gather a comprehensive list of objects and sites considered as 'cultural property', a qualification that is left to each state to define. In 2012, the Malian government provided a document containing maps and geographical coordinates of its historical and religious sites.

But in practice, this cooperation between a state and a foreign military may not occur, especially when the foreign military is perceived as a potential invader. For instance, in the spring of 2011, UNESCO with the ICOM provided a list of cultural sites in Libya not to be destroyed.[46] The Gaddafi regime obviously did not cooperate with Western armed forces to protect the sites. Likewise, in 2013, two NGOs, the Spanish Heritage for Peace and UK's National Committee Blue Shield released a public 'no-strike' list of archaeological sites in Aleppo. The two-page list of twenty sites was established with 'Syrian colleagues' and included geographical coordinates.[47] Notwithstanding the previous caveats, this information can help armed forces when they prepare their target planning process which defines a selection of objects and sites considered to have military significance. In other cases, the distinction between a military site and a cultural site might become uncertain. For instance, in 2012, Syrian rebels used the Krak des Chevaliers—a castle from the medieval crusades recognised by UNESCO as a World Heritage Site—to fight against the regime of Bashar al Assad.[48] However, according to international law, armed forces should exercise restraint in order, as much as possible, not to damage the site. A perfect example illustrating this obligation is the case of Malian insurgents in 2013 who used a house nearing the Djinguereber Mosque in Timbuktu, another UNESCO world heritage site. As a result, the Malian government and French forces ruled out the option of an airstrike and opted for artillery that allowed firing against the terrorists without harming the mosque.[49]

Recent operations such as the French intervention in Mali or the NATO air campaign in Libya seem to evidence positive developments in the integration of the defence of cultural heritage into the planning process. But this does not remove the challenge posed by non-state armed groups that are likely to keep targeting monuments which they see as obvious symbols of their opponents' culture or to use monuments as strategic locations. The rationale behind these destructions is not only extremist ideology that categorically denies the possibility of other cultures. It also sometimes follows a strategic logic: destroying historical and religious symbols can directly weaken the morale of the other side.

Preventive Asylum for Cultural Property?

Because of this enduring threat, one of the responses discussed by the international community is transferring cultural artefacts from a country in war to so-called safe havens abroad. Although there is not yet a legal definition of 'safe havens' in this context, it is understood to be a refuge zone where movable cultural property can be stored, maintained, and restored if needed.[50] The concept derives from the concept of 'right of asylum'. The transfer of artefacts has to be considered when a country is in a situation of armed conflict or political tension that could lead to war. The transfer can only be temporary and a way to prevent damage or destruction. In fact, the idea appeared for the first time in the 1954 Hague Convention (Article 18). The Abu Dhabi Conference of 2016 discussed the creation of a network of safe havens for movable cultural heritage as part of ALIPH missions. At the time, this proposal was met with doubt by some country representatives who were supposed to benefit from this initiative. Their cautious reaction highlighted the need for careful guidelines and for the definition of a legal, operational and ethical framework. Some observers have recommended examining the legal framework to work out ways to adapt national property laws.[51] For instance, the French law, through a bill passed in 2016,[52] enables the provision of safe storage for cultural goods endangered upon request of the state of origin or the UN Security Council. The goods can then be returned upon request of this state of origin. Switzerland had similar legal provisions. Consequently, initiatives promoting such networks of safe havens appeared in Switzerland or France, but without concrete effect or coordination with other organisations.[53]

Adapting the legal framework does not directly address the uncertainties that relate to the operational requirements of such a complex mission. Organising the transfer of cultural property out of a war zone implies several parameters. First, the appropriate moment to carry out the operation has to be identified. It means that armed forces and curatorial communities would work more closely to build an early warning database. In other words, the stakeholders—whether the UN, NGOs, or armed forces—should be able quickly to respond in case a crisis occurs in order to locate the cultural sites and to select exfiltration routes. This obviously could increase the fear of collusion for the heritage curators. Additionally, removing cultural objects from a war zone is likely to be a complex mission in terms of logistics. Search and rescue missions remain extremely risky missions to conduct, and we can wonder if a political leader from a Western country would bear such a risk for saving artefacts. Moreover, the experience in Mosul proved that the lives of the local members of conservation teams can be threatened by the collusion with external military actors.[54] As a result, this issue of collusion prevented measures to transfer the artefacts to a safe location. Similarly, defining the moment to return the precious collections can be as challenging as the transfer out of the war zone. In sum, heritage experts consider that the implementation of safe havens for cultural property should not be considered 'as a primary option but as a last resort, after all recourse to protect cultural property in situ has been exhausted' largely because of the complexity and the risk associated with the transfer of artworks in the context of armed conflict.[55] The resources of cultural organisations should in general therefore be focused on all other preventive measures to protect cultural property in situ—including the creation of safer storage within the country.

A final element of this discussion involved the fight against illicit trafficking of movable cultural property. In the context of security sector reforms, the training of police and customs forces is crucial to enforce national and international laws to prevent artworks from leaving the country. The coordination of international actors involved in fighting illicit trafficking can also prove efficient. The publication of the ICOM Red List has contributed to providing information on stolen and missing artworks. The training of border police, customs and other forces enabled the seizing in Spain, UK and Switzerland of an important amount of looted antiques from Afghanistan, Yemen, Iraq, Syria and Libya. In case the national institution in charge of the conservation of cultural heritage is not able to ensure their conservation, it is not suitable for these cultural goods to be returned to their country. Partnerships between institutions in the country of origin and the country where artworks would be located need to be initiated or extended to provide temporary storage for these artworks.

CONCLUSION

The protection of cultural heritage in conflict zones grew in earnest in recent years, primarily as the result of the assaults launched by organisations such as Daesh or Ansar al Din. However, as this chapter has demonstrated, the topic itself has a long history. Numerous legal documents and a myriad of international governmental and non-governmental organisations are dedicated to the defence of these artefacts. In fact, this new sense of urgency reflects the limited ability of the existing framework to tackle the contemporary challenges. As violent extremist organisations are unlikely to be deterred by laws, the strengthening of existing security measures becomes necessary. Initiatives such as ALIPH underline this reality.

But remarkably, this debate has occurred mostly among curators and only marginally involved armed forces. In that perspective, it appears that the priority of the stakeholders should be to bridge this gap between curators and soldiers. Such a gap is not inevitable. If one looks at the experience of stabilisation operations in the last two decades, humanitarian actors and armed forces barely knew each other before the 1990s. But since then, they have been more and more engaged together on the battlefield, as well as in conference rooms. Putting the defence of cultural property on the stabilisation agenda has an obvious significance: whereas security actors focus on the reconstruction of state institutions, those involved with the preservation of cultural artefacts play a role in the protection of a community's identity. But this means that cultural heritage has to be factored in at the three main phases of the stabilisation efforts: from the prevention of conflicts, the protection of monuments during conflicts and their restoration after the conflict. This has numerous policy implications. Establishing a process of governance that facilitates the coordination between armed forces, local museums, UN agencies and NGOs should be the first priority. Additionally, training soldiers and local security forces to consider the protection of cultural heritage in the three situations should become a norm ensured by national armed forces with the support of stakeholders such as curators. All in all, the momentum brought about by the contemporary wave of terrorist attacks targeting cultural sites should not peak with the establishment of new entities such as ALIPH. It should be used to turn the policy issue into an integral part—alongside security sector reform and the humanitarian and development efforts—of the stabilisation agenda.

Notes

1. BBC, "Timbuktu Mausoleums 'Destroyed'," 23 December 2012. http://www.bbc.com/news/world-africa-20833010. Accessed 10 April 2017.
2. Paul Veyne, *Palmyre, l'irremplaçable trésor* (Paris: Albin Michel, 2015).
3. United Nations Security Council, Resolution 2347, 24 March 2017. Document available at https://www.securitycouncilreport.org/atf/cf/%7b65BFCF9B-6D27-4E9C-8CD3-CF6E4FF96FF9%7d/s_res_2347.pdf.
4. UNESCO designates cultural artefacts as part of the tangible heritage of societies. They include 'buildings and historica places, monuments, arti-

facts which are considered worthy of preservation for the future (...) objects significant to the archaeology, architecture, science or technology of a specific culture'. Accessed at http://www.unesco.org/new/en/cairo/culture/tangible-cultural-heritage/.

5. For a comprehensive look at the stabilisation debate, see Saskia van Genugten, "Stabilisation in the Contemporary Middle East and North Africa: Different Dimensions of an Elusive Concept," EDA Working Paper, Emirates Diplomatic Academy, April 2018; Victor Gervais, "Variations on a Common Theme: Contemporary Approaches to International Stabilisation Efforts," EDA Working Paper, Emirates Diplomatic Academy, October 2018; and Philipp Rotmann, "Toward a Realistic and Responsible Idea of Stabilisation," Stability: International Journal of Security and Development, vol. 5, no. 1 (2016): 5.

6. Benedict Anderson, *Imagined Communities: Reflections on the Origin and Spread of Nationalism* (New York: Verso, 1983).

7. Robert Edsel, and Brett Witter, *The Monuments Men: Allied Heroes, Nazi Thieves and the Greatest Treasure Hunt in History* (New York: Center Street, 2010).

8. An electronic copy of the original document is available on the website of the French National Library: https://gallica.bnf.fr/ark:/12148/bpt6k48495b.

9. Article 27, Annex to the Convention (IV) Laws and Customs on War on Land, The Hague, 1907. Accessed at https://www.loc.gov/law/help/us-treaties/bevans/m-ust000001-0631.pdf.

10. Ibid.

11. Peace Treaty of Versailles, Article 247. Accessed at http://net.lib.byu.edu/~rdh7/wwi/versailles.html.

12. The Washington Pact is the only international legal instrument for the protection of cultural heritage in armed conflict ratified by the United States of America (USA). To date, the US have not ratified the 1954 Hague Convention.

13. UNESCO, Military Manual, op. cit., p. 2.

14. Convention for the Protection of Cultural Property in the Event of Armed Conflict with Regulations for the Execution of the Convention 1954, The Hague, 14 May 1954. Accessed at http://portal.unesco.org/en/ev.php-URL_ID=13637&URL_DO=DO_TOPIC&URL_SECTION=201.html.

15. The ICBS is composed of five professional associations ranging from museums, archives, audio-visual supports and libraries to monuments and sites. The five organizations are the International Council on Archives, the ICOM, the International Federation of Library Associations and Institutions, the International Council on Monuments and Sites and the Coordinating Council of Audiovisual Archives Associations.

16. UNESCO, "Report of the Blue Shield on the Situations Where Cultural Property Is at Risk in the Context of an Armed Conflict, Including Occupation," 2017. Accessed at http://unesdoc.unesco.org/images/0026/002601/260141E.pdf.

17. Ibid.

18. UN Security Council Resolution no. 2347, 24 March 2017. UN Document S/RES/2347. Accessed at https://www.un.org/sc/suborg/en/s/res/2347-%282017%29.

19. Ibid.

20. UNESCO Office in Dakar, "A Road Map to Fight Against the Illicit Trafficking of Cultural Property in the Sahel," 24 August 2017. Document available at http://www.unesco.org/new/en/dakar/about-this-office/single-view/news/a_road_map_to_fight_against_the_illicit_trafficking_of_cultu/.

21. Jean-Luc Martinez, *Cinquante propositions françaises pour protéger le patrimoine de l'humanité, Rapport sur la protection du patrimoine en situation de conflit armé, remis au Président de la République*, November 2015. Accessed at http://www.culture.gouv.fr/content/download/128740/1406550/version/2/file/Cinquante-propositions-francaises-pour-proteger-le-patrimoine-de-lhumanite.pdf.

22. G7 Ise-Shima Summit Side-event on "Terrorism and Cultural Property—Countermessage Against Destruction and Illicit Trade of Cultural Property by Terrorists." Accessed at https://www.mofa.go.jp/fp/is_sc/page3e_000497.html.

23. Abu Dhabi Declaration, Conference on Safeguarding Endangered Cultural Heritage, 3 December 2016.

24. Sophie Roselli, "Genève devient la capitale du patrimoine en péril," *Tribune de Genève*, 1 Mai 2017.

25. Emirates News Agency, "UAE and France Reunite for the Establishment of the International Alliance for Protection of Heritage in Conflict Areas," 20 March 2017. http://wam.ae/en/details/1395302604067. Accessed 10 April 2017.

26. ALIPH, *Protecting Heritage to Build Peace*, Paris Peace Forum, 12 November 2018.

27. French Presidency, Press Kit Visit by the President of the French Republic to Abu Dhabi, 2–3 December 2016. http://www.diplomatie.gouv.fr/IMG/pdf/16-3362-2_12_dossier_de_presse_abou_dabi_v5_2__ang_cle0954aa.pdf. Accessed 10 April 2017.

28. In early 1939, as the civil war escalated in Spain, artworks from the famous Prado Museum were moved to Switzerland where they stayed until the conflict reached its conclusion. Likewise, Switzerland also provided safe haven to the Afghanistan "Museum-in-Exile" from 1999 to 2007.

29. See https://www.aliph-foundation.org/en/our-grants. See also: AFP, "Protection du patrimoine dans les zones de conflits: appel à projets international," 16 January 2018.
30. The 1954 Hague Convention for the Protection of Cultural Property in the Event of Armed Conflict and its two (1954 and 1999) Protocols, p. 18. Available at http://unesdoc.unesco.org/images/0018/001875/187580e.pdf.
31. UNESCO, UNESCO's Response to Protect Culture in Crises, 2016, p. 3. Accessed at http://unesdoc.unesco.org/images/0024/002449/244984e.pdf.
32. Quoted in UNESCO, Protection of Cultural Property: Military Manual, 2016, p. 73. Accessed at http://unesdoc.unesco.org/images/0024/002466/246633e.pdf.
33. Geneva Call, "Culture Under Fire: Armed Non-state Actors and Cultural Heritage in Wartime," Report, October 2018.
34. Klaus Hufner, "The Financial Crisis of UNESCO After 2011: Political Reactions and Organizational Consequences," *Global Policy*, vol. 8, no. 5 (August 2017): 96–101. Heather Nauert, "The United States Withdraws from UNESCO," US Department of State, Press Statement, 12 October 2017.
35. NATO Joint Analysis and Lessons Center, "Cultural Property Protection in the Operations Planning Process," December 2012, p. 2.
36. Sarah Collinson, Samir Elhawary, and Robert Muggah, "States of Fragility: Stabilization and Its Implications for Humanitarian Action," HPG Working Paper, Humanitarian Policy Group, May 2010; Radha Iyengar Plumb, Jacob N. Shapiro, and Stephen Hegarty, "Lessons Learned from Stabilization Initiatives in Afghanistan: A Systematic Review of Existing Research," Working Paper, RAND Corporation, June 2017.
37. UK Parliament, "Written Evidence Submitted by Historic England," 2016. Accessed at https://publications.parliament.uk/pa/cm201617/cmpublic/CulturalProperty/memo/CPB14.pdf.
38. Cultural Protection Fund, *Annual Report 2017—2018*, 2018. Accessed at https://www.britishcouncil.org/sites/default/files/cultural_protection_fund_annual_report_1718.pdf.
39. Leah Binkovitz, "Q+A: How to Save the Arts in Times of War," *Smithsonian Magazine*, 24 January 2013. Accessed at https://www.smithsonianmag.com/smithsonian-institution/qa-how-to-save-the-arts-in-times-of-war-5506188/.
40. Ibid., pp. 89–90.
41. International Legal Materials, Prosecutor v. Ahmad Al Faqi Al Mahdi: Judgment and Sentence & Reparations Order (Int'l Crim. Ct.), 57, no. 1. Accessed at https://www.cambridge.org/core/journals/international-legal-materials/article/prosecutor-v-ahmad-al-

faqi-al-mahdi-judgment-and-sentence-reparations-order-intl-crim-ct/
E47EB6D000A07CAE48F47DFA0DDA201C/core-reader.

42. For a detailed overview of the case, see Milena Sterio, "Individual Criminal Responsibility for the Destruction of Religious and Historic Buildings: The Al Mahdi Case," *Case Western Reserve Journal of International Law*, vol. 49, no. 1 (2017): 63–73.

43. Hague Convention, Article 7 (2), p. 11. Accessed at http://unesdoc. unesco.org/images/0018/001875/187580e.pdf.

44. UNESCO, Military Manual, op. cit., pp. 20–21.

45. Ibid., p. 1.

46. Pita J. C. Schimmelpenninck van der Oije, "Saving the Past, Present and Future: Thoughts on Mobilising International Protection for Cultural Property During Armed Conflict," in Mariëlle Matthee, Birgit Toebes, and Marcel Brus, eds., *Armed Conflict and International Law: In Search of the Human Face*, 2013, Asser Press, The Hague, 195–230.

47. UK National Committee of the Blue Shield, Heritage for Peace, "No-Strike List," 2 June 2013. Accessed at http://www.ancbs.org/cms/images/ Aleppo_site_list_full_description.pdf.

48. Georges Malbrunot, "Syrie: le régime reprend le Krak des Chevaliers aux rebelles," *Le Figaro*, 20 March 2014.

49. UNESCO, Military Manual, op. cit., p. 37.

50. Peter Hellyer, "The UAE Could Become a Safe Haven for Antiquities," *The National*, 5 December 2016; UNESCO, "Federal Act on the Protection of Cultural Property in the Event of Armed Conflict, Disaster or Emergency Situations," June 2014, p. 2.

51. Thomas George Weiss, and Nina Connelly, "Cultural Cleansing and Mass Atrocities: Protecting Cultural Heritage in Armed Conflict Zones," J. Paul Getty Trust Occasional Papers in Cultural Heritage Policy, 1, J. Paul Getty Trust, 2017.

52. Loi n° 2016-925 du 7 juillet 2016 relative à la liberté de la création, à l'architecture et au patrimoine, Article 56. Accessed at https://www. legifrance.gouv.fr/affichTexte.do?cidTexte=JORFTEXT000032854341& categorieLien=id#JORFARTI000032854604.

53. "Mayor of Paris Proposes Turning Paris into a Refuge for Cultural Heritage," *Artforum*, 9 May 2018. Accessed at https://www.artforum.com/ news/mayor-of-paris-proposes-turning-city-into-a-refuge-for-cultural-heritage-75349. See also the network of cities-refuge: "Protection des droits humains et du patrimoine culturel: les villes signent la Déclaration de Genève," Ville de Genève, 28 March 2018.

54. Joshua Hammer, "The Salvation of Mosul," *Smithsonian Magazine*, October 2017. Accessed at https://www.smithsonianmag.com/history/ salvation-mosul-180964772/.

55. Blue Shield, 2017, op. cit.

INDEX

A

Abu Dhabi, 16, 130, 131, 140, 143, 146–148, 156, 157, 170, 171, 174, 176, 179–181, 314, 315

The Abu Dhabi Declaration, 315, 328

Afghanistan, 1–3, 8, 10, 14, 15, 26, 28, 41, 42, 44–49, 51–61, 68, 70, 80, 98, 99, 101, 104, 105, 113, 125, 127, 140, 182, 185, 188, 191, 192, 195, 211, 219, 246, 313, 320, 325, 328, 329

Al Abadi, Haidar, 170, 171, 175, 176

Al Assad, Bashar, 26, 239, 323

Al Assad, Hafez, 211, 239

Aleppo, 207, 211, 242, 323

Al-Faisal, Saud, 26, 35–37

Al-Hirak, 246, 248–250, 256

Ali, Ben, 185, 287, 288, 293, 294, 296

Al Jubeir, Adel, 171

Al Maliki, Nouri, 170

Al-Qaeda in the Arabian Peninsula (AQAP), 45, 46, 246, 250

Al-Qaeda in the Islamic Maghreb (AQIM), 84

Al-Qassimi, Sultan, 25

Ansar al Din, 307, 321, 325

Ansar Allah (Houthi rebels), 99, 101, 106, 107, 110, 112

Arab Gulf countries/Arab Gulf states, 8, 11, 12, 20, 32, 60, 121, 122, 126–129, 132, 133, 140, 145, 146, 168, 170–173, 176–179, 234

The Arab League – the League of Arab States, 35, 81, 85, 179, 252

Arab nationalism, 238, 267

Arab states, 10, 20, 21, 26, 27, 31, 129, 143

Arab Uprisings (Arab Spring), 9, 13, 23–25, 30, 34, 36, 95, 122, 133, 135, 136, 139, 141, 187, 196, 210, 235, 260, 285

Ataturk, Mustapha Kemal, 273, 274

Autonomy (regional), 13, 236, 237

© The Editor(s) (if applicable) and The Author(s), under exclusive license 331
to Springer Nature Switzerland AG, part of Springer Nature 2020
V. Gervais and S. van Genugten (eds.), *Stabilising the Contemporary Middle East and North Africa*, Middle East Today,
https://doi.org/10.1007/978-3-030-25229-8

332 INDEX

B

Baghdad, 12, 164, 165, 168, 170–173, 175, 176, 178, 209, 215, 216, 218, 236, 238, 248
Balkan wars, 2, 312
Barakat, Sultan, 14, 91, 214, 228
Belt and Road Initiative (BRI), 33, 146, 150, 156, 196
Benomar, Jamal, 247
Brahimi, Lakhdar, 86, 88
Buzan, Barry, 35

C

China, 12, 22, 29, 32, 33, 35, 37, 60, 70, 141, 143, 146, 150, 156, 186, 193, 195, 196, 200, 209, 249, 282, 315
China-Arab States Cooperation Forum (CASCF), 196
Civil-military actions, 67
Civil war, 20, 26, 52, 84, 99, 103, 142, 144, 188, 211, 217, 235–237, 241, 242, 245, 248, 251, 252, 255, 273, 285, 309, 312, 321, 328
Confidence-building, 109, 110, 112
Conflict-affected states, 8, 10, 42, 43, 55, 194
Counter-insurgency (COIN), 3, 4, 44, 50, 51, 208
Cultural property (heritage), 308–322, 324–330

D

Daesh, 11, 32, 84–87, 100, 116, 136, 150–152, 163–165, 167–170, 174–177, 180, 182, 190, 192, 211, 212, 233–236, 241, 243, 248, 250, 255, 307, 309, 314, 325
Decentralisation, 13, 151, 234, 235, 237, 240, 243

Democratic Union Party (PYD), 153, 156, 158, 239–242, 244, 252, 253
Democratisation, 2, 124
Diplomacy
  classical diplomacy, 70
  effective diplomacy, 68, 69
  multilateral diplomacy, 8, 68, 70
Disarmament, Demobilisation, Reintegration (DDR), 87, 144, 156, 217
DP World, 149, 199, 202

E

El Senussi, Abdullah, 291, 301
Erdogan, Recep Tayyip, 20, 27, 28, 152, 158, 260, 270–272, 274, 275, 277
Extremism, 25, 36, 82, 89, 163, 164, 169, 176, 183, 314

F

Fragile states, 10, 15, 42, 97, 134, 142, 321
Free Syrian Army (FSA), 151, 153, 154, 242

G

Gargash, Anwar, 31, 135, 169, 176, 180, 183
GCC-initiative (Yemen), 34, 131, 247
Global Coalition against Daesh (GCAD), 2, 127, 128, 164, 165, 167, 168, 179, 219, 227, 236
  Working Group on Stabilisation (WGS), 128, 164–167, 176
Government of National Accord (GNA), Libya, 106, 234
Gulen, Fethullah, 271–273
Gulf Cooperation Council (GCC), 10, 11, 22–26, 31, 32, 34, 35, 37, 121–135, 173, 245, 247

INDEX

H

Hadi, Abd Rabbu Mansour, 141, 247–250, 252
The Hague Convention, 310–312, 316, 317, 321, 322, 324, 327, 329, 330
Hedayah, 82, 314
Horn of Africa, 11, 33, 140–151, 155, 156, 197–199
Humanitarian
  aid, 15, 126, 131, 141, 143, 149, 152–154, 159, 193, 209, 212, 213
  assistance, 4, 6, 15, 34, 126, 145, 154, 165, 224, 321
  intervention, 89, 322
  response, 4, 5
Human rights, 2, 52, 69, 71, 72, 83, 84, 88, 89, 91, 104, 114, 141, 154, 170, 180, 265, 286, 293, 296, 321
Human security, 71
Hybrid approach, 67, 212

I

Instability, 1, 13, 15, 24, 34, 51, 70, 72, 74, 79, 81, 84–86, 88, 89, 104, 122, 124, 134, 144, 186, 187, 189, 209, 213, 218, 220, 223, 260–263, 266, 268–271, 275, 276, 284, 294
Insurgents, 4, 51, 54, 57, 58, 192, 307, 322, 323
Internally Displaced persons (IDP), 207, 216–218
International Alliance for the Protection of Heritage in Conflict Areas (ALIPH), 308, 315, 316, 318, 324, 326, 328
International Committee of the Blue Shield (ICBS), 312, 317, 327

International Committee of the Red Cross (ICRC), 211, 215, 224, 226, 227, 317
International Criminal Court (ICC), 281–283, 290, 291, 301, 321, 322
International law, 68–74, 88, 90, 215, 251, 291, 321–323, 325, 330
International Security Assistance Force (ISAF), 46
Iran, 20, 23, 26, 27, 30, 32, 35–37, 60, 80, 102, 128, 133, 141–144, 146, 148, 156, 164, 169–173, 176, 177, 181, 182, 198, 234, 235, 237, 238, 242–244, 249, 250, 254, 259
Iraq, 1–3, 8, 10–12, 14, 20, 26–28, 35, 42, 61, 68–70, 78, 80, 83, 100, 128, 136, 153, 156, 163–168, 170–174, 176–183, 185, 188–192, 201, 209, 210, 215, 216, 219, 220, 225, 227, 228, 233–240, 245, 246, 251, 255, 260, 262, 275, 307, 313, 314, 316, 320, 325
Israel, 21, 27, 30, 32, 35, 213, 216, 254, 259–261, 267

J

Justice
  retributive justice, 289, 290
  transitional justice, 13, 14, 247, 281–290, 292–295, 297–302
Justice and Development Party (AKP), 260, 270–272, 274–277

K

Kaplan, Thomas, 315
Kurdistan Democratic Party of Syria (PDKS), 239, 240
Kurdistan's Workers Party (PKK), 152, 239, 241, 242, 272, 273, 275, 277

L

Legitimacy, 4, 5, 24, 25, 45, 47, 52, 53, 58, 59, 71, 72, 74, 86, 88, 90, 96, 103, 111, 124, 126, 132, 135, 175, 216, 218, 224, 252, 277, 287, 288, 291, 298

Libya, 1, 2, 5, 10, 13, 23, 24, 29, 30, 61, 70, 78, 80, 83–87, 89–91, 99, 101, 102, 106, 110, 113, 122, 126–134, 136, 149, 156, 169, 185, 187–192, 194, 214, 234, 235, 251, 260, 281–283, 285, 290, 291, 298, 301, 317, 318, 320, 323, 325

Libyan Political Agreement, 87, 194

Libyan political dialogue, 85, 88, 104, 111, 117

Lynch, Marc, 24, 25, 31, 36, 37, 61

M

Mac Ginty, Roger, 14, 43, 44, 61, 79, 85, 91

Middle East, 11, 13, 19–29, 31–36, 61, 80, 83, 85, 95, 96, 121, 122, 134, 135, 140, 142, 143, 169, 183, 186, 196, 199, 201, 209, 216, 223, 233–236, 238, 244, 251, 255, 259–261, 267, 273, 278, 327

Middle East and North Africa (MENA), 1–3, 8–13, 19, 20, 22, 70, 80–83, 88, 89, 95, 140, 164, 169, 178, 185–189, 191, 193, 195, 196, 207, 209–211, 216, 282, 283, 285, 289, 292, 295, 320

Military assistance, 143, 144, 147, 152, 241

Militias, 26, 50–52, 57, 85–87, 99, 101, 106, 110, 113, 153, 175, 182, 240, 241, 245, 248, 250

Morsi, Mohamed, 197, 262, 264, 265, 268, 276, 277, 286, 299

Mosul, 15, 167, 174, 175, 177, 182, 183, 190, 211, 212, 215, 307, 308, 316, 325, 330

Mubarak, Hosni, 197, 261–268, 281, 286, 290, 300

Muggah, Robert, 5, 14–16, 79, 89, 90, 329

Multilateral diplomacy, 8, 68, 70

Muslim Brotherhood, 197, 240, 249, 262, 264, 276, 286, 287

N

Nasser, Gamal Abdel, 238, 266, 267

National Dialogue Conference (NDC), Yemen, 106, 110, 112, 247, 248, 256

NATO, 27, 37, 43, 46, 47, 57, 60, 77, 127, 129, 150, 241, 291, 318, 323, 329

Non-state actors, 10, 19, 20, 24, 26, 33, 50, 99, 100, 211, 212, 309, 317, 321, 322, 329

Non-State Armed Actors (NSAAs), 11, 95–115, 117

O

Öcalan, Abdullah, 239, 270

OECD, 4, 15, 73, 90, 189, 201

The Office of the Coordinator for reconstruction and Stabilisation (S/CRS), 43

Operation Enduring Freedom (OEF), 46

P

Palmyra, 308

Peacebuilding, 8, 43, 61, 75, 76, 97, 214, 217, 285

Peacekeeping (operations), 75–78, 82, 123, 125, 212, 319

Peace operations, 71, 76

Post-conflict recovery, 13, 165, 213, 214, 218
Proxies (proxy actors), 52, 80, 108, 243, 252
Puntland Maritime Police Force (PMPF), 148

Q

Qadhafi, Saif Al-Islam, 281, 282, 290, 291

R

Radicalism, 2
Reconstruction, 4, 11, 14, 16, 41, 44–46, 60, 61, 79, 82, 149, 153, 163–168, 170, 174, 176–178, 180, 189, 190, 192, 193, 196, 208, 209, 211, 213, 217, 220, 222, 223, 228, 289, 308, 312, 314, 317, 326
Reform, 5, 10, 23, 24, 30, 35, 36, 47, 48, 53, 54, 56, 74, 147, 151, 174, 177, 187, 200, 218, 255, 261, 265–268, 270, 271, 274, 275, 288, 293
Regional order, 22, 25, 26, 28, 31, 33
Regional security complex, 20, 33, 35, 169
Resilience, 4, 5, 75, 76, 79, 114, 134, 167, 209, 213, 218, 220, 221, 224, 228
Responsibility to Protect (RtoP), 71, 72, 89
Rotmann, Philipp, 15, 16, 79, 91, 133, 137, 170, 180, 226, 327

S

Saleh, Ali Abdallah, 108, 186, 244–249
Saudi Arabia, 2, 11, 20, 23, 24, 27, 30, 33, 37, 86, 99, 123, 125–128, 130, 132–136, 139–148, 150, 151, 155–158, 168, 170, 171, 173, 179, 181, 197, 198, 210, 225, 235, 245, 247–249, 254, 259, 315
Saudi-led military intervention, 142, 144
Security Sector Reform (SSR), 57, 58, 87, 106, 165, 172, 176, 217, 325, 326
Sisi, Abdel Fattah el-, 147, 197, 262, 266, 268, 276–278, 286
Skhirat agreement, 84, 87
Sovereignty, 28, 31, 46, 71, 72, 74, 81, 90, 99, 241, 255, 261, 266, 283, 290, 291
The Special Inspector General for Afghanistan Reconstruction (SIGAR), 4, 44, 48–50, 52–54, 58, 61–63
Stabilisation
  economic stabilisation, 194, 200
  stabilisation activities, 2, 4–6, 8, 9, 45, 50, 57, 58, 165, 166, 179, 180, 192, 196, 200
  stabilisation programme, 4, 44, 49, 52, 57, 149, 163, 214
Stability, 2, 3, 5–9, 12–16, 21, 23, 25–27, 31, 34, 35, 44, 57, 60, 70, 79, 80, 82–85, 88, 89, 97, 107, 113–115, 122–124, 126, 128, 133–135, 140, 144, 147, 151, 164, 165, 167–170, 173, 176–178, 180, 186, 188, 192, 193, 197, 198, 200, 209, 213, 224, 226, 235, 236, 243, 244, 246, 247, 249, 250, 252–254, 260–263, 265, 268–270, 272, 282–285, 287, 288, 290, 292–294, 297, 298, 301, 313, 320, 327
State-building, 7, 8, 10, 42–44, 46, 49, 55–57, 59, 60, 79, 87, 88, 98, 122, 131, 134, 164, 276, 308

336 INDEX

Supreme Council of the Armed Forces (SCAF), Egypt, 262, 264, 265, 286, 290
Sustainable Development Goals (SDGs), 75
Sykes-Picot Agreement, 233–235, 237, 238, 242, 243
Syria, 1, 11, 14, 20, 21, 24, 26, 27, 29, 30, 32, 35, 37, 70, 80, 100, 123, 126, 128, 132, 134, 140, 150–157, 159, 165, 180, 181, 185, 190, 192, 196, 207, 210, 216, 223, 225, 233–244, 250–253, 255, 260, 273, 275, 281, 282, 297, 307, 313, 314, 320, 321, 323, 325
Syrian National Council (SNC), 240, 252, 253, 255

T
Taliban, 26, 41, 45–48, 51–56, 58, 60, 98, 99, 104, 105, 114, 125, 128, 192, 195
The Truth and Dignity Commission (IVD), 288, 293, 294, 296
Tunisia, 13, 20, 23, 84, 85, 123, 169, 185–187, 189, 190, 281–283, 286–290, 292–294, 296, 298, 299, 301, 302, 320

U
UK Stabilisation Unit, 5, 14, 15, 43, 44, 97, 116, 137, 180
Unipolarity, 31, 33
United Arab Emirates (UAE), 2, 9, 11, 20, 23, 24, 27, 31, 33, 35–37, 80, 86, 123, 125–136, 139–144, 146–151, 155–158, 164–181, 183, 197–199, 235, 245, 248, 249, 255, 259, 314
United Nations, 8, 70, 74, 152, 166, 211, 299, 326

United Nations Development Programme (UNDP), 47, 137, 166, 167, 179, 209, 225
Funding Facility for Extended Stabilisation (FFES), 166, 167
Funding Facility for Immediate Stabilisation (FFIS), 166, 167
United Nations Educational, Scientific and Cultural Organization (UNESCO), 97, 116, 308, 311, 312, 314, 316–318, 321–323, 326–330
United States Agency for International Development's (USAID), 7, 14, 45, 194
Un Security Council, 35, 46, 59, 72, 74, 75, 77–81, 85, 86, 89, 91, 111, 247, 255, 281, 290, 301, 308, 313, 314, 324, 328
US Army, 213, 320

W
War economy, 108, 113, 115, 189, 191, 192, 200
Whole-of-government approach, 140, 154, 155, 321
World Bank, 73, 135, 187, 194, 200, 201, 226, 227

Y
Yemen, 1, 2, 8, 13, 23, 24, 27, 29, 61, 70, 99, 101, 102, 106, 107, 110, 112, 113, 116, 123, 125–128, 131–134, 136, 141, 142, 144–149, 155, 157, 169, 185–188, 192, 198, 235–237, 241, 244–252, 254, 320, 325

Z
Zaatari, 216, 227
Zintan, 291
Zyck, Steven A., 5, 14, 15, 79, 89, 91